AMERICAN NEOCONSERVATISM

JEAN-FRANÇOIS DROLET

American Neoconservatism

The Politics and Culture of a Reactionary Idealism

OXFORD
UNIVERSITY PRESS

OXFORD
UNIVERSITY PRESS

Oxford University Press, Inc., publishes works that further
Oxford University's objective of excellence
in research, scholarship, and education.

Oxford New York
Auckland Cape Town Dar es Salaam Hong Kong Karachi
Kuala Lumpur Madrid Melbourne Mexico City Nairobi
New Delhi Shanghai Taipei Toronto

With offices in
Argentina Austria Brazil Chile Czech Republic France Greece
Guatemala Hungary Italy Japan Poland Portugal Singapore
South Korea Switzerland Thailand Turkey Ukraine Vietnam

Published by Oxford University Press, Inc
198 Madison Avenue, New York, New York 10016

Published in the United Kingdom in 2013 by C. Hurst & Co. (Publishers) Ltd.

www.oup.com

Library of Congress Cataloging-in-Publication Data
Drolet, Jean-François.
American neoconservatism : the politics and culture of a reactionary idealism /
Jean-François Drolet.
p. cm.
ISBN 978-0-19-933345-5 (pbk.)
1. Conservatism—United States. 2. United States—Politics and govern-
ment—1945–1989. 3. United States—Politics and government—1989– I. Title.
JC573.2.U6D75 2013
320.520973—dc23
2013017013

1 3 5 7 9 8 6 4 2

Printed in India
on Acid-Free Paper

To My Parents

CONTENTS

ACKNOWLEDGEMENTS

This book draws on a doctoral dissertation researched and written in the congenial atmosphere of the Department of Politics and International Relations at the University of Oxford between October 2004 and May 2009. My thesis supervisors, Alexandra Gheciu and Yuen Foong Khong, provided invaluable academic guidance, and I am immensely grateful to both. Andrew Hurrell, Patricia Owens and Jennifer Welsh also offered thoughtful advice at crucial junctures during the development of the project. Needless to say, all remaining errors are my own.

Very special thanks are due to Michael C. Williams. His constructive criticism, encouragement and his own work on neoconservatism have been important sources of inspiration during the initial and final phases of the project. I am also deeply indebted to Marc Stears and Michael Cox, who examined the thesis rigorously and provided useful suggestions for the book, and to Christopher Coker and Kimberly Hutchings for stimulating intellectual exchanges and encouragement over the past eight years or so. For discussions of the ideas presented in this book and pointed criticism of various drafts, I would also like to thank Jeremy Allouche, Solon Barocas, Christopher Bickerton, Antoine Bousquet, Phil Cunliffe, Toby Dodge, Bart Edgerton, Philippe Fournier, Michael Freeden, Lee Jones, George Lawson, Peter Ramsey, William Scheuerman, Keith Stansky, David Williams and the two anonymous reviewers for Hurst.

My colleagues and students at City University (London) provided a stimulating and friendly environment for the completion of this long-drawn-out project, and I am very grateful for it.

This study would not have been possible without the generous financial assistance of the Fonds québécois de recherche sur la société et la culture, the Clarendon Fund (Oxford), and the Cyril and Phyllis Long endowment at Queen's College (Oxford). I am grateful to all three sponsors.

Parts of this book have been published elsewhere in various forms. Sections of an early draft of Chapter 2 were originally published in an article that appeared in *International Politics*. Parts of Chapter 3 were originally published in an article that appeared in *Millennium: Journal of International Studies*. An early and slightly different version of Chapter 5 appeared as an article in the *Review of International Studies*. And long sections of Chapter 6 were published in an article that appeared in the *Journal of Political Ideologies*. I am indebted to all four journals for allowing me to re-use and draw on material originally published in their pages.

Finally, very special and affectionate thanks to my parents, friends and family in Canada, the UK and Sweden for their unyielding moral (and often financial) support throughout my seemingly endless student career. Very special and affectionate thanks to Stina for her warm and loving support, and for sharing with me all the excitement and anxieties that have accompanied the production of this book.

'One should defend virtue from the preachers of virtue: they are its worst enemies. For they teach virtue as an ideal for everyone; they take from virtue the charm of rareness, inimitableness, exceptionalness and unaverageness—its aristocratic magic. Virtue has all the instincts of the average man against it: it is unprofitable, imprudent, it isolates; it is related to passion and not very accessible to reason; it spoils the character, the head, the mind—according to the standards of mediocre men'.

Friedrich Nietzsche, *The Will to Power*

INTRODUCTION

'We live in an ideological age—that is to say, an age in which human passions and frustrations find expression in politics rather than, as was once the case, in religion. We may deplore this phenomenon, wish it were otherwise, and hope it will eventually pass. But that we live in such an age is a fact, as it is a fact that, in such an age, the key political question is: Who owns the future?'

Irving Kristol[1]

On 18 September 2009, Irving Kristol, the founding father of American neoconservatism, died aged 89. Kristol was a passionate essayist and a remarkable ideological entrepreneur. He came to the Right with a Leftist background in the 1960s and re-articulated a conservative tradition that until then had limited appeal to a political community founded on Enlightenment values. Within less than a decade, Kristol and his like-minded colleagues such as Daniel Bell, Seymour Martin Lipset and Nathan Glazer had moved conservatism from the fringe to the mainstream. They had stripped it of its anti-intellectual character, plumped it with business-funded think tanks and taken the lead in public policy debates.[2] As the prominent Left-wing theorist Jürgen Habermas acknowledged at the height of the conservative revolution in the early 1980s, 'Neoconservatives made sure that for the first time in half-a-century conservatism has become a phenomenon to be taken seriously in the United States. It is an accomplishment of the neoconservatives that a conservative government is able to rely on theoretical points of view and not merely on pragmatic considerations and the general climate'.[3]

In recent years, however, it is mainly within the domain of foreign policy that Kristol and his followers have attracted the most attention to themselves. Neoconservatives took credit for the imperial ideological substance of the Bush administration's global war on terrorism. They also provided much political support for the invasion and ongoing occupation of Afghanistan and Iraq. Given the poor performance of the Republican Party in the 2008 presidential elections, many expected the neoconservative project to collapse with the demise of the Bush presidency. But this has simply not been the case. In spite of the whirlwind of torture-related scandals and high-level resignations which marked the end of the Bush era, neoconservatism has very much remained *the* main representative of the broader conservative movement in mainstream newspapers, cable news and radio talk shows. As one of their Right-wing critics noted with despair, 'Not even the feverish denunciation of President George W. Bush as a warmonger by *American Conservative*'s Old Right critics of the war, former Undersecretary of the Treasury Paul Craig Roberts and Pat Buchanan, has spurred the "liberal establishment" to reconsider its debating partners. Neoconservatives have not been told to vacate their spot in the authorised political conversation on TV in favor of what is sometimes called a "harder Right"'.[4]

Neoconservatives have not only retained a strong presence in the media. They have also launched a number a new political platforms, such as the Foreign Policy Initiative (FPI) and Global Governance Watch (GGW), from which they now lead the Republican opposition against the 'post-imperial' foreign policy of the Obama administration. As the FPI's mission statement makes clear, neoconservatives may have lost one of their leading intellectuals, but neoconservatism is alive, well, and undeterred by the turn of events:

> There are those who hope we can just return to normalcy—to pre-9/11 levels of defense spending and pre-9/11 tactics. They argue for a retreat from America's global commitments and a renewed focus on problems at home, an understandable if mistaken response to these difficult economic times. In fact, strategic overreach is not the problem and retrenchment is not the solution.... Our economic difficulties will not be solved by retreat from the international arena. They will be made worse. In this new era, the consequences of failure and the risks of retreat would be even greater than before. The challenges we face require 21st century strategies and tactics based on a renewed commitment to American leadership. The United States remains the world's indispensable nation—indispensable to international peace, security, and stability, and

indispensable to safe-guarding and advancing the ideals and principles we hold dear.[5]

This book seeks to come to terms with the politics and theory of American neoconservatism. It exposes and interrogates the ideational substance of this 'new' conservatism and offers a critical assessment of the implications for American democracy and American foreign policy. The aim is to generate a better understanding of neoconservative ideas and political sociology, in light of the historical events and changing social compacts that have created a demand for them over the past decades. The motivation for this enterprise is simple. As Michael C. Williams noted in the aftermath of the Iraq War, despite the important role that neoconservatism has played in American political life since the 1960s, theoretically-oriented literature within the field of politics and International Relations (IR) has remained remarkably scarce.[6] This study seeks to fill this important gap in the literature. It moves beyond recent debates over the implications and political intrigues of the Bush presidency to offer a deeper look at the intellectual premises of neoconservative political sociology. While animated by progressive politics, it seeks to understand the gaps that neoconservative politics appear to fill in American society, so as so encourage engagement and a more effective response.

Neoconservatism in Question

'The so-called liberals are being defeated by their enemies, but liberalism is being saved'.

Harvey Mansfield[7]

Neoconservatism owes its resilience and successes in US politics in great part to the fact that it is both a powerful retort to liberalism and a self-confident assertion of some of its most contested values. Indeed, according to neoconservatives, it is they who are the true heirs of the liberal tradition in America. Neoconservatism emerged and crystallised as a loose intellectual faction in the late 1960s early 1970s as a reaction to the cultural revolutions, the perceived failures of the welfare state and the subsequent rise of Left-wing intellectual movements such as multiculturalism, post-colonialism, post-modernism and feminism in American academia. First-generation neoconservatives had been supporters of the New Deal and the centre-liberal consensus that had kept America united in the face of the communist threat during the first two decades of the post-war period. By the mid 1960s, however, they had grown uncomfortable with the radicalism of the civil rights movement and the increasingly Left-wing tendencies of liberal discourses. Utopian and overly confident in the promises of rationalism and social engineering, New Deal liberalism had fostered a culture of heightened social expectations and rights claims that American institutions could not sustain. It made promises that it could not keep. Now the Left was criticising not the government but America as a nation for failing to live up to the Enlightenment ideals that it had historically claimed for itself.

As the Vietnam War escalated abroad and race and student riots broke out at home, neoconservatives became concerned with the loss of authority of state institutions and what they saw as the limitless demands of the counter-culture for the democratisation of the political process. Liberalism no longer recognised the limits of pluralist democracy. Consequently, it had become increasingly difficult for the government to make decisions that served the public interest and reflected common values in the face of conflicting demands. As Jeane Kirkpatrick (1926–2006) wrote in one of her very last essays, 'The extremes of this counter-culture had disappeared by 1976, but the residue was more lasting. Its effects on what has been called liberal politics were profound. The counter-culture was much broader than the anti-war movement with which it was associated and, I believe, constituted a sweeping rejection of traditional American attitudes, values, and goals'.[8]

Neoconservatives never got over the events of the 1960s. As Joshua Muravchik explains, 'The loose group of us who felt impelled by the antics of the 1960s to migrate from the political Left to Right must have numbered fewer than 100. And we were proven losers at Washington's power game: The Left drove us from the Democratic Party, stole the "liberal" label, and successfully affixed to us the name "neoconservative"'.[9] Today, more than four decades after the collapse of the liberal consensus, neoconservatives maintain that the adversarial ethos of the cultural avant-garde still dominates the *Zeitgeist* but it is no longer creative. It is incapable of generating a normative environment that provides individuals with a sense of ontological security and the community with a compelling narrative from which to formulate its hegemonic foreign policy: 'Just as we live in a "postmodern" era in art and philosophy because no new theme has replaced "modernist" ideas, so we live in a post-Cold War world because no new foreign policy has been developed for our age' (James Ceaser).[10] The problem, as neoconservatives see it, is that 'from having been the aggressive doctrine of vigorous, spirited men, liberalism has become hardly more than a trembling in the presence of illiberalism' (Harvey Mansfield).[11] American liberalism has abandoned its universalist commitments in favour of a divisive politics of identity that embraces multiculturalism and individual self-realisation with complete disregard for the republican legacy of the American Revolution and the preservation of the American creed: 'Liberalism has become the party of anti-Americanism, economic plunder, and immorality. By contrast, conservative policies are not only more likely to produce the good society, they are also the best means to achieve liberal goals such as peace, tolerance, and social justice' (Dinesh D'Souza).[12]

Neoconservatives thus see themselves as the guardians of a 'liberalism betrayed' by the events of the 1960s.[13] As Tod Lindberg explains, 'what is being conserved is *our* liberalism—its extension in time and space. Neoconservatism explores the history of liberalism and tries to make out when and why liberal political thinking has become a threat to its own fundamental principles of liberty, individualism and progress'.[14] Or in the words of Irving Kristol, neoconservatism is 'reformationist. It tries to "reach beyond" contemporary liberalism in the way that all reformations, religious or political, do—by a return to the original sources of liberal vision and liberal energy so as to correct the warped version of liberalism that is today's orthodoxy'.[15] According to Kristol, this is the main element of novelty in neoconservatism. It seeks to conserve a social order that is based on a set of progressive ideals: 'What is "neo" ("new") about this conservatism is that it is resolutely free of nostalgia. It, too, claims the future'.[16] Neoconservatism 'is hopeful, not lugubrious; forward-looking, not nostalgic; and its general tone is cheerful, not grim or dyspeptic. Its twentieth-century heroes tend to be TR, FDR and Ronald Reagan. Such Republican and conservative worthies as Calvin Coolidge, Herbert Hoover, Dwight Eisenhower, and Barry Goldwater are politely overlooked'.[17]

In foreign affairs, this 'forward-looking' conservatism has distinguished itself over the years by its rejection of the isolationist policies of the Old Right. Instead, neoconservatives favour a crusading style of foreign policy, combining liberal idealism with realist assumptions about power and the human condition. For the scholar trained to appreciate conceptual coherence, this ideological syncretism is perplexing. For neoconservatives, it is the mark of 'a new kind of politics suitable to govern a modern liberal democracy'.[18]

In the pages that follow, I examine this 'new kind of politics' and set out to demonstrate that American neoconservatism is not the mainstream 'liberal conservatism' that it pretends to be (and that many analysts have diagnosed). I argue that neoconservatism in fact owes a lot more to the counter-Enlightenment than to the liberal tradition that its protagonists allegedly want to reform and protect against its enemies.

Liberalism, of course, is a broad church constituted by many contending variants: classical liberalism, New Deal liberalism, pragmatic liberalism, neoliberalism, Rawlsian liberalism etc. Like all ideologies (including neoconservatism), each of these variants acquires its distinctive political and normative substance by virtue of the interpretative need to choose among a wide range of essentially contestable concepts and empty signifiers—e.g. freedom, democracy, sovereignty, rights, order, war, peace, self-determination—in order to attain control over the language that effects political action and forms the basis of a political identity.[19] These constellations of ideas are loosely held together not solely by 'reasons, values and claims about society, but by emotional and cultural appeals that may lead to inconsistent but nevertheless engaging political views'.[20] Although they can seem incoherent and irrational to external observers, individuals and groups who accept those views and act upon them confer an important justificatory dimension to ideology that expresses itself in the language of truth-claims.

As Peter Kuryla noted, in the United States, this ideological contest has generated a liberal tradition notorious for its tendency to evade a precise definition in favour of manifestly vague and aphoristic descriptions: 'American liberalism has been defined as much by its champions as by its critics, each having absorbed something of the other's perspective'.[21] Neoconservatism thrives on this muddled ideological terrain. And its claims to the tradition of liberal democracy must be assessed in light of the broad and imprecise meaning of liberalism in American public discourse. Yet for the term 'liberalism' to have any meaning at all, at least in the Anglo-Saxon context in which these debates take place, it must nevertheless refer to a cluster of Enlightenment values predicated on a distinctively modern conception of man and society. As John Gray explains:

Liberalism is individualist, in that it asserts the moral primacy of the person against the claims of any other social collectivity; egalitarian inasmuch as it confers on all humans the same moral status and denies the relevance to legal or political order of differences in moral worth among human beings; universalist, affirming the moral unity of the human species and according secondary importance to specific historical associations and cultural forms; and meliorist in its affirmation of the corrigibility and improvability of all social institutions and political arrangements.[22]

My contention is that to the extent that neoconservatism is committed to this discourse, these commitments are subordinated to an authoritarian form of cultural conservatism that is in fact ferociously predatory on liberal values—both in domestic and global politics. Over the years, analysts of all persuasions (including many neoconservatives) have used a variety of evocative Wilsonian slogans to describe the neoconservative approach to foreign affairs: 'Wilsonianism in boots'[23], 'hard Wilsonianism'[24], 'closet Wilsonianism'[25], 'Realistic Wilsonianism'[26], 'Wolfish Wilsonians'[27], 'Hobbes meets Kant'[28] etc. I argue here that these Wilsonian tropes are misleading. For they suggest that neoconservatism resorts to realist power politics to pursue a liberal vision and deepen the normative fabric of the global liberal order. This is simply not the case. Whether in domestic or in international politics, neoconservative attachments to liberalism are predicated on an atavistic conservative philosophy which is at the service of values—authority, hierarchy, elitism, nationalism, community, sacrifice—that are inimical to the transformative mechanisms of liberal governance and the progressive discourse of democracy and human rights.

To be sure, it could plausibly be argued that neoconservatism shares characteristics with certain nineteenth-century European traditions of national liberalism and liberal imperialism.[29]Protagonists of these traditions in Italy and Germany, for instance, were often aggressive in foreign policy, intolerant of dissent and cultural (and often racial) differences at home and abroad, and convinced of their right and duty to bring civilisation to the non-Western other.[30] Yet, from the perspective of the study of ideology, the alignment of contemporary neoconservatism with these nineteenth-century traditions is analytically superficial and does not really do justice to the complex, post-industrial and late-modern character of neoconservative political sociology. The main problem with such a rapprochement is that it misconstrues the relationship of these different ideological forces to liberal philosophy. The fact that liberal nationalists and imperialists in the nineteenth century often excluded people of colour, people without property, dissenters, women, atheists or Catholics from their enlightened political vision had nothing to do with the character of 'their liberalism'. Rather, it was an unwillingness to tackle existing prejudices with the full logic of their liberal beliefs and principles.[31] In the case of neoconservatism, however, it is not so much an unwillingness to address existing social problems and prejudices with the full logic of liberal principles, but a commitment to tackle societal problems with *conservative* practices and ideas. Neoconservatism is a claim that liberalism as an ideology is both unsuited to address the contradictions of the social world and often the very source of these contradictions.

That said, it should be stressed at the outset that the aim of this study is not to offer a normative defence of liberalism as such. Nor is it to exonerate liberal internationalist ideas from having anything to do with the failure of American foreign policy in the past decade.[32] Yet, situating neoconservatism within the broad church of liberal political theory tends to eclipse all that is specific to neoconservatism as an ideology. It endows this 'new conservatism' with a progressive ethical gloss that it simply does not deserve, and it muddles critical debates over the limits and desirability of liberal values and practices in contemporary world politics. American neoconservatism is not a conservative *variant* of liberalism but a *reaction* to liberal modernity and the cultural forces that the latter generates.

Liberal modernity is one of those multifaceted, essentially contestable concepts I borrow from Robert Latham to refer to the macro-historical principle of social formation which has underwritten the hegemonic order of Pax Americana since its inception in 1945. Liberal modernity is defined by the organisation of social existence according to liberal, democratic and capitalist principles of governance. This involves transnational relations between polities and other social actors in the context of open international economic exchange, domestic market relations, the governance of society according to liberal democratic principles, the formal separation between politics and economics and between the public and the private spheres, civil societies based on individual and group rights, and the right of collective self-determination.[33] According to neoconservatives, liberal modernity has done relatively well at the economic, administrative and technological levels. In their view the problem is confined to the realm of culture: i.e. the integrated set of attitudes, values, ideas, practices and shared knowledge that characterises an institution, organisation or group and depends upon the capacity for symbolic thought and social learning.[34]

Like Marxian and liberal theories, neoconservatism sees science and technology as a source of human empowerment and emancipation shaping social structures and moving history forward according to a principle of linear change and accumulation. This process is captured by concepts like productivity, growth, efficiency and functional rationality, which provide guidance to human societies in the expansion of their powers over nature within the respective value system of these societies. There is therefore progress in the realm of science and technology to the extent that the latter progressively removes the physical constraints on the material well-being of human societies. The problem, neoconservatives argue, is that this progress has no counterpart in the cultural sphere. Unlike science and technology, culture is not a cumulative enterprise. Rather, it is a perpetual return to the same fundamental questions generated by the tensions between the finite character of the human condition and man's constant desire to push all boundaries. These are perennial existential questions such as the meaning of life and death, the nature of obligations and the essence of the good life that have to be confronted by men and women in full historical consciousness, yet across all historical periods. History, therefore, cannot be the source of moral meanings for human societies since historical progress is not moral or metaphysical progress but simply the progress of man's control over nature.

In the past, religious cosmologies provided moral guidance and a *telos* that gave meaning to historical progress. But the privatisation of individual conscience encouraged by science and Enlightenment criticism has undermined this crucial source of normative stability. The liberal temperament today no longer allows for religious convictions in the public sphere. Instead, it embraces a decayed doctrine of tolerance based on the belief that the line between morality and immorality is rooted in the diversity of cultures. In its quest for 'one-worldism', modern liberalism has purged its ethics of all parochial ties. It has renewed its universalism in an abstract noumenal register which dissolves the civic bond of the community and devalues the primordial attachments of the family. It has introduced a parasitic epistemological shift that decouples all knowledge from metaphysics, and thereby affirms both the illusory nature of the past and the meaninglessness of the future. According to neoconservatives, this growing discrepancy between the 'technocratisation' of the economic-administrative sphere and the radical individualisation of the cultural sphere accounts for much of what is wrong with American society since the 1960s. As Daniel Bell explains in his classic formulation of the problem:

> Within this framework, on can discern the structural sources of tension in the society: between a social structure (primarily techno-economic) which is bureaucratic and hierarchical, and a polity which believes, formally, in equality and participation; between a social structure that is organised fundamentally in terms of roles and specialisation, and a culture which is concerned with the enhancement and fulfilment of the self and the 'whole' person. In these contradictions, one perceives many of the latent social conflicts that have been expressed ideologically as alienation, depersonalisation, the attack on authority, and the like. In these adversary relations, one sees the disjunction of realms.[35]

At the political level, neoconservatives argue that the internalisation of this cultural crisis into the political life of the country has transformed American democracy into what Allan Bloom famously described as a 'Disneyland version of the Weimar Republic'.[36] They argue that the rise of the counter-culture has emasculated the leadership quality of the elite, bred nihilism and subverted the unity of the general will. This in turn has led to the overcrowding of the political system with an ever-increasing number of special interest groups. These groups whittle away at the concrete power of the state in the name of all sorts of misguided egalitarian utopias, and promise to emancipate civil society from the politics of hierarchy and national security upon which this very same civil society in fact depends for its own prosperity. Hence with each new generation American liberalism degenerates and the American way of life becomes more vulnerable to its enemies. As William Kristol argues in his 'Eighteenth Brumaire of Barack Obama':

> The decade of the 1960s—the first appearance in full flower of modern American liberalism—was in many respects a tragedy. It was certainly a tragedy for American liberalism, which liberated itself from its previous (at least partial) mooring in common sense and the American tradition. It was to some degree also a tragedy for America. It took conservative politicians and policies decades to undo the damage of Great Society hubris, post-Vietnam weakness, and '60s cultural foolishness. Much wreckage still remains. Now we have the second appearance of '60s liberalism in the policies and personages of the Obama administration. Marx noted that in the France of his time, 'only the ghost of

the old revolution circulated', producing an 'adventurer' who claimed to be heir to the great Napoleon, but who was 'only a caricature of the old Napoleon'. Similarly, in the America of our time, we have a ghostly version of the liberalism of the 1960s, led by a man who is only a caricature of the vigorous if often mistaken liberals who once sought to reshape the nation.[37]

As we will see in the course of this study, the characterisation of conflict over the legitimacy of the prevailing order as a cultural crisis of nihilism generates a particularly volatile mode of political existentialism in which political notions such as inequality, domination, dissent, democracy, terrorism, war and revolution are read into cultural relationships. This elevates 'culture' as *the* main site of power struggle and imbues politics with a totalising character. Politics in this context is no longer about transforming the organisational basis of society, but about creating new forms of individual subjectivities.[38] This is what differentiates this new conservatism from the old limited style of politics of traditional Anglo-Saxon conservatism.[39] Burke, for instance, saw the values, habits, practices and beliefs that constitute a particular culture as organic and somewhat dispersed throughout society—pre-established norms of behaviour and unreflective prejudices that provide existing institutions with a minimum of social stability and bind past, present and future generations.[40] By contrast, neoconservatism envisages culture as a political object of systematic management that must be reformed, manufactured, exported or completely transformed. This intrusive cultural politics thus acquires a crusading character immensely taxing on the pluralist and individualising ethos of modern liberal institutions, practices and values.

The Spectres of Weimar

Approaching the neoconservative project from this political-sociological perspective draws attention to important systematic links between the domestic and international dimensions of our contemporary neoconservative politics. It also allows us to situate neoconservative theory in the context of intellectual debates over the nature and implications of the Enlightenment legacy that have become so important in IR theory, political theory and social philosophy since the 1980s.

In this respect, this study argues and demonstrates that neoconservatism is heavily influenced by a radical critique of liberalism and Enlightenment philosophy that harks back to the authoritarian intellectual circles of Weimar Germany. This is arguably *the* most controversial, misinterpreted and under-theorised issue in the existing literature on the movement. The main protagonist in those controversies is, of course, the German-Jewish political philosopher Leo Strauss. A gifted pupil of the proto-fascist political and legal theorist Carl Schmitt, Strauss came of age in the highly volatile political climate of the short-lived Republic of Weimar (1919–33). He left Germany amidst the turmoil of the early 1930s and eventually settled in America in 1938 where he taught political philosophy until his death in 1973. During his time as a teacher at the New School for Social Research (1938–49), the University of Chicago (1949–68), and St John's College in Annapolis (1969–72), Strauss earned himself a large following of dedicated students, many of whom went on to become teachers themselves in North American universities and contributed to the development of a 'Straussian' school in political science which is now at least three generations old. In more recent years, a significant number of so-called Straussians have preferred Washington's corridors of power to those of the university and went on to serve in high-ranking positions in Republican administrations (although a few have served with the Democrats) while others have become key players in the network of conservative and neoconservative think-tanks and media organisations, which is in great part responsible for the political success of the American Right since the 1970s.

Although Strauss had relatively little to say about America and the realm of international relations as such, the growth of Straussianism as a school of political thought and its link to the neoconservative movement and the Republican Party has led to a wide range of contentious claims about Strauss's alleged influence on American politics and foreign policy over the past twenty years or so. Conspiratorial charges against Strauss have been particularly extravagant in the aftermath of 9/11, as observers on both sides of the Atlantic identified him as the Machiavellian mastermind behind the imperialist policies of the Bush administration and the deceptive intelligence that led to the American invasion of Iraq in 2003.[41] According to Anne Norton, for instance, Strauss's teachings at the University of Chicago have sowed the seed of an 'enthusiasm for empire' in the mind of some of his brightest students which germinated into a fully fledged plan 'to establish a new world order to rival Rome' and eventually took American troops into Afghanistan and Iraq after 9/11.[42] Along similar lines, Shadia Drury maintains that the link between Strauss and the Iraq War is straightforward and hinges on two main facts. First, just as 'Leo Strauss was a great believer in the efficacy and usefulness of lies in politics', 'Public support for the Iraq War rested on lies about Iraq posing an immanent threat to the United States—the business about weapons of mass destruction and a fictitious alliance between al-Qaeda and the Iraqi regime'. And secondly, the political realism of Thrasymachus and Machiavelli that Strauss defends in his books is 'clearly manifest in the foreign policy of the current administration in the United States'.[43]

Needless to say, these allegations are at the very best intellectually lazy.[44] From a theoretical perspective, there is indeed something attractive about the identification of one single philosophical mastermind that would have inspired the most controversial aspects of the Bush administration's response to the attacks of 9/11. But this obscures the more mundane and more complex reality of a set of policies developed by statesmen who hardly had to read Strauss to justify deceit and mendacity in a situation of crisis.[45] On the other hand, it is a well-documented fact that Strauss had a crucial formative influence on many leading neoconservative figures, and that (intentionally or not) he provided the movement with vital intellectual ammunitions to fight the culture wars.[46] That is not to say that all neoconservatives are Straussians or that all Straussians are neoconservatives. But as one commentator argued, 'it is absolutely impossible to think of contemporary neoconservatism without references to Strauss'.[47]

And it is precisely because this issue of intellectual lineage is so important that it should not be unreflexively reduced to a momentary 'cabal' of well-positioned politicians willing to deceive the masses to fight an imperial war. For such conspiratorial interpretations of the Straussian legacy deceptively depreciate the intellectual depth of both Strauss's work and neoconservative thought. Ultimately, it prevents us from appreciating the more complex, diffused and perhaps more pervasive nature of Strauss's influence on one of the leading political factions within the American Right. While I wish to distance myself from the eccentricities of recent polemics surrounding the Iraq War, I argue here that by enrolling Strauss in their culture wars neoconservatives have indeed tapped into a distinctively Weimarian *Kulturkritik* (critique of modern civilisation), which is in no small measure indebted to the anti-liberal political theory of Strauss's early mentor, Carl Schmitt. As we will see, reading neoconservative discourses in the context of this issue of intellectual lineage provides a valuable entry point to understand the fusion of free-market economics, cultural authoritarianism and executive-centred governance underpinning the politics of neoconservatism.

Re-Constructing Neoconservatism

Mapping out the constellation of ideas and practices that constitute such a broad and cross-generational political project as neoconservatism is not without its difficulties. For one thing, one could legitimately question whether it makes sense at all to talk of a neoconservative project as such. As neoconservatives themselves like to remind us, neoconservatism does not constitute an intellectually unified movement or position.[48] When the socialist critic Michael Harrington first used the term in the US, it was meant as an insult.[49] At the time, most intellectuals who gravitated around disillusioned liberals like Irving Kristol, Norman Podhoretz, Daniel Bell, Nathan Glazer and Patrick Moynihan saw themselves as liberals or moderate social democrats. None of them wanted to have anything to do with either Harrington's label or with conservatism more generally.[50] Over the years, however, most came to recognise that they shared a distinctive attitude towards liberalism, which developed under Kristol's leadership and differed in many respects from traditional and libertarian conservatism.[51] Kristol and his colleagues came to accept the label without ever really feeling the need to defend or justify it. As Nathan Glazer explains, 'There is hardly one of us who has written an article explaining what neoconservatism is'.[52]

Yet while accepting the neoconservative label, statements such as 'there is no such thing as a neoconservative movement'[53] and neoconservatism is 'not an ideology with party-like planks on every issue of the day'[54] have remained common in neoconservative literature. Instead, neoconservatives prefer to describe their creed as an 'intellectual disposition'[55] or a 'sensibility'.[56] This is to emphasise that neoconservatism lacks the organisational features of a movement. According to Kristol, neoconservatism is a 'persuasion' based on 'a set of attitudes derived from historical experiences'. It is 'one of those intellectual currents that surface only intermittently... one that manifests itself over time, but erratically, and one whose meaning we clearly glimpse only in retrospect'.[57]

Yet as E. H. Carr once noted, 'To denounce ideologies in general is to set up an ideology of one's own'.[58] The claim that neoconservatism is a 'persuasion' rather than an ideological tradition is itself an ideological 'muddle' designed to mark a difference between the radical politics of socialism and the more temperate, elite-driven politics of post-war America with which neoconservatism associates itself.[59] Likewise, we should not be too surprised that neoconservatives resist the designation of 'movement' to describe their political and ideological enterprise. As one of them pointed out, neoconservatives 'spent their lives' lashing out on the 'communist movement', the 'peace movement' and the 'environmental movement'.[60] But the elaborate network of think tanks in which many neoconservative intellectuals have found a home over the years should raise serious doubts about the claim that neoconservatism lacks the platforms and the organisational features of a movement. These include the American Enterprise Institute, the Hudson Institute, the Manhattan Institute, the Project for a New American Century, the Foreign Policy Initiative, Global Governance Watch, Heritage Foundation, the Cato Institute, the Study of Economic Culture, the Institute for Contemporary Studies, the Institute on Religion and Public Life, the Study of Economic Culture, the Ethics and Public Policy Center, the Center for Strategic and International Studies, the Center for Security Policy, the Georgetown Center for Strategic Studies, and more. One would also have to add to this list the extensive number of journals set up and edited by neoconservative intellectuals over the years. These include *The Public Interest*, *The National Interest*, *Commentary*, *The American Enterprise*, *The Weekly Standard, The American Interest*, *The New Criterion*, *The Journal of Democracy*, *Public Opinion*, *First Things*, *Orbis*, *Society*, *The New Leader*, *Foreign Policy*, *Defense Review*, *Crisis*, *Encounter* (UK). Neoconservatives are also very well represented in mainstream publications and news channels like *Newsweek*, *Reader's Digest*, *The New Republic*, *Atlantic Monthly*, *Vanity Fair*, *Esquire*, *Harper's Magazine*, *The Washington Monthly*, Fox News and CNN.

Francis Fukuyama is one of the few neoconservative intellectuals who has acknowledged that neoconservatism does indeed constitute a relatively united ideological faction (his post-Iraq quarrels with other prominent neoconservative figures undoubtedly being a contributing factor to this admission).[61] In his own words, neoconservatism is 'a coherent set of ideas, arguments, and conclusions from experience ...

a confluence of intellectual streams that have resulted in areas of ambiguity or disagreement among neoconservatives'.[62] Along those lines, this study maintains that although neoconservatives often disagree with each other on particular issues, there is a core body of ideas, values and assumptions about the nature of modern liberal politics that cuts across generations and unites this group of essayists, politicians, sociologists, political scientists and media commentators under the label of neoconservatism.

'The neoconservative' that I am presenting in this study is therefore a rational reconstruction of neoconservative thought based on a wide range of sources such as books, journal and newspaper articles, think-tank policy recommendations as well as conference transcripts. 'The neoconservative' is like 'the liberal', 'the Marxist' or 'the empiricist'. He is not to be identified with any particular neoconservative intellectual. Neither is he the average neoconservative who has been deprived of the opinions that distinguish him or her from his peers, or who does not take side on divisive issues. Rather, he is the ideal type neoconservative who represents the most perceptive view to be assembled from the actual writings of a relatively wide pool of neoconservative and Straussian ideological travellers who have contributed importantly to shaping the contours of this political project over the years.[63]

For analytical purposes, the neoconservative project can be broken down into three closely interrelated dimensions:

Capitalism: The dismantling of the domestic and international architecture of the post-war economic settlement (Keynesianism and Bretton Woods) and the restoration/maintenance of corporate power.

Nationalism: The cultivation and maintenance of a homogenous national identity—a universal 'Americaneity'—based on the subordination of minority cultures to the enduring worldview of the white Anglo-Saxon majority culture.

Imperialism: The consolidation, maintenance and deepening of America's economic, political, cultural and global military supremacy.

The analysis that follows will take us into each of these three dimensions of neoconservative politics. Chapter 1 provides a historical overview of the development of neoconservatism as a distinct ideological faction from the end of the Second World War to the early 1980s. The narrative explains how and why first-generation neoconservatives slowly turned against liberalism to become the champions of a new and explicitly 'ideological' mass conservatism during this important formative period.

Chapter 2 exposes and analyses Leo Strauss's controversial critique of modernity and highlights the elements of this intellectual legacy which, as will be demonstrated in the subsequent chapters, came to have a significant impact on this new conservatism over the past decades. Of particular importance here is a political existentialist reading of Hobbes that Strauss developed in the context of his intellectual exchange with Carl Schmitt, and which, I contend, looms large in the politics and theory of American neoconservatism today.

Chapter 3 moves on to explore the manifestation of this neo-Hobbesian politics in the context of neoconservative discourses on the liberal state and regimes of citizenship. It exposes the main axes of the neoconservative critique of both the neo-liberal 'New Right' and the post-1960s 'New Left' and analyses the political programme that follows from these intellectual interventions. It is argued that neoconservative domestic governance hinges on the cultivation of a politics of enmity that tends to elide the material basis of social conflict and expand the management of political and societal questions in terms of security and various forms of cultural antagonisms. While this facilitates the re-articulation of class interests in favour of market forces, it generates an executive-driven style of politics which tends to undermine the substantive value-neutrality of the liberal state and extend its disciplinary reach deep into the American household. Most importantly, the devaluation of democracy and redistributive welfare measures that underlies this programme deprives the 'neoconservative state' of important sources of legitimation. This invites the exploitation of foreign policy to make up for this cohesive deficit and sublimate the contradictions of this post-welfarist socio-economic order through the militarisation of American civil society.

The following two chapters look at the external, foreign policy dimension of this neo-Hobbesian politics. Chapter 4 analyses the theoretical and political fabric of neoconservative democracy promotion discourses. It traces the conceptual evolution of those discourses from the early 1970s until today, and then offers a critical analysis of their implications in the context of America's ongoing global war on terrorism. The analysis demonstrates that neoconservative views on democracy promotion over the years have been driven by a reactive modernisation narrative, which is determined as much by nationalist anxiety over America's declining will to power as by a genuine belief in the viability of democratic peace theory. It is argued that the democratic import of this long-drawn-out foreign policy campaign is in fact limited and inimical to the normative thickening of the global liberal order that it promises.

Chapter 5 analyses the neoconservative defence of American sovereignty against the advances of human rights regimes and the constitutionalisation of the global liberal order. It offers a conceptual interpretation of the neoconservative case against global liberal governance and draws out the main political and ethical implications for American foreign policy and international society more generally. It argues that the neoconservative critique of global governance rests upon a decisionist interpretation of the normative order that weaves together democracy, individual rights and national autonomy through a volatile identity politics which is fundamentally at odds with both the pluralist character of 'Westphalian' diplomacy and the universal order of rights envisaged by cosmopolitan advocates of global liberal governance.

Finally, Chapter 6 concludes with a critical assessment of the peculiar synthesis of realism and idealism that characterises the neoconservative mode of engagement with the world. It draws on the findings of the previous chapters to expose the atavistic and nihilistic core of this unstable ideological fusion and highlights the extent to which the emancipatory ideals that neoconservatism claims for itself in fact lend themselves to the justification for restrictions on these very same ideals.

1

A NEW CONSERVATISM

'In the modern world, a non-ideological politics is a politics disarmed'.

Irving Kristol[1]

American neoconservatism has its origins in the predominantly Jewish and New York-based intelligentsia generally referred to as the 'New York intellectuals'. The New York intellectuals were an aggregation of remarkably prolific anti-Stalinist Left-wing social critics who exerted a great deal of influence in the political and cultural debates of the post-war period. They are responsible for setting up and contributing to the success of some of the most important periodicals of the time, such as *The Partisan Review*, *Commentary* and *Dissent*. Some of their most well-known representatives include Sidney Hook, Irving Howe, Dwight MacDonald, Alfred Kazin, Saul Bellow, James Burnham, Mary McCarthy, Philip Rahv, Hannah Arendt, C. Wright Mills, Lionel Trilling, Susan Sontag, Michael Walzer, as well as would-be neoconservatives Irving Kristol, Daniel Bell, Seymour Martin Lipset, Elliot Cohen, Melvin Lasky, Gertrude Himmelfarb, Midge Decter, Hilton Krammer, Nathan Glazer and Norman Podhoretz.[2]

Like many other New York intellectuals, although by no means all of them, neoconservatives had been student radicals associated with the Trotskyist and socialist movements at the City College of New York. Gathering in a small section of the cafeteria called Alcove One, which housed the non-communist socialist activists, they honed their theoretical and rhetorical skills through bitter arguments among themselves and with the Stalinist communists of Alcove Two. While sharing many socialist ideals with their Stalinist counterparts, 'would-be neoconservatives' waged a war of words with the latter over their refusal to recognise what Trotskyists saw as the inhumanity of Soviet totalitarianism. The holistic approach to politics and the adversarial style of argumentation that they cultivated during those early years of endless debates in Marxist social theory would later become a distinctive feature of neoconservative discourses, as well as a valuable asset in the culture wars from the 1960s onwards.[3]

Kristol and his colleagues discarded their radicalism and abandoned their socialism at an early age. They were all from poor immigrant backgrounds, and they came of age at a time when the political hopes of the lower strata of American society were very much tied to the fate of socialism. But for them, even before the Nazi-Soviet Pact of August 1939, events like the Moscow Trials and the liquidation of anarchists and Trotskyites in Spain had made it clear that the rise of totalitarianism was inexorably linked to the failures of grand socialist ideals. As Bell explained in a commemorative essay, his generation 'is a generation that finds its wisdom in pessimism, evil, tragedy, and despair', not in humanist utopias.[4]

By the end of the Second World War, 'would-be neoconservatives' had become strong supporters of the liberal anti-communist ideological consensus that was to dominate intellectual circles and policy debates until the mid 1960s or so. This consensus was the product of bitter factional infightings within the Left between communists, non-Stalinist socialists and liberals that took place before, during and in the immediate aftermath of the Second World War.[5] At the organisational level, the liberal consensus operated under the umbrella of the Americans for Democratic Action (ADA) created in 1947 by Harvard historian Arthur Schlesinger Jr., the realist theologian Reinhold Niebuhr and other prominent Democratic Party activists such as John Kenneth Galbraith, Eleanor Roosevelt and former Vice President Hubert Humphrey to rally liberals behind the strong anti-communist position of the Truman administration. The liberal consensus was eventually dubbed the 'vital centre' after the publication of Schlesinger's famous book in 1949. As Schlesinger explains there, the vital centre had been forged by purging progressive ranks of 'sentimentalist self-delusions' about the true nature of Soviet intentions.[6] If there was one fundamental belief holding this centrist coalition together, it was that Left-wing dictatorships were of the same aggressive breed as Right-wing dictatorships. For Schlesinger and his followers, isolationism was no longer an option. America could not maintain peace without being willing to risk war.

Until the mid 1960s, liberal anti-communist intellectuals enjoyed unprecedented political power through the ADA and contributed enormously to shaping the contours of the United States' post-war hegemonic grand strategy.[7] This grand strategy was determined by the belief that, after nearly half a century of military conflicts and economic instability, long-term peace and prosperity necessitated the abandonment of economic nationalism along with the political and military props that had supported it. Only the global integration of free markets could realise the potential of capitalism for prolonged growth and the pacification of international relations.

Vital centrists, however, also believed that for capital, goods, people and ideas to move freely within this projected liberal space the US would have to expand the reach of its political and military power to ensure that the norms and rules underpinning this new geopolitical pact would be adhered to by all actors involved. As Robert Latham explains, both intellectuals and practitioners conceived of military power as a mediating force between autonomy and governance—a form of 'embedded militarisation'—that enabled politics within the West to be played out in a liberal key: 'With military force constituting the predominant form of social control at the international level, more thickly institutionalised political relations of governance could be avoided, and a certain degree of relative autonomy for actors in the international system could be preserved'.[8]

At the geopolitical level, this liberal grand strategy had both an East-West and a East-South dimension. The East-West dimension was determined by the doctrine of containment. Containment not only aimed at containing Soviet expansion but also at controlling the recovery of Germany and Japan and at keeping the other European allies aligned.[9] The North-South dimension concerned the development, extension and maintenance of what was to become a maturing post-colonial international capitalism under US leadership.[10] This particular dimension became especially important following the denouement of the British Empire in the Eastern Mediterranean in the late 1940s. NSC-68, for instance, stated explicitly that the main objective of US foreign policy was not only to 'foster seeds of destruction within the Soviet Union' but also to create 'a world environment in which the American system can survive and flourish'. 'Even if there was no Soviet Union', the document explains, 'we would face the great problem of achieving and maintaining order and security'.[11] The Third World was crucial to US grand strategy as a source of raw materials and investment opportunities, as well as an additional market for finished products from Western economies. It played a key role in the revival of the industrial productivity of Japan and Europe, and thus provided the latter with the financial means to meet the huge demands for American imports. As Thomas McCormick explains, 'In general, the United States saw Third World economies as important, integral strands in the overlapping triangular trades that were the warp and woof of global multilateralism'.[12] The East-West and North-South dimensions of the US's grand strategy were therefore inexorably linked with one another. If America could demonstrate that the liberal modernisation of the South could be achieved, then communism would lose a great deal of its appeal everywhere.

In domestic politics, the liberalism of the vital centre remained very much attached to the preservation of the politically successful alliance of organised labour, farmers, intellectuals, blacks and southern whites that formed the 'New Deal' coalition. This coalition had its roots in the series of welfare reform programmes initiated by President Franklin D. Roosevelt in the 1930s. Prompted by the economic crisis of 1929, the intensification of class conflicts, and the emergence of America as a dominant player on the world stage during the first half of the twentieth century, the New Deal sought to address the pressing problems of mass unemployment and racial discrimination through public policies designed to favour social, multicultural and multiracial integration. By the time Truman had taken over from Roosevelt, New Deal liberalism evoked nearly two decades of Democratic leadership driven by a faith in the wisdom and legitimacy of state intervention to distribute wealth and power to traditionally subordinate classes and ethnic groups.[13] The New Deal had rescued America from the worst economic depression of its history. Now that pressing problems of basic economic subsistence had been overcome, New Deal liberalism sought to expend social welfare policies and civil rights legislation to improve the quality of life of the greatest number of Americans and put an end to racial segregation.[14]

'Would-be neoconservatives' were active supporters of both containment and New Deal liberalism. But like most other New York intellectuals, they jealously guarded their relative independence from the particular interests of organised labour and the vagaries of elite bargaining and electoral politics. The objectives of their small group of essayists were more general. But their discourses were more coherent and, above all, less compromising than those of the election-oriented ADA. This, however, did not prevent them from occupying key organisational positions within anti-communist associations. This included Sidney Hook's American Committee for Cultural Freedom (ACCF) and its international counterpart the Congress for Cultural Freedom (CFF), which, as the *New York Times* would reveal at the time of its dissolution in 1966, was secretly funded by the CIA.[15] Kristol, Lasky, Bell and Podhoretz also served as editors of CFF-affiliated journals and magazines such as *The New Leader*, *Partisan Review*, *Commentary* and *Encounter* (UK-based).

'Would-be neoconservatives' wrote on a wide variety of subjects related to culture, public policy and, not least, anti-communism. Most of them opposed McCarthyism, at least in its crudest form. But their opposition was heavily qualified and often had less to do with concerns over civil liberties than with McCarthy's methods and incompetence. In their view, liberal freedoms were more threatened by 'liberal forbearance' than by McCarthyism as such.[16] Kristol, for instance, believed that McCarthy was a 'vulgar demagogue'. But he believed that the fact that Western intellectuals were developing 'a bad conscience about opposing communism' was a proof that communist propaganda was succeeding.[17] Likewise, Glazer expressed regret that a man like McCarthy was ever allowed to enter politics in the first place. Yet he could 'not see that it is an imminent danger to personal liberty in the United States'.[18] The communist movement was, in Bell's words, 'a conspiracy, rather than a legitimate dissenting group'. Communists were therefore not entitled to the same rights as other dissidents.[19] Bell and his colleagues believed that concerns over civil liberties dangerously obscured the nature of the real threat. They believed that liberals who neither feared communism nor hated it unreservedly had failed to grasp the unappeasable and existential nature of communist hostility to liberalism. As Podhoretz later explained in *Making It* (1967):

> [T]he Soviet Union was a totalitarian state of the same unqualified evil character as Nazi Germany, and as such could not be expected to change except for the worse.... The Soviet Union was incorrigibly committed to the cause of world revolution, to be furthered by military means when necessary, and when

possible by a strategy of internal subversion directed from Moscow; only American power stood in the way of this fanatical ambition to destroy freedom all over the world, and only American awareness of the threat could generate policies that would thwart it.[20]

In domestic politics, by contrast, 'would-be neoconservatives' envisaged the second half of the twentieth century as an era of incremental socio-economic development that would raise America and the West above the 'trivialities' of class politics. With socialism discredited and excluded from policy-making circles, only the anti-New Deal Right remained a potential disturber of the liberal status quo. But the Right emerged from the Second World War with relatively few supporters. Its reactionary character seemed to be completely out of step with the triumphant and forward-looking mood of the post-war period. Indeed, according to George Nash's sympathetic history of the conservative movement, American conservatism at that time 'was almost an underground phenomenon'.[21] American conservatism had not experienced the political tumults that marked the collapse of the Ancien Regime and informed the conservatism of prominent European thinkers like Edmund Burke, Joseph De Maistre and Juan Donoso Cortés. It was therefore more the work of grassroots-based activism than intellectuals. Its political programme was characterised by racial and religious discrimination against minorities, by uncompromising isolationism in international affairs, and by a hatred for the New Deal that bordered on the fanatical.[22] Lionel Trilling made particular note of the obtuse and moribund character of American conservatism in the opening pages of his influential *The Liberal Imagination* in 1950. Although he was himself committed to the liberal consensus of the post-war period, Trilling lamented the absence of a powerful conservative intellectual tradition that could keep liberalism in check and prevent its degeneration into a naïve and facile utopianism. In his view, 'the conservative impulse and the reactionary impulses' did not, 'with some isolated and some ecclesiastical exceptions, express themselves in ideas but only in action or in irritable mental gestures which seek to resemble ideas'.[23]

Trilling's arguments were reiterated by Bell, Lipset and a number of their colleagues throughout the 1950s and 1960s in a series of polemics against the anti-New Dealers and what they saw as the 'extremism' of the 'radical Right'.[24] The use of terms like 'radicals' and 'extremists' to designate Right-wing anti-New Dealers betrays the attachment to the political status quo of these authors. 'Would-be neoconservatives' were part of a broader group of scholars who embraced what one commentator describes as the 'new political theory' of the post-war liberal academia: 'interest politics to trump dangerous ideologies, rational choice to trump the excesses of democracy, expertise-based policy-making to trump messy participatory options, liberal consensus to hold it all together'.[25]

The 'new political theory' was both a product and a source of broader debates and controversies associated with the famous 'end of ideology' thesis. The end of ideology thesis itself emerged out of intellectual debates within the CFF and between the CFF and some of their European critics. These included Jean-Paul Sartre, Georg Lukács, Ernst Bloch, Bertolt Brecht and other such prominent Left-wing intellectuals who saw Third World revolutionary movements and Khrushchev's 1956 de-Stalinisation speech as the resumption of the march of history.[26] The end of ideology thesis came in many variants.[27] But it is Bell who ultimately popularised it for a wider audience in 1960 in his highly influential and much debated book *The End of Ideology: On the Exhaustion of Political Ideas in the Fifties*.[28] A work of remarkable erudition, *The End of Ideology* argued that the grand humanistic ideologies of the Enlightenment were exhausted and giving way to a middle-ground compromise on the virtues of a mixed economy and the welfare state. According to Bell, enlightenment ideologies had until the mid twentieth century functioned as compensatory devices for the erosion of religious worldviews. But their hubristic entrepreneurial outlook had now been completely discredited by the experience of Nazi and Soviet totalitarianism.[29] Bell therefore maintained that the 1960s would be a decade in which technical experts would tackle issues of social justice unimpeded by partisan hostilities. He predicted 'not only the shrinking of the industrial working class but the break-up of economic class as the fundamental axis of social division'.[30] For Bell and the end of ideologists, it was the global conflict with the Soviet Union that had become the ultimate source of domestic transformations:

> Politics today is not a reflex of any internal class divisions but is shaped by international events. And foreign policy, the expression of politics, is a response to many factors, the most important of which has been the estimate of Russian intentions. This estimate, the need for containment, made initially by Kennan, Acheson, and Truman and followed, with little fundamental change, by the succeeding administration, has set in its wake a whole consequent of political and social changes: the military build-up, regional military

alliances, the creation of a 'dual economy', a new role for science and scientists—all of which have reworked the map of American society.[31]

The 'Civil Wars' of the 1960s

Claims that the West had 'weathered the storm of ideology' could not have been less timely. Far from being the era of consensual politics predicted by end of ideologists, the 1960s turned out to be the most tumultuous decade in the history of post-war American politics. The stagnation of the world economy, the Vietnam War, the radicalisation of the civil rights movement, the cultural revolutions—together these events led to a 'renewal' of labour militancy and an unprecedented proliferation of new modes of resistance within American society. Indeed, at no other time since the American Civil War of 1861–5 have the domestic lines of enmity been so multiple. As Maurice Isserman and Michael Kazin explain in their history of this revolutionary decade:

> In the course of the 1960s, many Americans came to regard groups of fellow countrymen as enemies with whom they were engaged in a struggle for the nation's very soul. Whites versus blacks, liberals versus conservatives (as well as liberals versus radicals), young versus old, men versus women, hawks versus doves, rich versus poor, taxpayers versus welfare recipients, the religious versus the secular, the hip versus the straight, the gay versus the straight—everywhere one looked, new battalions took the field, in a spirit ranging from that of redemptive sacrifice to vengeful defiance.[32]

Amidst this political turmoil, both a New Right and a New Left emerged to pose serious ideological challenges to the liberal consensus. These would forever change the attitude of those who would become associated with the neoconservative movement towards the liberal establishment. On the Right, a serious body of conservative thought led by prominent European émigrés such as Friedrich von Hayek, Joseph Schumpeter, Leo Strauss and Eric Voegelin had begun to emerge in the 1950s. As suggested above, this body of thought had a rather modest impact on the political and intellectual disposition of the Right as a social movement in the immediate aftermath of the war. But by the end of the 1950s, the 'intellectual conservatism' of these European exiles had reached a wide audience. It had become a point of reference for many conservative activists and public intellectuals. Together with the 'neo-Burkean' traditionalism of the American philosopher Russell

Kirk and the distinctively conservative (and often messianic) anti-communism cultivated by William Buckley's *National Review*, this new body of conservative thought would become a crucial source of inspiration for the modernisation of the Old Right. As Sarah Diamond explains, the transformation of post-war American conservatism hinged on a flexible 'fusionist' compromise between the different strains of conservatism that existed in the US at the time. 'Fusionism, simply put, was the historical juncture at which Right-wing activists and intellectuals focused, diversely, on the libertarian, moral-traditionalist, and emerging anticommunist strains of conservative ideology, recognised their common causes and philosophies, and began to fuse their practical agendas'. Fusionism was *the* 'breakthrough ideological transformation' that led the Right out of the political impasse of the immediate post-war period.[33]

The changing fortunes of the Right were also in great part due to mounting discontent with the large-scale welfare programmes of the New Deal and the Great Society. As the US economy began to run out of steam from the late 1950s onwards, many Americans began to perceive a rise in the costs of minority gains. Increased state interventionism had unavoidably raised the tax burden of America's large white middle class. At the same time, racial integration and civil rights policies had contributed to undermining the legitimacy and dominance of the country's Anglo-Saxon and Protestant majority culture.[34] Traditionalists all across the country directed their anger at the federal government for enacting laws deemed to be too lenient towards crime. They also resented the government for passing legislation that banned officially sanctioned school prayers, authorised school busing and increased the cost of running a business by making record-keeping mandatory in view of potential legal actions over racial and gender discrimination.[35] As Republican pollster Kevin Phillips argued in *The Emerging Republican Majority*, the Democratic coalition began to fracture because its 'Negro socioeconomic revolution ... carried [the Democrats] beyond programmes taxing the few for the benefit of the many (the New Deal) to programmes taxing the many on behalf of the few (the Great Society)'.[36]

All of this bred a high level of frustration among the White working class-majority, especially in the increasingly populous Southern and Western states such as Arizona, Texas, Florida and California which form what Phillips famously termed the 'Sun Belt'. This populist backlash became the source of large-scale political support for the New

Right's agenda during the presidential race of Republican Senator Barry Goldwater in 1964. Although Goldwater lost by a landslide to President Lyndon B. Johnson, he won nearly 40 per cent of the vote. His campaign turned out to be the catalysing event for the emergence of a 'new' movement conservatism that became the motor of the Republican Party and that has grown steadily ever since.[37]

By comparison, the challenge of the New Left was relatively short-lived. But its immediate political shock on the American social compact was much more disruptive. The New Left was a multifaceted movement. Its agenda and political makings were too loose and vague to be defined in a coherent and consistent manner. It had its sources in the Old Left and in new political currents that began to take shape during the 1950s from within the liberal consensus. The New Left represented less a precise set of political doctrines than a new political awareness reflecting a changing social environment.[38] These were mainly men and women who increasingly felt alienated from the conformist bourgeois culture of their parents, and who had grown impatient with the moderate, reformist approach of the liberal elite. Unlike the liberalism of the establishment, which prized stability above all else, their liberalism was adversarial, self-righteous and eager to redress social injustices. As this new generation was slowly taking its place in American public life, new social movements began to emerge and raised questions about established authority in both the public and private spheres. The civil rights movement exposed the double standards of American society regarding social equality. The environmental and consumer protection movements exposed the dishonesty, greediness and heedlessness of powerful business interests. The feminist offensive on ascribed gender roles and other challenges to sexual conventions undermined authoritative wisdom about politeness and appropriate behaviour.

Still, as the 1950s drew to an end, there were in fact few signs of the radical insurgency that was about to take place. It was not until late in 1963 that the first indications of this radicalisation began to appear, as students mobilised under the umbrella of numerous activist organisations such as the Student Nonviolent Coordinating Committee (SNCC), the DuBois Clubs, the Young Socialist Alliance, the May 2nd Movement, and the Students for a Democratic Society (SDS). The SDS was the largest and arguably the most influential of these organisations. In its famous 1962 Port Huron Statement, it committed itself to the creation of a 'New Left' that would have the universities as its main agent of social change. The chief concerns of the document were nuclear weapons, poverty and the civil rights of African Americans. It emphasised the gulf between ideals such as 'all men are created equal' and the 'facts of Negro life in the South and the big cities of the North', and insisted that militarism abroad and anti-democratic practices at home were inexorably linked to one another. After acknowledging the overly bureaucratised and hierarchical character of the Old Left, the statement called for a new activism driven by the ideals of participatory democracy and rational deliberation.[39]

The Port Huron Statement sought to express the sense of urgency and exasperation felt by the 'people of this generation' and the New Left as a whole over the apathy of the average American. All in all, it was a relatively moderate call to action. Indeed, many of the demands that were put forth there would eventually be realised as part of the Johnson administration's Great Society programmes. But as the 1960s progressed, the New Left's demands and attacks on the establishment grew increasingly radical, and its militancy grew more and more adversarial. Tens of thousands of American students rose up against America's imperialist policies in South East Asia and against the universities' attempts to limit political activism on university campuses. They mobilised against the educational system, bureaucracy and the manipulation of information by the media. They also warned against the growing meaninglessness of work and the decline of organised labour generated by automation. Finally, they protested against the increasingly close ties between universities, business interests and the military industrial complex, and against the existential meaninglessness of a university experience driven by the demands of the market and the arms race.

By the mid 1960s, the New Left began to abandon its earlier commitments to non-violence and rational persuasion. Instead it favoured a new strategy of joint struggle with the Third World liberation movements, using the methods of revolutionary leaders like Che Guevara, Frantz Fanon, the Viet Cong and the Palestinian Liberation Front. This ultimately led to the bombings, arson and vandalism that would mark student protests thereafter. By going down this road, the New Left was following the movement for Black equality. Under the leadership of SNCC organiser Stokely Carmichael and the influence of the charismatic Black nationalist leader Malcolm X (assassinated in February 1965), the movement for Black equality had abandoned both non-violence and inter-racialism in 1966 in favour of armed self-defence and the slogan of 'Black Power'. The adoption of violent tactics like armed displays, rioting, kidnapping and murder by the Black Panthers and other such Black militant groups encouraged many among the more prosperous White population to leave urban centres for the suburbs. Those who could not afford such a move lived mainly in ethnic ghettos. They had to contend with the threat posed by a growing Black minority and the socio-economic decay of the city generated by the radicalisation of black militancy. This gave rise to White backlash movements in cities like Boston, Cleveland and many others where the majority of the White population had a relatively low income and faced the prospect of sending their children into a dilapidating school system under intense Black pressure for school integration. Black Power was an ideologically vague battle cry that meant different things to its supporters. But for many White Americans after the bloody race riots of the 'long hot summers' of 1966 and 1967, it came to signify a declaration of full-scale race war.[40]

The confrontations climaxed in 1968. This momentous year was marked by the Tet offensive in Vietnam; massive and particularly violent student protests in Ivy League universities like Columbia, Yale, Harvard, Cornell and Chicago (as well as in many European universities and metropolitan centres around the world); the assassination of Robert F. Kennedy and Martin Luther King, followed by large-scale urban race riots; President Lyndon Johnson's decision not to run for re-election; and the police riots against anti-war protesters outside the Democratic national convention in Chicago. This was also the year when the New Left began to disintegrate. The increasingly violent and sectarian character of its activities from then on reflected its mounting frustration at failing to achieve specific goals and finding constituents.

To many, the New Left often appeared more preoccupied with criticising US imperialism than with the immediate economic concerns of the White working class. The working class in the US lacked the degree of political consciousness and institutional organisation that had facilitated the alliance of students and Left-wing trade unions during the general strike in France in May 1968. Moreover, the rancorous rhetoric and the confrontational style of anti-war protesters often vexed the Americanist sentiment of many of its constituents: 'Both the manner and the privilege of many antiwar protesters antagonised millions of Americans who otherwise had little interest in supporting the war except as a patriotic reflex. Too often criticisms came across as scorn for the United States, for its history and its promises'.[41] Students, on the other hand, were the bearer of an energetic utopianism that served the New Left well in the early to mid 1960s. But they were a transient social force.[42] As William O'Neill argues, the majority of them were well-educated teenagers who came from liberal middle-class families. They soon realised the difficulties of using universities and participatory democracy to bring about the type of socio-political changes pursued by Third World revolutionaries in a country where the majority of the population supported the government. The most radical and frustrated among them who went on to join violent anarchist or Marxist-Leninist factions like the Weatherman, the Mad Dogs, the Crazies and the Motherfuckers were also confronted with the futility of revolutionary action in a country where the government has the monopoly on legitimate violence.[43]

Revolutionary terrorism, student protests and other forms of 'counter-cultural subversion' continued well into the next decade. Indeed, student militancy after the invasion of Cambodia was particularly disruptive. But by then the New Left had more or less collapsed, leaving behind a mass anti-war movement of alienated young people with very few plausible common political denominators.

To the Right

The collapse of the liberal consensus in the 1960s is the single most important event in the history of neoconservative thought. As the neoconservative literary critic Joseph Epstein explains:

> The sixties, I have come to believe, are something of a political Rorschach test. Tell me what you think of that period and I shall tell you what your politics are. Tell me that you think that period both good and bad, with much to be said for and against it, and you are, whether you know it or not, a liberal. Tell me that that you think the sixties a banner time in American life, a period of unparalleled idealism, a splendid opportunity sadly missed, and you are doubtless a radical, sentimental or otherwise. Tell me that you think the sixties a time of horrendous dislocation, a disaster nearly averted, a damn near thing, but a thing nonetheless for which we are still paying and shall continue to pay.... Well, I am not sure what you are precisely, but your views, friend, are close to mine and I am pleased to meet you.[44]

First-generation neoconservatives like to think of themselves as conservatives by default. Intellectually, their conservatism was born out of reflection on the reasons why American liberalism had fallen prey to what they saw as the misguided utopianism and destructive cultural relativism of the counter-culture. Politically, their conservatism was born out of frustration with the liberal elites for having allowed the New Left to flourish and gain influence over the Democratic Party. As Jeane Kirkpatrick recalled decades later:

> The 'neoconservative' designation puzzled me. I had never thought of myself as a conservative of any kind. What is a neoconservative? I asked my friend, Irving Kristol, who was widely described as the godfather of the neoconservative movement. He responded without hesitation that a neoconservative was a liberal who had been mugged by reality. That is, I thought, a person with a liberal past. It was the liberal past that distinguished a neoconservative from a traditional conservative, say Russell Kirk or Bill Buckley and all the others who had begun their political lives as traditional conservatives. The neocon had embraced liberal values and quite possibly never abandoned them, but was unhappy with the political turns taken by many in liberal ranks. Voila!, I thought, the neoconservative was born from a reaction to the counter-culture that dominated American politics through the sixties and seventies.[45]

The consolidation of neoconservatism as a loose ideological faction took place between the early-mid 1960s and the early 1970s in the pages of *Commentary* and *The Public Interest*. Although the term 'neoconservative' would not really be used until the early 1970s, those who wrote in these publications during the 1960s formed a distinct group of increasingly disillusioned liberals who became known as the neoconservatives during the 1970s. The neoconservatives' alienation from liberal ranks was driven mainly by two sets of issues. The first had to do with the causes and consequences of government failure and the view, held by many in liberal circles, that the state could and should play a more active role in effecting greater social equality. The other concerned what neoconservatives perceived as the failure of liberalism to understand the nature and political implications of the counter-cultural offensive of the 1960s. The two, of course, were not unrelated.

As suggested earlier, during the first half of the 1960s, the Democratic Party had provided a hospitable home for liberal intellectuals and their centrist, problem-solving approach to policy-making. The behaviouralist revolutions and the phenomenal growth of the social sciences in American universities had nurtured the belief among liberals that with sufficient resources and the help of well-designed studies the modernisation process could be controlled and its negative effects progressively eliminated. It is in this spirit that Bell and Kristol had founded *The Public Interest* during the fall of 1965. The aim was to generate social scientific knowledge and policy prescriptions that operated 'beyond ideology'.[46] But as student protests escalated and mass urban riots exploded in the face of the Democrats' Great Society agenda, optimism about the potential contribution of the social sciences to governmental problem-solving soon turned to caution and scepticism.

Neoconservatives began to direct their readers' attention towards the inner-city revolts and the public disillusionment that ensued from the shortcomings and perceived failures of the ambitious social programmes of the Great Society. In their view, this was evidence that even the best-intentioned and best-designed social scientific studies could not foresee the potentially damaging outcome of government action. In a complex and interdependent society like post-war America, government actions in one domain often have unexpected consequences in other domains. This tends to decrease the expected benefits of actions, and sometimes even produce the opposite of the desired objectives. This is what neoconservatives called the 'law of unintended consequences': 'the unanticipated consequences of social action are always more important and usually less agreeable than the intended consequences'.[47]

From the mid 1960s onwards, *The Public Interest* published a wide range of studies that sought to 'throw cold (or at least cooling) water on reformist enthusiasm' by exposing the unintended results of social policy. This included what neoconservatives saw as the destructive impact of welfare on the poor American family, the idleness allowed for in government jobs programmes, the homelessness cultivated by rent control etc.[48] Although they had all been supporters of the New Deal and the early civil rights movement, neoconservatives were growing increasingly alarmed by what they saw as the militance and culture of dependence bred by the so-called 'war on poverty'—especially among African-Americans, Puerto Ricans and other such large non-White ethnic minorities.

In their seminal 1963 study on ethnicity, *Beyond the Melting Pot*, Glazer and Moynihan had expressed scepticism about the integrationist policies pursued by liberal policy-makers. They warned that race issues could prove to be beyond the ability of the government to solve. Their scepticism stemmed from their belief that ethnicity and race have always formed—and will always form—the basis of precisely the type of involuntary negative associations that pose obstacles to liberal conceptions of integration. Although they supported anti-discrimination laws, they insisted that many reasons other than discrimination accounted for the socio-economic depravation of ethnic minorities. As measures get implemented, they argued, '[w]e may discover that discrimination is only the first crude barrier to integration, and that people are more complicated than either racists or those who deny the reality of race believe'.[49] Yet in spite of this scepticism, Glazer, Moynihan and most other neoconservatives continued to support the civil rights movement until at least the mid 1960s. It was only when many within the civil rights movement began to push for a shift from integrationism to demands for equality of results that they revised their position from one of half-reluctant support to outright opposition.

The publication of Moynihan's study *The Negro Family: The Case for National Action* in March 1965 turned out to be a defining moment in that respect.[50] The study was produced for the Office of Policy Planning while Moynihan was in his function as Johnson's Assistant Secretary of Labor. It argued that anti-segregation and voting rights laws alone could not remedy the historical conditions that would prevent African-Americans from taking advantage of newly created opportunities. Years of slavery and subordinate positions in the labour market had created unstable conditions for Black families—often the absence of a strong father figure, teenage pregnancies and illegitimate births, juvenile delinquence—that would perpetuate poverty and welfare dependence irrespective of the new civil rights legislation. Moynihan's study was an 'ambiguous' case for equality of results. It was targeting precisely those barriers to integration that formal legal measures alone could not address. But the timing of the study, and the fact that it appeared to blame victimised Black families for their own plights, antagonised the African-American community and the civil rights movement as a whole. Newspapers and the New Left accused Moynihan of fuelling racist and moralising stereotypes at a time when racial tensions were rife and the government was struggling to meet the rising economic expectations of African-Americans. Indeed, many critics blamed what became known as 'The Moynihan Report' for the large-scale race riots that broke out in the Watts area of Los Angeles two months later.[51]

This was a bruising experience for Moynihan. And it was an important formative experience for his neoconservative colleagues. Neoconservatives furiously denounced the failure of liberals to defend Moynihan against Left-wing 'radicals' who, in their view at least, unjustly accused him of racism. They believed that liberals in universities, the media and elsewhere knew very well that Moynihan was not a racist. But liberals would no longer stand for their beliefs and defend existing institutions against student radicalism and black militance, strictly out of fear of being perceived as reactionary. According to neoconservatives, radicals were creating an intellectual climate in which open intellectual debates and dissent from mainstream liberal views on race and many other issues like Vietnam and education had become impossible. As James Q. Wilson wrote of his experience at Harvard:

> [It is] within higher education that one finds today many ... of the most serious threats to certain liberal values—the harassment of unpopular views, the use of force to prevent certain persons from speaking, the adoption of quota systems either to reduce the admissions of other kinds, and the politicisation of the university to make it an arena for the exchange of manifestoes rather than a forum for the discussion of ideas.[52]

What infuriated neoconservatives was that, in their view, liberals preached tolerance without understanding that what was being tolerated was a destructive attack on the essence of their own profession and mode of existence.[53] The Moynihan episode and other similar instances of liberal 'failure of nerves' within academic and policy-making communities only increased the resolve of neoconservative intellectuals to speak out against liberal orthodoxies on social policy matters. Neoconservatives worried about what they saw as the socially divisive effects of social welfare programmes. They argued that Johnson's welfare programmes exacerbated demands for group rights as opposed to individual rights and thereby mobilised 'American against American, class against class, race against race, ethnic group against ethnic group'.[54] Suddenly, American values and institutions were no longer the solution that had to be exported to solve the problem of order in world politics. They had become the very source of East-West animosity and Third World misery. These were charges that neoconservatives simply could not accept. As Podhoretz recalled in a 1989 article:

> Somewhat to our own surprise, we found that we simply could not stomach the hatred of 'Amerika' that increasingly pervaded the New Left and the counterculture. And this revulsion led to a process of reflection and reconsideration that gradually brought us to a new appreciation of the virtues of the American political system and of its economic and social underpinnings. So profoundly

affected were we by this new appreciation that we have been devoting ourselves ever since to defending America against the defamations of its enemies abroad and the denigrations of its critics at home. Almost every idea espoused by the neoconservatives relates back to this central impulse to defend America against the assaults of the left.[55]

Most neoconservatives opposed the Vietnam War from the very beginning. Yet none of them believed that Vietnam had anything to do with the political, economic or cultural fabric of American society and institutions. Neoconservatives opposed the war on realist grounds. Like Hans Morgenthau, they believed that the war was the product of a flawed analysis of the geostrategic environment and a misinterpretation of the national interest. They believed that it was a reckless and irresponsible use of American power informed by liberal zeal and geopolitical miscalculations.[56] As Podhoretz explains, for neoconservatives it was the 'wrong war in the wrong place at the wrong time' but for very different reasons from those put forward by the New Left. For the New Left:

American intervention in Vietnam was not a mistaken extension to Asia of the strategy of containment that had worked so well in holding the Soviet Union back in Europe; it was a criminal act of imperialism aimed at suppressing the legitimate national aspirations of a downtrodden dark-skinned people. It was the 'wrong war' not because it was a wasteful and imprudent use of American power, but because it was morally evil; it was the 'wrong place' not because it was a foolishly chosen political and military field on which to hold the line against the spread of Communism, but because the fight being conducted by the Communists there was a fight for freedom that deserved our sympathy, not our opposition; and it was the 'wrong time' not because conditions in the United States were unfavourable to the building of support for such a war, but because *any* time was the wrong time for such a war.[57]

Again here, what infuriated neoconservatives the most was that liberals did not understand that the aim of the New Left was not only to stop the Vietnam War. The New Left's aim was to institute a completely new social contract which, according to neoconservatives, challenged all conventional wisdom about the nature of the social world. As Kirkpatrick wrote at the time:

The New Politics is the expression of the political counter-culture; it is united by its opposition to the traditional political culture, and it challenges that culture's central beliefs: the belief that politics if based on self-interest; that conflict is a permanent feature of politics; that the pursuit of individual purpose is socially beneficial; that freedom is rooted in law; that equality of opportunity and individual achievement constitute a just basis of reward; that power is an instrument necessary to social and international peace... that those who cannot work should be supported by public funds and those who will not should be treated less generously; that authority rests on force as well as consent ... that work (read discipline) has intrinsic value for persons and societies; that citizenship requires obedience to laws with which one disagrees; that violation of the law should be punished; that order is a prerequisite to both liberty and justice; that patriotism is a social virtue; that the U.S. is basically a decent and successful—though imperfect—society.[58]

In a famous *Commentary* article, Theodore Draper invoked 'The Specter of Weimar' and warned that American democracy could be 'destined to suffer the fate of Weimar Germany'.[59] Just as 'liberal tolerance' had prevented many within the Democratic Party from recognising the existential character of the Soviet enemy during the early days of the Cold War, so liberals now failed to understand the truly radical and uncompromising character of the cultural revolutions that were devouring America's youth. More importantly, they failed to understand that their liberalism provided the liberties that were in the process of destructing the political system that made liberal freedoms possible in the first place. Abandoned by liberal intellectuals, bourgeois society was yielding to the cultural revolutions and absorbing the very ideas that would eventually lead to its collapse. As Kristol wrote in 1970:

One wonders: how can a bourgeois society survive in a cultural ambiance that derides every traditional bourgeois virtue and celebrates promiscuity, homosexuality, drugs, political terrorism—anything, in short, that is in bourgeois eyes perverse... there is something positively absurd in the spectacle of prosperous suburban fathers flocking to see—and evidently enjoying The Graduate—or of prosperous, chic, suburban mothers unconcernedly humming 'Mrs. Robison' to themselves as they cheerfully drive off to do their duties as den mothers. This peculiar schizophrenia, suffusing itself through the bourgeois masses of our urban society, may be fun while it last; but one may reasonably suppose that, sooner or later, people will decide they would rather not die laughing at themselves, and that some violent convulsions will ensue.[60]

By the early 1970s, neoconservatives had effectively abandoned their liberal credentials. Although some were less keen to admit it than others, the mutation of their early scepticism towards social policy into outright acceptance of the inevitability of social inequality placed those disgruntled liberals well within the realm of conservative political philosophy. As Kristol explains in his memoirs, his 'neoconservatisation' was more a discovery than a radical transformation. For him, the move to conservatism and the new identity that this move afforded him turned out to be 'an experience of moral, intellectual and spiritual liberation': 'I no longer had to pretend to believe—what in my heart I could no longer believe—that liberals were wrong because they subscribe to this or that erroneous opinion on this or that topic. No—liberals were wrong, liberals are wrong, because they are liberals. What is wrong with liberalism is liberalism—a metaphysics and a mythology that is woefully blind to human and political reality'.[61]

After the defeat of the Left-leaning Democratic presidential candidate George McGovern in 1972, a number of neoconservative intellectuals led by Jeane Kirkpatrick, Ben Wattenberg and Democratic Senator Henry Scoop Jackson's aide, Richard Perle, united with discontented Democratic politicians, university professors and trade union leaders to form the Coalition for a Democratic Majority (CDM). As Lipset recalls, the CDM was 'the one important neoconservative organisation during the seventies and early eighties'.[62] The stated aim of the CDM was to undermine McGovern's support and counter the growing influence of the Left's 'New Politics' within the Democratic Party.

Neoconservatives used the term 'New Politics' to refer to Left-wing activists and social movements who were willing to work from within the party system. In their view, the 'New Politics' promoted 'forces and ideas unrepresentative of traditional Democratic principles'.[63] These principles included affirmative action, unpatriotic opposition to the Vietnam War and what many labour officials considered to be an offensive lack of support for trade unions. In 1969, McGovern and his 'New Politics' supporters had introduced new rules within the party concerning the selection of delegates. The aim was to render the process more representative of the gender and racial composition of the American electorate. Neoconservatives and other critics within the party saw this as a form of positive discrimination in favour of Blacks, women and young adults at the expense of labour representatives and party diehards who primarily represented the interests of the White working class. The 'New Politics' was perceived as a new kind of liberalism inspired by the activism of the 1960s and alienating the traditional constituency of the Democratic Party.[64] It was the liberalism of young, educated and affluent activists who 'championed the poor but not the working class; who admired African Americans but not the white lower-middle class; who believed in education and equality but not the trials of home ownership and playing by the rules; who believed in a new cultural agenda but not the family; who believed in an upper-middle-class bohemianism but none of the values of the simple bourgeoisie'.[65]

The creation of the Coalition for a Democratic Majority marked the beginning of a major political realignment from which the Democratic Party would never recover. This realignment had its roots in the growing gap between organised labour and the new social movements. It took place throughout the 1970s and eventually led to the migration of many Democrat voters and neoconservative intellectuals to the Republican Party.

The 'Return' to Ideology

The consolidation of neoconservatism as a political faction, along with its reluctant realignment with the Republican Party during the 1970s and early 1980s, were characterised by two main developments: a 'return' to ideology and an increased involvement in foreign policy debates.

As American society faltered out of the 1960s, neoconservatives had come to the conclusion that the rationalist-positivist approaches to the social sciences which they had endorsed earlier were partly responsible for the disasters of the closing decade. The social sciences profession had failed to recognise that the success of its policy prescriptions depended upon the existence of a widely shared value consensus which could no longer be taken for granted. What this meant was that political science would have to give way to political philosophy.

Neoconservatives found much intellectual support for the legitimisation of their political objectives in the work of Leo Strauss and other conservative thinkers like Friedrich von Hayek, Russell Kirk and Eric Voegelin. Yet because of its elitist nature and its sceptical attitude towards all established social truths, political philosophy was thought to be of relatively limited use to fight a culture war against a Left which owed its popular appeal to its utopian aspirations. In a country driven by technological innovation and economic growth, the anti-modern and nostalgic character of traditional conservative political philosophy offered few resources for the mobilisation of public opinion. Neoconservatives wanted American conservatism to abandon defensive politics. It wanted conservatism to overcome its disdain for visionary politics and become more ideological.[66]

In practical terms this implied that the American Right would have to put politics in front of economics and take its fight into the realm of culture. This would not be a question of direct lobbying power as such, but of cultural definition and redefinition. It would be a populist fight to rebuild a community consensus on certain values and lifestyles that could serve as a basis for the assimilation of individuals into a common hegemonic identity. This is what Kristol called 'American bourgeois populism':

> Any ideology that gives politics a priority over economics is bound to have a populist hue, since most ordinary people—in this day and age at least, and perhaps always—see things in that same order. The 'conservatism' of neoconservatism leads naturally to an insistence on standards of excellence and virtue; it is anything but populist in that respect, and indeed would seem to be what we have come to call 'elitist'.... But the 'neo' in neoconservatism is its insistence that the American people have always had an instinctive deference toward such standards, and that American democracy has never been egalitarian in this sense. Economic and cultural egalitarianism—as distinct from the social and legal egalitarianism essential to a viable democracy—has been a passion of the intellectual class, never of the people.... Our intellectuals may feel 'alienated' from the orthodoxy represented by the 'American way of life'; they may feel homeless and hopeless in the world this way of life has created. The American people, in their overwhelming majority, do not feel so alienated, homeless, or hopeless. It is the self-imposed assignment of neoconservatism to explain to the American people why they are right, and to intellectuals why they are wrong.[67]

Neoconservatives had come a long way from the 'non-ideological and non-partisan' attitude to knowledge professed by *The Public Interest* in 1965. For them, what logically followed from this politicisation of knowledge was that they had to build their own knowledge industry geared towards conservative ends. They proceeded to recruit conservative thinkers of all stripes (especially Straussians) and courted experts' sympathy for conservative ideas by convincing the corporate elite to fund research and all sorts of educational projects.[68] According to neoconservatives, America's growing appetite for social equality was fuelled by a growing 'animus towards the business class' amongst a 'new class' of intellectuals and professionals who had a vested interest in the growth of the 'welfare industry' (see Chapter 3). As a member of the *Wall Street Journal*'s board of contributors, Kristol took it upon himself to convince the business community that it had to take ideas seriously. He argued that foundations, which were in great part funded by the money of businessmen who had been successful in the past, should start investing in 'the survival of the corporation itself as a relatively autonomous institution in the private sector' rather than funding ill-conceived social programmes.[69]

Kristol's recommendations did not fall on deaf ears. Neoconservatives, along with their incipient free marketer New Right allies, became both facilitators and beneficiaries of a major political mobilisation of big business. This mobilisation led to the revitalisation of the American Enterprise Institute (AEI) and the Hoover Institution, along with the creation of a whole range of other anti-egalitarian think thanks and foundations. These became home to prominent free market ideologists like Milton Friedman, Friedrich von Hayek and Jude Wanniski. They also distributed research grants and stipends to influential Straussian scholars like Ralph Lerner, Allan Bloom, Walter Berne, Thomas Pangle, Joseph Cropsey and Clifford Orwin in universities across North America.[70] According to Sara Diamond, 'In 1977, about 200 corporations provided 25 per cent of AEI's $5 million budget; by 1981, 600 corporate donors accounted for 40 per cent of a $10 million budget'. In 1978 Kristol and William Simon, the Secretary of the Treasury under Nixon, founded the Institute for Educational Affairs (IEA) to promote free market ideas and values across different academic disciplines. 'With initial grants of $100,000 each from the John M. Olin Foundation, the Scaife Family Trusts, the JM Foundation and the Smith-Richardson Foundation, IEA assembled a donor base of dozens of corporations, including Bechtel, Coca-Cola, Dow Chemical, Ford Motor Company, General Electric, K-Mart, Mobil, and Nestlé. The idea was for corporations to donate directly to IEA, whose board of largely neoconservative intellectuals then dispensed grants to applicants'.[71] (The IEA is the ancestor of the neoconservative National Association of Scholars created in 1987 after Allan Bloom's unlikely bestseller, *The Closing of the American Mind*, 'alerted Americans to the ravages wrought by illiberal ideologies' and the 'post-modernist evisceration of the humanities' on university campuses.)[72]

According to Paul Gottfried, neoconservative enterprise from the 1980s onwards became dependent on annual funding from philanthropic foundations 'well in excess of 50 million dollars, plus patronage from the World Unification Church, Australian press baron Rupert

Murdoch, and foreign governments opposed to American protectionism'.[73] This mobilisation of corporate power has therefore allowed neoconservatives to build an impressive intellectual infrastructure for the dissemination of their ideas. As *American Conservative* editor Scott McConnell wrote in 2005, 'One thing the neocons have that both other factions of conservatives and liberals don't have is they can employ a lot of people. AEI provides a seat for the kind of midlevel intellectuals who can produce op-ed pieces. It's 50 to 100 people with decent prose styles or Ph.D.s and they form a critical mass. They help create the reality of being the dominant strain of conservatism'.[74] Through this far-reaching ideological network, neoconservatives have been able to influence academic trends and thereby complement their direct policy lobbying better than any other political factions in the US.[75]

As suggested earlier, this turn towards ideology was accompanied by an increased involvement in foreign policy debates. This was in great part a reaction to the increasingly obvious prospect of an American defeat in Vietnam and the consequences of that defeat for the broader struggle against the Soviet Union. For it was not the conduct of the war itself that predominantly preoccupied neoconservatives. Rather, it was what Podhoretz would come to call the 'culture of appeasement' that it supposedly fostered among a liberal elite whose political leadership had allegedly been compromised by the 'New Politics' and the subversive influence of the adversary culture. The 'culture of appeasement' was characterised by un-Americanism, lack of resolve, 'unmanly' deference to public opinion, and misplaced 'liberal guilt' generated by the Vietnam War over the plight of the Third World as a whole.[76]

Neoconservatives were particularly anxious about the warm reception that the 'third-worldism' of the American Left found in the UN General Assembly. They 'noted that the same liberals who had substituted collective guilt for individual accountability with the criminal justice system and affirmative action in the United States were now blaming the problems of the Third World on the West'.[77] Neoconservatives saw redistributive resolutions such as the Programme of Action on the Establishment of a New International Economic Order (1974), the Charter of Economic Rights and Duties of States (1975), and the Constitution of the United Nations Industrial Development Organization (1979) as symptoms of misplaced liberal guilt which recently decolonised countries were only too happy to exploit.[78] The US was now outnumbered and no longer capable of dominating the General

Assembly. It found itself on the defensive and condemned for its implicit and explicit support of decayed European empires in Africa and Asia.

Anti-American and anti-Western posture in the General Assembly reached its climax in November 1975 with the approval of the famous UN resolution 3379. Resolution 3379 stated that Zionism was 'a Form of Racism and Racial Discrimination'. It had been sponsored by 25 states, including some particularly brutal dictatorships. In a speech that would earn him a standing ovation, the Ugandan dictator Idi Amin called upon Americans 'to rid their society of Zionists'. He demanded nothing less than 'the expulsion of Israel from the United Nations and the extinction of Israel as a State'.[79] For neoconservatives, resolution 3379 became a symbol of the irreversible moral bankruptcy of the UN. It also confirmed the political irrelevance of what had once been a key instrument for the maintenance of American hegemony. Moynihan, who was US ambassador at the UN at the time (1975–6), fervently condemned the resolution as a revolting manipulation of the enlightened ideals enshrined in the UN Charter. He blamed liberal forbearance for the hopeless decay of the world organisation.[80] Likewise, Kirkpatrick, who would later also serve as US ambassador to the UN (1981–5), argued that liberals made the mistake of treating UN multilateralism as a form of consensus-seeking diplomacy. She maintained that the UN and other multilateral institutions could be useful tools of statecraft if they served American values and interests. But once they fell under the spell of a Marxian 'Third World Ideology', anti-Americanism became the flavour of all UN deliberations in a way that elevated all national and regional issues into issues of complex global interdependence.[81]

During the 1970s, the idea of 'complex interdependence' had become one of the key concepts of liberal thought in international relations.[82] The idea anticipated much of what today falls under the category of 'globalisation'. 'Complex interdependence' denoted a progressive and more pronounced interconnectedness between states, civil societies and markets, driven mainly by technological development and the advances of mass communications. Central to 'complex interdependence' was the notion that greater interconnectedness and technological advances in the area of weaponry had radically increased the unpredictability and destructive potential of organised violence. This generated an imperative for nuclear arms regulation and collective security agreements of all sorts. Since the beginning of the Cold War, both the US and the USSR had accumulated enormous nuclear stockpiles under the strategic logic of 'mutually assured destruction' (MAD). The US maintained a lead until the late 1960s. But by the early 1970s the Soviet Union had achieved nuclear parity. This led to the Strategic Arms Limitation Talks (SALT). The talks were designed to prevent the arms race getting out of control and reduce the risk of global nuclear annihilation.

Neoconservatives criticised arms limitations and arms reduction agreements on both strategic and moral grounds. Strategically, they pointed at the technical deficiencies of the SALT treaty and argued that the limits imposed on US nuclear weapons granted a de facto nuclear advantage to the Soviets which the latter would exploit without hesitation. They condemned deterrence and 'nuclear sufficiency' on the basis that such doctrines abandoned the traditional objective of strategic primacy and thereby placed the security of the United States into the hands of its enemy. Strategic interdependence undermined the credibility of American resolve in the eyes of both its enemies and its allies, and it limited the agency and decision-making capacity of the executive. Strategic interdependence was also deficient at the moral level, because it conferred de facto legitimacy on the Soviet Union and thereby put both superpowers in a relationship of moral equivalence.[83]

Neoconservatives opposed détente for a similar set of reasons. Détente and the turn to realism under Kissinger during this tumultuous period were a response to the relative decline of American power and the disorienting socio-cultural experience that accompanied that process. With the rise of accusing voices in the Third World and the emergence of new centres of power in Europe and Asia, détente promised a cheaper and less burdensome form of containment that would allow the US to extricate itself from Indochina with a certain degree of respectability. With most economic indicators in decline and US public diplomacy in tatters, many within the foreign policy community greeted Kissinger's Metternichean diplomacy as a sound strategy to keep control of events within America's sphere of influence—but not the neoconservatives.

First, neoconservatives believed that the depreciation of ideology in Kissinger's framework had led him to misunderstand the nature of the Soviet enemy. As Podhoretz wrote in the early 1980s, Kissinger 'saw the Soviet-Union as a nation-state like any other, motivated by the same range of interests that define and shape the foreign policy of all nation-states'.[84] By contrast, neoconservatives insisted that the Soviet Union was not a traditional state. It represented 'a radically different idea about how to organise social, political, and economic life on this earth'. The Soviet Union was a prisoner of its own ideology in a way that forced its elite onto an expansionist path and defied traditional understandings of the national interest. Neoconservatives argued that although communist leaders might no longer believe in Marxism-Leninism, it remained their only source of legitimation in the domestic sphere. Hence they could not be satisfied with strictly maintaining the status quo; their own political survival depended on the establishment of subdued satellite states.[85]

Secondly, given the predominantly Jewish composition of neoconservative ranks, neoconservatism has always been deeply committed to the defence of Israel. As détente unfolded, neoconservatives feared that the relaxation of superpower tension could lead the US to reduce its commitments to the survival of Israel—at the same time as the Soviet Union would maintain or strengthen its own commitments to Israel's enemies. The Arab-Israeli War of October 1973 appeared to lend credence to these anxieties. For although the US provided Israel with crucial material assistance, and despite the fact that Nixon put the military on high alert worldwide when the Soviets threatened to intervene, America ultimately joined the Soviet Union in co-sponsoring a UN resolution demanding a ceasefire before Israel could complete its encirclement of the Egyptian army. The US then also threatened to interrupt its material assistance if Israel did not put an end to its violations of the ceasefire and agree to negotiate a truce. As McCormick explains:

> The lesson drawn by Israel supporters from these developments was not that détente had failed; that they would have welcomed. On the contrary, despite the Soviet-American tension during the American military alert, détente by and large worked. It worked, however, in ways contrary to Israel's long-term desire to maximise its freedom to pursue its own security. Détente in operation had demonstrated that the two superpowers might collude in ways inimical to chosen Israeli policy. It also demonstrated increased sensitivity by American leaders to the economic clout manifested in the OPEC oil embargo during the war. Taken together, Russian-American détente and OPEC solidarity seemed to pro-Israelis to pose a situation far different and far less satisfactory than the earlier epoch (the 1967 Six Days' War, for example) when they

could count on simple, uncompromisingly pro-Israeli, anti-Soviet policy by the United States.[86]

Neoconservatives deplored the 'abandonment' of the only liberal democracy in the Middle East. They saw this as the manifestation of a broader foreign policy shift towards a relativist style of *Realpolitik* that was just as 'un-American' as its main architect. As Walter Lacquer put it in a vicious attack on the newly promoted Secretary of State in December 1973, Kissinger 'is an unassimilated outsider ... a European by heritage and cultural choice, a cosmopolitan by circumstance, and American by deliberate (and hazardous) calculation ... he revealed the derivative nature of his national identity in an almost pathetic fashion'.[87] And this was yet another important source of neoconservative discontent with détente. Neoconservatives saw Kissinger's materialist redefinition of the national interest as a negation of the ethical essence of the nation. No less than New Left accusations of imperialism, Kissinger's realism both reflected and exacerbated the rapid cultural degeneration of American civil society since the early 1960s. Kissinger's own account of his feud with the neoconservatives is worth citing at length:

> The radical opponents of the Vietnam War had ascribed the failures in Indochina to moral defects and had preached the cure of abdication to enable the United States to concentrate on self-improvement. The neoconservatives reversed the lesson, seeing in moral regeneration the key to reengagement. Nixon and I agreed with the neoconservative premise, but we also believed that the Wilsonianism of the early 1960s had lured us into adventures beyond our capacities and deprived us of criteria to define the essential elements of our national purpose. Those of us who had been mauled by the Vietnam protests were deeply concerned with avoiding a repetition of this paralysis. We therefore searched for a more sober approach to American foreign policy that would—as we repeatedly stated—avoid the oscillations between abdication and overextension that had marked the previous period.
>
> The neoconservatives insisted that such an approach did not do justice to the moral dynamism of a society that had turned its back on the callous calculations of the Old World. In the process, they put forward not so much a new dispensation—as they claimed—but a return to a militant, muscular Wilsonianism. The fundamental aim of foreign policy as they saw it was the eradication of the evil presented by the Soviet Union without confusing the issue with geopolitics.
>
> Whereas Nixon (and I) saw the greatest danger in creeping Soviet expansionism abetted by Soviet superiority in conventional forces, interior lined of com-

munication, and the umbrella of vast and growing strategic nuclear force, the neoconservatives' stated nightmare was some apocalyptic showdown over world domination. The Nixon team viewed the conflict with Moscow as a long-term geopolitical contest in which, together with our allies, we would wear down the Soviet system. The neoconservatives argued that it was possible to overcome communism with a burst of ideological elan.[88]

Domestic politics thus played a crucial role in this contest over foreign policy. As the Cold War historian Jeremy Suri argued, détente was a profoundly conservative strategy that sacrificed domestic reforms for the sake of international stability. Yet it grew in great part out of an increasing urge for domestic stability among leaders who could no longer assume that they commanded legitimacy in the eyes of their own citizenry. Brandt, de Gaulle, Nixon, Brezhnev and Mao all used the prospects of great power cooperation to denounce domestic unrest and argue that their respective domestic opponents threatened international peace.[89]

Although détente had to a certain extent succeeded in calming domestic unrest, neoconservatives complained that the 'anti-ideological' and secretive manoeuvring with which Kissinger conducted his realist diplomacy had isolated domestic opponents from the political process without ever re-assimilating them. After having failed to gain the support of trade unions and link with the formal organisations of the Old Left in the 1960s, the new social movements emerging out of the defeated democratic surges rejected formal organised representations altogether.[90] Instead, they favoured postmodern discourses of individuated emancipation driven by a deep distrust of party and state bureaucracy and a pronounced scepticism of all collective forms of political subjectivity. This new identity politics asked not for tolerance but for the public affirmation of individual and group differences—not as pathological deviations to be accepted reluctantly by the majority, but as worthy ways of leading individual and collective life. In the eyes of its advocates, this represented a fight for self-determination and human dignity against the false universalisms of the establishment and the hegemony of the heterosexual, White Anglo-Saxon majority culture. For neoconservatives, it was a cultural and moral tragedy, a relativist and self-defeating celebration of difference for difference's sake that lethally undermined exceptionalist meta-narratives of US diplomacy.

As the war scholar Christopher Coker pointed out, the 'social surges of individualisation' of the 1970s brought America's collective will to power into question. It undermined its readiness to assert that will against an 'other' whom individual Americans increasingly perceived to be constitutive of their own identity. 'Of the 2 million young men who were called up for Vietnam', Coker reminds us, 'an unprecedented 139,000 refused to be drafted'. The ethos of 'manifest destiny' that had underwritten American power throughout the twentieth century was self-referential, self-absorbed and self-regarding. It 'barely took into account other people or nations or individuals, or when it did it subsumed the latter into larger categories to be redeemed or rescued, or even punished, as the power that was "willing" saw fit'. The 1970s changed all that. The growing sense of interdependence generated by the revolutions in the spheres of culture and communications undermined the self-referentiality of American exceptionalism, and with it the capacity of the elites to give meaning to the projection of American power.[91] As Bell wrote at the time, 'In the heyday of the imperial republic, the quiet sense of destiny and the harsh creed of personal conduct were replaced by a virulent "Americanism," a manifest destiny that took us overseas, and a materialist hedonism which provided the incentives to work. Today that manifest destiny is shattered, the Americanism has worn thin, and only hedonism remains. It is a poor recipe for national unity and purpose'.[92]

Neoconservatives were particularly concerned that the defeat in Vietnam and the identity politics of the 1970s might lead to a crippling lack of will when the time came again to use military power to defend vital American interests—the so-called 'Vietnam syndrome'. As Midge Decter recalls, for neoconservatives 'domestic policy was foreign policy, and vice versa'.[93] When they became convinced that the elite no longer had the nerve to defend American values and institutions against the 'relativistic lunacies' of the Left, neoconservatives began to suspect that this same elite would also be lowering its guard vis-à-vis its external enemies.[94] Peter Steinfels has well captured the logic of the argument in his 1979 book on the movement:

> The United States must have a strong, confident elite willing to employ American power swiftly and decisively if the nation is to cope with international danger. But international danger exists, *ipso facto*, if the United States is lacking in a strong, confident elite willing to employ its power. The argument is not quite circular, but ultimately rests on the more or less permanent state of international rivalry that exists between great powers rather than on specific events as cause for concerns. With the exception of the precarious situation of Israel, in Angola or Afghanistan, are less important in themselves than as

markers of how far America has fallen from the necessary strength of will. Thus neoconservatives are undoubtedly sincere in their anxiety over international affairs, at the same time as the essential source of that anxiety is not military or geopolitical or to be found overseas at all; it is domestic and cultural and ideological.... The existence of an ideologically armed and intact elite is the crucial ingredient, and its role in resisting external pressure is only the reverse side of its role in resisting internal disintegration.[95]

The Carter presidency turned out to be particularly exasperating for neoconservatives in this respect. Carter was also a proponent of détente who, even more than his two predecessors, played down the importance of the Cold War as the overarching framework determining America's foreign affairs. Although they found him less offensive than McGovern, neoconservatives were dismayed by Carter's appeasing attitude towards communism. Just around the time of his election, the Coalition for a Democratic Majority (CDM) had joined forces with the newly revived Committee on the Present Danger (CPD). The CDP was a hard-line anti-communist organisation dominated by conservative Republicans. It sought to revive containment militarism as the core of American foreign policy.[96] After the election, the CPD and the CDM lobbied Carter for a prompt return to proactive containment militarism. They presented him with a list of 60 leading neoconservatives whom they wanted to see appointed to high-ranking positions in his administration. Carter, however, was resolute in seeking détente with the Soviets. He wanted little to do with the Cold War-mongering of neoconservatives, despite the fact that many of them had campaigned for him.[97]

Carter's refusal to appoint neoconservatives further alienated neoconservatives from the Democratic Party. It eventually led them to form an alliance with the fusionist New Right in an attempt to force Carter to reverse his détente policies and mobilise support against the SALT II disarmament treaty.[98] Carter eventually gave in during the second half of his term, partly because of intense Right-wing pressures and partly because his policies had been implemented inconsistently. After the Soviet invasion of Afghanistan, he authorised a massive increase in military spending, reinstated draft registration and imposed trade sanctions on the USSR at the same time as the Iranian Revolution disrupted oil supplies and generated an inflationary spiral that sank the US economy.[99]

Ronald Reagan won a landslide victory in 1980 on the back of Carter's foreign policy failures and the disaffection of traditional

Democrat voters since the early-mid 1970s. Neoconservatives were quick to take credit for his victory. Indeed, according to Podhoretz, neoconservatives were the intellectual power brokers who made his rise to power possible:

> If the grip of the conventional liberal wisdom and leftist orthodoxies in the world of ideas had not been loosened by the criticisms of the neoconservatives; if a correlative willingness to entertain new ideas had not thereby been created; and if these new ideas had not been plausibly articulated and skilfully defended in the trials by intellectual combat that do so much to shape public opinion in the United States—if not for all this, Ronald Reagan would in all probability have been unable to win over the traditionally Democratic constituencies (blue-collar workers, white-ethnic groups like the Irish and the Italians and a surprisingly high percentage of Jews) whose support swept him into the White House.[100]

Reagan vowed to regenerate confidence in governmental power. He promised to reinvigorate America's sense of purpose in the world by rallying the nation behind an anti-communist crusade abroad and fighting big government at home. What this meant in practice was that he would expand government powers where necessary to fight the so-called 'Second Cold War', while simultaneously deregulating markets, privatising the state's service-providing functions and rolling back the welfarist measures introduced by the Great Society programmes. This would stimulate capitalism, allow for a transfer of state spending into the military sector and restore the power of the White Anglo-Saxon majority culture in the educational system.[101] Reagan reasserted the old certainties of the early Cold War and used this military escalation to launch a domestic counter-offensive against the new social movements and discipline trade unions whenever the latter appeared to pose a threat to the vitality of American capitalism.[102]

It is not difficult to understand why neoconservatives were so fond of this former Hollywood actor. In a way, Reagan was the embodiment of the neoconservative aversion for liberal tolerance and relativism. His 'bourgeois populist' appeal, his ability to distinguish friend from enemy clearly, and his unconditional support for missile defence quickly earned him the utmost respect among neoconservative ranks. Reagan, Podhoretz wrote cheerfully in January 1981, would finish off the 'New Politics' and implement the agenda fought for by neoconservatives throughout the 1970s: 'economic policy that will unleash the productive energies of an artificially hampered people and thereby foster growth; a programme of rearmament that will make our defense invulnerable; a legal structure that will encourage the revitalisation of the values of "family, work, and neighbourhood"'.[103] Most neoconservatives who, unlike Kristol and Podhoretz, had not campaigned vigorously for Reagan during the previous year joined the Republican Party after his victory. The attraction between Reagan and the neoconservatives was mutual. After his election, over 60 members of the CDM were appointed to important posts in his new administration.[104] For the first time, neoconservatives were no longer wielding influence strictly through conferences, books, magazines and newspaper columns but from within the government through important roles at the national administrative level.

To be sure, Reagan's diplomatic overtures to the Soviet Union and his move towards disarmament during his second term would turn out to be a huge disappointment for his neoconservative supporters. Indeed, many would begin to express their discontent already by the beginning of Reagan's second year in office, as the realist wing of Reagan's foreign policy entourage became more assertive and threatened to 'hijack' the foreign policy agenda.[105] But today all this is forgotten. Rightly or wrongly, neoconservatives hail Reagan as one of their own—as the man whose assertive policies brought the downfall of communism and consecrated the rise of a new conservatism on the mainstream political scene.

The ideational substance of this new conservatism will be exposed and analysed in the forthcoming chapters of this book. But in order fully to appreciate its nature, implications and theoretical underpinnings, we first turn to a man who has provided much of the intellectual impetus for its development since the 1970s.

2

LEO STRAUSS, LIBERALISM AND THE 'CRISIS OF OUR TIMES'

'The theme of political philosophy is mankind's great objectives, freedom and government or empire—objectives which are capable of lifting all men beyond their poor selves'.

Leo Strauss[1]

Leo Strauss is arguably *the* most single important source of theoretical influence on the development of neoconservatism since the 1970s. Other Cold War intellectuals such as James Burnham, Max Shachtman, Sidney Hook, Reinhold Niebuhr and Lionel Trilling played a significant role in the early intellectual life of first-generation neoconservatives. Yet the impact of all of these thinkers taken together on the course of neoconservative politics over the past four decades arguably remains less significant than that of Strauss alone.[2]

Contrary to what some of his critics have claimed, Strauss's meticulous readings of the great texts of political philosophy did not bequeath an ideological system that can directly inform government policy in any significant manner. But Strauss's critique of the modern liberal democratic state has provided neoconservatives with vital intellectual ammunition in their struggle to reform the political culture of the United States after the events of the 1960s.[3] As Irving Kristol explained in the *Wall Street Journal* in 1995:

To the surprise of most observers, the critique of liberalism by neoconservative intellectuals, scholars, and publicists was far more effective than the older attack on 'statism'. Paradoxically, precisely because there was no socialist movement—no ideological 'statist' movement—in the United States, the neo-conservative critique went deeper, and was more radical, than conservative critiques in Britain or Western Europe. Oakeshott has evoked little active response in the United States, but the writings of Leo Strauss have been extraordinarily influential. Strauss's analysis of the destructive elements within modern liberalism, an analysis that was popularised by his students and his students' students, has altered the very tone of public discourses in the United States. Who would have thought it possible, thirty years ago, that in 1995 one third of the American public would designate itself as conservative while only 17 per cent designated itself as liberal—with the rest claiming the label 'moderate'. To bring contemporary liberalism into disrepute—its simplistic views of human nature, its utopian social philosophy, its secularist animus against religion—is no small achievement.[4]

Yet while Kristol and his colleagues talk candidly about their indebtedness to Strauss's intellectual legacy, they are much more guarded and evasive about its meaning and political implications. For if it is impossible to think of neoconservatism without reference to Strauss, it is also impossible to think of Strauss without reference to Carl Schmitt. And Schmitt, of course, is not someone to be associated with in polite society—especially in America. Strauss's American followers have therefore been keen to distance the master from the so-called 'Nazi crown jurist' by insisting that Strauss broke with his former mentor after leaving Germany in 1932. As Kristol explains in his autobiographical memoirs, Strauss 'never allowed his aristocratic mode of thinking to determine, in any simple and linear way, his political opinions. Himself a victim of Nazism, he defended liberal democracy as the best alternative among modern political regimes, even while keeping it intellectually at a distance. He was no Right-wing ideologue, as some of his critics have claimed, nor did he fit easily into contemporary conservative discourse'.[5]

Such refutations, however, are both philosophically naïve and politically mendacious. Strauss was indeed a brilliant and provocative thinker who conducted his investigations for his own purpose. But his political opinions—like his political theory—remained unambiguously conservative, anti-democratic and contemptuous of human rights discourses throughout his entire academic career. As Alan Gilbert pointed out:

Strauss was always on the right in American politics. With his students Robert Goldwin and Walter Berns, he organised public policy conferences that affirmed state's rights against the Brown v. Board of Education decision? With Berns and Allan Bloom, Strauss supported an American 'patriotism' which included McCarthyism. Strauss also allied with Willmoore Kendall, a political scientist with strong interests in theory, but an outspoken admirer of Franco and McCarthy... Advising Presidential candidate Senator Charles Percy of Illinois—a mirror of the Athenian stranger counseling Klinias in Plato's Laws—Strauss recommended that the US be as brutal as its Soviet enemy. Even after the Cuban missile crisis, he urged that the US should conquer Cuba as the Russians had Hungary.[6]

As for his experience with Nazism, this only made him more resentful of liberalism. Indeed, at the time of emigration, Strauss defended Italian-style fascism as the best antidote to Nazism and the 'effete' liberalism of Weimar. As he told his friend Karl Löwith in a letter he wrote from Paris in May 1933 after the Nazi takeover:

The fact that the new right-wing Germany does not tolerate us [Jews] says nothing against the principles of the right. To the contrary: only from the principles of the right, that is from fascist, authoritarian and imperial principles, is it possible with seemliness, that is, without resort to the ludicrous and despicable appeal to the *droits imprescriptibles de l'homme* to protest against the current state of affairs. I am reading Caesar's *Commentaries* with deep understanding, and I think of Virgil's *Tu regere imperio... parcere subjectis et debellare superbos*. There is no reason to crawl to the cross, neither to the cross of liberalism, as long as somewhere in the world there is a glimmer of the spark of the Roman thought. And even then: rather than any cross, I'll take the ghetto.[7]

Strauss's letter to Löwith was published in German for the first time in 2001 in the third volume of his *Gesammelte Schriften*. It was then translated into English in 2006 on the website *Balkanization* and subsequently appeared in a number of other academic publications.[8] Not surprisingly, some of Strauss's most devoted followers have responded to this new round of controversy with their own interpretation of the document in question. According to Harvey Mansfield, for example, Strauss's flirtation with fascism in the letter is not evidence of his anti-liberal political disposition, but an early manifestation of his 'trans-political' and existential commitment to philosophy. Mansfield's intervention is worth citing at length, if only as an example of the degenerative character of those debates:

The philosopher would choose between liberalism and conservatism not because he is sceptical like a liberal or claims truth like a conservative but because one or the other better protects and tolerates the philosopher's way of life. This concern with his own self-interest gives the philosopher a certain elevation over normal, non-philosophical politics, an elevation that can appear as uncalled-for levity in a serious situation.... Strauss says that the "men of science," including himself, have no place to stay but only seek (*non habemus locum manentem, sed quaerimus*). It is as if they, from their platform above, were refuting Nazi "natural right" with Roman rather than liberal natural right, replacing vicious right-wing principles with benign ones.... Instead of making a "laughable and pathetic" appeal to the rights of man—the fixed truths of liberalism—Strauss proposes resorting to the principles of the Roman empire, in Virgil's words, "to spare the subjects and subdue the proud'. ... The letter certainly confirms Strauss's disgust with the liberalism of Weimar Germany, a pitiful and cowardly liberalism unable to defend itself against the Nazis because it had abandoned its own fixed truths and absorbed much of the relativism of German nihilism.[9] According to Strauss in a 1941 lecture, German nihilism was the enemy, not liberalism; but Weimar liberalism, having abandoned Enlightenment liberalism in favor of historicist relativism, had shown itself to be powerless against the enemy. Obviously this was not the case with all liberalism in 1933, for Strauss fled the Nazi enemy to France, then England, and finally, the United States—all liberal democracies and the last two, it turned out, not incurably infected with appeasement.

The obvious problem here is that Mansfield projects back to the 1930s opinions and analyses that Strauss progressively developed over a long period of research and writing after he settled in the United States. What he is telling us, in essence, is that the young Strauss was not really a supporter of fascism but some sort of neoconservative '*avant la lettre*' . As Scott Horton noted, Mansfield is 'presenting Strauss as a dynamic new kind of liberal, who is prepared to act robustly (and militarily) to defend democratic institutions. This argument presents a strange contortion of liberalism, just as the main themes of neoconservatism present a departure from the traditional conservatism of the Anglo-American world. But it seriously distorts Strauss's attitude towards fascism at the time of emigration'.[10]

In this chapter, I expose Strauss's critique of liberalism against the background of his coming of age in the short-lived Republic of Weimar and his close intellectual connection to Schmitt. I examine the proto-fascist reading of Hobbes that Strauss and Schmitt developed in their intellectual dialogue during the Weimar years and highlight the strong elements of continuity in Strauss's American writings. I then conclude with a short discussion of the reception of his ideas in the United States since the 1960s. Strauss's influence on the theory and politics of neoconservatism will be emphasised and discussed where relevant in the subsequent chapters.

The Theological-Political Question

Leo Strauss was born into an assimilated orthodox Jewish family in 1899 in Kirchain, Hessen, a rural area of Germany. He made his intellectual debut in Zionist circles where he published a number of texts on Jewish religion and politics after serving in the German army during the First World War. Strauss wrote his doctorate dissertation under the supervision of the neo-Kantian philosopher Ernst Cassirer in Hamburg. As he was to explain later, however, it is from Nietzsche and Heidegger that he learned the most during those early days.[11] Strauss left Germany in 1932 to conduct research on Hobbes in France until 1934, and then moved to England where he lived until 1937. The Nazi takeover and the subsequent outbreak of the Second World War prevented him from returning to Germany. This eventually compelled him to seek refuge in the United States, where he settled and remained until his death in 1973.

Like Hannah Arendt, Hans Morgenthau, Eric Voegelin and a number of other Jewish émigré intellectuals who came of age in Weimar Germany, Strauss saw America with continental eyes. He arrived in the United States with vivid memories of total war and ethnic hatred, as well as a first-hand experience of the vulnerability and weaknesses of liberal democracy in the face of such upheavals.[12] As he recalls in the 1965 preface to his study of Spinoza's biblical criticism, the Weimar Republic aimed at striking 'a balance between the dedication to the principles of 1789 and the dedication to the highest German tradition'. It was of a 'moderate and non-radical character' and in many respects offered many new opportunities for German Jewry. But the enlightened spirit of its constitution was paired with a chronic lack of political will. In the absence of a well-rooted liberal democratic political culture, this proved to be a great source of danger for the Jews.[13] Unlike the 'Old Germany', Weimar was 'justice without a sword'. He who had the 'the strongest will or single-mindedness, the greatest ruthlessness, daring, and power over his following and the best judgement about the strength of the forces in the immediately relevant political field was the leader of the revolution'.[14]

The collapse of the Weimar Republic on the night of the Reichstag fire was a grim deception for all Jews. Thought to be the regime that would guarantee not only the security of Jews but of all minorities, liberal democracy had been welcomed by most as a progressive move away from the state-sponsored religious discrimination of previous eras. For the first time, Jews were granted equal rights and full citizenship without having to relinquish their right to remain Jews. Yet by confining religion to the private sphere and endorsing a 'universal human morality', Weimar in fact created a space for the unconstrained pursuit of private interests in which one was free to discriminate and hate at will. According to Strauss, this privatisation of moral conscience had been one of the conditions of possibility for the emergence of a political regime that 'had no other clear principle than murderous hatred of the Jews'.[15]

Strauss thus came to see Weimar as a tragic symbol of the Enlightenment's failure to secularise politics and assert the absolute authority of science over religion. In its pursuit of rational scientific truths, enlightenment scepticism concluded that one could not travel the road of reason and faith at one and the same time. Either one follows reason on the path of atheism or one chooses faith and abandons reason. But Strauss argued that this was a misconceived dilemma that had led modern rationalism to its own destruction. Since rationalism cannot answer the question of the meaning of life, it is ultimately unable to ground the legitimacy of its own activity in reason. According to Strauss, this is why no one ever succeeded in demonstrating the impossibility of God's existence by appealing to principles derived from human reason alone. The Enlightenment's refutation of religious orthodoxy relied on premises that are just as arbitrary or irrational as the claims of revelation. Faith and reason never succeeded in refuting one another.[16]

Strauss therefore saw enlightenment as a question of choice. It was the ethical choice of particular and historically situated societies in the face of the 'theological-political problem'. As he explained, 'philosophy, the quest for evident and necessary knowledge, rests itself on an unevident decision, on an act of will, just as faith. Hence the antagonism ... between belief and unbelief, is ultimately not theoretical, but moral'.[17] But like all ethical decisions, the choice of enlightenment over religion had serious consequences. According to Strauss, the Enlightenment's doctrinal worship of reason had led to a world without any commanding truth in which all opinions are deemed of equal worth and uninhibited individualism is the norm. This created a moral void at the heart of modern societies; and in Weimar it facilitated the rise of Hitler.

This led Strauss to embark on a genealogical investigation of rationalism in the hope of finding alternative or forgotten strains of thought from which twentieth-century societies could learn. As he explained, the possibility of a turn to obscurantism and a number of:

> other observations and experiences confirmed the suspicion that it would be unwise to say farewell to reason. I therefore began to wonder whether the self-destruction of reason was not the inevitable outcome of modern rationalism as distinguished from pre-modern rationalism, especially Jewish-medieval rationalism and its classical (Aristotelian and Platonic) formulation.[18]

Strauss's reflections on the self-destructive tendencies of modern rationalism and his desire to reinstate the respectability of revealed religion in the face of enlightenment thus led him back to the Greeks and ancient rationalism. As he explained in his autobiographical essay, this 'change of orientation found its first expression, not entirely by accident', in the course of his intellectual debate with Carl Schmitt on the political philosophy of Thomas Hobbes.[19]

The Hobbesian Moment

The Schmitt-Strauss exchange on Hobbes is one of the most important moments in the political theorisation of Weimar Germany.[20] As David Dyzenhaus noted, it was important because (i) it underpinned the whole of Schmitt's Weimar political theory; (ii) Schmitt's political theory became exemplary of *the* dominant political-legal paradigm in Weimar; and (iii) it was later put to the test by the Nazis.[21] The Schmitt-Strauss exchange is also important for the present study because, as we will see in the following chapters, the critique of liberalism and the modern liberal state developed and debated in this dialogue anticipates many aspects of our contemporary neoconservative politics.

The Hobbes that we find in this 'informal dialogue' is rather different from the Hobbes found in contemporary liberal Anglo-Saxon political philosophy. In the Anglo-Saxon world, Hobbes is the rationalist theorist of negative liberty who set the basis of an ethics of individual right to life in order to emancipate people from the lawless politics of the state of nature. Those who work within this tradition today, David Gauthier and John Rawls for example, celebrate the rationalist method and libertarian underpinnings of Hobbes's contractual theory. They dismiss both its vitalist-existentialist anthropology and its political authoritarianism as historical particularities that can and must be tamed or eliminated from the framework of contemporary liberal politics. By contrast, both Schmitt and Strauss saw in Hobbes the potential for an authoritarian, existentialist solution to the political crisis that afflicted the young liberal democracy of Weimar. For them, it was precisely Hobbes's rationalist scientific method and his libertarian ethical premises that stood in the way of their shared enterprise.[22]

The exchange takes its cue from Schmitt's famous critique of liberalism in *The Concept of the Political*.[23] Schmitt's *Concept of the Political* was aimed at the pluralist theories of the state and precarious parliamentary practices that characterised post-Versailles Germany. In essence, Schmitt argued that the pluralist nature of the liberal state allows an interpenetration of state and society that is conducive to the disintegration of the state's centre of sovereignty. He saw this as a negation of the conditions necessary for the existence of 'the political' as a decisive entity.[24] Schmitt argued that pluralism of association necessarily leads to a situation in which one 'association is played off against another and all questions and conflicts are decided by individuals' rather than by the sovereign.[25] Writing in the near civil war context of Weimar, he maintained that the pluralistic conjectures of liberal theories and practices fail to appreciate the 'objective nature and autonomy of the political' from all other spheres of human activity: economics, ethics, aesthetics etc. Schmitt argued that liberalism had transformed civil society into a sort of second Hobbesian state of nature in which the 'war of all against all' is projected at the level of inter-group conflicts. So that in his neo-Hobbesian world, the rationale of sovereign power no longer consists of providing the condition for domestic peace, but of establishing the content of the cultural community by deciding on the distinction between friend and enemy: an activity which defines the political as such.

Crucially, Schmitt stressed that the enemy is not 'the private adversary whom one hates' but the public enemy. And it is the state as the organised political entity that decides for itself upon the friend-enemy distinction.[26] Schmitt valued this sovereign moment of decision as a normatively unfounded act of political creation, which effected a welcome break with the formal legalism and rationalising tendency of liberal modernity.[27] Echoing Nietzsche and Weber, Schmitt saw liberal modernity as a disenchanting process of secularisation, bureaucratisation and technological instrumentalisation, which neutralises human agency and seeks to subject politics to the demands of ethics, commerce and rational deliberation. However, Schmitt believed that this attempt at de-politicising the world was ultimately doomed to failure.

Against liberalism, he insisted that common agreement reached through rational deliberation and exchange of opinions was only possible *within the remit of accepted categories* sustained by sovereign power and the decision on friend and enemy.[28] Schmitt saw forced exclusion and decisive conflict as a constitutive feature of the human condition—the essence of the political. In his view, the liberal assumption that war and political violence could be progressively eliminated through rational debates and exchange of opinion was dangerous and deeply misleading. For, all political solutions arrived at through compromise are bound to be only temporary, never decisive. And when perpetually deferred or masked by ethical universal pretences, the political always re-surfaces in a more destructive form.[29] As the Straussian scholar Joseph Cropsey explains:

> Whereas according to an understanding that could claim to be self-evident, political society exists to promote peace among men, Schmitt argued that the essence of the political is polemic. He did not mean that there is a tragic defect in the ground of our being that condemns us forever to internecine hatred, and to give effect to that hatred with higher efficiency by organising ourselves in polities. Much to the contrary, he argued that the human beings are divided, and woe to them if they should ever cease to be divided, over the issues that go to the heart of humanity's existence.... Schmitt can agree with those who have perceived the human record as a history of bloodshed, but far from interpreting the fact as a sign of God's neglect or punishment, he sees it as an evidence of God's providence. By a dialectic of conflict, of 'ideals' that men take seriously enough to contend over, and not by mere dialectic or reason, mankind is preserved from the lassitude of indifference that is the soul's death.[30]

Because he saw conflict as a constitutive feature of the social world, Schmitt insisted that the friend-enemy distinction had to remain uncontaminated by moral and rational justifications. The enemy for Schmitt had no normative content: 'The political enemy need not be morally evil or aesthetically ugly; he need not appear as an economic competitor, and it may even be advantageous to engage with him in business transactions. But he is, nevertheless, the other, the stranger; and it is sufficient for his nature that he is, in a specially intense way, existentially something different and alien, so that in the extreme case conflicts with him are possible'.[31]

It is on the basis of this last claim that Strauss engages with Schmitt's treatise. Strauss's *Notes on the Concept of the Political* remains one of the most incisive commentaries on Schmitt's work to this day. It is both reproving and flattering at one and the same time. Like Schmitt,

Strauss had little time for the illusory security of a liberal world of leisure and comfort. In his essay, he praises Schmitt for asserting the primacy of the political and for his defence of the state against liberalism's culture of entertainment, which by constantly deferring quarrels about the most fundamental issues is stripping the world of all its seriousness. In a passage that sums up what would become one of the founding propositions of Straussian political philosophy, he reformulates Schmitt's emphasis on the primacy of the political with words that capture both his appreciation of Schmitt's thesis as well as the essence of his criticism:

[Schmitt] certainly does *not* mean that in the nineteenth and twentieth centuries politics is to a less extent destiny than in the sixteenth and seventeenth centuries; today, no less than in earlier times, humanity is divided into 'totalities that have the real possibility of fighting one another'. A fundamental transformation has occurred, not in *the fact* that men quarrel but in *what* they quarrel *about*. What men quarrel about is what is considered important, authoritative; in the sixteenth century, theology was authoritative; in the seventeenth, metaphysics; in the eighteenth, morals; in the nineteenth, the economy; and in the twentieth technology. Basically: in every century a different 'domain' is the 'central domain'. The political, because it has 'no... domain of its own, is never the "central domain". Whereas the 'central domain' changes, the political constantly remains destiny. But as human destiny the political is dependent upon what ultimately matters for man.... The exact meaning of the de-politicisation that is characteristic of the modern age can thus be discerned only if one understands which law rules in the 'succession of changing central domains'. This law is the 'tendency towards neutralisation', that is, the striving to gain a ground that 'makes possible security, clarity, agreement, and peace'. Agreement and peace here mean agreement and peace at all costs....

The speciousness of this neutrality reveals the absurdity of the attempt to find an 'absolutely and definitely neutral ground' to reach agreement at all costs. Agreement at all costs is possible only as agreement at the cost of the meaning of human life; for agreement at all costs is possible only if man has relinquished the question of what is right; and if man relinquishes that question, he relinquishes being a man. But if he seriously asks the question of what is right, the quarrel will be ignited, the life-and-death quarrel: the political—the grouping of humanity into friends and enemies—owes its legitimation to the seriousness of the question of what is right.[32]

Strauss accepts Schmitt's de-politicisation thesis, but he rejects the relativist ethics that underpin his analysis. In his view, the political cannot be affirmed simply by virtue of its persistence through history. It must be asserted because it forces reflection upon the most fundamental and most serious questions concerning right and wrong: 'The affirmation of the political is in the final analysis nothing other than the affirmation of the moral'.[33] And this is *why* a political world is morally superior to a de-politicised world of ease and entertainment. Strauss's critique revolves around the fact that Schmitt's attack on liberalism and his grounding of the political in otherness 'as such' rely on relativist assumptions that are in fact perfectly in line with the neutralising spirit of liberalism. As he explained in his autobiographical essay some thirty years later:

> Whoever affirms the political as such, respects all who are willing to fight; he is quite as tolerant as liberals, but with the opposite intention. Whereas the liberal respects and tolerates all 'honestly held' convictions, so long as these respect the legal order or acknowledge the sanctity of peace, whoever affirms the political as such respects and tolerates all 'serious' convictions, in other words, all decisions leading up to the possibility of war. Thus the affirmation of the political as such proves to be liberalism preceded by a minus sign.[34]

To be human, Strauss argues, is to be able to reflect and make choices about what is right. And these choices are often a matter of life and death that forces a distinction between friend and enemy. Strauss agrees with Schmitt that the political 'remains constantly determinative of man's fate'. But he insists that the enemy's attempt to negate one's way of life necessarily implies a certain notion of good and evil and of right and wrong.[35] One cannot in good conscience engage in a life and death struggle with an enemy if one is not convinced that the principles for which the enemy is fighting are fundamentally wrong. According to Strauss, Schmitt did not go far enough in demonstrating the naturalness of the political. He recognised that the political was grounded in human nature, but his formulation suggests that 'the political is something *subsequent* or *supplementary*' to historical institutions like the church or the state.[36] Cropsey again:

> Strauss saw that if Schmitt applauded strife itself as humanising simply because it preserves mankind from the moral torpor of the technological terrarium, then Schmitt was no better than the value-free liberals he condemned. Schmitt might stipulate for a higher, i.e., a more violent, commitment to the adopted value, read 'faith', but Strauss made it clear that that would be a distinction without a significant difference. On the other hand, if Schmitt escaped the stigma of crypto-liberal relativism by positing religious faith as the absolute object of the commitment that defines the political and inspires men to kill and die, then Strauss was there to rejoin that nature, especially human nature, was a more primordial category than faith. The definition of the political should

then be elicited from the ground of nature, as philosophers had been seeking to do from antiquity on.[37]

Strauss attributes the deficiency of the Schmittian doctrine to its Hobbesian genesis. In the first instance, Strauss welcomes Schmitt's return to Hobbes's solution to social order as a necessary attempt to 'bring the political out of concealment' and instil in man again 'the mutual relation between Protection and Obedience'.[38] 'Schmitt's task', he explains, 'is determined by the fact that liberalism has failed'. Its failure stems from its poor understanding of the relationship between culture and nature. According to Strauss, liberal theories understand culture as 'the totality of "human thought and action" which is divided into "various, relatively independent domains" and emerges somewhat spontaneously in society independently from the state'. But what is forgotten is that '"culture" always presupposes something which is cultivated: culture is always cultivation of nature; that is, the cultivation of human nature'.[39] And it is the state, in establishing order and the foundation upon which society *subsequently* emerges, that cultivates the state of nature.

Strauss therefore recognises Schmitt's return to the Hobbesian state of nature as a legitimate effort to ask the question of the state seriously again.[40] Yet, in his view, Schmitt failed to appreciate that Hobbes's own approach to the cultivation of nature was in fact paradigmatic of modern liberalism. As he explains, for the ancients the cultivation of nature 'means, primarily, that culture develops the natural disposition; it is careful nurture of nature—whether of the soil or of the human spirit makes no difference; it thus *obeys* the orders that nature itself gives'. By contrast, the modern liberal understanding sees culture 'not so much [as] the faithful cultivation of nature as the harsh and cunning fight against nature'. With Hobbes, this takes the form of 'a disciplining of human will, as the *opposite* of the *status naturalis*'. In other words, instead of recognising the natural irrationality and dangerousness of people and educating them so that they can govern themselves accordingly, Hobbes opted for the conquest of the 'external' natural world and the promises of a safe and comfortable commercial civilisation.[41] He appealed to people's physical sensuous perception and, with the help of science, commerce and technology, founded liberalism against the illiberal natural individual.[42]

Like Schmitt, Strauss appreciated the value of Hobbes's defence of sovereignty and his view of human nature as being essentially evil. But he believed that Hobbes's understanding of evil was fundamentally flawed and that this undermined the stability of his theoretical construction. According to Strauss, Hobbes erroneously based his interpretation of the individual's natural dangerousness on a morally innocent 'animal evil' (derived from human will and physical sensuous disposition) rather than on a 'moral evil' (derived from natural law):

> Hobbes understood man as 'evil like the beast'. Hobbes had to understand evil as innocent 'evil' because he denied sin; and he had to deny sin because he did not recognise any primary obligation of man that takes precedence over every claim *qua* justified claim, because he understood man as by nature free, that is, without obligation; for Hobbes, therefore, the fundamental political fact was natural right as the justified claim of the individual, and Hobbes conceived of obligations a *subsequent* restriction upon that claim. If one takes this approach, one cannot demur in principle against the proclamation of human rights as claims of individuals upon the state and contrary to the state, against the distinction between society and state, against liberalism.... And once one understands man's evil as the innocent 'evil' of the beast, but of a beast that can become astute through injury and thus can be educated, the limits one sets for education finally become a matter of mere 'supposition'—whether very narrow limits, as set by Hobbes himself, who therefore became an adherent of absolute monarchy; or broader limits such as those of liberalism; or whether one imagines education as capable of just about everything, as anarchism does. The opposition between evil and good loses its keen edge, it loses its very meaning 'as soon as evil is understood as innocent "evil" and thereby goodness [i.e. the state] is understood as an aspect of evil itself'.[43]

Strauss's point here is that Hobbes's desire to ground natural right in an earthly and unlimited individualist claim against the state emptied the relationship between protection and obedience of all moral and metaphysical content beyond the preservation of individual human life. With Hobbes, 'the right of securing life pure and simple [i.e. 'mere life' irrespective of its moral or immoral substance] ... takes precedence over the state and determines its purpose and its limits'.[44] Through this revolutionary negation of political theology, Hobbes undermined the absolute authority of the sovereign decision on the friend-enemy distinction: the 'morally demanding decision'. According to Strauss, it is this subjective individual right against the state that grew exponentially over the centuries and progressively empowered society against the state, until the latter effectively became an impotent slave to society. Had Hobbes recognised that the dangerousness of man originates not in his 'beastlike' character but in the moral baseness of his distinctively *human* nature, he would have seen the limits of rational education. He would have understood that man's dangerousness reveals itself as a natural 'need of dominion' inimical to the individualist starting point upon which he founded liberal political modernity.[45]

Strauss pursues this line of argument further in his own book on Hobbes, which he had started in Weimar and completed in England in 1936. There, Strauss argues that reason is precisely what renders man the most dangerous animal of all: 'The specific difference between man and all other animals is reason. Thus man can envisage the future much better than can animals; for this reason, he is not like animals hungry only with the hunger of the moment, but also with future hunger, and thus he is the most predatory, the most cunning, the strongest, and the most dangerous animal'.[46] Strauss then goes to great lengths to demonstrate that, despite what Hobbes tells his readers, what really pushes Hobbesian man into a dangerous power struggle to 'have all the world ... to fear and obey him' is not the physical sensuous mechanism he shares with all the other animals. For, 'animals who also perceive and desire do not aspire to absolute dominion'.[47] 'Human appetite is essentially distinguished from animal appetite in that the latter is nothing but a reaction to external impressions, and, therefore the animal desires only finite objects as such, while man spontaneously desires infinitely'.[48] In Strauss's view, Hobbes's 'mechanistic' sensuous conception of human appetite does not corroborate the vitalist interpretation of human nature that has rendered his work so relevant today. A person who is guided by a strictly animal appetite would certainly engage in a struggle for power in order to ensure his self-preservation. But he would content himself with the power necessary to ensure his self-preservation. This quest for power would therefore be rational and permissible, as Hobbes suggests, because it would be driven by a morally neutral sensuous mechanism that can be educated. This is why the individual's irrational and impermissible appetite for absolute dominion cannot have its source in sensual perception. Rather, it has its source 'in the pleasure which man takes in the consideration of his own power, i.e. in vanity'. And only fear of violent death can neutralise human vanity.[49]

Strauss then goes on to give a vivid neo-Hegelian reinterpretation of Hobbes's state of nature to show how man's vain desire for recognition leads to the deliberate intention to harm others. It is worth citing at length:

> The vain man, who, in his imagination, believes himself superior to others, cannot convince himself of the rightness of his estimate of himself; he requires

the recognition of his superiority by the others... Now, either the others take his claim seriously and feel themselves slighted, or they do not take his claim seriously and he feels himself slighted. In either case, the making of the claim leads to contempt. But to be slighted is the greatest *animi molestia*, and from the feeling of being slighted arises the greatest will to injure... The one slighted longs for revenge. In order to avenge himself he attacks the other, indifferent whether he loses his life in so doing. Unconcerned as to the preservation of his own life, he desires, however, above all that the other should remain alive; for 'revenge aimeth not at the death, but at the captivity and subjection of an enemy... revenge aimeth at triumph, which over the dead is not'. The struggle which thus breaks out, in which, according to the opinion of both opponents, the object is not the killing but the subjection of the other, of necessity becomes serious, because it is a struggle between bodies, a real struggle. From the beginning of the conflict the two opponents have, without realising and foreseeing it, completely left the imaginary world. At some point in the conflict, actual injury, or, more accurately, physical pain, arouses a fear for life. Fear moderates anger, puts the sense of being slighted into the background, and transforms the desire for revenge into hatred. The aim of the hater is no longer triumph over the enemy, but his death. The struggle for preminence, about 'trifles', has become a life-and-death struggle.[50]

The implications of Strauss's existentialist reconstruction of the Hobbesian state of nature are twofold. First, it suggests that the state of nature is not a distant historical condition but a true possibility that haunts the modern state at all time. Secondly, it suggests that the Hobbesian theory of the state is not based on Hobbes's 'mechanistic' natural scientific method but on vitalist political philosophical insights: fear of violent death is a prerequisite to rational education. Strauss's suggestion here is that a viable state must constantly warn its citizenry about the possibility of violent death and a return to the state of nature: 'The bourgeois existence which no longer experiences these terrors will endure only as long as it remembers them'.[51] According to Strauss, it is Hobbes's privileging of the scientific elements of his theory at the expense of its vitalist human substance that has led to the failure of his leviathan state. As John McCormick argues, Strauss criticises Hobbes for choosing 'physics over anthropology, and hence ultimately technology over political philosophy'.[52] Hobbes emphasised reason and appealed to science, commerce and other such technologies to neutralise the characteristics that render humankind such an irredeemably dangerous species. And yet, although reason refutes the quest for glory, it 'justifies the striving after power, possessions, gains, wealth, since these provide the means to gratify the underlying desire for pleasures of the senses' to which Hobbes appeals to bring man out of his dangerous natural condition.[53] Eventually, it is precisely those technologies of government that undermine the stability of the social order. For the more that people indulge in commodious life, the less they perceive the need for discipline and restraint, and the less they understand the primordial role of the state in the founding of the social order.

Strauss's critique of Hobbes had a profound impact on Schmitt's own interpretation of Hobbes after 1933. In his 1938 book on Hobbes, which also influenced Strauss's post-Weimar views on Hobbes, Schmitt draws heavily on Strauss's analysis of the tension between the vitalist and the liberal mechanistic elements of the Leviathan (without ever explicitly acknowledging his debt to his former Jewish pupil).[54]

Following Strauss, Schmitt reverses the views he had expressed in *The Concept of the Political* and reads Hobbes as the founder of the de-politicised liberal order that he loathed so much. Schmitt now argues that the Hobbesian 'concept of the state became an essential factor in the four-hundred-year-long process of mechanisation, a process that with the aid of technical developments brought about a general "neutralisation" and especially the transformation of the state into a technically neutral instrument'.[55] To be sure, Hobbes's *Leviathan* remains for Schmitt the most powerful defence of the sovereign's absolute right to determine the public validity of norms and opinions against the 'indirect powers' of sectarian religious and ideological forces. But Schmitt now argues that the mechanistic, rationalist character of Hobbes's thought has historically neutralised the organic dimension of his leviathan state. This progressively allowed for a complex interpenetration of politics and economics, which in turn facilitated the re-affirmation of the 'indirect powers' of civil society over the absolutist international order of Westphalia.

Schmitt wrote his *Leviathan* at a time when he feared for his life after falling out of favour with the Nazis over academic opinions. He therefore uses Hobbes's voice throughout the book to express his own subdued disappointment about National Socialism. Schmitt had initially supported the Nazis after the latter gained the upper hand over the aristocrats whom he supported during the Weimar period. He joined the Prussian State Council opportunistically in July 1933 at the invitation of Hermann Göring. He had done so because he believed that the Nazis would put an end to the 'pluralistic' disintegration of the neutralised state of Weimar and re-assert the sovereign unity of the German state.[56] But five years later, Schmitt insinuates that the Nazis have failed to forge the 'qualitatively total state' that he envisaged in his Weimar writings as a way out of the interwar crisis.

Schmitt's 'qualitatively total state' stood strong above civil society. It was based on a strict separation between civil society and the state that allowed the state to secure its autonomy from private interests. For Schmitt this was necessary in order for the state to preserve its monopoly on the political distinction between friend and enemy. He believed that only a strong autonomous state with a total monopoly on the friend-enemy distinction could withdraw from the economy and allow the free market and other 'non-state affairs' to operate according to their own immanent principles. Schmitt's 'qualitatively total state' was an authoritarian, culturally substantive bourgeois state. What the Nazis had forged was a 'quantitatively totalitarian state': 'This kind of total state is one that penetrates all domains and all spheres of human existence, one that knows of no state-free sphere because it can no longer discriminate. It is *total in a purely quantitative sense, in the sense of pure volume and not in the sense of intensity or political energy*'.[57]

Schmitt had initially developed his theory on the 'quantitatively total state' as a representation of Weimar's liberal democratic welfare state. But now he insinuates that the all-intrusive, ever-interfering Nazi state is no more capable of distinguishing anything and drawing the distinction between friend and enemy than the pluralistic welfare state of Weimar. Indeed, Schmitt hints that Nazi Germany is worse than Weimar in that respect. For it completely derides the contractual relationship between protection and obedience underpinning the neo-Hobbesian solution that he had envisaged years earlier. As he put it in a suggestive passage: 'Hobbes' theory of the state would certainly have been a peculiar philosophy of state if its entire chain of thought had consisted in propelling poor human beings from the utter fear of the state of nature only into the similarly total fear of a domination by a Moloch or Golem'.[58]

Schmitt's book on Hobbes is therefore more than just an erudite scholarly enterprise. It is also an account of the origins and crisis of the classical European state that hints 'esoterically' at the impending failure of the National Socialist solution to this crisis. The originality of Schmitt's reading of *Leviathan* rests in great part on the emphasis that he puts on the function of myth in Hobbes's theoretical construction. Schmitt interprets the Hobbesian state as a trinity: the representative person, the machine and the mythical monster. According to him, the organic totality of this trinity rests on the capacity of this mythical new god to act as a fearsome representative power which transcends the 'mechanically' aggregated individual wills of the state of nature and keeps those wills in a state of peaceful awe from above:

> The terror of the state of nature drives anguished individuals to come together; their fear rises to an extreme; a spark of reason flashes and suddenly there stands in front of them a new god.... The decisive element of the intellectual construction resides in the fact that this covenant does not accord with medieval conceptions of an existing commonwealth forged by God and of a pre-existent natural order.... Fear brings atomised individuals together. A spark of reason flashes, and a consensus emerges about the necessity to submit to the strongest power.... The sovereign representative person is much more than sum total of all the participating particular wills.[59]

The image of the biblical sea monster is therefore a mythic symbol of the rational collective agency that establishes the sovereign as their sole representative. But it also symbolises the dissolution of this popular sovereignty into a submissive multitude immediately after the political creation of this all-powerful 'earthly god'. Hobbes's leviathan state generated a specifically modern order that prevailed between the mid seventeenth century and the nineteenth century. This order was characterised by the reorganisation of Europe's public space into two clearly separated domains: a domain of political authority reserved for the sovereign and governed by the principle of *raison d'état*, and a subordinate domain of apolitical subjects where culture, morality and commerce developed according to their own immanent principles. Crucially, Schmitt argues that 'the image of the Leviathan—a mix between a great beast and a great machine—achieves its highest degree of mythical force' by ensuring the preservation of an external space of permanent existential danger. There, sovereign states affirm their 'force and vitality' against one another and remind their subjects of the dangerous character of human nature:

> Although covenants are concluded in the state of nature, they always reflect great existential reservations that prevent a rational and legal security from emerging in place of a state of insecurity... The state absorbs all rationality and all legality. Everything outside of the state is therefore a 'state of nature'. The thoroughly rationalised mechanisms of state command confront one another 'irrationally'. The more complete the internal organisation of a state

is, the less feasible it is for it to engage in mutual relations on an equal basis. The more thoroughly each state is developed, the less it is able to maintain its state character in interstate relations. There is no state between states, and for that reason there can be no legal war and no legal peace but only the pre- and extralegal state of nature in which tensions among leviathans are governed by insecure covenants.[60]

Once instituted, the 'supra-sectarian' order of absolutism engendered a new sense of mutual recognition between sovereign states that cut across the plurality of religious faiths, and to which only the consciences of the sovereigns were subject. According to Schmitt, the rules and norms that emerged out of this new sense of obligation were genuinely political because they lacked powers of enforcement and were free of moral arguments beyond *raison d'état*. The absorption of all rationality and legality by Hobbes's absolutist state therefore had two important ramifications for international relations. The first is that those who face one another as enemies no longer do so as religious or ideological foes, but as states according to the purely secular dictate of *raison d'état*: 'Wars become pure wars between states'. Secondly, it follows from this that one can no longer talk of 'just wars' between states. For 'such an interstate war is just as incommensurable as the question of just resistance within the state. By contrast to religious, civil, and factional wars, wars between states cannot be measured with the yardsticks of truth and justice'. This is so, Schmitt explains, because the juridical categories of the system of international law no longer take their bearing from a transcendent theology, but from the concept of the state and its immanent ethics of *raison d'état*: '*Ordo hoc non includit*. The state has its order in, not outside, itself. What is therefore essential to international law, which governs relations between states, is law that does not distinguish between just and unjust, a non-discriminating concept of war'.[61]

Schmitt considers the de-moralisation of warfare as one of the great humanising achievements of the age of absolutism. For, in his view, the 'pure wars between states' of the *Jus Publicum Europaeum* were waged with much more restraint and much less indiscriminate violence than the 'just war' that decimated Germany and Europe between 1914 and 1918: 'only the just war is the true "total" war'.[62] Yet, like Strauss, he now believes that it is precisely the absence of a genuinely transcendent political theology in the leviathan state that would eventually lead to the decline of the absolutist order. Schmitt's point here is that although the leviathan transcends the sum of the individual wills in the state of nature, the transcendence of this sovereign representative has no real metaphysical legitimacy. Consequently, it cannot provide 'anything like a foundation, in the sense of an intellectual demonstration' that will give meaning to the relationship between state protection and individual obedience. The Hobbesian peace was a strictly man-made rational construction that could be deconstructed at will:

> To be sure, the accumulated anguish of individuals who fear for their lives brings a new power into the picture: the leviathan. But that affirms rather than creates this new god. To that extent the new god is transcendent vis-à-vis all contractual partners of the covenant and vis-à-vis the sum total, obviously only in a juristic and not metaphysical sense. The intrinsic logic of the man-made, artificial product 'state' does not culminate in a person but a machine. Not the representation by a person but the factual, current accomplishment of genuine protection is what the state is all about.[63]

The thrust of this Schmittian-Straussian narrative is that the leviathan state owes its failure to the strict separation between morality proper and the self-referential ethics of the state upon which Hobbes founded the absolutist order. Under the doctrine of *raison d'état*, Hobbes's leviathan took leave from all moral norms and subordinated all religious and rational claims of individual morality to political necessity. But in doing so, it created a foothold for the emergence of a private realm autonomous from the state where a well-financed and intellectually influential civil society would grow and acquire a monopoly on 'morality proper'. In other words, Hobbes's absolutist state set the social basis of the Enlightenment, and thereby sowed the seed of the critical spirit that would eventually bring absolutism to an end.

Schmitt knew very well that Hobbes could not have foreseen that this would happen. For in Hobbes, freedom from politics is the ultimate moral good. The emergence of a bourgeois civil society could therefore not have appeared to him as a potential threat since civil society's self-understanding was moral rather than political. And yet, it is precisely this moral rejection of politics that established a comfortable critical vantage point from which the immoral substance of the absolutist order would eventually be put into question by a civil society emancipated from the state of nature. For as the secularising process continued to unfold in the seventeenth, eighteenth and nineteenth centuries, the new bourgeois public sphere progressively turned its attention away from religion and began to exercise its critical spirit on earthly matters. It slowly extended itself into politics through legal criticism enunciated from within the realm of government, until it eventually turned against the state itself.[64]

According to Schmitt, Hobbes's leviathan fell short of serving its ordering function because its mythical element failed to identify a clear public enemy. It failed to establish a clear political distinction between 'us and them' which transcends the public-private distinction and cultivates the cultural homogeneity of the political community. Schmitt saw this antagonistic feature as the pivotal element in the relationship between protection and obedience. He argues that the moralising character of the Enlightenment's revolt against the absolutist politics of the state also prevented its agents from establishing a new, viable model of the political. Schmitt's suggestion here is that the heterogeneous elements of 'society' could only be maintained as long as the 'civil society versus state' line of enmity existed. When this strict opposition progressively dissolved, enlightenment criticism failed to reconcile its anti-political morality with the perennial amorality of the political realm. As a mode of social integration, moral critique could not succeed without succumbing to the autonomy and primacy of the political. It could only lead to the heterogenisation of the domestic order and the re-assertion of the sectarian forces suppressed by Hobbes's absolutist solution:

> Hobbes's thought prevailed in the positivist statute state of the nineteenth century, but only in a rather apocryphal manner. The old adversaries, the 'indirect' powers of the church and of interest groups, reappeared in that century as modern political parties, trade unions, social organisations, in a phrase, as 'forces of society'. They seized the legislative arm of parliament and the statute state and thought that they had placed the Leviathan in a harness. Their ascendancy was facilitated by a constitutional system that enshrined a catalogue of individual rights. The 'private' sphere was thus withdrawn from the state and handed over to the 'free', that is, uncontrolled and invisible forces of 'society'.... From the duality of state and state-free society arose a social pluralism in which the 'indirect powers' could celebrate effortless triumphs.... This typically indirect method *à deux mains* enables them to carry out their actions under the guise of something other than politics—namely, religion, culture, economy, or private matter—and still derive all the advantage of the state. They were thus able to combat the leviathan and still avail themselves of the animal until they destroyed the big machine.... The institutions and concepts of liberalism became weapons and power positions in the hands of the most illiberal forces. In this fashion, party pluralism has perpetrated the destruction of the state by using methods inherent in the liberal law state. The

leviathan, in the sense of a myth of the state as a 'huge machine', collapsed when a distinction was drawn between the state and individual freedom. That happened when the organisations of individual freedom were used like knives by anti-individualistic forces to cut up the leviathan and divide his flesh among themselves.[65]

The authoritarian import of this Schmittian-Straussian critique of Hobbes is obvious but no less troubling. By arguing that even the minimal subjective determination of self-conservation led to the destruction of the existing order by the indirect powers of society, both Schmitt and Strauss deprived themselves of individualistic premises in their intellectual reconstruction of the state. As Dyzenhaus argues with regard to Schmitt (but the argument also applies to Strauss), Schmitt's authoritarianism was more radical than Hobbes. 'It was more radical because it excluded the rational argument for absolute authority [self-preservation] that Hobbes provided in his appeal to individual rationality. Such arguments are, Schmitt thought, excluded by the very context of politics, the pluriverse of competing myths, and by a retrospective look at the consequences of individualism'. But in doing so, this Schmittian-Straussian project completely undermined the relationship between protection and obedience that legitimises the leviathan state.[66] This is why Schmitt's self-exonerating critique of the Nazi 'Moloch' is highly unconvincing. For Schmitt's Weimar constitutional theory had advocated the strengthening of executive power. It had called for the instauration of a *Reichspräsident* as some sort of neutral leviathan in order to discipline the competing factions which had turned Weimar into a near civil war. Yet as Schmitt knew very well (and his legal critics reminded him all the time), although this leviathan was deemed to be neutral with regard to the conflicting parties, there was nothing to prevent it from abusing its power and indiscriminatingly oppressing all participants. As McCormick argues, the whole neo-Hobbesian project of Schmitt and Strauss grounds the state's duty to protect subjects 'not in the "right to protection" of those subjects but in the state's "responsibility to do so". The onus is on the state, and hence the initiative to act (when and how) is its own prerogative and not a response to the demands of or manipulation by particular social forces'.[67] More than anything else, Schmitt feared for his life in 1938 because he fell victim to his own fascistic solution to the constitutional crisis of Weimar.

Recovering Natural Right

Unlike Schmitt, Strauss did not get to taste his own medicine. His research on Hobbes led him to undertake a study trip abroad in 1932 after receiving a Rockefeller grant upon Schmitt's recommendation. This ultimately saved his life. Strauss settled in the US in 1938 and became a naturalised American citizen in 1944. In the stability of America's comfortable commercial civilisation, he abandoned the neo-Hobbesian project that he shared with Schmitt in favour of an intellectual recovery of the wisdom of the ancients. Hobbes remained central to Strauss's American writings. However, as he explained in his last indirect response to the *Leviathan* of his disgraced mentor in 1959, 'respectable people, to remain silent about others', no longer study Hobbes to find a solution to the crisis of the modern state. They study Hobbes more seriously than ever because he is the source of both the progress and the decay of modernity: 'For Hobbes presents himself at first glance as the man who first broke completely with the pre-modern heritage, the man who ushered in a new type of social doctrine: the modern type'.[68]

In Strauss's American writings, Hobbes is therefore no longer an ally in the regeneration of the absolute sovereignty of the state, but one of the main intellectual figures responsible for the crisis of modernity. Strauss understood the crisis of modernity as an intellectual crisis beginning with Machiavelli and Hobbes and culminating in the nihilistic and value-relativist philosophy of Nietzsche and Heidegger. I cannot go into the fascinating details of Strauss's narrative in the little space that I have available here. But the nub of the argument goes as follows.

Classical rationalism understood the ultimate end of human life as the contemplation of the order of the cosmos and the rightful place of humankind within this order. Ancient philosophers knew that achieving this ideal life was practically impossible. For no sciences or arts could provide effective guidance in establishing the kind of socio-political order that would allow for the realisation of this way of life. Nevertheless, the ancients remained faithful to the idea that the best life was one guided by utopian reflections upon the nature of the good life. Strauss argues that moderns, beginning with Machiavelli and Hobbes, rejected the classical view. Instead, they favoured an interpretation of the ultimate end of human life that is no longer based on the imaginary kingdoms of Plato or God, but on the satisfaction of man's natural desires and passions here and now. Modern rationalism wishes to make man 'the master and owner of nature'. It seeks to liberate humanity 'completely from all non-human bonds'.[69] But by 'lowering' its sight as to what type of socio-political order can actually be achieved in this earthly life, modern rationalism reduced the scope of political philosophy from an investigation into moral and political problems to a technical enterprise. Along the way, thanks to Rousseau and German idealism, what is distinctively human came to be seen not as a 'gift of nature' but as 'the outcome of what man did… in order to overcome or change nature'.[70] As the moral laws as laws of freedom were severed from man's fundamental experience of existence in nature and graphed upon the historical process, reason (pure in Kant and historicised in Hegel) became the sole source of moral judgement. Nietzsche finally completed the moral debasement instigated by Machiavelli and Hobbes centuries earlier. For him the disquieting abandonment of transcendent natural standards could not be eased by the cowardly assumption that the historical process had any intrinsic rational meaning. He exposed the 'human, all too human' origins of all values, and ushered in a new era of existential anxiety and terrifying meaninglessness.[71]

According to Strauss, this sense of meaninglessness was responsible for the crisis of nihilism which had led to the decimation of Germany in the first half of the twentieth century. Now he believed that this same crisis was looming over the West and threatened to undermine its will to fight a long protracted war against communism.[72] Strauss was particularly anxious about the degeneration of liberal democracy into a 'creeping conformism'.[73] He believed that modern liberalism had transformed democracy into a degenerative form of government and mass rule that gratifies the lowest desires of society. Originally, democracy 'meant to be an aristocracy which has broadened into a universal aristocracy'.[74] By this he meant a democracy in which everybody has had the benefits of 'liberal education': the type of knowledge, virtues and intellectual capacities which provide the restraint and sobriety necessary for democracy to be viable in the long run. Strauss attributed the decay of liberal democracy to the egalitarian impulse of modern liberalism. In his view, liberal education presupposes a certain hierarchy of intellectual aptitudes. It is inevitably elitist and therefore incompatible with egalitarian principles. Strauss offered no easy way out of this predicament. As he argued, 'We must not expect that liberal education can ever become universal education'.[75] For the elitist nature of liberal education necessarily limits both its appeal and its transformative power. Our best hope, Strauss believed, rested with the nurturing of an 'aristocracy within mass democratic society'.[76]

In his magnum opus *Natural Right and History* (1953), Strauss appears to be suggesting that America is the best candidate to lead the re-orientation of Western civilisation. He argues that the American regime has some classical antecedents which have been important sources of stability since its founding in 1776. However, he warns that the growing prestige of positivism in American universities, coupled with the waning of religious support and republican virtues, was disturbing the fragile balance of modern and pre-modern beliefs which had for so long protected American democracy against the excesses of modern rationalism.

Yet if Strauss abhorred positivism for its mediocre understanding of the social world, it is above all historicism that he saw as the main intellectual force responsible for the decline of the West. His *Natural Right and History* makes a case for the continuing relevance of the classical understanding of natural right. It proposes to renew our appreciation for the pre-philosophic experience of nature as the universal ontological foundation for all philosophical knowledge. The prose and argumentative style of *Natural Right and History* are dense and sometimes difficult to follow. But at the heart of Strauss's narrative is the claim that there exists by nature a universally 'best life' which, once freed from the 'experience of history' and the artifice of modern scientific construction, we can discover by following our most intuitive sense of nobility and baseness:

> The 'experience of history' and the less ambiguous experience of the complexity of human affairs may blur, but they cannot extinguish, the evidence of those simple experiences regarding right and wrong which are at the bottom of the philosophical contention that there is a natural right. The fundamental problems, such as the problem of justice, persist or retain their identity in all historical change, however much they may be obscured by the temporary denial of their relevance and however variable or provisional all human solutions to these problems may be.[77]

Obviously, Strauss does not deny that our understanding of the world and our framing of daily political problems are dependent on historically conditioned conventions. What he suggests is that conventions are not all there is. Conventions are counterposed with pre-theoretical settings that are part of 'an eternal and unchangeable order within which history takes place, and which is in no manner affected by history'.[78] These pre-theoretical settings establish the terms and conditions of possibility for conventionalism.

More importantly, Strauss does not claim with certainty that there is in fact a transcendent natural right waiting to be discovered (or recovered) by means of intellectual investigation. As he explains, 'The fact that reason compels us to go beyond the ideal of our society does not yet guarantee that in taking this step we shall not be confronted with a void or with a multiplicity of incompatible and equally justifiable principles of "natural right"'.[79] Rather, his argument is that the nihilistic consequences of abandoning the possibility of natural right are much worse than being confronted with an assortment of competing and equally justifiable claims about the good life:

> To reject natural right is tantamount to saying that all right is positive right, and this means that what is right is determined exclusively by the legislators and the courts of the various countries... Many people today hold the view that the standard in question is in the best case nothing but the ideal adopted by our society or our 'civilisation' and embodied in its way of life or its institutions. But, according to the same view, all societies have their ideals, cannibal societies no less than civilised ones. If principles are sufficiently justified by the fact that they are accepted by a society, the principles of cannibalism are as defensible or sound as those of civilised life... And, since the ideal of our society is admittedly changing, nothing except dull and stale habit could prevent us from placidly accepting a change in the direction of cannibalism.[80]

Strauss's recovery of natural right is heavily influenced by the phenomenology of Husserl and Heidegger. It rests on the suggestion that moderns have created through education and training over time a set of emotional and intellectual habits, a sort of artificial screen, which distorts how participants engaged in political life actually make sense of this experience. This consequently leaves them at a loss with respect to the most fundamental questions about how one ought to live one's life.[81]

Yet despite the pivotal role of the concept of nature in his work, Strauss does not offer a clear and straightforward definition of what constitutes the 'natural'. In fact, he argues that it is neither possible to grasp the notion of nature in all its determinations nor to come to a fully achieved natural right doctrine.[82] Strauss's ontological enterprise takes the form a critical examination of the givens of human experiences. It proceeds dialectically through pre-philosophic political life to show how the ancient sought access to nature. It seeks to demonstrate how from prejudices, intellectual disputes and the exposition of inconsistencies and contradictory 'opinions about the whole' one can ascend to 'knowledge about the whole'.[83] As he explains:

> It is this ascent which Socrates had primarily in mind when he called philosophy 'dialectics'. Dialectics is the art of conversation or of friendly dispute. The friendly dispute which leads towards the truth is made possible or necessary by the fact that opinions about what things are, or what some very important groups of things are, contradict one another. Recognising the contradiction, one is forced to go beyond opinions towards the consistent view of the nature of the thing concerned. That consistent view makes visible the relative truth of the contradictory opinions; the consistent view proves to be the comprehensive or total view. The opinions are thus seen to be fragments of the truth, soiled fragments of the pure truth.[84]

Natural right therefore arises out of a fundamental clash of opinions concerning what constitutes the good and the just life. These opinions, Strauss insists, are not mere preferences. They are derived from the way different people *live* the experience of right and wrong in their everyday life: 'The disagreement regarding the principles of justice thus seems to reveal a genuine perplexity aroused by a divination or insufficient grasp of natural right, a perplexity caused by something self-subsistent or natural that eludes human grasp'.[85] The classic natural right teaching emerges out of this awareness of the limits of one's knowledge and the need to respond to this perplexity. Natural right, in other words, is the way that nature shows itself in politics.[86]

So we see here that the natural right to which Strauss appeals to ground his normative enterprise has in fact nothing to do with the traditional notion of a transcendent natural law: i.e., a set of moral principles grounded in man's most elementary physical needs and desires, especially his desire for self-preservation. Neither, however, is it congruent with Kant's attempt to disconnect moral laws from man's most basic instincts and link them to motives that could be completely independent from nature, i.e., established purely on the basis of a spiritual or intellectual causality (the Kantian categorical imperative). As John Gunnell noted, the natural in Strauss refers not so much to a specific set of moral principles as to the 'demands that [are] coincident with the naturalness or givenness of the political and its relationship to other orders of existence such as the social and religious'.[87] In other words, men are by nature just as bent on accumulating power and pursuing their interests as they are naturally constituted by their thoughts on justice. But justice is derived from the political. It cannot transcend the political order and therefore remains grounded in the particularities of a given political society. Hence, just as politics for Machiavelli could not be aligned with the demands of Christian morality, so political life for Strauss cannot be aligned with the demands of philosophy. Although the best life is the philosophical life, what is right is what is in tune with the demands of the political life. Or as Strauss puts it in his study of Thucydides, 'The Athenians's assertion of what one may call the natural rights of the strong as a right which the stronger exercises by natural necessity is not a doctrine of Athenian imperialism; it is a universal doctrine; it applies to Sparta for instance as well as to Athens'.[88]

Strauss's appeal to nature is in fact an endorsement of Aristotle's claim that 'all natural right is changeable', and that 'it is just to deviate even from the most general principles of natural right' out of political necessity. As he explains, 'Natural right is that right which must be recognised by any political society if it is to last and which for this reason is everywhere in force. Natural right thus understood delineates the minimum conditions of political life, so much so that sound positive right occupies a higher rank than natural right'.[89] In sum, Strauss's appeal to natural right is an Aristotelian reformulation of his commentary on Schmitt's decisionist concept of the political. Natural right is dictated by the necessity of statecraft and the life-and-death struggle over what is right in concrete political situations. As he put it in a key passage of *Natural Right and History*:

Let us call an extreme situation a situation in which the very existence or independence of a society is at stake. In extreme situations there may be conflicts between what the self-preservation of society requires and the requirements of commutative and distributive justice. In such situations, and only in such situations, it can be said that the public safety is the highest law. A decent society will not go to war except for a just cause. But what it will do during a war will depend to a certain extent on what the enemy—possibly an absolutely unscrupulous enemy—forces it to do. There are no limits which can be defined in advance, there are no assignable limits to what might become just reprisals. But war casts its shadow on peace. The most just society cannot survive without 'intelligence', i.e., espionage. Espionage is impossible without a suspension of certain rules of natural right. But societies are not only threatened from without. Considerations which apply to foreign enemies may well apply to subversive elements within society. Let us leave these sad exigencies covered with the veil with which they are justly covered. It suffices to repeat that in extreme situations the normally valid rules of natural right are justly changed, or changed in accordance with natural right; the exceptions are just as the rules.[90]

Those keen to distance Strauss from Schmitt's decisionism insist that Strauss's 'theory' of natural right is grounded in a universal ethics.[91] But it is important to emphasise that the foundations of Strauss's enterprise are not derived from a transcendent natural law as traditionally understood. Strauss's attempted recovery of natural right is grounded in philosophy's failure to validate itself and refute revelation through reason alone. As Laurence Berns noted, like the ancients, Strauss understands the natural pre-philosophic cognition 'to be constituted at its core by an inalienable tension between the demands of piety and the divination of an impersonal nature that leads to philosophy and science'.[92] Although he sometimes seems to suggest that philosophy and religion are antithetical alternatives, Strauss in fact maintains that the two are locked into a mutually sustaining relationship which has for hundreds of years accounted for the vitality of Western civilisation.[93] This tension is therefore natural not only in the sense that it constitutes the 'natural consciousness', but also in the sense that it is good for society.

Faced with the epistemological dilemma posed by the mutual irrefutability of reason and revelation, Strauss argues that philosophy must remain open to the inconclusive challenge of both. Philosophy must remain 'zetetic'. Zetetism rests on a sceptical alertness to the insufficiencies of any philosophical systems and solutions. It is based on the Socratic awareness that any attempt at resolving the permanent problems that beset humanity can only lead to a dangerous form of ideological dogmatism. As Strauss put it in his famous exchange with Alexandre Kojève, 'the philosopher ceases to be a philosopher from the moment that his "subjective certitude" of the truth of a solution becomes stronger than the consciousness that he may have of the problematical character of this solution. At this moment, the sectarian is born'.[94]

Politicising Philosophy

Strauss's zetetic move is in fact a more or less concealed admission that he cannot ground his ascent from convention to nature in any foundations whatsoever which could be validated discursively. As he himself warns at the beginning of *Natural Right and History*, 'Even by proving that a certain view is indispensable for living well, one proves merely that the view in question is a salutary myth: one does not prove it to be true'.[95] All that philosophy can provide is knowledge and wisdom about the nature of the political; and the most important insight that philosophy can teach us is that politics is a contest of opinions.

As Stanley Rosen argues, because he is incapable of discursively defending philosophy in its own terms, Strauss is forced to defend it by appealing to the pre-philosophical situation: 'Since nature is, as it were, theoretically invisible, Strauss attempts to find it in practice'. Yet, the pre-philosophical situation to which Strauss appeals is both implausible and incredible. It is implausible because the pre-philosophical situation contains 'everything', i.e. both the unphilosophical and the philosophical. And it is incredible because to believe that the neutral observer could make the distinction between the unphilosophical and the philosophical would be a manifest endorsement of the very positivism that Strauss so vehemently criticised. On the other hand, however, Strauss's pre-philosophical turn conveniently allows for the philosophical construction of an exoteric form of political philosophy potentially capable of sustaining a world fit for both the philosopher and the non-philosopher citizen.[96]

We are now getting at the very core and most controversial aspect of Strauss's 'political' philosophy. According to Strauss, enlightenment criticism, in its effort to make moral autonomy available to all, confused moral equality with natural equality. It failed to recognise the unbridgeable gap between the wise and the non-wise and wrongly assumed that everyone could be a philosopher. Philosophy, for Strauss, is not a set of beliefs but a way of life. It refers to the existential condition of the individual philosopher who by an act of pure will and in full awareness of the limits of his own perspective piously dedicates his life to the quest for the unattainable knowledge of 'the whole'.[97] This is not a life that is suitable for everyone. When ordinary citizens become aware that their principles rest upon a comprehensive order that can no longer be recognised as right, they find themselves unable to defend their most valued and identity-conferring beliefs. The responsible philosopher is therefore compelled to become political and construct an exoteric rhetorical foundation. This rhetorical foundation will support the city and mediate between his passionate 'quest for the eternal order' and his love for his own city.[98]

Strauss's entire intellectual enterprise rests upon his belief that the contradictions between the ways of life and practices of one's society could perhaps be resolved in thought but not in practice. As he explained in the course of his debate with Kojève, 'There is no adequate solution to the problem of virtue or happiness on the political or social plane'.[99] In his view, modern philosophy's connivance with power to bring about a world governed by ideals had led to its own destruction. For at the very moment that it yields to the demands of society, philosophy becomes ideological dogmatism. To the extent that philosophy must have a public face, its politics ought to remain moderate—especially in conditions of mass rule. The philosopher, therefore, 'will not engage in revolutionary or subversive activity. He will try to help his fellow man by mitigating, as far as in him lies, the evils that are inseparable from the human condition'.[100]

To the extent that his critique of liberalism sought to 'protect liberal democracy from itself', Strauss primarily sought to problematise the status of individuality and how the latter pertains to the stability of the political community.[101] Strauss was well aware that the ancients did not have more access to the natural world than we do today. But he believed that ancient rationalism was more viable existentially, and that it provided a better basis for ordering the political community. The difference between ancient and modern rationalism ultimately hinged on their respective conceptions of happiness, understood as the ultimate end of human life. Although both agree that happiness is individual and not political, they disagree fundamentally in their understanding of what happiness actually is. Whereas the ancients found happiness in the contemplative life, the moderns find happiness in physical individuality. In this disagreement, Strauss sees the basis for two very different conceptions of the state.[102]

Strauss argues that by consigning happiness and virtue to the private sphere, modern liberalism has rendered impossible the notion of a common good to which the political community must aspire. In these conditions, the purpose of the modern state is limited to guaranteeing human life while refraining 'from imposing on its members happiness of any sort'.[103] The city of the moderns, as first instituted by Hobbes, is like the 'city of pigs' described by Plato in *The Republic*. It is 'a society which is sufficient for satisfying the natural wants of the body, i.e. of the naturally private'.[104] Again here, Strauss's critique of the modern 'Hobbesian' state unfolds as an Aristotelian reformulation of his Weimar dialogue with Schmitt on liberalism:

We shall say that society as distinguished from the state first comes to sight as the market in which competitors buy and sell and which requires the state as its protector or rather servant. On this basis the 'political' comes to be understood eventually as derivative from the 'economic'. The actions of the market are as such voluntary whereas the state coerces. Yet voluntariness is not a preserve of the market, it is above all of the essence of genuine, as distinguished from merely utilitarian, virtue. From this it was inferred in modern times that since virtue cannot be brought about by coercion, the promotion of virtue cannot be the purpose of the state; not because virtue is unimportant but because it is lofty and sublime, the state must be indifferent to virtue and vice as such, as distinguished from transgressions of the state's laws which have no other function than the protection of the life, liberty, and property of each citizen...

We note in passing that this reasoning does not pay sufficient attention to the importance of habituation or education for the acquisition of virtue. This reasoning leads to the consequence that virtue, and religion, must become private, or else that society, as distinguished from the state, is the sphere less of the private than of the voluntary. Society embraces then not only the sub-political but the supra-political (morality, art, science) as well. Society thus understood is no longer properly called society, nor even civilisation, but culture. On this basis the political must be understood as derivative from the cultural: 'culture is the matrix of the state'... [Yet] 'culture' as commonly used now differs from the original notion decisively because it no longer implies the recognition of an order of rank among the various elements of culture. From this point of view Aristotle's assertion that the political element is the highest or most authoritative element in human society must appear to be arbitrary or at best the expression of one culture among many.[105]

As he had done in his exchange with Schmitt, Strauss deplores the debilitating ethico-political paradox underpinning the modern liberal state. On the one hand, the liberal state comes into being by means of an absolute and constitutive right to sovereignty. On the other hand, it legitimates itself by virtue of an absolute human right to life (irrespective of the moral substance of that life). The problem, as Strauss sees it, is that 'liberal sovereignty' deprives the state of its right to demand that the individual abandons his right to life to defend the political community in times of war: 'When armies fight, there is on one side, or both, a running away: yet when they do it not out of treachery, but fear, they are not esteemed to do it unjustly, but dishonourably'. Hobbes preferred to allow for individual 'natural timorousness' rather than nurturing the civic and martial virtues of the citizenry. Yet in doing so, he 'destroyed the moral basis of national defense'.[106]

This is why Strauss believed that Hobbes's 'political hedonism' inevitably pointed towards the creation of a global leviathan. But he warned that such an enterprise demanded a faith in politics and history that contradicts man's natural experience. In America as in Weimar, Strauss insisted on the particularistic nature of statecraft. In his view, institutional projects which accommodate a variety of competing answers to the theological-political problem—like the League of Nations and the United Nations, for example—necessarily involve the abandonment of a standard of right and wrong independent of positive right. And it was this standard which for Strauss made politics possible and imbued life with meaning. Strauss saw the universal state as a de-humanising dystopia.[107]

Like the Schmitt of *Leviathan*, the mature Strauss had come to the conclusion that there was no real solution to the political impasses of the Hobbesian state. This is why he idealised the classical idea of the state. Classical political philosophy rests on the premise that people have needs which are hierarchically ordered by their natural constitution. According to the classics, man's natural constitution allowed for the differentiation between the needs of the human body and those of the human soul. The needs of the soul being higher than corporal needs, it is only when life conforms itself to reason and human intelligence that it concurs with man's natural hierarchy of needs. But human nature 'as such' and its perfection are two different things: 'Human nature "is" in a different manner than its perfection or virtue. Virtue in most cases, if not in all cases, as an object of aspiration and not as fulfilment. Therefore, it exists in speech rather than in deed'.[108] The best regime will therefore never be realised completely and will always remain an ideal. Nevertheless, although justice in its most ideal form can never be attained, the well-ordered soul will tend towards its realisation. Natural right in this context imposes restraint on the fulfilment of corporal needs and limits exercise of individual liberties: 'Man's freedom is accompanied of a sacred awe, by a kind of divination that not everything is permitted'.[109]

This is the central lesson that Strauss seeks to recover from the ancients. In its most perfect form, the republic requires that man's corporal needs be subordinated to those of his soul. For it is the needs of his body that lead him to expand his own private sphere and elevate his individuality at the top of the hierarchy of human ends. Strauss turns his back on the moderns because they have abandoned the utopian city of the ancients to found the city on the needs of the body. Whereas the moderns sought to expose the natural condition of man and re-arrange society according to it, the ancients thought it necessary to veil this original condition. This was the function of Plato's 'noble lie' introduced by Socrates in *The Republic*.[110] The good city rests upon a crucial silence about the natural condition of man. It requires that man be elevated above nature. The good citizen must sacrifice his individuality and accept that he is constituted by the city in all its particularity. By trading his individuality for political virtue and obeying the law of the city, the good citizen becomes more human as he opens himself up to a whole that goes beyond his natural desire for self-preservation.[111]

The American Legacy

Strauss's intellectual enterprise is constituted at its core by an irresolvable tension between his Platonic moral authoritarianism and the anti-dogmatic, moderating nature of his zetetic epistemology—i.e. 'human knowledge is knowledge of ignorance'.[112] As we have seen, his zetetic position was mainly a reaction to historicism and what he saw as a series of misconceived and irresponsible attempts to put philosophy at the service of politics and social transformation. Yet, if one follows the multiple rhetorical twists of his narrative, Strauss in fact authenticates the experience of history. He remains well within the intellectual parameters of German historicism. As Robert Pippin pointed out, his belief that 'thought could reach in historical time a culmination, that that culmination should be a kind of self-consciousness, together with the implication that we needed experience this culmination before we could understand properly what modern thought involved, all sound unmistakable Hegelian notes'. Strauss, Pippin argues, was something of a 'middle-of-the-road Hegelian'.[113] He tacitly accepted the Kantian identification of the human condition as a split between the natural and the ideal, and he followed in the path of German idealism in his belief that ideas were the motor of history. Unlike Hegel, however, he denied that the sense of loss and alienation caused by the decline of religions and mythical folklores was a necessary step towards human emancipation. Here Strauss sided with Nietzsche. He rejected the belief that, once freed from the moral laws of nature, self-legislating human subjects would spontaneously realise themselves as the rational society.[114]

In spite of all his misgivings about the relativist and post-moral character of Nietzsche's philosophy, Strauss in fact never refuted its radical historicist premises. What he thought he had refuted was its ethical conclusions. For Nietzsche, the realisation that self-legislated reason was nothing but an expression of man's will to power demanded bravery and self-overcoming. For Strauss, it demanded moderation and called for a recollection of the relationship between human experience and philosophy as understood by the ancients—a 'noble lie'.

It is nevertheless important to emphasise that, unlike Nietzsche's, Strauss's Platonic elevation of the philosopher above the city is predicated on a belief in the permanent, trans-historical and restrictive tension between philosophy and the city. Many of Strauss's critics who depict him as a closet Nietzschean radical fail to recognise this point and consequently underestimate the genuinely conservative character of his political philosophy.[115] As Leo Lampert argues, Strauss's esotericism is derived from two basic Nietzschean premises: (i) the fabric of society is unalterably opinion, and (ii) philosophy seeks to 'dissolve the elements in which society breathes' and therefore threatens its stability. Yet whereas Nietzsche believed these truths to be timeless, he denied the timeless necessity of esotericism. Nietzsche believed that 'modern opinion necessitates what it also makes possible, the attempt to bring society's opinion into accord with philosophy's character, not by making society wise but by making its opinions reflect rather than contradict the truth'. In his view, if God was dead, there was no point in making concessions to a discredited worldview. Strauss, by contrast, denied that scientific progress or any other human advancements or catastrophes had altered the terms and conditions under which the philosopher must operate.[116]

Strauss was a man of his time. And, as Pippin noted, complaints about his Platonic elitism very often tend to ignore the fact that his intentions were 'at least ambiguous'.[117] He did condone lying in politics, and he did advocate an archaic and anti-democratic executive-centred moralisation of politics. But he also emphasised that true statesmanship is 'free from all fanaticism because it knows that evil cannot be eradicated and that one's expectations from politics must be moderate'.[118] Those who associate him too directly and unreflectively with the Bush administration's democratic crusades tend conveniently to overlook the scepticism that defines his intellectual enterprise.[119]

And yet, Strauss is ultimately solely responsible for this rapprochement between his work and the crusading politics of American neoconservatism. For, to the extent that his Platonic practices were a means to exercise his responsibility as a philosopher, it was a deeply anachronistic intellectual strategy. It was completely unsuited to an audience of young American students who did not possess the intellectual baggage and experience to appreciate the nature of his apprehensive attitude towards historicism.[120] On the other hand, Strauss's rhetorical style was perfectly designed for American use. As John Gray noted, 'His claim that political order rests on the acceptance of moral constraints that lie outside the human sphere matched the creedal character of American public life. America has always been hospitable to the belief that its values are God-given, and so long as he was not read too closely Strauss could be seen as suggesting that the United States was the best regime'.[121] By deciding to found a 'philosophical school' and opting for the false comfort of reified metaphysical foundations, Strauss rendered his experimental ontological recovery of nature perfectly amenable to the type of sectarian ideological politics he criticised in his debate with Kojève.[122]

As Mark Lilla noted in an insightful article on the subject, during the 1950s and early 1960s, Strauss's followers devoted themselves to the study of the great books. They adapted their master's aristocratic interpretation of philosophy to the setting of American democracy in a manner which, although imbued with missionary and rhetorical zeal, was more or less consistent with Strauss's teachings. But the student revolt of the 1960s changed all that. The implosion of the American university radicalised and politicised a great number of influential Straussian scholars. Many of them never got over what they saw as the intellectual levelling resulting from this assault on the establishment. Although many Straussians to this day remain non-partisan and have stayed away from daily political debates, others began to congregate around neoconservative circles after Strauss's death in 1973.[123] As Irving Kristol explained in a 2001 lecture at the American Enterprise Institute, 'We in America fought a culture war ... and neoconservatives brought Strauss in'.[124]

Considering that many in neoconservative circles had studied with Strauss or some of his best students during the 1960s, the Straussian-neoconservative convergence was somewhat of a natural affair. Prominent Straussian scholars like Allan Bloom, Thomas Pangle, Harry

Jaffa, Harvey Mansfield, Ralph Lerner, Joseph Cropsey, Carnes Lord, Donald Kagan, Martin Diamond, Clifford Orwin and Walter Berne helped reinforce the neoconservative project intellectually. Neoconservatives in turn provided Straussians with a political and media machine to spread their ideas.[125] As we will see in the coming chapters, in the process Strauss's intellectualisation of the crisis of modernity became an integral feature of the neoconservative persuasion. Whether Strauss would have approved or not of this political-intellectual merger is no longer the question. American neoconservatism has become an important aspect of his legacy.

3

CAPITALISM, CULTURE WARS AND THE NEOCONSERVATIVE STATE

'The modern world, and the crisis of modernity we are now experiencing, was created by ideas and by the passions which these ideas unleashed.... The truth is that ideas are all-important. The massive and seemingly-solid institutions of any society—the economic institutions, the political institutions, the religious institutions—are always at the mercy of the ideas in the heads of the people who populate these institutions'.

Irving Kristol[1]

'The distance from Hobbes to the "spirit of 1776" and to modern liberal democracy is a very short one... Liberal democracy in its Anglo-Saxon variant represents the emergence of a kind of cold calculation at the expense of earlier moral and cultural horizon. The liberal state growing out of the tradition of Hobbes and Locke engages in a protracted struggle with its own people. It seeks to homogenise their variegated traditional cultures and to teach them to calculate instead their own long-term self-interest. In place of an organic moral community with its own language of "good and evil," one had to learn a new set of democratic values: to be "participant," "rational," "secular," "mobile," "empathetic," and "tolerant". These new democratic values were initially not values at all in the sense of defining the final human virtue or good. They were conceived as having a purely instrumental function, habits that one had to acquire if one was to live successfully in a peaceful and prosperous liberal society. It was for this reason that Nietzsche called the state the "coldest of all cold monster" that destroyed peoples and their cultures by hanging "a thousand appetites" in front of them'.

Francis Fukuyama[2]

For nearly half a century, neoconservatives have been engaged in a relentless culture war over the meanings and symbols that constitute and reconstitute the liberal state in America. Drawing on Strauss's critique of liberalism, as well as a wide range of other sources, neoconservatives have sought to reconnect the American citizenry with its republican roots and recover an 'older' form of public philosophy capable of revitalising American democracy in the face of rapid capitalist modernisation. Although this offensive has mainly taken place on the terrain of civil society, neoconservative intellectuals have provided an important set of ideas and arguments to legitimise reforms in regimes of citizenship and new modes of statecraft designed to facilitate the re-structuring of the welfare state and the 'neoliberalisation' of market relations in the US.

This chapter examines neoconservative discourses on capitalism and the modern liberal state. The first section surveys a set of essays by Irving Kristol, Daniel Bell, Jeane Kirkpatrick and other influential neoconservative intellectuals. It does so in order to expose the main axes of the neoconservative critique of both New Right neoliberalism and the post-war Left in the context of what its protagonists see as the crisis of American liberal democracy. I then analyse the ethico-politics underpinning this critique and call attention to the extent to which it has translated into an expressive politics of security, facilitating the re-articulation of class interests and the advancement of market forces since the late 1970s. I argue that this politics is animated by a distinctively Schmittian-Straussian rationale that resonates strongly with the neo-Hobbesian narrative of statecraft surveyed in the previous chapter, and that tends towards the sublimation of domestic crises through the militarisation of American foreign policy.

Capitalism on Trial

Neoconservatism's relationship to capitalist development is heavily influenced by the rise of neoliberalism as a hegemonic discourse on the appropriate relationship between the market, the state and civil society since the early 1970s. Indeed, neoconservatives themselves often describe neoconservatism as both a qualified accolade and a riposte to neoliberalism—a cross between the conservative political philosophy of Leo Strauss and the neoliberal economics of Friedrich von Hayek and Milton Friedman.[3] It is therefore useful to begin the present discussion with a few words on the main ideological characteristics of neoliberalism so as to appreciate better the nature and particularities of neoconservative arguments.

Neoliberalism as an ideology itself emerged in the early 1970s as a pro-business challenge to what is commonly referred to as 'embedded liberalism', i.e. the set of Keynesian policies, socio-political constraints and legal regulations that surrounded market processes and corporate activities and framed industrial and economic relations in Western liberal democracies during the post-war period.[4] 'Embedded liberalism' was a class compromise between capital and labour. In the US, it grew in great part out of the New Deal and the tradition of 'welfare liberalism' with which the latter became associated.

'Embedded liberalism' sought to ensure peaceful class relations in the domestic realm and prevent another global economic meltdown like the one that nearly destroyed the capitalist order during that tumultuous interwar decade. It delivered the goods during the best part of the two decades that followed the Second World War, mainly because the United States had been willing to run deficits with the rest of the world and to absorb the surplus of market products. By the end of the 1960s, however, signs of a serious crisis of capital accumulation became apparent everywhere at the international and domestic level. High unemployment and inflation plagued most Western economies. This led to a global phase of 'stagflation' that would last throughout the 1970s. Tax revenues fell drastically while social expenditures kept increasing. Keynesianism was no longer working, and various states found themselves in a serious fiscal crisis. At the international level, the Bretton Woods system of fixed exchange rates supported by gold reserves collapsed after US dollars flooded world markets and escaped US control. Gold could no longer be used as the basis of international money and fixed exchange rates had to be abandoned in 1971.[5] Neoliberalism came forward in this gloomy political-economic climate and presented itself as the pro-business cure to the ills of Keynesian economics. Privatisation of state assets, deregulation, low taxation and a disengagement of the state from many areas of social provision were proposed as the key principles of a neoliberal public policy agenda that promised to revitalise economic growth and re-affirm the superiority of capitalism over socialism.[6]

As it turns out, neoliberalism is another intellectual legacy of Weimar Germany. Neoliberalism as a theory of political economic practice has its roots in the 'ordoliberalism' of the so-called Freiburg School, which is also often referred to as 'German neoliberalism'.[7] Ordoliberalism was a conservative, authoritarian form of economic liberalism promoted in the late 1920s and early 1930s by a group of Freiburg University political economists led by Wilhelm Röpke, Walter Eucken, Franz Böhm, Hans Grossmann-Doerth and Alexander Rüstow. Its central tenet was that the state should form an economic order instead of directing economic processes. Ordoliberals argued that the state must create and enforce a strong legal environment so that the economy can maintain a high level of competition through measures that abide by market principles. Not unlike Carl Schmitt, ordoliberals believed that a sound economy required a strong state that stands above the particular interests of civil society and actively guards against the politicisation of the economy. The main concern here was that if the state failed to enforce active measures to generate competition, economic monopolies and oligopolies would emerge. This would undermine both democracy and the advantages offered by the market economy, since strong economic power always tends to translate into strong political power, or so ordoliberals (quite correctly) believed.[8]

The basic principles of German ordoliberalism found their way to the United States mainly via the Austrian-British economist and political philosopher Friedrich von Hayek. Hayek was a student of the Austrian libertarian economist Ludwig von Mises, as well as an attentive reader of Schmitt. He contributed frequently to the main ordoliberal journal, *Ordo*, during the 1930s.[9] Hayek taught at the London School of Economics between 1931 and 1950 and then moved to the United States to become professor of political philosophy at the University of Chicago. There he taught alongside the champion of free market economics Milton Friedman. Together with a number of their colleagues of the Mount-Pelerin Society (an intellectual forum Hayek founded in 1947 to counter the influence of Keynesian economics), they laid the theoretical basis of what is today known as American neoliberalism.

Like ordoliberalism, neoliberalism maintains that human welfare is best achieved by promoting individual entrepreneurial freedoms and skills within a socio-economic setting based on free markets, private property rights and free trade. From this perspective, the role of the state should be to guarantee the rule of law, the functioning of the markets and the institutions that will allow for the individual to pursue his interests freely and thereby ensure the organic reproduction of the socio-political order. Neoliberalism sees market exchange as 'an ethic in itself, capable of acting as a guide to all human action, and substituting for all previously held ethical beliefs'.[10] Its core normative claim is that the common social good will be best served by maximising the flow of market transactions. It therefore aims at bringing all fields of human activity under the aegis of the market, and proposes that the state should create markets where they do not exist: health care, social security and education, for example. But neoliberalism is adamant that this is where state intervention should stop. Unlike ordoliberals, neoliberals do not believe that the state should actively intervene in the economy to stimulate competition. In their view, the state does not possess enough information to anticipate market signals; by intervening the state is more likely to produce unforeseen and undesirable results. Neoliberalism therefore rejects some of the more interventionist premises of its German predecessor. Instead, it favours a more laissez-faire approach that in practice has favoured the development of a monopolistic-oligopolistic form of capitalism—just as the ordoliberals had anticipated.[11]

Although Hayek and his followers had been promoting their ideas in academic circles for decades, it was not until the mid 1970s that their work took centre-stage in policy circles. In the US, neoliberal ideas were nurtured by influential corporate-funded conservative think tanks such as the Heritage Foundation and Hoover Institutions. They came to form the intellectual basis of a concerted effort to restore the pre-New Deal power of the business elite.[12] By the mid 1980s, neoliberalism had become the economic orthodoxy in most industrialised liberal states as well as at the World Bank and the International Monetary Fund (IMF).[13]

The affinity between neoliberal and neoconservative political-economy stems from a shared enthusiasm for free markets, as well as from what both see as the unprecedented level of personal freedoms and class mobility generated by capitalist social relations. Like neoliberals, neoconservatives are deeply suspicious of government intervention in market processes. Over the years, most of them have become staunch advocates of the neoliberal remedy to the perceived failures of 'embedded liberalism'—i.e. privatisation, deregulation, and low taxation.[14] As a journalist on the *Wall Street Journal* and later as editor of *The Public Interest*, Irving Kristol played a pivotal role in the publication of works of people like Robert Mundell, Arthur Laffer, Jude Wanniski and George Gilder who laid the basis of what would become known as supply-side 'Reaganomics' in the 1980s.[15] Put simply, the theory of supply-side economics posits that government revenues increase when tax rates are low but begin to decrease when rates peak to a high level. It assumes that people work harder when they are allowed to keep their money and that, since people make more money when they work harder, the government will have more money to tax. As Mark Gerson explains cheerfully, in supply-side economics, neoconservatives found the basis of a communitarian doctrine of capitalism that 'manifests a vision of instilling the power of creative economic possibility into the hands of the ordinary citizen with the vision and the determination to transform into reality'.[16]

This concern with nurturing a communitarian basis for the cultural embedding of capitalist socio-economic relations also constitutes the main difference between neoliberalism and neoconservatism. For, in spite of all their praises for capitalism, neoconservatives are profoundly anxious about the strains which market forces and corporate culture tend to inflict on the American social compact. According to neoconservatives, the neoliberal capitalist state fares rather well on the economic and administrative level. Its fatal weakness lies in the realm of culture. Or more precisely, the problem lies in the structural incongruity between capitalism's entrepreneurial philosophy of accomplishment and the subversive character of late-modern cultural trends sustaining and stimulating material consumption in post-industrial societies. Whereas the former is based on deferred gratification and the reasonable forbearance that underwrites Protestant ethics, the latter encourage experiential immediacy, materialist entitlements, sensual fulfilment and expressive rather than purposive forms of subjectivity.

This foundational neoconservative argument in fact echoes a well-known thesis first advanced in the mid twentieth century by Frankfurt School theorists like Theodor Adorno, Max Horkheimer, Eric Fromm and Herbert Marcuse. Between the early 1940s and the mid 1960s, these Leftist scholars wrote extensively about the manner in which capitalism had narrowly averted a fatal systemic crisis of legitimacy in the 1930s by co-opting the modernist counter-culture and turning it into a commodity. They analysed the ways in which this emerging 'culture industry' went on to become a vital tool for the administrative creation of demands for consumer goods ('consumerism'). This in turn insured the continuity of capitalist exploitation under America's hegemonic leadership in the post Second World War period.[17]

From a similar analysis, neoconservatives draw different conclusions. Neoconservatives celebrate the continued reign of capitalism as an idea. But they complain that the success of consumerism and the commodification of the counter-culture have led to the internalisation of a subversive impulse into the normative fabric of the capitalist system. In their view, this threatens the long-term reproductive capacity of liberal capitalist societies and the republican vitality of American democracy. This is what Daniel Bell famously identified as *The Cultural Contradictions of Capitalism* in the mid 1970s:

> The culture has been dominated (in the serious realm) by a principle of modernism that has been subversive of bourgeois life, and the middle-class lifestyles by a hedonism that has undercut the Protestant ethic which provided the moral foundation for the society. The interplay of modernism as a mode developed by serious artists, the institutionalisation of those played-out forms by the 'cultural mass', and the hedonism as a way of life promoted by the marketing system of business, constitutes the cultural contradiction of capitalism. The modernism is exhausted, and no longer threatening. The hedonism apes its sterile japes. But the social order lacks either a culture that is a symbolic expression of any vitality or a moral impulse that is a motivational or binding force. What, then, can hold the society together?[18]

> A society given over entirely to innovation, in the joyful acceptance of change, has in fact institutionalised the avant-garde and charges it, perhaps to its own eventual dismay, with constantly turning up something new. In effect, 'culture' has been given a blank check, and its primacy in generating social change has been firmly acknowledged.[19]

Irving Kristol gives a similar account in an influential essay first published in the early 1970s, '"When Virtue Loses All Her Loveliness"—Some Reflections on Capitalism and the "Free Society"'.[20] There, Kristol explains that historically capitalism has drawn its appeal from three promises. First, it promised an unprecedented improvement of people's material condition. Second, it promised a degree of individual freedom that likewise has never been attained in human history. And third, it promised that amidst this newly acquired liberty and material affluence, the individual would be able to live 'a virtuous life that satisfies the demands of his spirit ... and that the free exercise of such individual virtue would aggregate into a just society'. Echoing Strauss, Kristol explains that the novelty here is that, unlike all previous modes of socio-economic organisations, bourgeois capitalism has 'lowered its sights' so as to make its best civilisational attributes accessible to all citizens rather than just a small aristocratic elite. This 'amiable philistinism' inevitably led to the depreciation of 'high culture', since by its very nature 'high culture' is aristocratic. And this is why, in Kristol's view, artists and intellectuals were bound to be hostile to bourgeois society: 'This antagonism was irrepressible—the bourgeois world could not suppress it without violating its own liberal creed; the artists could not refrain from expressing their hostility without denying their most authentic selves'. Kristol argues that as long as capitalism fulfilled its three promises, the hostilities between the bourgeois world and the artistic and intellectual 'counterculture' could, and were, kept under control. But as capitalism strove to deliver on its first two promises of wealth and liberty, it produced culturally destructive dynamics. These progressively undermined its own capacity to deliver its third promise of a virtuous and just society and eventually raised doubts about its legitimacy as a system.[21]

According to Kristol, it is this cultural dimension that neoliberalism and its libertarian supporters underestimate in making their case for capitalism. In a famous critique of Hayek, Kristol argues that Hayek's libertarian defence of capitalism rests on the erroneous notion that the idea of social justice in a market economy is ultimately meaningless. In his interpretation, Hayek's argument is that people are not necessarily against inequality per se, but against the fact that the differences in reward do not match any perceivable differences in the merit of the recipients.[22] From this, Hayek concludes that the notion of social justice is based on the idea that a just society is one in which rewards are proportional to recognisable differences in merit. The problem with this reasoning for Hayek is that in practice no human being has the knowledge and competence necessary to assess objectively the extent of an individual's moral merit. Consequently, any attempt to match material recompense to moral merit amounts to the arbitrary imposition of a particular system of values by a political actor endowed with the power to take the final decision on who is worthy of what. In a market society, since differentials in wealth and income 'are not the effect of anyone's design or intentions, it is meaningless to describe the manner in which the market distributed the good things of this world among particular people as just or unjust' (Hayek).[23]

According to Kristol, Hayek's reasoning is overly rationalistic, and therefore unrealistic. In his view, a free society and a just society cannot be put in such stark opposition on purely epistemological ground. Kristol argues that people cannot live in a free society if they do not believe that it is also a just society. Collective freedom is a subjective condition that ought to be grounded in a widely accepted notion of social justice:

> Who wants to live in a society in which selfishness and self-seeking are celebrated as primary virtues? [....] My reading of history is that, in the same way as men cannot for long tolerate a sense of spiritual meaninglessness in their individual lives, so they cannot for long accept a society in which power, privilege, and property are not distributed according to some morally meaningful criteria. Nor is equality itself any more acceptable than inequality—neither is more 'natural' than the other—if equality is merely a brute fact rather than a consequence of ideology or social philosophy. This explains what otherwise seems paradoxical: that small inequalities in capitalist countries can become the source of intense controversy while relatively larger inequalities in socialist or communist countries are blandly overlooked ... [P]eople's notions of equality and inequality have extraordinarily little to do with arithmetic and almost everything to do with political philosophy ... I believe that what holds for equality also holds for liberty. People feel free when they subscribe to a prevailing social philosophy; they feel unfree when the prevailing social philosophy is unpersuasive; and the existence of constitutions or laws or judiciaries have precious little to do with these basic feelings.[24]

Kristol argues that it is only relatively recently that capitalism has abandoned its claim to be the 'most just social order the world has ever witnessed'. This claim was based on the fact that capitalism replaced an aristocratic system in which power, property and wealth were distributed arbitrarily, and that capitalism reorganised the distribution of those goods on the basis of personal merit, abilities and virtues. This was the bourgeois society at its apogee. It was an era when the Protestant or Puritan ethic prevailed and power and wealth were seen as corollaries of bourgeois virtues: 'a willingness to work hard to improve one's condition, a respect for law, an appreciation of the merits of deferred gratification, a deference towards religion, a concern for family and community, and so on'.[25]

Kristol argues that neoliberalism is fundamentally flawed as an ideology because it has no 'extra-market' moral anchor. Neoliberalism translates the liberal *ontological* claim about the persistence and determining role of economic rationality in human affairs into a *normative* claim about the pervasiveness and desirability of economic rationality. It seeks to advance this normative claim and disseminate market values to all spheres of human activity by fostering institutional practices and a system of penalties and rewards to reproduce and sustain this way of life. Whereas classical liberalism posits different criteria for individual moral, political and economic actions, neoliberalism *constructs* the individual actor as a calculating entrepreneur in all areas. It equates morality with the individual's capacity to fulfil his own desires and ambitions autonomously through a rational cost-benefit analysis. It then tries to steer society by moralising the consequences of individual freedom according to these rational economic criteria.[26]

For neoconservatives, the market cannot be considered as a set of ethics in itself. When released from the constraints of religion and the bourgeois ethos, the self that is being realised through liberal capitalism becomes manipulative and overly materialist. It develops a whole range of vices that undermine its contribution to the common good and to the maintenance of a social system which organically weds order to liberty.[27] As Kristol argues, by replacing bourgeois virtue with the idea of individual liberty in their defence of capitalism, both Hayek and Friedman have no principled ground from which to oppose attacks on the liberal values presupposed by their defence of the free market: 'What if the "self" that is "realised" under the conditions of liberal capitalism is a self that despises liberal capitalism, and uses its liberty to subvert and abolish a free society? To this question, Hayek—like Friedman—has no answer'. The libertarian tradition that informed the neoliberal paradigm, Kristol argues, was too naive. 'It never really could believe that vice, when unconstrained by religion, morality, and law, might lead to viciousness. It never really could believe that self-destructive nihilism was an authentic and permanent possibility that any society had to guard against. It could refute Marx, effectively, but it never thought it would be called upon to refute the Marquis de Sade and Nietzsche'.[28]

Kristol argues that until the 1960s capitalism lived off the 'accumulated capital' of the moral and spiritual traditions of Christianity and Judaism. 'But with each generation that capital stock was noticeably depleted, had to be stretched ever thinner to meet the exigencies of life'.[29] Liberal modernity's insistence on the privatisation of moral conscience undermined the public status of religion. In doing so, it destroyed the moral beliefs which in earlier times allowed Americans to make a distinction between liberty and license, and which provided them with a sense of stoical resignation to face the inevitable existence of poverty and economic inequality.[30] Secularism transformed America into a mindless materialistic society, which 'insists that an 18-year-old girl has the right to public fornication in a pornographic movie—but only if she is paid the minimum wage'.[31] It substituted technology, industry, science and history to the transcendent powers of religion. Yet as these new gods failed one after the other to deliver on their promise of a meaningful, emancipated and rationally organised world society, 'the West' was left without beliefs. So that whatever is left of the 'moral and spiritual capital stock' accumulated by religion in the past is in the process of being wiped off by the 'hurricanes of twentieth century nihilism'.[32] Bell makes a similar argument in *The Cultural Contradictions of Capitalism*:

> The realm problem of modernity is the problem of belief. To use an unfashionable term, it is a spiritual crisis, since the new anchorages have proved illusory and the old ones have become submerged. It is a situation which brings us back to nihilism; lacking a past or a future, there is only a void. Nihilism was once a heady philosophy, as it was for Bazarov, when there was something to destroy and something to put in its place. But today what is there left in the past to destroy, and who has the hope for a future to come? [...] What holds one to reality, if one's secular system of meanings proves to be an illusion? I will risk one unfashionable answer—the return in Western society of some conception of religion... What religion can restore is the continuity of generations, returning us to the existential predicaments which are the ground of humility and care for others.[33]

The reader will surely have noted the strong similarities between these arguments and the Straussian narrative surveyed in the previous chapter. According to neoconservatives, 'the enervation of strong religious beliefs has demoralised society'. Since 'nothing else has been found to substitute for it', a return to religion in public discourse is necessary to counter the 'new nihilism' and tame the 'basest appetites, passions and impulses' of the citizenry (William Bennett).[34] And all this despite the fact that no one can discursively 'prove' that religion is a sound basis upon which to build a society. As Kristol explains, 'One accepts a moral code on faith... Pure reason can offer a critique of moral beliefs but it cannot engender them'.[35] For neoconservatives, the fact that it has helped maintain order in the past is a good enough reason to embrace it. In their view, the instrumentalisation of religion is a perfectly legitimate response to a liberal capitalist culture that embraces nihilism as a business opportunity. As Kristol tells us, Americans 'don't bother with theology...The fact is that the moral dimension of religion is what counts for Americans'. This is why, according to Kristol, neoconservatives are 'pro-religion even though they themselves may not be believers': 'Whether you believe or not is not the issue—that's between you and God—whether you are a member of a community that holds certain truths sacred, that is the issue'.[36]

Echoing Strauss, neoconservatives argue that the crisis of governability which has been periodically hovering over America since the 1960s can be traced back to Hobbes's reversal of the ancient hierarchy between reason and human will. For in subordinating reason to man's animal instincts and desires, Hobbes removed all moral constraints on the quest for self-gratification. In doing so, he laid the foundations for a society based on the unrestrained satisfaction of psychological wants. The success of Hobbes's leviathan state progressively led to the elevation of individual aesthetic experience as the only source of meaning and existential authenticity. As Bell explains:

> In Western consciousness there has always been tensions between the rational and the nonrational, between reason and will, between reason and instinct, as the driving force of man. Whatever the specific distinctions, rational judgment was traditionally thought to be superior in the hierarchy, and this order dominated Western culture for almost two millennia.... Modernism dirempts this hierarchy. It is the triumph of the spirited, of the will. In Hobbes and Rousseau, intelligence is a slave to appetite and the passions. In Hegel, the will is the necessary component of knowing. In Nietzsche, the will is fused with the aesthetic mode, in which knowledge derives most directly ('apprehended, not ascertained', as he says in the first line of the Birth of Tragedy) from intoxication and dream. And if aesthetic experience alone is to justify life, then morality is suspended and desire has no limit. Anything is possible in this quest of the self to explore its relation to sensibility.[37]

According to neoconservatives, the hedonistic logic of this cultural politics has introduced an overly materialistic form of rationalism in the socio-political life of the country. This materialistic rationalism tends to outstrip the state's capacity to satisfy the demands of the citizenry and to devaluate republican virtues—i.e. 'the willingness of the good democratic citizen, on critical occasions, to transcend the habitual pursuit of self-interest and devote himself directly and disinterestedly to the common good'.[38] As Kristol explains, like religion and the bourgeois ethos, republican virtue was an important source of restraint in the American tradition. But modernism transformed the 'bourgeois citizen into the bourgeois consumer'. It dissolved the moral and ideational framework that kept unreasonable expectations under control and prevented the pursuit of private economic interests from dominating and corrupting the political sphere, the *res publica*: 'One used to be encouraged to control one's appetites; now one is encouraged to satisfy them without delay. The inference is that one has a *right* to satisfy one's appetites without delay, and once this 'right' is frustrated, as it always is in some way or other, an irritated populace turns to the state to do something about it'. The unconstrained pursuit of self-interest dissolves the citizens' sense of obligations to each other and eventually erodes their commitment to the values embodied by the state. The effort of economic interests to promote themselves through the electoral system falsifies the genuinely political nature of the national interest by forcing on it concerns which ultimately belong to the private realm. Under such conditions, democracy ultimately becomes a threat to the reproduction of the liberal capitalist state.[39]

Following Strauss, neoconservatives see the contemporary liberal state as the latest institutional manifestation of Hobbes's political hedonistic dystopia. As Kristol observes, the liberal state derives its legitimacy not from its capacity to transcend the individual wills and unite them into a representative whole, but strictly from its capacity to maintain order and adapt its domestic institutions to the caprices of the global economy. It rests on a technocratic ethics that puts the entire burden of legitimation on the elites' capacity to generate and sustain economic growth. Yet the success of the elites in boosting the economy and developing national industry is more often than not achieved at the expense of the environment and large sections of the workforce. For that reason, Kristol observes, a successful business community may bring benefits to a portion of the population. But it cannot provide anything that approximates to the 'public good' and thus cannot be relied upon to legitimate the capitalist system.[40] According to Kristol, the legitimacy deficit built into the liberal state is one of the main sources of the crisis that has been looming over the American political system since the late 1960s. The American citizenry no longer recognises itself and its values in state institutions because the latter no longer reflect the private moral code that 'presumably' governs the life of the average American individual:

> The 'outside' of our social life has ceased being harmonious with the 'inside'—the mode of distribution of power, privilege, and property, and hence the very principle of authority, no longer 'makes sense' to the bewildered citizen. And when institutions cease to 'make sense' in this way, all the familiar criteria of success or failure become utterly irrelevant ... An idea of self-government, if it is to be viable, must encompass both the private and the public sectors. If it

does not—if the principles that organise public life seem to have little relations to those that shape private lives—you have 'alienation', and *anomie*, and a melting away of established principles of authority.[41]

As in the Schmittian-Straussian narrative, the main problem with the 'Hobbesian' liberal state for neoconservatives is that it fails to mobilise fully the individual conscience of the citizen. It envisages citizen obligations strictly as a set of negative constraints, and therefore cannot simultaneously aspire to absorb the will of its subjects into an existential community of values transcending the sum of the individual wills. As Fukuyama argues, 'Beyond establishing rules for mutual self-preservation, liberal societies do not attempt to define any positive goals for their citizens or promote a particular way of life as superior or desirable to another. Whatever positive content life may have has to be filled by the individual himself'.[42] In pre-modern times, he goes on:

Each of the peoples of the earth had its own 'language of good and evil', which their neighbors could not understand. What constituted the essence of man was the act of valuing itself, of giving oneself worth and demanding recognition for it. The act of evaluating was inherently inegalitarian, for it required distinguishing between better and worse. The terrible consequence of modernity was the effort of its creators Hobbes and Locke to strip man of its evaluative power in the name of physical security and material accumulation.[43]

Fukuyama's mentor, Allan Bloom, mounts a similar critique in *The Closing of the American Mind*:

Hobbes and Locke gave the plebs equal rights to selfishness. The ruled are not directed by nature to the rulers any more than the rulers naturally care only for the good of the ruled. Rulers and ruled can consciously craft a compact by which the separate interests of each are protected. But they are never one, sharing the same highest end... There is no body politic, only individuals who have come together voluntarily and can separate voluntarily without maiming themselves.[44]

In sum, neoconservatives contend that the legitimation problems of post-war liberal capitalism are tied to a more generalised legitimation crisis that cannot be addressed simply by confronting what Hayek called the 'mirage of social justice' with the neoliberal mirage of endless material accumulation. The crisis of American democratic capitalism is a crisis of public philosophy. And it is a crisis that New Right neoliberalism in fact exacerbates by depriving conservatism of a solid normative ground from which to defend existing institutions against the 'new politics' of the post-war Left and what neoconservatives call the 'new class'.

The New Class

The concept of the new class is another important linkage between American neoconservatism and the political sociology of interwar Europe. It grew out of Trotskyist and anarchist critiques of Stalinism in the late 1920s, which described the Soviet regime as a form of state capitalism managed by a 'new class' of professional and self-interested bureaucrats.[45] The concept then evolved into a critique of the role of intellectuals in public life originating in a set of arguments first made by Joseph Schumpeter, who migrated to the United States from Central Europe (via Weimar) in the early 1930s and had a brilliant academic career there.

Schumpeter was a frustrated conservative liberal. Although this is rarely acknowledged in the mainstream literature, his work was heavily influenced by the proto-fascist political theory of late-nineteenth- and early-twentieth-century European intellectuals such as Gaetano Mosca, Vilfredo Pareto, George Sorel and, not least, Carl Schmitt, who was one of his close colleagues at the University of Bonn during the 1920s.[46] As William Scheuerman noted in a brilliant intellectual exegesis on the subject, just as Schmitt criticised modern rationalism for having divested politics of decisive agency, Schumpeter complained that it had led to the disappearance of the charismatic firm manager capable of inspiring and disciplining the workforce. In his view, this was slowly transforming capitalism into a soulless form of bureaucratic management that he associated with the rise of the welfare state.[47] Schumpeter also complained that the increasingly monopolistic character of capitalism in the early twentieth century had eroded the function of the individual heroic entrepreneur. He assumed that in these conditions people would prefer state regulation and provision to unfettered private enterprise. Thus although he was a fervent supporter of capitalism, Schumpeter believed that the future belonged to socialism.

According to Schumpeter, however, the demise of capitalism would not ensue from the actions of the working class but from those of intellectuals. In *Capitalism, Socialism and Democracy* (1942), he argued that, under conditions of advanced modernity, intellectuals 'develop group attitudes and group interests sufficiently strong to make large numbers of them behave in a way that is usually associated with the concept of social classes'.[48] Steeped in the culture of modern rationalism, and eager to avoid jobs that would leave its intellectual and financial appetite unsatisfied, the intelligentsia tends to adopt egalitarian anti-capitalist views out of self-interest: 'The intellectual groups cannot help nibbling [at the foundations of capitalist society] because it lives on criticism and its whole position depends on criticism that stings'. According to Schumpeter, this is why public policy was destined to become increasingly hostile to capitalism. And since intellectuals appeal to the very same liberal freedoms to undermine capitalism that capitalism needs to thrive, the capitalist class could do little to reverse this state of affair.[49] As he put it in a famous passage that anticipates the neoconservative 'cultural contradictions' thesis presented earlier:

> [C]apitalism creates a critical frame of mind which, after having destroyed the moral authority of so many other institutions, in the end turns against its own; the bourgeois finds to his amazement that the rationalist attitude does not stop at the credentials of kings and popes but goes on to attack private property and the whole scheme of bourgeois values ... Unlike any other type of society, capitalism inevitably and by virtue of the very logic of its civilisation creates, educates and subsidises a vested interest in social unrest.[50]

Schumpeter's argument was reprised by Hayek in 'The Intellectuals and Socialism' (1949)[51], and then by Lionel Trilling in *Beyond Culture* (1965) where he identified the so-called 'adversary culture' of the 1960s.[52] There, Trilling argued that cultural modernism is characterised by an adversary intention whose purpose is to give a vantage point to the intellectual 'from which to judge and condemn, and perhaps revise, the culture that has produced him'. Although he welcomed this critical spirit as a bulwark against mindless conformism, Trilling warned that as the adversary culture was gaining in number, cohesion and political influence, it was manufacturing its own conformity and undermining its autonomy from society and public institutions.[53]

Neoconservatives use the concept of the new class as a mixture of all of the above interpretations. The new class refers to the growing stratum of Left-leaning intellectuals who came of age during the cultural revolutions and today find themselves in positions of economic and political power—supported by the advent of a technologically driven post-industrial 'information society'. Members of the new class range from corporate executives to university lecturers, lawyers, computer programmers and bureaucrats of all sorts who make a living from ideas and social criticism. These are professionals who allegedly have a vested interest in the 'war on poverty', progressive reforms, bureaucratic expansion, and the growth of international institutions and the NGO sector.[54] According to neoconservatives, academics are the most influential and subversive of all since (i) they are statistically more likely to adopt radical views than any other social groups, (ii) their work has a direct impact on public policy and (iii) the student market is steadily increasing.[55] Not far behind academics are journalists and media commentators whose critical gaze and capacity to shape public opinion have grown massively since the 1960s. As Samuel Huntington wrote in the mid 1970s, the media 'increasingly came to conceive of themselves in an adversarial role vis-à-vis the executive government. At stake were not merely conflicting personalities and differing political viewpoints, but also fairly fundamental institutional interests. The media have an interest in exposure, criticism, highlighting and encouraging disagreement and dissatisfaction within the executive branch'.[56]

The new class is one of the main *raisons d'être* of neoconservatism. As Gertrude Himmelfarb wrote in the mid 1990s, although the concept was adapted and developed in the 1970s, it has over the past decades become more relevant than ever for neoconservative politics. Indeed, Himmelfarb argues that the designation 'new' should be abandoned altogether since the new class has simply become 'the mirror image of the underclass'. Although they do so for different reasons and with different consequences, both the new class and the underclass reject the cultural values and bourgeois public philosophy that she claims account for the exceptional political and economic success of the American nation-state.[57] And this, neoconservatives tell us, is the main characteristic of the new class: it does not wield influence through financial power or human capital but through the interpretation of cultural symbols. As Kirkpatrick argued, 'the new class can be recognised not by its socioeconomic characteristics but by its relation to culture: to the meanings that constitute a culture and to the symbols through which those meanings are expressed'.[58]

According to neoconservatives, the new class has soiled public discourse with a set of utopian and distinctively modern ontological and epistemological assumptions that have forever disturbed the frame of intelligibility through which Americans have historically understood their political experience. New class discourses are a repudiation of the political wisdom that has characterised American politics since the Founding Fathers in favour of a rationalist conception of politics that no longer recognises the limits of the human condition. As Kirkpatrick put it in the early 1980s:

> Failure to distinguish between the domain of thought and experience, of rhetoric and politics, is, of course, the very essence of rationalism. Rationalism encourages us to believe that anything that can be conceived can be brought into being. The rationalist perversion in modern politics consists in the determined effort to understand and shape people and societies on the basis of inadequate, oversimplified theories of human behavior... Rationalism not only encourages utopianism, but utopianism is a form of rationalism. Utopianism shares the characteristic features of rationalism: both are concerned more with the abstract than the concrete, with the possible more than the probable, both are less concerned with people as they are than as they might be (at least as rationalist think might be).[59]

Particularly disconcerting for neoconservatives is the egalitarian spirit that underpins the rationalist outlook of new class politics. As Aaron Wildavsky explains, the new class is driven by a radical egalitarianism that seeks to eliminate all distinctions of status, of authority, of income, of gender, of right and wrong etc... It sees the state as a 'vastly expanded compensatory mechanism whose purpose is to make up for past inequalities'.[60] Along similar lines, Kristol protests that the new class has blurred the traditional distinctions between the political and the social. He speaks of the thematisation of poverty as a ploy by a 'new class of self-designed "intellectuals" [who] pursue power in the name of equality'. Identifying John Rawls as one of the leading new class intellectuals, Kristol argues that the idea that social justice hinges on the elimination of inequality is a rationalist heresy.[61] '[A] just and legitimate society', he retorts, 'is one in which inequalities—of property, or station, or power—are generally perceived by the citizenry as necessary for the common good'.[62] According to Kristol, new class politics express a characteristically un-American 'divorce between rationality and reasonableness': a perversion of the spirit of 1776 in the name of the same hubristic humanism that sent the French Revolution to its doom.[63]

The minimisation of the impact of the French Enlightenment on the American experience is a common rhetorical strategy in neoconservative discourses. It is designed above all to discredit egalitarianism, rationalism and other contemporary intellectual movements that cultivate Left-wing political allegiances on university campuses.[64] Again here, the structure of the argument is characteristically Schmittian-Straussian. Neoconservatives argue that the abstract universalisms that have given meaning and sustained the unity of the state over the years are being politically exploited by the indirect powers of civil society (the new class) in order to pursue their own cosmopolitan utopias against the established order. They argue that the 'utopian rationalism' introduced by the new class has polarised the citizenry. It has led to the decay of integrative institutions like the churches, the party system, trade unions and the presidency; and it has empowered divisive actors like single-issue special interest groups, the new social movements and the critical media. To the 'old pragmatic style of politics that once allowed the democratic party system to build consensus and foster political stability, the new class has substituted a politics driven by a tendency to distrust authority, to prefer the new, and to seek conflict in the form of "confrontation"'. It has introduced a 'rationalistic, moralistic, and reformist approach... dominated by intellectual questions and concerned with matters of justice and justice in history'.[65] This new politics, neoconservatives complain, envisages democracy as a forum where voters can be presented with alternatives rather than as a bargaining process between elites over elite-determined policies.[66] The new class also appeals to postmodern cosmopolitan categories to sponsor multiculturalism and the internationalisation of US domestic law (see Chapter 5). This indirect 'method *à deux mains*' devours the concrete power of the state and subverts the qualitative unity of the general will. It allows for an interpenetration of state and civil society that increases the power of the unrepresentative liberal elite within state institutions, and gives this elite the financial power, skills and education that it needs to take advantage of the average American.

According to neoconservatives, the rationalism of the liberal elite is a dangerous political hypocrisy. It presents itself as an ethical type of 'apolitical' utopian politics morally superior to the Right's more sober, realist and elite-driven politics of hierarchy, law and order. But in the process, existing political institutions come to be judged by utopian ethical standards that no longer take account of the real and hard constraints of politics. As Kirkpatrick argues:

> The rationalist orientation creates disenchantment with concrete people, places, and practices ... The habit of measuring existing practices against abstract principles inevitably leads to discontent with the status quo, and the belief that reality can be brought into conformity with principles creates a

predisposition to act to remedy unsatisfactory situations. Rationalism, optimism, and activism have been and still are the source of liberal and radical political action. They also are characteristics of the politics of the new class.[67]

For neoconservatives, political utopianism is an oxymoron. At the theoretical level, it takes its cue from the same political categories and constraints that it seeks to subvert in practice. And because it inevitably fails to provide a viable alternative to the politics that it challenges, it leads to a de-legitimation of state institutions and generates a 'constant fear and suspicion that power and/or authority, whether in government or out, is being used to frustrate the "will of the people"'.[68] Kristol sees it as a prime source of nihilism and civil disobedience:

> One cannot continue in a condition in which reality is always offending our expectations. That is an unnatural condition, and sooner or later people will be seeking relief from it... The utopian impulse, in the end, must actively seek its own liquidation because it is impossible to sustain indefinitely; the psychological cost becomes too great. Utopianism dreams passionately of a liberation from all existing orthodoxies—religious, social, political—but, sooner or later it must wearily and gratefully surrender to a new orthodoxy which calms its passions even as it compromises its dreams.[69]

From Welfare to Security State

Since the 1970s, and in the light of the analysis presented above, neoconservatives have been insisting that the restructuring of the welfare state ought to be accompanied by radical reforms in regimes of citizenship designed to reconcile the alienated citizen with the values embodied by state institutions. To this end, they urge the reconstruction of a widely accepted public philosophy that will facilitate the reconstitution of the state as an order of meaning in the face of rapid socio-economic modernisation. In more practical terms, this has translated into a campaign of devaluation of cultural modernity which targets liberal intellectuals as bearers of values conflicting with the functional imperatives of the state and the capitalist economy. It has also led to a more or less concerted effort to transform the political rationales underpinning state intervention in civil society, so as to foster a consensus on the political and moral values deemed necessary to ensure the peaceful coexistence of capitalism and democracy.

As we have seen, at the intellectual level, the neoconservative offensive hinges on an alleged disjuncture of the cultural sphere from the political, economic and administrative spheres of human activity. At the concrete political level, this then allows neoconservatives to displace the burden for the negative effects of accelerated modernisation and economic neoliberalisation onto the ground of culture. As Habermas noted in the 1980s, neoconservatives want to preserve one-sidedly the economic, administrative and technological aspects of modernity at the expense of its moral and aesthetic accomplishments. They welcome the penetration of the instrumental logic of economic forces and state administration into the 'lifeworld'—the informal and non-instrumentalised domain of everyday life that we share with other human beings (the family and non-marketised civil society)—inasmuch as the capitalist economy and state administrative forces impose a set of externally determined objectives on social actors. For this keeps the latter within pre-established patterns of instrumental action and advances the technical demands of system maintenance. At the same time, neoconservatives seek to avoid a crisis of legitimacy and authority of state institutions by gaining control over the sphere of cultural reproduction, lowering social expectations and minimising the demands of normative justification on the political system.[70]

From both a theoretical and political perspective, the main problem with this programme is that it envisages the cultural sphere as a set of values and moral truths disembodied from the production processes that shape the community's socio-economic life. As Richard Wolin noted, cultural modernity's unquenchable thirst for novelty and aesthetic self-fulfilment cannot be so conveniently separated from the dynamics of modernity as a socio-economic phenomenon: 'the ceaseless dynamism that necessitates the dismantling of all traditional ways of life, the disruption of all fixed values and norms, the obsessive concern with progress and development at all costs—all of these values correspond to the entrepreneurial ethos, the Faustian striving in which "all that is solid melts into air"'.[71]

Not so surprisingly, this disembodied interpretation of culture bears a close resemblance to the one that prevailed in the conservative intellectual circles of interwar Germany. Herbert Marcuse and his Frankfurt School colleagues at the time referred to it as 'affirmative culture'. Affirmative culture 'plays off the spiritual world against the material world by holding up culture as the authentic values and self-contained ends in opposition to the world of social utility and means'. It lifts the ideational world 'out of its social context, making culture a false collective noun and attributing (false) universality to it'.[72] In an analogous manner, the neoconservative identification of alienation, anomie and nihilism with subjective loss of meaning in the cultural sphere conveniently ignores the 'objective' sources of alienation in the commodity form as a structured and structuring social practice. The latter is predicated on the coerced rationalisation and instrumentalisation of labour as an a priori and necessary condition for the modernisation of liberal capitalist societies. As David Frisby argues, alienation in late-modern capitalism does not refer to intersubjective anomie as such. It refers to the perceived independence of social phenomena created by agents (in response to their own needs) who progressively experience a sense of helplessness in controlling the developmental dynamics of these same phenomena.[73]

Nevertheless, to the extent that this reification of culture works to neutralise the antagonisms that oppose democracy to capitalism, it has allowed neoconservatives to enlist the support of large segments of the business class, while at the same time allowing it to court the Christian Right and cultivate a broad popular base among the largest and least organised social class in the United States: the White working class.[74] While it is the liberal intellectual class that is being held responsible for the cultural crisis that looms over America, it is mainly those whom neoconservatives see as the victims of liberal ideas spread during the 1960s and 1970s—the 'demoralised poor' and 'urban underclass'—who have been made the object of this re-articulation of interests. According to neoconservatives, the counterculture and the social welfare programmes of the 1960s have eroded the value of hard work at the heart of the American value system. Although well intended, these experiences in social engineering in fact created a culture of dependence on drugs and welfare and completely eroded the sense of responsibility of the citizenry. Rather than helping the poor, the programmes have undermined their capacity to help themselves out of poverty.[75] Indeed, according to Himmelfarb, the new class's demoralisation of American culture has now replaced the socio-economic causes of crime: 'Today in inner cities there is a correlation between unemployment and crime, but it is not a causal one. Or if it is causal, it is not unemployment that causes crime so much as a culture that denigrates or discourages employment, making crime seem more normal, natural, and desirable than employment'.[76] Harvey Mansfield gives the argument a racial tone:

> America has had a frightening, demoralising increase in crime that has caught everyone's attention but is as yet unchecked. Not only is crime more frequent among blacks, but for many of them it has also become, through the indulgence of whites, their specialty—or, in the sixties lingo, their identity. Crime makes blacks threateningly, hence thrillingly different. Its romanticisation by sixties white lingers on in the diminished form of sympathy or at least toleration of criminals.[77]

Since the 1980s, neoconservatives have come to the conclusion that the legislative apparatus of the state should be used to enforce particular moral codes and ways of life so as to re-adjust the moral balance of American society. Against anti-statist libertarian conservatives and neoliberals, neoconservatives argue that simply dismantling welfare regimes so as to shift responsibility for welfare back to the individual and allow the market to discipline the poor will not be effective since the cultural conditions necessary for the maintenance and reproduction of the liberal state no longer exist.[78] Thus although neoconservatives are strongly in favour of welfare retrenchments, unlike neoliberals, they do not seek its complete dismantling. What they want is what Kristol calls a 'conservative welfare state' that provides a safety net for those suffering from illness and old age who cannot actively take part in the country's economy, *and that is consistent with traditional American values*. The conservative welfare state is not geared towards tackling poverty as such but towards the elimination of the culture of welfare dependency and residual commitments to social democracy:

> The plain truth is that if we are ever going to cope with the deficit and the social programmes that inflate it, we are going to have to begin with a very different view of human nature and human responsibility in relation to such issues as criminality, sexuality, welfare dependency, even medical insurance. Only to the degree that such a new—actually very old—way of looking at ourselves and our fellow citizens emerges can a public opinion be shaped that will candidly confront the fiscal crisis of the welfare state. Presidential calls for 'sacrifice', meaning a willingness to pay higher taxes, are a liberal cop-out. Why don't we hear something about self-control and self-reliance? It's the traditional spiritual values that we as individuals need, not newly invented, trendy ones.[79]

The neoconservative 'welfare state' is a moral tutor. It condemns 'vulgar' and 'promiscuous' lifestyles. It promotes family values and hard work, and it rewards households capable of managing their finances wisely.[80] In effect, it substitutes the 'rehabilitative' and 'solidarist' rationale that underpinned the post-war approach to social security for a retributive one by which welfare and social security benefits are made conditional upon certain moral behaviours—sexual, alcohol and drug abstinence, for example—and can be withheld or withdrawn in cases of 'moral misconduct'.

This is a far cry from the laissez-faire attitude of neoliberalism. As Kristol explains, 'Neocons do not like the concentration of services in the welfare state and are happy to study alternative ways of delivering these services. But they do not feel that kind of alarm or anxiety about the growth of the state in the past century, seeing it as natural, indeed inevitable. People have always preferred strong government to weak government'.[81] The neoconservative state, therefore, is just as interventionist in maintaining capitalist social relations as the Keynesian social democratic welfare state. What changes is the governmental rationale and political objectives of this interventionism. Rather than actively participating in the economy through state-owned enterprise and the enforcement of certain redistributive mechanisms, the neoconservative state seeks to enhance private sector accumulation by creating and maintaining regulatory control over a set of quasi-markets in health, education and other social services. The role of the state in this context is to enhance the capacity of the private sector to provide public goods. At the same time, it seeks to increase the capacity of the workforce to individualise the provision of its own reproduction needs by rewarding and punishing certain lifestyles. In other words, neoconservatism does not 'downsize' the state. Rather, it seeks to transform its role and increase the scope of its reach into civil society and the American household.

Not surprisingly, neoconservatism's retributive attitude towards the 'demoralised' and 'undeserving' segments of society in welfare polices has been matched by a similar approach to crime control. Neoconservative discourses have sought to shift compassion for the offender (which has traditionally moderated the severity of punishment) to sympathy for the victims and fearful potential victims. They advocate harsh retributive measures of crime control that increase disincentives—e.g. the death penalty—and often lead to the segregation of the social groups that pose a risk to the rest of the population. According to neoconservatives, the failure of the Great Society programmes is inexorably linked to the high crime rates in America today. Penal expertise here is seen as a deplorable symptom of late-modern relativism—a lack of moral clarity that epitomises the progressive zeal of the

1960s and the failure of rehabilitative programmes to understand the 'true' nature of crime and human beings.[82]

Over the past decades, neoconservatives have expressed dismay at the fact that tolerance to crime in the US has increased steadily to match the rising crime rates. In 'Defining Deviancy Down', for instance, Patrick Moynihan argues that America is living in denial because it deals with the soaring level of crime and social deviance by lowering the threshold for what society is prepared to accept as normal so as to keep the volume of crime and deviance within manageable proportions.[83] Charles Krauthammer follows Moynihan in 'Defining Deviancy Up'. There, he adds that 'as part of its vast project of moral levelling', the liberal elite has simultaneously defined deviance up so as to raise the bar of normality for the ordinary bourgeois: 'while for criminals and the crazies deviancy has been defined down.... [N]ormal middle-class life then stands exposed as the true home of violence and abuse and a whole catalogue of aberrant acting and thinking'.[84]

Now, as the critical theorist Thomas McCarthy pointed out, to the extent that neoconservative discourse on the socially dysfunctional behaviour of the underclass relies on psychological and cultural patterns to explain social structures and processes (rather than inversely or reciprocally), it operates according to the same logic as the biological racial theories of society and development discredited in the second half of the twentieth century:

> Like racist discourses in the past, neoracist discourses today attempt to explain away entrenched injustices by reference to their victim's own shortcomings, which are now taken to be cultural rather than biological in origin. In an influential neoconservative version, differences in social mobility or societal modernisation are said to be due to behavioural deficiencies in the disadvantaged underclass or underdeveloped societies. While the historical origins of these deficiencies in slavery, colonialism, or the like may be acknowledged, this is not understood as a causal account of the inequalities in question, but at most a confession of the sins of our fathers.[85]

The 'neoconservative state', of course, is an ideal type. It has never found full expression in American state institutions. Nevertheless, numerous studies have shown that neoconservative culturalist discourses on welfare and crime have had a significant impact on American public policy since the late 1970s and early 1980s.[86] For example, many studies have highlighted the moralising slant of welfare retrenchments since the first Reagan administration and demonstrated how this moralising approach to welfare has taken an acute racial bent over the last two decades or so. Martin Gilens' disturbing *Why Americans Hate Welfare*, for one, has shown how the American people's views of the welfare state correspond strongly to their views of African Americans—with racist individuals being the most hostile to welfare regimes and seeing welfare beneficiaries as Black, slothful, promiscuous and undeserving.[87] Other studies have observed a similar process of racialisation in criminal justice policy. Here, research has shown how the shift from rehabilitation to retribution has been accompanied, or even driven, by a sustained moral critique of deviant social groups—personified by the poor urban Black population—and demonstrated compellingly that growth in mass imprisonment in the US has been matched by racial inequality.[88]

As Bruce Western argues, it is by no means implausible that the racial bent of American welfare and crime policy since the 1980s is linked to politics as much as it is to crime: 'Civil rights protests, the political achievements of voting rights, affirmative action and the development of legal protections against discrimination are all plausible bases for a punitive sentiment among white suburban voters'.[89] The extension of market freedoms and the dismantling of welfare regimes that have characterised the neoliberalisation of post-war American capitalism have produced a significant increase in economic inequality. This has led to a great deal of economic and social insecurity among large segments of the population since the early 1980s. The deregulation of markets has increased the freedom of those with the financial capabilities to take advantage of it. But it has also created high levels of unemployment for the most vulnerable sectors of the labour force. This contributed in undermining the more solidarist class politics of the post-war period and opened sharp racial divisions. This increased disparity has led those who can afford it to turn to a booming market in commodified services, which has developed in tandem with the dismantling of the welfare state. Similarly, a huge private security industry has grown alongside the criminal justice system and thereby commodified security as well.[90] Indeed, one of the main characteristics of the 'Reaganomics' of the 1980s is that it has redistributed income from the poor to the rich by reinvesting the money saved through welfare retrenchments into arms production, the security industry and other such capital-intensive sectors.[91] As the criminologist David Garland explains, this has contributed greatly to discrediting the welfare system in the eyes of the middle classes. Since the 1980s, they have been inclined to perceive it as a costly and inefficient machinery that redistributes 'the hard-earned income of people in employment to an undeserving mass of idle and feckless recipients'. Yet although the rich and some segments of the middle classes benefited greatly economically from these transformations, they were also affected by the social costs and frustration of those marginalised by the reforms and the high crime rates inherent in deregulated society.[92] This has produced a defensive cultural climax of insecurity and group hostility that generated a fixation for control, and which contrasts sharply with the solidarist spirit of the post-war era:

> In the political reaction against the welfare state and late modernity, crime acted as a lens through which to view the poor—as undeserving, deviant, dangerous, different—and as a barrier to lingering sentiments of fellow feeling and compassion. In this reactionary vision, the underlying problem of order was viewed not as a Durkheimian problem of solidarity but as a Hobbesian problem of order, to which the solution was to be a focused, disciplinary version of the Leviathan State.[93]

American (Neo)Hobbesism

> *'In politics, being deprived of an enemy is a very serious matter'.*
>
> Irving Kristol[94]

As both Émile Durkheim and Michel Foucault have shown, each in their own characteristic ways, the cultural and pedagogical effects of punishment on society are not to be underestimated.[95] Retributive regimes enact a powerful symbolic politics of security that enables the authoritative allocation of values and responsibilities while at the same time diverting attention from the state's inefficiency in other areas. As William Connolly noted, the failure of harsh punishment as an instrument of deterrence is 'trumped by its success in symbolising the state as a potent agent of public revenge in a world of high anxiety'. By associating 'liberal' clemency with the idleness of welfare recipients and the cruelty of rapists and murderers, retributive regimes work as a key site of mobilisation in the culture wars.[96] They appeal to popular emotions to mitigate social and economic struggle at the symbolic level rather than through rational collective action.

Now, David Garland is absolutely right to suggest that retributive regimes of welfare and crime control have reconfigured the underlying problem of domestic order from one of Durkheimian solidarity to a Hobbesian problem of security, control and sovereign command. However, as I have suggested throughout this discussion, neoconservative Hobbesian practices of statecraft have in fact more to do with the neo-Hobbesism of Schmitt and Strauss than with Hobbes himself.

As we have seen in Chapter 2, the fundamental difference here has to do with the place of culture in the relationship between protection and obedience. According to Schmitt, we will remember, Hobbes failed to give sufficient cultural substance to the leviathan myth that is supposed to unite individuals with state institutions into an organic whole. He devised his social contract on a purely rationalistic and corporal fear of violent death. This consequently set the basis of a strict distinction between the public realm (the political) and the private realm (the social), and confined cultural beliefs to the latter. None of this, of course, is to say that culture does not play an important role in the establishment of the Hobbesian state. To the contrary, it is Hobbes's sensitivity to the radical indeterminacy of the state of nature that underpins his case for the establishment of an overarching sovereign authority who will adjudicate between competing moral, cultural and epistemological claims.[97] For in the state of nature, 'everyman is his own judge, and differeth from other concerning the names and appellations of things, and from those differences arise quarrels, and breach of peace'.[98] Hobbes's reliance on fear and self-preservation is an appeal to a common denominator which transcends philosophical, moral, religious and ideological conflicts and thereby allows for civilisation to emerge and prosper. Hobbes believed that through rational education any individual could be made to see that it is in his own interest to trade a substantial amount of his freedom in return for a space where he can safely pursue his own material interest and conception of the good life.

Schmitt was well aware of the cultural and irrational dynamics that underpinned Hobbes's materialistic enterprise. Yet he believed that by constructing subjectivity along such rationalist and materialistic lines Hobbes fatally hollowed out the cultural substance of his leviathan. He transformed the state into a mere administrative machine vulnerable to capture by a multitude of civil society interest groups, all organised around their own myths and values. In this reading, the Hobbesian myth fell short of serving its ordering function because it failed to identify a public enemy that would (i) mark the fundamental political distinction between 'us and them', (ii) transcend the public-private distinction and (iii) cultivate the cultural homogeneity of the political community.[99] Schmitt (and Strauss) saw this antagonistic feature as the pivotal element in the relationship between protection and obedience that the leviathan is meant to sustain as a myth.

It is this antagonistic cultural slant that distinguishes the Schmittian solution to the problem of order from that of Hobbes. And it is this crucial distinction that underpins the politics of the neoconservative state. Neoconservatism negotiates the tension between its commitment to market capitalism and liberal democracy on the one hand, and its commitment to conservative socio-cultural values on the other by means of a symbolic politics of security that places the myth of the undesirable other and the enemy of society at the centre of public policy debates. By doing so, neoconservative practices of statecraft translate into an executive-centred conception of politics in which the elite must produce social order through the sovereign allocation of right and wrong. Whether it is the demoralised street criminal, the welfare cheat, the illegal immigrant, the godless communist or the religious fanatic, the moment of antagonism and unease prompted by the identification of the enemy forces the liberal state to abandon its claim to value neutrality and give normative substance to the relationship between protection and obedience. It forces a transcendent element of irrationalism not admitting of compromise into the public sphere that negates liberal and pluralist conceptions of politics altogether.[100] Insofar as this aestheticisation of politics draws on the power of symbol and images to discipline and steer society, it replaces persuasive rational argumentation by strict demonstration and institutes fear and loathing of the undesirable other as the main organisational social bond.[101]

As hinted above, this politics of enmity also constitutes an important contact point between neoconservative domestic and international politics. Over the years, the elevation of the friend-enemy dialectic to mythical proportion in foreign policy discourse has provided neoconservatives with a prime mobilising resource in their effort to conciliate the growing gap between the political elite and an increasingly heterogeneous polity. As Peter Steinfels noted in the late 1970s:

> Neoconservatives are shrewd students of social dynamics who know well the interaction of foreign and domestic politics. Their renewed emphasis on foreign affairs emerged after the New Left and the 'counterculture' had dissolved

as convincing foils for neoconservatism, and just after Watergate had proved an embarrassment. Their determination to find an overseas opponent, whether Idi Amin, Fabian socialism, Eurocommunism, or Soviet power, seemed constant despite the vast differences in the military and geopolitical factors. Their emphasis on the power of Communist—and then even socialist—ideology... aimed at discrediting radical social and economic criticism in the United States and rather easily shaded into a defense of the American economic establishment.[102]

The foreign policy aspect of this neo-Hobbesian politics will be analysed in the coming chapters. For the moment, I simply want to draw attention to the fact that the normative content of the neoconservative state does not emerge out of the conciliation of antagonisms and the regulation of conflicting interests under the coercive guarantee of the state. The neoconservative political community presupposes conflict. It comes into being and acquires its normative content by facing and overcoming the undesirable other.

This antagonistic politics of otherness introduces an inherently expansionist element into the neoconservative contest over the liberal state, linking public policy and foreign policy in a disquietingly systematic manner. As we have seen, the neoconservative 'revolution' in public policy hinges on the transmutation of the war on poverty into a culture war on a demoralised underclass. Whereas the 'New Deal state' sought to foster solidarity and social cohesion by providing welfare among the popular classes, the neoconservative state is the state of monopoly capitalism that allocates moral values from above and re-channels its expenditures into the penal, policing and security industry. It is a security state that, after having significantly diminished its welfare providing functions and privatised its service providing capacities, falls back on security and foreign policy to legitimise its authority and mobilise the republican conscience of the citizenry. As Robert Kagan and William Kristol explained in their 1996 neo-Reaganite manifesto:

American conservatism cannot govern by domestic policy alone. In the 1990s conservatives have built their agenda on two pillars of Reaganism: relimiting government to curtail the most intrusive and counterproductive aspects of the modern welfare state, and reversing the widespread collapse of morals and standards in American society. But it is hard to imagine conservatives achieving a lasting political realignment in this country without the third pillar: a coherent set of foreign policy principles that at least bear some resemblance to those propounded by Reagan.... There could be further efforts to involve more citizens in military service. Perhaps the United States has reached the point where a return to the draft is not feasible because of the high degree of professionalisation of the military services. But there are other ways to lower the barriers between civilian and military life. Expanded forms of reserve service could give many more Americans experience of the military and an appreciation of military virtues. Conservatives preach that citizenship is not only about rights but also about responsibilities. There is no more profound responsibility than the defense of the nation and its principles.[103]

In this militarisation of civil society, the 'political' repressed by the neoliberal de-politicisation of the economy and the transmutation of material relations of conflict into a culture war on nihilism re-surfaces in its most radical form. It leads to another negation of the political that devaluates pluralism and contestation among friends and seeks to relegate conflict outside of the political community.[104] In this process, foreign policy simply becomes the continuation of the culture wars by other means. This is where culture as an object of control reaches its full, totalising potential. As the political theorist Sheldon Wolin noted, in this type of cultural politics:

[e]verything—authority, obedience, social norms and practices, industry, education, and military power—seem to depend, ultimately, on 'values' and their accompanying practices, and to be subsumed under what a postmodern writer [Maurice Blanchot] would refer to as 'the total cultural fabric'. Culture, then, as the ultimate paradox, a 'whole' with no clear boundaries; culture as all-enveloping yet immaterial, powerful yet ideal; culture as a totality before and after the fact of totalitarianism.[105]

And this is precisely why these Schmittian tactics cannot succeed in regenerating the civic culture of the American republic. As Hannah Arendt noted in her own critique of Hobbes's leviathan state, a vibrant and genuinely republican politics draws its ethical substance and normative authority from the multitude itself independently of the state. It shapes state institutions and cultivates national unity from below through democratic deliberation and contestation over the ends that the community wishes for itself.[106] By contrast, neoconservatism places the onus on a state that tends towards the absorption of democratic agency and the devaluation of ethical criteria from which civil society can make normative demands on state power. To paraphrase Arendt, the neoconservative state is not a republican commonwealth but an impotent Behemoth that must constantly provide itself with new props from the outside.[107] It hinders critical subjectivity through a prescriptive rendering of collective identity that appeals to individual citizens not as autonomous agents but as a mythic cultural community—a sort of 'Gemeinschaft capitalism'—constituted by the careful nurturing of antagonistic otherness.

4

THE DEMOCRATIC MIRAGE OF NEOCONSERVATIVE INTERNATIONALISM

'In the end the fundamental problem for America is that its foreign policy is democratic. This is something the world has not witnessed since ancient Athens, where a democratic foreign policy led to one disaster after another. On the other hand, Athens was never the great power the U.S. is today, and its version of democracy had far fewer ways of shaping, refining and even sometimes thwarting popular opinion. Still, American foreign policy will surely remain, as it always has been, an exasperating enigma to the rest of the world as well as to our academic analysts, who will never cease to believe that a foreign policy should be analytically coherent'.

Irving Kristol[1]

On 20 March 2003, the United States launched a full-scale military operation against Iraq for the second time since the end of the Cold War. The war was a bid to eliminate weapons of mass destruction that were never found. It also promised to plant the seed of a regional democratic revolution that quickly turned into a costly embarrassment to American democracy. Justified on the basis of 'flawed' intelligence and undertaken without UN Security Council authorisation, the war has cast serious doubts over the future of multilateral frameworks restricting use of force and strained transatlantic relations to a degree that many today consider beyond repair.[2]

Neoconservatism was by no means the only political force behind the invasion. Conservative nationalists, Christian fundamentalists and liberal hawks have all contributed towards building the case for war and rationalising the ensuing occupation.[3] But neoconservative 'democratic globalism' provided much of the ideological impetus for 'Operation Iraqi Freedom'. Its protagonists have also happily taken credit for the so-called Bush Doctrine and the content of the controversial National Security Strategy of 2002, which set out the terms for the United States ongoing 'war on terrorism'—terms from which the Obama administration has so far found it difficult to depart significantly.[4]

'Democratic globalism' is the phrase I borrow from Charles Krauthammer to refer to the democracy promotion discourses cultivated by neoconservative intellectuals since the early 1970s.[5] As a practice of statecraft, 'democratic globalism' is the external, expansionist dimension of the neo-Hobbesian politics of security surveyed in the previous chapter. As a foreign policy doctrine, 'democratic globalism' envisages American national security in global terms as a modernising operation targeting domestic political systems with liberal democratic transformations and neoliberal economic restructuring in regions poorly integrated with the liberal core of international society.

According to Francis Fukuyama, during the Cold War this 'was seen as a means of inoculating populations from the appeal of communism, a way to stabilise allies and anchor American influence around the world'. After 9/11, it became 'a way of fighting terrorism, a means of 'draining the swamp' that fed Muslim rage and alienation'.[6] Today, in spite of the blatant failures of American foreign policy in the Middle East under Bush, 'democratic globalism' has remained central to the neoconservative critique of Obama's foreign policy.[7] As Robert Kagan argued in his appraisal of Obama's first year in office:

> Obama and his foreign policy team have apparently rejected two of the main pillars of this post-World War II strategy. Instead of attempting to perpetuate American primacy, they are seeking to manage what they regard as America's unavoidable decline relative to other powers. They see themselves as the architects of the 'post-American' world... The new strategy requires, in their view, accommodating the world's rising powers, principally China and Russia, rather than attempting to contain the ambitions of those powers... This may seem like realism to some, because accommodating allegedly stronger powers is a hallmark of realist foreign policy. Henry Kissinger practiced it in the years of Vietnam and détente... But there is also in this approach a remarkable idealism about the way the world works that Kissinger would never have endorsed... The Obama Doctrine is about 'win-win' and 'getting to yes'. The new 'mission' of the United States is to be the great convener of nations, gath-

ering the powers to further common interests and seek common solution to the world's problems... Administration officials play down the idea that great powers have clashing interests that might impair cooperation. This extends to the question of ideology, where the administration either denies or makes light of the possibility that autocratic powers may have fundamentally different perceptions of their interests than democracies... The new American posture they propose is increasingly one of neutrality. In order to be the world's 'convener', after all, the United States cannot play favorite, either between allies and adversaries, or between democrats and tyrants.[8]

This chapter traces the historical and conceptual development of the neoconservative doctrine of 'democratic globalism' from the early 1970s to the present. I expose the reactive narrative of modernisation by which it has been constituted over the years, and then offer a critical assessment of its political and normative implications for US foreign policy and international society. Looking at the theoretical underpinnings and discursive fabric of this core element of neoconservative foreign policy, I argue that its democratic import is in fact very limited, and that its transformative ethos is inimical to the progressive normative developments that it promises on the international stage.

Domesticating Anarchy: The Critique of Realism

As suggested in Chapter 1, democracy as an abstract ideal and worthy objective of US foreign policy emerged as a determinant feature of neoconservative discourse in the early 1970s in response to Henry Kissinger's attempted 'de-ideologisation' of American foreign policy. Over the years, this critique has grown into a more general critique of realism as such and served as a powerful rhetorical *point d'appui* for the rationalisation of democracy promotion initiatives. At the most basic level, this critique revolves around the claim that realists tend to underestimate the importance of cultural values, identity and moral principles in the construction of action in international relations. In a sense there is really nothing new here. Constructivists and critical theorists of all kinds have made this point repeatedly and to different effect since the early 1980s.[9] What should detain our attention, however, is the ways in which neoconservatives instrumentalise and politicise that knowledge.

According to neoconservatives, realism lacks an adequate understanding of the crucial role of foreign policy in fixing the cultural content of citizenship and constructing the forms of subjectivities necessary to sustain a hegemonic foreign policy. In their view, realism's insistence on ideological sobriety and the exclusion of universal moral values from foreign policy-making leaves its proponents incapable of articulating a vision for America that goes beyond narrow strategic calculations. In turn, this incapacity to link moral and identity issues to American power and international engagement fosters distrust and pessimism towards politics within the population and ultimately leads to the subordination of foreign policy to private and individual concerns. Hence, far from providing a sound basis for statecraft and foreign policy-making, realism's reactive and materialistic outlook ultimately fails to generate the domestic commitments necessary for the pursuit of even the most basic foreign policy objectives, such as the defence of so-called 'vital interests'.[10] As Robert Kagan and William Kristol argue:

> Without a broad, sustaining foreign policy vision, the American people will be inclined to withdraw from the world and will lose sight of their abiding interest in vigorous world leadership. Without a sense of mission, they will seek deeper and deeper cuts in the defense and foreign affairs budgets and gradually decimate the tools of U.S. hegemony... Without a broader, more enlightened understanding of America's interests, conservatism will too easily degenerate into the pinched nationalism of Buchanan's "America First," where the appeal to narrow stir-interest masks a deeper form of stir-loathing. A true "conservatism of the heart" ought to emphasise both personal and national responsibility, relish the opportunity for national engagement, embrace the possibility of national greatness, and restore a sense of the heroic, which has been sorely lacking in American foreign policy—and American conservatism in recent years.[11]

Against realists, neoconservatives insist that a democratic social order that is no more than the summation of the egoistic interests of individuals or social groups is unsustainable and bound to collapse into political, social and moral decay. A society incapable of linking morality and identity with power and generating a compelling notion of the public interest will rot from within and be unable to assert itself in the international sphere.[12] As Krauthammer argues, 'America cannot and will not live by *Realpolitik* alone. Unless conservatives present ideals to challenge the liberal ideal of a domesticated international community, they will lose the debate. Which is why among American conservatives, another, more idealistic, school has arisen that sees America's national interest as an expression of values'.[13] According to neoconservatives, the materialistic, rationalistic and individualistic sociology of realism betrays the republican aspirations of the average

American. As Irving Kristol argues, 'the American people are simultaneously individualistic and communal in their outlook. They really do believe that there is such a thing as the "public interest"—a *res publica* that is something more than the summation of individual interests'.[14] This is why the construction of action in American foreign policy 'must go well beyond a narrow, too literal definition of "national security". It is the national interest of a world power as this is defined by a sense of national destiny'.[15]

Neoconservatives also criticise realism for its overly static interpretation of history and understanding of the causes of war in world politics. First, they disagree categorically with the fundamental assumptions of structural realism. For them, the idea that war and competition between states are the inevitable by-product of the anarchical character of the international system as such is a positivist heresy that bears witness to the decay of American universities. Against such relativistic follies, neoconservatives insist (quite correctly) that the structural realist thesis in fact rests upon a set of a priori assumptions about the self-interested and competitive character of human nature without which the war-prone, self-help logic of anarchy posited by structural realists would make no sense at all.[16] Neoconservatives share the classical realist view that war and conflict are ultimately rooted in man's natural drive for self-preservation, competition, vain glory and, importantly, universal recognition. Against classical realists, however, they insist that these natural impulses are cultivated, mediated and channelled by historically evolving institutions, ideology and cultural norms. Consequently, each state will relate differently to the international struggle for power depending on its size and on the nature of its political regime: i.e. on the character of its institutions, its cultural make-up and the degree of modernisation that it has achieved. Fukuyama offers the classic statement in *The End of History and the Last Man*. It is worth citing at length:

> The international order described by realists closely resembles the state of nature of Hobbes, where man is a state of war of all against all. But Hobbes's state of war does not arise out of the simple desire for self-preservation, but because self-preservation co-exists with vanity or the desire for recognition. Were there not some men who desired to impose their views upon others, particularly those imbued with a spirit of religious fanaticism, then Hobbes himself would argue that the primordial state of war would never arise in the first place. Self-preservation alone is not sufficient to explain the war of all against all... The realist contention that states perceive each other as threats and arm

themselves accordingly does not arise from the system so much as from a hidden assumption that human societies in their international behaviour tend to resemble Hegel's master seeking recognition, or the vainglorious first man of Hobbes, rather than the timid solitary of Rousseau... The realist, then, can deduce nothing at all from the bare facts of the distribution of power within the state system. Such information becomes meaningful only if he or she makes certain assumptions about the nature of the societies constituting the system, namely, that at least some of them seek recognition rather than mere self-preservation... In sharp distinctions to every other aspect of human and political social life, realism portrays international relations as isolated in a timeless vacuum, immune from the evolutionary processes taking place around it. But those apparent continuities in world politics from Thucydides to the Cold War in fact mask significant differences in the manner in which societies seek, control, and relate to power.[17]

The reader will have recognised the Straussian tropes of this neo-Hobbesian account. The importance of regime type in shaping both domestic and world politics is one of the most important connections between Leo Strauss and neoconservatism. According to the Straussian theory of regime, each regime is the 'outcome of a struggle over which human type or types will be morally preponderant', and each regime advances a notion of justice and the common good that will guide political action towards particular ends. Whereas a neoliberal, commercially-driven regime will produce a hedonistic and morally corrupted citizenry, an oppressive regime that suppresses free association through violence will produce a violent opposition and a citizenry with violent tendencies since participation in this oppressive regime will be based on the potential for violent compulsions.[18] Because the regime of a country 'shapes the "way of life" more than any other formative factor except for human nature itself', the struggle between those who wish to define the regime is 'the supremely important contest in human existence'—the essence of the political.[19] As Steven Lenzner and William Kristol explained in the immediate aftermath of the Iraq War, 'To understand political life in terms of regimes is to recognise that political life always partakes of both the universal (principles of justice or rule) and the particular ("our" borders, language, customs, etc.). President Bush's advocacy of "regime change"—which avoids the pitfalls of a wishful global universalism on the one hand, and a fatalistic cultural determinism on the other—is a not altogether unworthy product of Strauss's rehabilitation of the notion of regime'.[20]

From this perspective, the realist precept that friends and enemies ought to be chosen on the basis of balance of power rather than ideology is strategically self-defeating. For, realists who seek to maintain international order through a balance of military power often paradoxically find themselves accommodating and sometimes even in alliance with powerful regimes who have a long-term existential interest in undermining American hegemony to bolster their domestic legitimacy. Thus, although 'no doctrine of foreign policy can do away with the need for judgement and prudence, and for weighing competing moral considerations', realism cannot be a viable path in the long term.[21] Democracy promotion is not only an end but also an indispensable geostrategic instrument for securing American interests. As Paul Wolfowitz explains:

> Today, it's hard to understand why realists remain so confident about their doctrine, given that changes in the nature of states have benefited the U.S. national interest in so many instances—not only the peaceful collapse of the Soviet empire and the end of apartheid in South Africa, but also with the many transitions from dictatorship to democracy that have deepened security in almost every region of the world. Moreover, there are so many other instances where a disregard for such issues has set back the national interest.[22]

Reactive Modernisation

As hinted above, the neoconservative critique of realism draws on a high modernist narrative of linear historical development which is generally referred to as modernisation theory. This takes us back to the Cold War liberalism of the late 1950s, and early 1960s.

Modernisation theory was the liberal vital centre's response to Marxist theories of social change. Heavily influenced by the functionalist social theory of Talcott Parsons and Joseph Schumpeter's *Capitalism, Socialism and Democracy* (1942), it was developed in the 1950s and early 1960s by liberal and proto-neoconservative 'end of ideologists' close to the policy-making community such as Walt Whitman Rostow, Max Millikan, Gabriel Almond, Edward Shills, Daniel Lerner, Daniel Bell and Seymour Martin Lipset.[23] Modernisation theory was both a foreign policy doctrine and a social theory of development.

As a foreign policy doctrine, it stipulated that the threat of communism came as much from the social failures of capitalist development in the South as from the threat of the Soviet armed forces in Eastern Europe. For modernisation theorists—and for the liberal vital centre more generally—the consolidation of the US-led liberal order depended on both the credibility of US military power and America's ability to secure governments that were politically stable and supportive of economic internationalism in the Third World.[24] Already by the early 1950s, the sweeping influence of nationalist movements in the Third World was posing a serious challenge to the social classes and self-serving elites to which US interests were tied. The fact that conservative orders began to weaken and unravel created complex new situations. It was perceived by Washington as a test of its will and military resources to control those processes.[25] Following the Cuban revolution in 1959 there were growing concerns in US foreign policy circles that the Soviet Union was slowly expanding its sphere of influence in Latin America and the Third World more generally. In search of the appropriate response, Kennedy and his advisers came to the conclusion that America had to become more actively involved in the development of the Third World. The Kennedy administration thus proceeded to set up the Peace Corps and the US Agency for International Development (USAID) in 1961 to coalesce and coordinate all American foreign aid initiatives. In the beginning, the great majority of American aid went to the Alliance for Progress, an initiative which had also been set up by Kennedy in 1961 and which called upon all governments in the Western hemisphere to participate in the political and economic development of Latin America. But soon this strategy was extended to Indochina and other regions in the Third World.[26]

As a theory of development, modernisation theory played a key legitimating function in this enterprise. Although it came in many variants, the core thesis of this body of work was that history could be read as a linear series of developmental stages that would ultimately lead to the functional, ideological and institutional convergence of all human societies towards American-style liberal democracy. According to modernisation theorists, the passing from traditional agricultural society to industrialism hinged upon a thorough transformation in cultural and political values. Its theorists did not necessarily believe that modernisation eradicated cultural differences per se. But they believed that modernisation was in the final analysis only compatible with secularism, rationalism and a liberal democratic political culture. As Millikan and Rostow explained in the opening pages of their manifesto, modernisation theory rests on the 'observation' that America's political, social and economic techniques had been more successful than those of any other nation in the world 'for realising widespread popular desires for change without either compulsion or social disorganisation'.[27] The general idea here was that by studying the history of the United States and other industrialised nations, developing states could identify the steps that had brought the modernisation process forward as well as those that had uselessly slowed it down. This would then offer an implicit set of directives as to which steps must be taken and which must be bypassed in order to bring the Third World to the desired level of development and secure governments that were politically stable and supportive of economic internationalism.

Following Schumpeter, modernisation theorists came to the conclusion that it was the entrepreneurial culture of a stable middle class that generates the kind of sustained risk-taking investment needed for continual economic growth, which in turn leads to democratisation. The main implication for US foreign policy was that economic aid had to be accompanied by technology, education, market reforms, technical expertise and social engineering know-how. This attempt to create a US-style entrepreneurial middle class depended on a relatively high level of Keynesian state involvement in the market. This ranged from tariff barriers, subsidies and dual exchange rates to a comprehensive effort to improve education, health care and other social services. In many countries, it was accompanied by programmes aiming at modernising the military in order to increase its capacity to fend off potential communist revolutions.[28]

Modernisation theory was very much a reflection of how Americans understood themselves, their identity and their own relationship to modernity as a liberal society in the 1950s and early 1960s. Its theorists promoted 'a high-concept version of Americanism: materialism without class conflict, secularism without irreverence, democracy without disobedience. In the process of making Americanism respectable by equating it with modernisation, the modernisation theorists reflected on the meaning and place of the United States in the world arena'.[29] But this ambitious modernisation project incurred immense costs for Third World governments. Soon many of them found themselves completely overwhelmed, both financially and administratively. By the 1970s levels of foreign debt had risen dramatically while state bureaucracies, oversized and often run by corrupted elites, had become ineffective.

Growing discontent with US modernisation narratives found expression in neo-Marxist dependency theories developed by Latin American economists, and spread in many other parts of the world by scholars such as Andre Gunder Frank and Samir Amin. Against modernisation theory, dependency theorists demonstrated that 'underdevelopment' in the Third World was not a 'moment' in the history of the region that would be overcome with the help of Western technological and financial assistance. Rather, 'underdevelopment' and dependency were preconditions of Western prosperity. They were inherent and necessary characteristics of an exploitative and deeply integrated world capitalist system in which capital flowed perpetually from the Third to the First World only to be borrowed back by the Third World to finance its own development.[30]

As the war in Vietnam kept escalating, the supposedly 'non-military' character of America's nation-building strategy in the Third World appeared increasingly deceitful and the limits of US-led modernisation more and more obvious.[31] Far from demonstrating the relevance of modernisation theory for US foreign policy (as Rostow thought it would in the early 1960s), the Vietnam War highlighted the reactionary character of American power and exposed the shallowness of America's commitments to democracy and human rights. At the same time, the implosion of the American universities, the racial violence of the late 1960s, the revolt against tradition, the perceived failures of the Great Society Programmes, the transformation of the nuclear family, and attacks on core social modernist beliefs such as rationalism, secularism and scientism all contributed towards undermining the optimistic reading of modernity that sustained modernisation theory. As Nils Gilman explains, 'As the reality of a consensual, liberal, rational, secular, technocratic, welfare-oriented United States broke down, so did the vision of a consensual, liberal, rational, secular, technocratic, welfare-oriented modernism as a model for Third World development'.[32]

Democratic globalism as advocated by neoconservatives today can be seen as both a pessimistic reaction to the misfortunes of modernisation theory in the 1960s and a simultaneous desire to pursue its transformative course of action.[33] As we saw in Chapter 1, although neoconservatives supported the war effort, they did not see Vietnam as a crucial front in the war against communism and had advocated an immediate withdrawal right from the start. Many of them had made important contributions to the body of thought that underpinned modernisation theory in an American context. However, most were highly sceptical about the prospect for democracy and liberal modernisation in Indochina. As Kristol wrote in 1963:

> The plain truth is that South Vietnam, like South Korea, is barely capable of decent self-government under the very best of conditions. It lacks the political traditions, the educated classes, the civic spirit that makes self-government workable... No amount of American aid, no amount of exhortation, no amount of good advice can change this basic condition... The most we can hope for in Sought Vietnam is what we have achieved in South Korea; that is, to remove this little, backward nation from the front line of the cold war so that it can stew quietly in its own political juice.[34]

Samuel Huntington, another neoconservative *avant la lettre*, was also critical of liberal modernisation narratives. In his influential *Political Order in Changing Societies* (1968), Huntington sought to demonstrate that modernisation was as likely to generate political decay as peaceful liberal democratic societies. His argument, in a nutshell, was that rapid socio-economic modernisation tends to over-inflate expectations, outrun political development, and then frustrates expectations to the point where it often leads to disorder, violence, insurgencies, military coups and weakened governments. Huntington surveyed the situation in the newly independent states of the Third World and maintained that most of them were in fact heading for political disintegration and disorder rather than democracy and stability. As a rejoinder to modernisation theory, he proposed a theory of 'modernising authoritarianism', whereby a modernising dictatorship provided political order, a rule of law, and the conditions for successful socio-economic development. Once this was in place, democracy and political participation could be added.[35]

By the early 1970s, Huntington's thesis that the goods of modernity often work at cross-purposes had become a signature neoconservative theme in the domestic culture wars. As we saw in the previous chapters, neoconservatives spent the best of that decade fighting to maintain the status quo and the integrity of American political institutions against what they saw as the 'democratic distemper' of the student movement, the participatory 'democratic utopia' of the New Left, and the 'democratic opportunism' of the new class. Yet although engaged in a protracted ideological war against democracy at home, most neoconservatives could simply not bring themselves to abandon the rhetoric of the democratic peace in foreign policy debates. In line with the critique of realism discussed earlier, they insisted that, for America, democracy was not just a mode of political organisation but an existential vocation. It is in this context that the defence of democracy in the world became one of the main themes driving the Coalition for a Democratic Majority's 'Come Home Democrat' Campaign in 1972 and continued to figure prominently in *Commentary* throughout the 1970s.[36]

In reality, however, democracy remained very much subordinated to the global struggle against communism. As Podhoretz wrote in the early 1980s, 'Certain authoritarian regimes and Right-wing dictatorships were included in the [anti-Communist] alliance. But in view of the fact that such associations were important in holding back the single greatest and most powerful threat to freedom on the face of the earth, they could be justified as an unfortunate political and military necessity'.[37] This was also the basis of Jeane Kirkpatrick's famous critique of Carter's ethical foreign policy in 'Dictatorships and Double Standards' (1979). There, Kirkpatrick argued that by making human rights and democracy the cornerstone of his Third World strategy Carter had implicitly aligned the US with extremists and Soviet clients: 'The American effort to impose liberalisation and democratisation on governments confronted with violent internal opposition not only failed, but actually assisted the coming to power of new regimes in which ordinary people enjoy fewer freedoms and less personal security than under the previous autocracy—regimes, moreover, hostile to American interests and policies'.[38] Echoing Huntington's theory of modernising authoritarianism, Kirkpatrick castigated the Carter administration for failing to recognise the crucial difference between authoritarian regimes and communist regimes:

> Although there is no instance of a revolutionary 'socialist' or Communist society being democratised, right-wing autocracies do sometimes evolve into democracies—given time, propitious economic, social, and political circumstances, talented leaders, and a strong indigenous demand for representative government... There are systemic differences between traditional and revolutionary autocracies that have a predictable effect on their degree of repressiveness. Generally speaking, traditional autocrats tolerate social inequities, brutality, and poverty, whereas revolutionary autocracies create them.[39]

According to Kirkpatrick, Carter was, '*par excellence*, the kind of liberal most likely to confound revolution with idealism, change with progress, optimism with virtue'.[40] He and his advisers interpreted the modernisation process through a contemporary version of the rationalist philosophy of history developed by thinkers like 'Condorcet, Comte, Hegel, Marx, and Weber' whose 'idea of progress has traumatised Western imaginations since the Enlightenment'.[41] In a companion essay, 'The Hobbes Problem', Kirkpatrick insisted that it was not moral reason that established state legitimacy but a rational fear of death at the hand of the overwhelming power of the sovereign. She reprimanded Carter for making military aid to El Salvador conditional on the implementation of social and human rights reforms on the grounds that such conditionality ignored the fact that 'competition for power' which was rooted in 'the nature of man' was the basis of all politics. Salvadorans had to be taught to respect the sovereign before the sovereign could be asked to respect human rights—even if this implied US support for the use of death squads.[42] Against Carter's naïve identification of the US national interest in the Third World with the 'putative end of the modernisation process', Kirkpatrick defended the status quo. Her point was not that America should not promote liberal values but that the promotion of human rights and democratic values had to be firmly subordinated to geopolitical considerations. As she put it, 'Liberal idealism need not be identical with masochism, and need not be incompatible with the defense of freedom and the national interest'.[43] Effectively this meant taking human rights off the US foreign policy agenda and supporting ruthless Right-wing dictatorships and military juntas in Central and Latin America, South Africa, Iran, Afghanistan, Cambodia, the Philippines and wherever it was deemed necessary to advance America's geostrategic interests.[44]

All in all, it is only fair to say that until the early to mid 1980s, neoconservative commitments to democracy in foreign policy were little more than a rhetorical device designed to mobilise domestic support for American leadership in the struggle against the Soviet Union. Whilst neoconservatives were *in principle* committed to the *defence* of democracy in the world, it is only since the early to mid 1980s that neoconservatives began to seriously talk about proactively *exporting* democracy as a viable foreign policy objective. In fact William Kristol admitted so much in an interview with James Mann during the build-up to the Iraq War: 'I don't think that neoconservatives at that time [prior to the 1980s] were particularly strong supporters of democracy'.[45]

Regimenting Democracy

The 'democratic turn' in neoconservative foreign policy discourse in the mid 1980s was part of a broader policy shift instituted by the Reagan administration. The aim was to move away from covertly supporting Right-wing authoritarianism (wherever and whenever it suited the national interest) towards promoting democracy through the newly and purposively established National Endowment for Democracy. As various analysts have argued, this shift was above all a pre-emptive measure to secure elite and American interests against more radical changes in light of the mass mobilisation of anti-authoritarian movements that took place during the 1970s and early 1980s.[46] Already by the mid 1970s, there were growing concerns in Centre-Right intellectual circles that, under conditions of globalisation and complex interdependence, supporting authoritarian regimes might no longer be a viable means to contain socialism and generate the stability necessary for economic growth in the periphery. In fact, as early as 1972 the neo-modernisation theorist William Douglas (who would eventually help the Reagan administration set up its democratisation programme in the 1980s) had argued that US geopolitical and geoeconomic interests in the Third World would be better served by promoting a 'regimented' form of democracy that would appeal to mass audiences. In his view, this would help boost pro-American sentiment and skim off some of the popular support enjoyed by the most radical transformative forces in those regions.[47] The Trilateral Commission made a similar set of arguments in its famous 1975 report, *The Crisis of Democracy*, published in the immediate aftermath of the Vietnam War.[48] The report warned of a crisis of elite rule which tied the industrialised North with the developing South into a global 'crisis of governability'. It called for a 'basic mutation in the mode of government' based on 'more flexible models that could produce more social control with less coercive pressure'.[49]

As far as neoconservatism is concerned, the turn towards democracy promotion in the early 1980s owed as much to the imminent crisis of authoritarianism in the South as to the declining legitimacy of communist regimes in the East. After the revolt of Gdansk and the rise of the Solidarity movement in Poland in December 1981, neoconservatives began to worry that the US could be losing the war of ideas against the Soviet Union if America did not align itself clearly with the forces of democracy at this important historical juncture.[50] After

Alexander Haig resigned as Reagan's first Secretary of State and Elliot Abrams became Assistant Secretary for Human Rights in the summer of 1982, the State Department became increasingly concerned with the incoherent fit between the Reaganite rhetoric of American exceptionalism and the public repudiation of Carter's human rights legacy. The strategy then became to harmonise the two by conflating the defence of human rights with the promotion of a controlled form of elitist democracy.[51]

Neoconservatives adopt the so-called 'polyarchic' definition of democracy. According to neoconservatives, democracy is 'the formation of a political elite in the competitive struggle for the votes of a mainly passive electorate'.[52] Hence, 'a country is democratic if it grants its people the right to choose their own government through periodic, secret-ballot, multi-party elections, on the basis of universal and equal adult suffrage'.[53] As Seymour Martin Lipset and Jason Lakin explain in *The Democratic Century* (2006), 'this is a minimalist definition of democracy inspired by Joseph Schumpeter's classic elitist conception of democracy as professed in *Capitalism, Socialism and Democracy*'.[54]

In *Capitalism*, Schumpeter argued that the socio-cultural homogeneity assumed by the classical model of democracy had been undermined by the complexity and heterogeneous cultural composition of advanced industrial societies. In his view, the only kind of democratic consensus that could realistically be envisaged in such conditions was one fashioned from above by the ruling elite through propaganda and the manipulation of public opinion. This process would then be legitimised through some sort of popular mandate achieved through the manufacture rather than the execution of the general will.[55]

Schumpeter's elitist model of democracy is another legacy of the conservative intellectual milieu of interwar Europe. In the 1920s, Carl Schmitt had famously sought to redefine democracy as that institutional arrangement by which the masses have the opportunity of either accepting or rejecting the policies proposed by their rulers. During the following decades, Schumpeter redefined democracy as that institutional mechanism by which 'the people have the opportunity of accepting or refusing the men who are to rule them'.[56] As William Scheuerman noted, to a large extent, 'Schumpeter's "democratic elitism" simply reformed an onerous tradition of Central European authoritarianism in order to make it more palatable to an American audience. Whitewashed of its more openly antidemocratic rhetorical flourishes, Schumpeter's contribution to this tradition proved an attractive starting point for historically and philosophically naïve political scientists seeking an "empirical" alternative to the classics of normative theory'.[57]

From the mid 1950s onwards, prominent American political scientists such as Robert Dahl, Gabriel Almond, Sidney Verba, Bernard Berelson, Paul Lazarfeld and William McPhee drew upon Schumpeter's democratic elitism and adapted it to the American political context.[58] The polyarchic interpretation of democracy grew out of this ideological assimilation. Dahl first used the term 'polyarchy' in the early 1970s to distinguish from a more utopian form of democracy, 'one of the characteristics of which is the quality of being or almost completely responsive to all its citizens'.[59] The concept was subsequently developed and elaborated upon during the following decades by Seymour Martin Lipset, Samuel Huntington, Larry Diamond, Marc Plattner, Juan Linz, Alfred Stepan, Adam Przeworski and other neoconservative and liberal democratisation experts affiliated with the National Endowment for Democracy (NED) since its creation in 1983.[60]

Like the Schumpeterian model from which it takes its cue, polyarchy turns the notion of representative democracy on its head. For the purpose of polyarchic elections is not to select representatives who will execute the policy choices and preferences of the voters, but to authorise rulers to decide on the content of policies and legislation.[61] As the neo-Gramscian scholar William Robinson argued, polyarchy promotion as a foreign policy practice allows for the removal of authoritarian regimes that have become increasingly incapable of managing the expansive forms of transnational social interaction generated by globalisation.[62] The whole enterprise hinges on the promotion of formal electoral democracy whilst at the same time limiting the transformative capacity of democracy. The aim of promoting polyarchy:

> is to construct in intervened countries an exact replica of the structure of power in the United States. This is done by strengthening existing political parties and other organisations identified as congenial to U.S. interests, or by creating from scratch new organisations where ones do not already exist. With few exceptions, the leaders of these organisations are drawn from the local elite and their efforts are aimed at competing with, or eclipsing, existing broad-based popular organisations and neutralising efforts by popular sectors to build their own organisations in civil society.[63]

Aside from its elitist character, the other particularity of the polyarchic model is that it sees no inconsistency in democratic processes characterised by pronounced socio-economic inequality. As Lipset and Lakin argue, democracy 'is a system that by definition guarantees no redistribution of wealth, but it does separate wealth from power, by giving votes (political power) to those who do not have wealth...'.[64] According to polyarchists, the separation of the economic sphere from issues of governmental structure eliminates unrealistic normative expectations from the definition of democracy and therefore makes the study of democratisation processes more reliable and relevant for policy-making.[65] As Diamond explains in a widely circulated study, 'the incorporation of social and economic desiderata into the definition of democracy—an approach fashionable in the 1960s and 1970s—has waned considerably in the past two decades. By and large, most scholarly and policy uses of the term democracy today refer to a purely political conception of the term, and this intellectual shift back to an earlier convention has greatly facilitated progress in studying the dynamics of democracy...'[66]

Diamond, Lipset and their NED colleagues are correct that the polyarchical model has become dominant in democratisation literature since the 1980s. However, we should be clear here that the hegemonisation of this 'working definition' is by no means a mere issue of academic modelling. Democratisation, if it is to be seen as a progressive political development, must be an inclusive, transformative process geared towards the alleviation of socio-economic, political and cultural factors that prevent equal access to the policy-making process. It may very well be that polyarchy does formally 'separate wealth from power' by giving one vote to those who do not have wealth. But in reality, socio-economic inequality invariably tends to translate into political inequality. As Dahl acknowledged in a 1985 publication, 'Ownership and control contribute to the creation of great differences among citizens in wealth, income, status, skills, information, control over information and propaganda, access to political power ... differences like these help in turn to generate significant inequalities among citizens in their capacities and opportunities for participating as political equals in governing the state'.[67] In sum, polyarchy belittles democratic citizenship as it lowers popular expectations from democratic politics and makes it harder to assemble majorities to overcome the resistance of well-entrenched and privileged minorities. Although one should not disparage the normative distinction between authoritarian and polyarchic political systems, the point is that the policy goal of promoting low-intensity democracy remains essentially the same as that of previous policies of supporting authoritarian regimes. And that is to maintain 'essentially undemocratic societies inserted into an unjust international system'.[68]

In addition to this very important systemic dimension, Reagan's democratic offensive also had an important domestic function. As the diplomatic historian David Ryan argues, 'Reagan possessed an uncanny ability to connect with the American psyche'. This new crusade for democracy, fought mainly through proxies and therefore without great risks to US morale and life, 'allowed the president to recreate an image of a strong, determined, resolute nation ... The process of healing US "wounds" after Vietnam and the crippling confusions of the Carter administration was enhanced through the effective use of symbols closely associated with the national narrative'.[69] Despite evidence to the contrary, this democratic campaign, for which neoconservatives claim credit today, reduced all activity in the periphery to the bipolar conflict. It used the rhetoric and symbols of democracy and self-determination to re-enforce the identity and ideological basis of the nation. Even Irving Kristol, who had been highly sceptical of American efforts at exporting democracy during the previous decades, lent his voice to this new 'ideological élan'. As he argued in *The National Interest* at the time:

> American foreign policy, hitherto reactive, is bound to become more activist. This activism, if it is to have popular support, will necessarily have a significant ideological dimension. Those who make American foreign policy will discover—may already be discovering—that any viable conception of the United States's 'national interest' cannot help but be organically related to that public philosophy—ideology, if you wish—which is the basis of what we have come to call 'the American way of life'.[70]

This new 'ideological élan' in US foreign policy under Reagan marked the inconspicuous return of modernisation theories of development in US foreign policy discourse—albeit this time with a pronounced neoliberal, anti-welfarist spin. As we have seen earlier, the first generation of modernisation theorists understood modernisation as a form of collective action to spread the welfare state and universalise its progressive values. By contrast, the modernisation narratives of the 1980s tended to devalue indigenous processes and rejected the idea of the rational meliorist state. Instead, they envisaged liberal democratic modernisation as the convergence of all human societies towards a globalised economic system based on trust in well-trained managerial elites in which the state has little or no incentive to intervene, except to provide the environment for market institutions to operate freely.

Promoting polyarchy and neoliberal economics in this context became two sides of the same programme to re-assert American leadership and integrate the Third World in the global capitalist economy on US terms after the troubled 1970s. During its first year in office, the Reagan administration had already established market capitalism as the primary conditionality for all US foreign assistance in the Third World. This involved an unconditional commitment from the part of the receiving states to re-orient their institutions towards monetarism and market solutions at both the domestic and international level. Eager to minimise US commitments to a United Nations besieged by demands for a New International Economic Order (NIEO), Reagan and his advisers proceeded to transform the IMF and the World Bank into mediums through which its programmes of stabilisation and structural adjustment could be forced upon the indebted Third World. By 1983, 'adjustment' (trade liberalisation, end to government quotas and subsidies, devaluation, budget austerity, privatisation and often total dismantling of public services) had been established as the basis of what came to be known as the 'Washington Consensus'.[71] By the end of the Cold War, the Third World as an idea had lost all its meaning and political leverage. As one historian put it:

> For all the high hopes in the 1970s, the sad irony was to be that further Third World integration into the world economic system was to be postponed until the 1980s onwards, and was to be the direct consequence of Third World *weakness*, not of strength. Its integration was to occur, not on its own terms, but on those set by the West and its panoply of international financial institutions. Far from being an expression of the autonomy of the Third World, in which state control and national development were top priorities, the terms of engagement denoted the final capitulation of the Third World's struggle for separate national development in the face of a more competitive, and importunate, international economic system. Instead of the NIEO symbolising the new political order, the old political order managed to thwart the NIEO.[72]

Democracy at the End of History

For neoconservatives these were great victories. As Muravchik boasted in the opening page of his *Exporting Democracy* (1991), 'America has won the Cold War—almost without trying ... It won, not on the strength of its arms or the skill of its diplomats, but by virtue of the power of the democratic ideas on which the American system is based and the failure of the Communist idea'.[73] This was also the thrust of Fukuyama's influential 'end of history' thesis, which was first published as an article in *The National Interest* in 1989 and then extended into a book in 1992.[74] There, Fukuyama maintained that the collapse of the Soviet Union under the force of the democratic ideal and the unprecedented level of material well-being brought about by science and capitalism had resolved the contradictions of the historical process. Heavily influenced by Kojève's reading of Hegel and Strauss's Nietzschean critique of modernity, Fukuyama argued that the inevitable spread of the West's hedonistic market civilisation through globalisation would create a world of ease and comfort in which human societies would lose their appetite for war, ideological struggle and vainglorious conquests. The victory of market democracy over communism marked the end of man's ideological evolution—the end of history.

Underneath the triumphalist pomp, however, neoconservatives during the 1990s were not so comfortable with the world that they had just 'won' for themselves. As Fukuyama concluded at the end of his treatise, the end of history marked the beginning of 'sad and austere times': 'the struggle for recognition, the willingness to risk one's life for a purely abstract goal, the worldwide ideological struggle that called forth daring, courage, imagination, and idealism, will be replaced by economic calculation, the endless solving of technical problems, environmental concerns, and the satisfaction of sophisticated consumer demands'.[75] Fukuyama's intellectual mentors concurred:

> The enemy protected us from too much depression on ourselves. The global nature of the conflicts we were engaged in imposed an unprecedented uniformity on the world. It has been liberalism—or else ... Now, however, all bets are off. The glance back towards ourselves ... is likely to be not entirely satisfying.
>
> Allan Bloom[76]

> With the end of the Cold War, what we really need is an obvious ideological and threatening enemy, one worthy of our mettle, one that can unite us in opposition. Isn't that what the most successful movie of the year, "Independence Day," is telling us? Where are our aliens when we most need them?
>
> Irving Kristol[77]

Americans have constructed their creedal identity in contrast to an undesirable 'other'... If there is no evil empire out there threatening those principles, what indeed does it mean to be an American?

Samuel Huntington[78]

Although neoconservatives remained united on the domestic front, the discomfort created by the collapse of European communism generated a momentary split within their ranks in foreign policy debates. On one side, a minority of the founding members like Irving Kristol, Jeane Kirkpatrick, Nathan Glazer and Robert Tucker no longer saw the need for democratic crusades and called for a more limited interpretation of the national interest. They advocated a defensive case-by-case approach oriented towards the prevention of the emergence of a rival superpower. In their view, the fall of the Soviet Union represented a 'return to normal times', which meant that the US could go back to being a 'normal nation' that focused on public policy at home rather than costly and futile efforts to promote democracy abroad.[79] Democracy promotion, Kristol wrote in the *Wall Street Journal*, was above all an ideological ploy designed to contain and undermine communism. It served its purpose well during the Cold War, but now the world had changed:

The only innovative trend in our foreign-policy thinking at the moment derives from a relatively small group, consisting of both liberals and conservatives, who believe there is an 'American mission' actively to promote democracy all over the world. This is a superficially attractive idea, but it takes only a few moments of thought to realise how empty of substance (and how full of presumption!) it is. In the entire history of the U.S., we have successfully 'exported' our democratic institutions to only two nations—Japan and Germany, after war and an occupation. We have failed to establish a viable democracy in the Philippines, or in Panama, or anywhere in Central America.[80]

By contrast, the great majority of neoconservatives sought to provide the ideological blueprint for a new and assertive democratic globalism that would take Cold War geopolitical doctrines into the twenty-first century. Led by Ben Wattenberg, Norman Podhoretz, Michael Novak, Carl Gershman, Gregory Fossedal, Michael Leeden, Kenneth Adelman, Charles Krauthammer, Francis Fukuyama, Joshua Muravchik, Paul Wolfowitz, Robert Kagan and other second- and third-generation neoconservatives, this faction argued that the collapse of the Soviet Union represented a long-awaited opportunity for America to fulfil its democratic destiny and insure American security by disseminating America's values to every region of the globe. For these self-professed global democrats, the collapse of the Soviet Union and the swift victory of the United States in Iraq in 1991 were irrefutable confirmations of America's status as the sole superpower. They insisted on the growing power differential between America and all of its great power competitors and saw this as a rare opportunity for the United States to institute unilaterally a new *Pax Americana*.[81] It is this globalist faction that came to have the upper hand as Kristol, Kirkpatrick, Tucker and the other 'isolationists' found themselves incapable of adapting their interpretative framework to the geopolitical realities of the post-Cold War era.

The re-articulation of the neoconservative foreign policy agenda took place throughout the 1990s on the back of a relentless critique of the liberal internationalist diplomacy of the Clinton administration. Although they approved of Clinton's internationalist posture, Clinton's multilateral and legalist approach to military intervention dismayed the neoconservatives.

Debates over America's intervention in the Balkans had a decisive formative influence in that respect. The intervention in Bosnia highlighted the complexities of deploying military force through a multilateral forum rather than unilaterally. Neoconservatives criticised Clinton for unnecessarily risking lives and jeopardising the military campaign by subjecting American-led NATO operations to legal requirements and the vagaries of great power politics within the UN command. The UN command had a veto power on all NATO operations. Since France and Britain contributed the largest amount of resources to UNPROFOR, this gave them a de facto power to control NATO air strikes and to interpret NATO's ultimatums to the Bosnian Serbs according to their own evaluation of the situation on the ground. Neoconservatives (and many other analysts) argued that the subordination of NATO's air power to legalism, coupled with Paris's and London's reluctance to use decisive force, encouraged Bosnian Serb violations of safe areas and the continued shelling of civilian targets in Sarajevo and elsewhere.[82] They therefore felt vindicated when the United States finally assumed leadership in the summer of 1995 and NATO's Implementation Force (IFOR) resolutely bombed the Bosnian Serbs to the negotiation table in just three weeks. For them this was proof that the central role of the UN and its disjointed command structure had been a costly hindrance to the success of military operations. It had facilitated European obstruction and jeopardised the credibility of Western leadership in international society.

The Kosovo War three years later appeared to confirm the lessons of Bosnia. Only this time it was not the decision-making process and the war-fighting capability of the UN that was the object of neoconservative criticism but that of NATO itself. NATO's Operation Allied Force was to a very large extent an American operation. Two-thirds of the air strikes were conducted by American aircrafts; practically all of the precision-guided weapons were launched from American platforms; and nearly all of the targets hit during the operations were identified by American intelligence. The growing discrepancy in military capability between the transatlantic partners rendered European interference highly frustrating for American decision-makers.[83] Neoconservatives concluded from this that the transatlantic alliance had simply become more of a burden than anything else. As Robert Kagan later explained in *Of Paradise and Power* (2003):

> In fact, the Kosovo war showed how difficult it was going to be for the United States and its European allies to fight any war together... The fact is that by the end of the 1990s the disparity of power was subtly rending the fabric of transatlantic relationship. The Americans were unhappy and impatient about constraints imposed by European allies who brought so little to a war but whose concern for 'legal issues' prevented the war's effective prosecution. The Europeans were unhappy about American dominance and their own dependence. The lesson for Americans including the top officials in the Clinton administration, was that even with the best intentions, multilateral action could not succeed without a significant element of American unilateralism, an American willingness to use its overwhelming power to dominate both war and diplomacy when weaker allies hesitated.[84]

Neoconservatives interpreted America's increasing military capability during the 1990s as a vindication of the strategic vision of Albert Wohlstetter. Wohlstetter was a conservative nuclear strategist and professor of political science at the University of Chicago. He had a decisive influence on the development of neoconservative strategic thinking (neoconservatives like to refer to him as 'Saint Albert'). Wohlstetter became known during the Cold War for his intellectual contribution to America's increased capability in high-technology warfare and precision targeting. He promoted the adaptation of nuclear delivery systems to conventional weapons and the development of high-precision military technology that would maximise strike capability and minimise collateral damage. During the Cold War, Wohlstetter argued that more accurate weapons which could target Soviet defences rather than civilians would allow American decision-makers to intervene in regional conflicts without provoking nuclear retaliation.[85] After the collapse of the Soviet Union, neoconservatives came to see the convergence of systemic unipolarity with America's increased surgical and specialised weapon capabilities as the foundation for a new logic concerning the use of force for the post-Cold War era.[86] By minimising collateral damage and putting relatively few American lives at risk, this new American way of warfare represented a fusion of strategy with ethics that would lower the burden of domestic legitimation and overcome the potential problem of public reticence. It would allow the executive to deploy military force promptly everywhere and at a different intensity. As Robert Devigne noted, for neoconservatives, this new technology '[made] presidential high politics in foreign policy possible. Public and congressional debates [would] now follow, not precede or accompany, most military action'.[87]

Although some in neoconservative circles had seen potential in the interventionist stance that Clinton promised during his first electoral campaign, all had become ferocious critics by the end of his first year in office. Neoconservatives criticised Clinton for his wavering approach to the crises in Somalia, Rwanda, Haiti and the Balkans. They also criticised his administration for its failure to formulate a compelling narrative that would give meaning to American power beyond the purely reactive task of crisis management. They resented the Clinton administration for its directionless foreign policy, and for 'cashing in' on the benefits of an assertive foreign policy that was no longer pursued.[88] As Robert Kaplan argued in *Atlantic Monthly* in 1994, US foreign policy under Clinton was like a doughnut: 'lots of peripheral interests but nothing at the centre'.[89] As a result, American civil society had assimilated the naïve economistic worldview of its president and lost all interest in the foreign affairs of the republic. Americans had become inward looking. They had 'come to take the fruits of their hegemonic power for granted'.[90]

It is in this spirit that the neoconservative think tank Project for a New American Century (PNAC) was established in June 1997, and that a more or less unified neoconservative foreign policy vision for the post-Cold War era began to emerge. Drafted by Kristol and Kagan, and signed by 25 other associates, the PNAC's Statement of Principles declared:

Does the United States have the vision to build upon the achievements of the past decades? [...] We are living off the capital—both the military investments and the foreign policy achievements—built up by past administrations... We seem to have forgotten the essential elements of the Reagan Administration's success: a military that is strong and ready to meet both present and future challenges; a foreign policy that boldly and purposefully promotes American principles abroad; and national leadership that accepts the United States' global responsibilities... If we shirk our responsibilities, we invite challenges to our fundamental interests.[91]

The PNAC's statement outlined five broad objectives: (1) 'challenge regimes hostile to our interests and values', (2) 'increase defense spending significantly', (3) 'promote the cause of political and economic freedom abroad', (4) 'strengthen our ties to democratic allies', and (5) 'accept responsibility for America's unique role in preserving and extending an international order friendly to our security, our prosperity and our principles'.[92] To a large extent, the statement was a slightly toned down reformulation of a set of ideas first developed and exposed in the controversial *Defense Policy Guidance* memo that had been prepared by Paul Wolfowitz's office at the Pentagon and leaked to the *New York Times* on 8 March 1992. The memo in question proposed to replace the post-war strategy of 'collective internationalism' with the notion of 'benevolent domination by one power'. It made 'the case for a world dominated by one superpower whose position can be perpetuated by constructive behaviour and sufficient military might to deter any nation or group of nations from challenging American primacy'.[93] The idea, as Paul Wolfowitz later explained, was 'to prevent any hostile power from dominating a region whose resources would, under consolidated control, be sufficient to generate global power'.[94]

A New Cold War...

9/11 gave democratic globalism an appeal and credibility in Washington that it simply did not have during the 1990s. At last, the rise of a new existential enemy would allow America to trade 'the anxieties of affluence for the real fears of war'.[95] As Podhoretz wrote in the *Weekly Standard* a month after the attacks, Al Qaeda brought a new myth of struggle and enmity into being that would save the republic from decadence:

More than just revenge, Americans crave a 'new birth' of the confidence we used to have in ourselves and in 'America the beautiful'. But there is only one road to this lovely condition of the spirit, and it runs through what Roosevelt and Churchill called the 'unconditional surrender' of the enemy. If we go on dithering, our lives will remain at permanent risk. So, too, will something deeper than the desire for physical security that has been stirred and agitated by the ferocious wound we received on September 11: a wound that is still suppurating and sore for lack of the healing balm that only a more coherent and wholehearted approach to the war will bring. What I mean is that nothing less than the soul of this country is at stake, and that nothing less than an unambiguous victory will save us from yet another disappointment in ourselves and another despairing disillusion with our leaders. Only this time the disappointment and the despair might well possess enough force to topple us over just as surely as those hijacked planes did to the twin towers of the World Trade Center.[96]

Neoconservatives thus greeted the Bush administration's declaration of a global war on terrorism as a welcome return to America's grand strategic purpose after 'the dumb decade' of the 1990s.[97] In the weeks following the attacks, they re-articulated their democracy promotion agenda as a civilisational struggle to hive off the terrorist *potentiality* of an Arab and Islamic political culture perceived to be particularly resistant to the globalising forces of liberal modernisation. According to neoconservatives, the rise of Islamic terrorism is rooted in 'the cauldron of political oppression, religious intolerance, and social ruin in the Arab-Islamic world—oppression transmuted and deflected by regimes with no legitimacy into virulent, murderous anti-Americanism'.[98] In this 'new' security environment, democracy promotion is now 'about America "coming ashore" to effect a "pan-Arab reformation" ... and change the very culture of the Middle East, to open its doors to democracy and modernity'.[99]

Although explanations vary in the details, most neoconservatives attribute terrorism to the alienation and extreme poverty often generated by the failure of many Islamic societies to adapt to globalisation and cope with what Kirkpatrick called the 'modernising imperative'.[100] As Krauthammer explains, 'This feeling of a civilisation in decline—and the adoption of terror and intimidation as the road to restoration—is echoed in a recent United Nations report that spoke frankly of the abject Arab failure to modernise. It is one thing for the Arabs to have fallen behind the West. But to fall behind South Korea—also colonised, once poor and lacking any of the Muslim world's fantastic oil wealth—is sheer humiliation'.[101] Along similar lines, Fukuyama explains Islamic terrorism as a nihilistic crisis of identity. In his view, this crisis is caused by the socio-cultural shocks incurred by rapid modernisation and the failure of many Islamic societies to achieve the 'attractive package' offered by the post-historical world 'combining the material prosperity of market economies and the political and cultural freedom of liberal democracy'.[102] As he explains in the 2006 afterword to *The End of History*:

> Radical Islamism is not the reassertion of some traditional Islamic cultural practice, but should be seen in the context of modern identity politics. It emerges precisely when traditional cultural identities are disrupted by modernisation and a pluralistic democratic order that creates a disjuncture between one's inner self and external social practice... Modernisation has from the beginning created alienation and thus opposition to itself, and in this respect contemporary jihadists are following in the footsteps of anarchists, Bolsheviks, fascists, and members of the Baader-Meinhof gang in earlier generations.[103]

Robert Kaplan offers another influential interpretation of this 'failed modernisation' thesis. Since the late 1980s, Kaplan has published a series of influential books, commentaries and articles on the dark sides of globalisation and the patterns of overpopulation, poverty and national fragmentation which, so he argues, have plunged many Arab, African and Southeast European states into barbarism.[104] According to Kaplan, the polities inhabiting the failed states of those regions are afflicted by a number of cultural limitations that have rendered them slave to their natural environment and incapable of managing their resources 'responsibly'.[105]

In light of such analyses, neoconservatives have sought to extend the scope of the humanitarian doctrine of 'sovereignty as responsibility to protect' advocated by cosmopolitan scholars and practitioners since the late 1990s to deal with the threat of terrorism and state failure.[106] In a nutshell, the idea is that in the same way that the norms of sovereignty and non-intervention should be made conditional upon a state's capacity to ensure the basic well-being and human rights of its citizens, a government that directly or indirectly supports terrorism de facto forfeits its right to rule without external interference. As Kagan explained in a call for US intervention in Pakistan in December 2008, 'nations should not be able to claim sovereign rights when they cannot control territory from which terrorist attacks are launched. If there is such a thing as a "responsibility to protect," which justifies international intervention to prevent humanitarian catastrophe either caused or allowed by a nation's government, there must also be a responsibility to protect one's neighbors from attacks from one's own territory, even when the attacks are carried out by "non-state actors"'.[107] Thus although the primary motives of neoconservatives are different from those of cosmopolitan norm entrepreneurs (self-defence for the former and human security concerns for the later), both share the view that the Westphalian norm of sovereign statehood should only apply to states that can produce order and that are constituted internally by liberal democratic standards of civilisation: i.e. human rights, democratic governance and the rule of law.

These reactive narratives of modernisation were synthesised and given a particularly idiosyncratic treatment by Thomas Barnett in a set of articles, interviews and presentations that received a great deal of attention in Washington during the Bush presidency.[108] Barnett first exposed his grand strategic vision in a 2003 article written for *Esquire* entitled 'The Pentagon's New Map', which he then extended into two books and recently updated in another *Esquire* piece, 'Obama's New Map of the World'.[109] There, Barnett divided the world into two zones: a 'functioning Core' and a 'non-integrating Gap'. The 'functioning Core' is made up of developed and developing states and characterised by stable 'rule sets', thick connections to globalisation and a low level of US military involvement. The 'non-integrating Gap', on the other hand, is made up of poor and 'underdeveloped' countries ruled by repressive and unstable regimes where the US has had to intervene repeatedly since the end of the Cold War and is likely to continue to do so in the future. '[T]his new world', Barnett argued, 'must be defined by where globalisation has taken roots and where it has not':

> Show me where globalisation is thick with network connectivity, financial transactions, liberal media flows, and collective security, and I will show you regions featuring stable governments, rising standards of living, and more deaths by suicide than murder... But show me where globalisation is thinning or just plain absent, and I will show you regions plagued by politically repressive regimes, widespread poverty and disease, routine mass murder and—most important—the chronic conflicts that incubate the next generation of global terrorists.[110]

Although Barnett did not exclude the risk of a confrontation with China and Russia, he announced that US military action in the coming decades was most likely to be provoked by those that are either 'losing out to globalisation or rejecting much of the content flows associated with its advance'. In his view, there are two main reasons why those living within the 'bloody boundaries' of the 'seam states' that constitute the Gap resist the civilisational 'content flows' of globalisation: abject poverty and deficient political-legal culture.[111] Barnett argued that containment must therefore be replaced by aggressive engagement, integration and a new strategic sound bite: 'Disconnectedness defines danger'. According to him, the periphery has become a 'strategic threat environment' in great part because it has failed to harmonise its 'internal rule sets' with the global 'rule sets' of the Core, which rests upon the principles of 'democracy, transparency, and free trade'. He therefore maintained that the US was free to disregard the norm of equal sovereignty when intervening, sometimes pre-emptively, in the periphery to enforce its own liberal 'rule sets'.[112] 'To accomplish this task', Barnett argued, America must 'be explicit with both friends and foes alike about how it will necessarily differentiate between its security role within the Core's burgeoning security community and the one it assumes whenever it intervenes militarily in the Gap. Seeking two sets of rules for these different security roles is not being hypocritical but honest and realistic'.[113]

Imperial Delusions

It has now been nearly a decade since the United States enacted the Bush Doctrine in Iraq in a bid to implement a national security strategy heavily influenced by the geopolitical discourses surveyed above. Save for a small minority of diehard partisans, the great majority of analysts today are in agreement that the Iraq War is likely to be remembered by historians as one of the most monumental fiascos in the history of contemporary American foreign policy.

According to neoconservatives, it is the incompetence of the Bush administration and the lack of troops in the post-invasion phase of the war that are to blame for this debacle—not neoconservative ideas and policy prescriptions as such.[114] Indeed, according to the Straussian-neoconservative scholar Robert Reilly (chairman of the Committee for Western Civilisation and senior adviser to the Iraqi Ministry of Information during the Operation Iraqi Freedom), America's failures in Iraq and the wider war on terror are rooted not in the shortcomings of neoconservative ideas but in the relativist intellectual currents haunting American public diplomacy:

The rifts in the broad consensus that is necessary for a successful public diplomacy arise from the fact that the fundamental teachings of our civilisation are widely disputed in American society, especially in academia and the media. These disputes have taken various forms, all of which one way or another deny the existence of an objective moral order... Our freedom is no longer dependent upon conforming ourselves to a reality that exists independently of our desires—the very 'Laws of nature and of Nature's God' on which the Declaration declares the United States into existence... The regression is not accidental. Relativism inevitably concludes in nihilism, and the ultimate expression of nihilism is the supremacy of the will. Those who promote 'multiculturalism', another form of relativism, have chosen the surest way to the destruction of diversity, the very thing they claim to celebrate. The extent to which America has changed in this way is the extent to which it has lost its moral authority, both at home and abroad. Radical Islam has not done this to us; we have done it to ourselves. This is the real, internal crisis of public diplomacy.[115]

Over the past three years or so, neoconservatives have re-adjusted their focus and renewed their activity in making the case for a 'league of democracies'. In their view, this would allow the world's democrats to promote and defend their values and principles in a more systematic and organised fashion.[116] It is in this optic that Robert Kagan, William Kristol and Dan Senor founded the think tank Foreign Policy Initiative (FPI) in the spring of 2009. In its mission statement, the FPI lists a familiar series of threats to the US, including 'rogue states', 'failed states', 'autocracies' and 'terrorism'. But it also puts a particular emphasis on the 'challenges' posed by 'rising and resurgent powers' of which only China and Russia are named. Echoing the objectives of the defunct Project for a New American Century, the FPI's mission statement calls for 'continued engagement—diplomatic, economic, and military—in the world and rejection of policies that would lead us down the path to isolationism; a strong military with the defense budget needed to ensure that America is ready to confront the threats of the 21st century; and robust support for America's democratic allies and opposition to rogue regimes that threaten American interests'.[117]

The self-exonerating rhetoric and continuity in neoconservative thinking after Iraq bears witness to the lack of humility and incapacity for introspection of its protagonists. There is no doubt that the post-invasion phase of the war has been grossly mismanaged by the Bush administration. But the failures of US foreign policy under Bush cannot be so casually disassociated from the hubristic geopolitical vision surveyed in this chapter. Democratic globalism provides many opportunities for criticism. Here, I will limit myself to three closely interrelated points that are symptomatic of neoconservative thought more generally, and which can help us understand the ways in which its advocates make use of progressive ethical rhetoric to pursue their own conservative ends in the contemporary geopolitical environment.

The first point concerns the relationship between security, democracy, neoliberal economics and globalisation posited by neoconservative discourses. As we have seen, neoconservatives see global terrorism and state-failure today as correlates of slow or absent economic growth in the 'non-integrating periphery' caused by the cultural blockages that afflict indigenous population. Aside from its grotesque ethnocentricity, the problem with this argument is that there is no causal relationship between deprivation and violence—only higher statistical probability. Generalisations over the economic root causes of terrorism fail to capture the specific context and dynamics of each zone of conflict and thus cannot explain in what way and to what extent economic factors matter.[118] As Mark Berger argued, contemporary discourse about violence and state-building in the post-colonial world must be set in the context of the 'universalisation of the nation-state system and the ways in which the subsequent spread of globalisation has, in an increasingly uneven and incomplete fashion, pushed nation-states in many parts of the world to the limits of their potential as a vehicle for security and development'.[119]

Neoconservative democracy promotion discourses are cast in a complete historical and political void. It is only in the linkage to past policies and interventions that the economic and cultural sources of the terrorist violence directed at the United States and its allies today gain significance. By locating the 'root cause' of terrorism in the late or delayed structural development of Arab and other non-Western societies, neoconservative security discourses establish a false spatio-temporal discontinuity with the geopolitics of the Cold War. This elides the extent to which religious terrorism today is in many ways linked to past US and Soviet policies on the periphery.[120] This then deceitfully situates the locus and motivation of post-colonial violence within the psyche and socio-cultural milieu of the agents.[121] As Simon Dalby argues, once violence is understood in this unreflective manner, '[r]esponsibility for the difficulties to which military strategies are the answer is designated as originating in an external unrelated space. This radical separation, the spatialised "Othering" of threats, acts to perpetuate geopolitical knowledge practices that emphasise conflict and militarised understanding of security'.[122] In turn, simplistic conflation of poverty and inequality with conflict in public discourse inevitably nurtures the popular view that conflict and terrorism are a developing country problem. This confines the origins of terrorism and economic misery to geographically distant regions, while concealing the fact that the problem of terrorism and poverty is *genuinely* global, both in its origins and scope. The linkage between the 'globalisation of terror' and abject poverty in neoconservative discourse thereby cultivates xenophobia and public fears about migrants and asylum seekers. Ultimately, it helps muster support for stringent Right-wing immigration and border control policies and for foreign policy ventures to 'securitise' the remote frontiers of globalisation.

This de-historicisation of the terrorist threat is at one with the de-politicised interpretation of democracy underpinning democratic globalism. And this is my second point. As we have seen, neoconservatives envisage the promotion of democracy as the establishment by force of a set of institutions and electoral mechanisms designed to manufacture consent from above and lull civil society into accepting the rationality of an externally imposed neoliberal infrastructure.[123] In this Straussian-Schumpeterian framework, democratic institutions are not seen as regulating arenas for power competition that may be restructured from the bottom up as the competing groups see fit. Rather, they are top-down socialising mechanisms designed to generate new forms of political subjectivities and confer a new political character to individual citizens without any concerns for the political legitimacy of the new regime among the indigenous population. In other words, neoconservatives envisage the new democratic communities that they want to create in terms of cultural and ethical values rather than as the political representation and expression of the conflicting interests of their constitutive social forces. The limits of such an approach have been exposed in a most dramatic manner in Iraq. The French specialist of political Islam Olivier Roy has well captured the nature of the problem:

> By attributing the problems of the Middle East to cultural and societal blockages, which one should ignore or circumvent to democratise the region, those discourses casually bypass the political dimension of those problems—especially all that is related to US foreign policy (resentment created by US domination of the region and American passivity in the Israel-Palestine conflict). But more than anything else, such discourses ignore the fact that there can be no democracy without legitimacy. And political legitimacy presupposes that actors

are firmly grounded in the history, traditions and general social fabric of a country. The notion of 'civil society' envisaged by theorists of democratisation is out of step with society as it really exists on the ground. The fundamental issue has to do with the political legitimacy of the actors suddenly put forward to bring this new democracy into being... [T]hey are most of the time perceived either like businessmen of a new type, or like the 'agents of American and Zionist imperialism'... In effect, Washington's politics of democratisation has opened up the political space and allowed various political forces to express themselves and gain political force by drawing on the two main pillars of political legitimacy in the Middle East: nationalism and Islam.[124]

And this brings us to my third and final point: democratic globalism dislocates ethics from the play of political interests and re-articulates conflicts between states and social forces as a set of existential antagonisms grounded in ethical and cultural categories. This discursive move follows a similar pattern to the discourses on crime and welfare analysed in Chapter 3. For both locate the causes of disorder in the cultural habits of the social group concerned, independently of the socio-political patterns that structure the relationship between agents. Thus whereas domestic discourse on crime and welfare seeks to mobilise moral values for the policing of a demoralised and unruly civil society, the discourse on counter-terrorism and the promotion of democracy mobilises ethical values for the policing of a 'non-integrating periphery' whose 'cultural blockages' are thought to have become a threat to 'the West'. Not unlike Huntington's 'clash of civilisation' thesis[125], this transforms the 'cultural' understood as an indicator of difference into 'culture' as an axis of enmity that associates 'terrorist potentiality' with the uneasy fit between non-Western values and global liberal modernisation.[126] By attributing causality to the 'cultural' in this manner, neoconservative discourse renders terrorism, 'rogue states' and 'state-failure' amenable to the disciplinary force of the civilising process and the ethical language of humanitarianism. Once understood as 'liberal', violence can be represented as a progressive force geared towards the establishment of the normative conditions of a democratic peace. It can also be legitimated outside the formal legal structure of the liberal order if necessary, since it is precisely the liberal character of this order that is at stake in this civilisational struggle. As Kagan and Kristol explain, when it comes to dealing with undemocratic, 'rogue' or 'failed' states, the US:

will not succeed in persuading them to play by the existing—which is to say American—rules of the game ... We cannot hope to stem their aggression by appealing to their consciences and asking them to accept the 'norms' of the civilised world. For those 'norms' serve as obstacles to their ambitions and even threats to their existence. They have, and will continue to have, a clear and immutable interest in flouting them.[127]

This normative distinction between states thus institutes a zone of exceptionalism and non-law at the heart of international society, which invites the deployment of military force. In this normative setting, a state can be subjected to intervention not solely on the basis of a previous aggression or a legal transgression but on the basis of its 'deficient' political culture, or of its failure to manage its resources and control its populations 'responsibly'. This establishes a continuum of intervention ranging from preventative economic and technical assistance to the establishment and maintenance of formal and informal protectorates—either directly through security guarantees or indirectly through dense business networks, arms trading and military training—and outright regime change and occupation. As it shifts the burden of justification from the intervening actors to the state subjected to intervention, this expansionist politics disinvests the liberal order from commitments to the norm of sovereign existential equality and formal processes of interest mediation in contemporary international society.[128] The normative order thereby ceases to transcend culture and ideology and is re-articulated on the basis of a new contractual form of justice, which is no longer established by an order of rights among equals but strictly by conventions established by the American hegemony. (Barnett talks of a 'Global Leviathan' without the actual consent of the peoples concerned.)[129]

In sum, neoconservative internationalism gestures towards a radical departure from the anti-imperialist 'Charter liberalism' that has legitimated the hegemonic order of Pax Americana since 1945. When Pax Americana emerged out of the rubble of Pax Britannica more than half a century ago, the ideological separation between politics and economics that served capitalism so well in the nineteenth century had been blurred by hard-fought social democratic struggles and the end of European imperialism during the first half of the twentieth century.[130] The catastrophic failures of balance of power diplomacy and neo-Smithian economic doctrines created the need for multilateral institutions to facilitate the management of political violence and cooperation over the administration of the global capitalist economy. In these circumstances, multilateralism became both a key component of the historical structure of Pax Americana and the main process by which conflicts over the modalities that determine the operating principles between the global capitalist economy and various regimes of state sovereignty in international society are regulated and institutionalised.[131]

To be sure, post-war multilateralism was not the product of a benevolent liberal progressivism, but an essentially conservative political development. It was established by the US and the club of Western liberal democratic states as a mode of social and economic protection against the threats of revolution, instability and nuisance caused by the social democratic struggles and the process of decolonisation as they unfolded after the First World War. As Ian Clark put it, 'While society had to be protected from the unregulated global market, in the interests of restoring domestic and international political stability, so the core states of the international system sought to guard their existing privileges in the unregulated global state system by deploying the institutions of the embedded liberal solution at the international level also'.[132] Nevertheless, multilateralism established a progressive normative structure that embedded the market into a comprehensive political structure. This allowed for a more inclusive representation of conflicting interests and values, enabled political struggles for civil rights and national independence, and allowed demands to be made to redress the irrationality of the existing order. This normative structure linked the constitutionalisation of labour in the West with the demands for equal recognition and power redistribution of the global South. It also served as a standard for both the critique of ideology and great power *Realpolitik*. Clearly, the emancipatory potential of Charter liberalism is much more limited than liberal internationalists would like to admit. But it nevertheless endowed global politics with what Martti Koskenniemi calls a 'horizon of universalism embedded in a culture of restraint, a commitment to listening to others', that provides a more inclusive basis for the continued production of norms and *could* lead to more benign political developments. At any rate, this 'culture of formalism' operates as a precondition and a set of regulative ideals for the further development of international law and a mediation of particular ethical decisions that prevents the unmediated moralisation of relations between political adversaries.[133]

It is this 'horizon of universalism' that hangs in the balance in our contemporary neoconservative politics. As the liberal internationalist scholar John Ikenberry observed, neoconservative internationalism hinges on the belief that you can do democratic engagement 'without committing to the values, institutions, and mutual responsibilities of the wider democratic community... For neoconservatives, democracy promotion is a goal partly because it will create an international environment that will free the US from the need to build and commit to multilateralism'.[134]

Ikenberry has his own questionable political agenda.[135] Nevertheless, public statements by key neoconservative figures closely involved with the planning of the Iraq War during the Bush presidency appear to confirm his assessment. Consider the following examples:

> Contrary to the view of many critics of the war, we did not go into Iraq mainly to impose democracy by force in some grand, ambitious (and naive) scheme to transform Iraq and then the region as a whole into a collection of happy democracies ... There is a larger picture with respect to Iraq ... We have demonstrated in Iraq that we will act to protect ourselves. We have shown that we will fight terrorists where we find them, even when the cost is high. We, and now much of the world, have begun to take terrorism seriously. This is in good measure because we have been willing, in Iraq and Afghanistan, to go beyond the instruments of law enforcement and plaintive pleas of ineffective international institutions on which we relied. We have, as the always wise Fouad Ajami put it, created, 'from Egypt to Kuwait and Bahrain, a Pax Americana [that] anchors the order of the region. In Iraq, the Pax Americana, hitherto based in Sunni Arab lands, has acquired a new footing in a Shiite-led country'.
>
> Richard Perle (2008)[136]

> [T]he purpose of the war was to remove a threat to national and international security. Whether the Iraq War was right or wrong, it was not about imposing democracy, and the decision to establish a representative government afterward was the most realistic option, compared with the alternatives of installing another dictator or prolonging the U.S. occupation.
>
> Paul Wolfowitz (2009)[137]

As these post-facto rationalisations suggest, democratic globalism in Iraq was as much about promoting polyarchy as it was about dissuading future challenges to American global supremacy by putting the US's overwhelming military superiority on display. Neoconservatives believe that 'power is its own reward' (Krauthammer).[138] They are haunted by the thought that if the US does not decisively exert force at regular intervals, its global leadership will lose significance.[139] Yet the mounting death toll in Iraq and Afghanistan and the steady decline of

American prestige since 2003 bear witness to the shortsightedness of this political psychology. When invoking the Machiavellian maxim that 'it is better to be feared than loved' to mock the pacifist and law-abiding sensitivity of their critics, neoconservatives conveniently omit the crucial proviso that qualifies Machiavelli's counsel to the prince.[140] And that is that 'the prince must none the less make himself feared in such a way that, if he is not loved, at least he escapes being hated'.[141]

5

THE NEOCONSERVATIVE CRITIQUE OF GLOBAL LIBERAL GOVERNANCE

'Obama is inspired by the religion of humanity. The desire to act on behalf of humanity betrays impatience with the contentiousness of politics within nations, where life is always both inspired and bounded by partisan and national loyalties. Over time the devotees of progressive politics discover that they can do away with domestic political differences only through a globalisation that does away with national differences. That is why multiculturalism—which is today's downsized term for the religion of humanity—is both a domestic and a foreign policy'.

Harvey Mansfield[1]

In April 2008 the American Enterprise Institute, in conjunction with the Federalist Society for Law and Public Policy, launched its web-based resource centre, Global Governance Watch (GGW). The aim of the GGW project is to monitor the ways in which the agenda of international organisations impact on domestic politics and the US national interest. Since its inauguration, GGW has directed its audience towards a wide range of political commentaries and scholarly analyses of four 'pillars of global governance: development; global regulation, which includes climate change, health, and intellectual property; human security; and national security'.[2] The launch of GGW marked the escalation of a neoconservative campaign to re-assert the virtues of sovereignty and the liberal democratic nation-state against the cosmopolitan project of global liberal governance. As its sponsors explain, GGW 'keeps an eye on American sovereignty'.[3] It raises awareness about the fact that 'the mainstream American left has come to internalise the core arguments of global governance and redefined them as "American leadership"'.[4]

The neoconservative reaction against global governance (or 'world federalism' as it was called at the time) has its origins in the 1970s. However, it really began to take shape during the 1990s under the leadership of a number of political scientists, jurists, diplomats and media commentators organised around think tanks such as the American Enterprise Institute, the Hudson Institute and the Heritage Foundation. Against the background of an uneven and incomplete transition to globalisation and the emergence of a unipolar world, neoconservatives criticised the woolly legalism of the Clinton administration and urged a re-orientation in foreign policy that would put American sovereignty at the heart of the international liberal order and beyond the reach of legal regimes of global liberal governance at one and the same time. Sovereigntist arguments eventually came to play a crucial role in shaping the Bush administration's outright rejection, refusal to ratify, or unilateral withdrawal of high-profile multilateral legal initiatives such as the International Criminal Court Statute, the Kyoto Protocol, the Mine Ban Treaty and the ABM Treaty. They also contributed a great deal towards setting the unilateralist tone of the Bush administration's response to the attacks of 9/11, and informed its dubious re-interpretation of the Geneva Conventions and Convention on Torture to fight terrorism. Since 2008, they have provided much support for the critique of the Obama administration's approach to international law, multilateralism and climate change.[5] Indeed, according to John Fonte, one of the leading neoconservative intellectuals behind the sovereigntist cause, the struggle between liberal nationalists and 'global progressives' will be the main ideological event of the century:

> The liberal democratic nation-state in general and American constitutionalism in particular will confront what is perhaps the greatest challenge ever to their moral authority and legitimacy from the ideology and forces of global governance. This challenge is 'existential' because it challenges the existence of the American constitutional democratic regime. It is formidable because it comes from within the Enlightenment thought and Western civilisation. It will be the great challenge of the twenty-first century.[6]

This chapter offers a conceptual interpretation of the neoconservative case for US sovereignty against global governance and draws out the main political and ethical implications for American foreign policy and American democracy. I argue and demonstrate that the neoconservative critique of global governance rests upon a decisionist interpretation of the normative order that weaves together democracy, individual rights and national autonomy through a volatile identity politics which is fundamentally at odds with both the pluralist character of 'Westphalian' diplomacy and the universal order of rights envisaged by advocates of global governance. As we will see, the neoconservative challenge to the contemporary liberal order goes well beyond the virtues of unilateralism and multilateralism in international affairs. It expresses deep-seated ideological beliefs about the modalities of political power, the extent of individual rights, the nature of political conflict and the legitimacy of liberal democracy as a modern political regime that transcend party divisions and are bound to remain major sources of friction between the US and its liberal democratic allies during the coming decades.

The 'Internationalisation' of the Domestic Legal Order

In essence, neoconservative discontent with global liberal governance has to do with the extent to which the latter is transforming international law from a mechanism designed to regulate inter-states relations (a law of nations) into a mechanism designed to regulate the relationship between states and their citizens (a cosmopolitan law of human rights).[7] Here, neoconservatives have been able to draw on the emergence of a juridical revisionism since the late 1990s which is deeply hostile to the internalisation of international law in US domestic courts. This juridical revisionism is led by a number of conservative jurists associated with the University of Chicago, the AEI and the Federalist Society, such as Curtis Bradley, Jack Goldsmith, Eric Possner, John Yoo, Lee Casey, David Rivkin and many others.

During the past fifteen years or so, revisionists have mobilised against what they see as the increasingly intrusive and unmediated incursion of international law in the American legal system. Central to their campaign is the complaint that the rules and norms of customary international law may now be introduced into domestic courts directly by judges without having been subject to approval by Congress. They argue that these developments simply go against the core features of the American Constitutions: the separation of powers, representative democracy and federalism.[8] Revisionists also complain that recent practices by some federal judges of relying upon the decisions of foreign and international tribunals in their opinions and for guidance in interpreting the American Constitution go against the original intentions of the framers.[9] Yoo refers to this phenomenon as the 'outsourcing of American law':

> Outsourcing in American law is proceeding. Foreign law has made its controversial appearance in the Supreme Court's decisions on individual rights. Some customary international law has become a part of federal law through the 1789 Alien Tort Statute. The laws of war have provided the rules of decision for the cases on the Bush administration's policies in the war on terrorism. Advocates of these developments would like to see even more use of foreign and international law in U.S. judicial decisions and the American legal system more broadly.[10]

The revisionists owe their name to their effort at reversing the trend established by the *Restatement of the Foreign Relations Law of the United States*, a document widely accepted as authoritative within the American juridical community and which asserts that international law is indeed part of American federal law.[11] In their view, large segments of international customary law are illegitimate because (1) they concern matters like human rights that are the property of the domestic and not the international realm, and (2) because they are not 'customary' since in several cases they do not correspond to state practices but simply express various forms of international agreements.[12] John Bolton, George W. Bush's former Ambassador to the UN (2005–6), gave a particularly flamboyant rendering of this argument in his keynote address at the inauguration of GGW in April 2008:

> 'Customary international law', or as I prefer to call it, 'customary international custom' is really the embodiment of state practice. This is something that evolves over decades, and it reflects a common-sense appreciation of the process involved as to what norms ought to be to govern behavior... But what has actually happened in the past several decades is that customary international law and the function of norming have become the captives of international law professoriate, a dangerously underemployed group of people, who spend their lives developing new customary international law that does not derive from decades or centuries of state practice but comes from their own political agenda... If this professoriate and their outriders were prepared to argue that customary international law derives from the natural law tradition, then I would be prepared to grant some additional legitimacy to their lien of argument... I doubt, however, that there are many members of the law professoriate who believe in God, let alone are prepared to argue that international law

as it has evolved over the centuries from the natural law tradition represents something from heaven. Instead, it is a creation of their own overactive intellects, and it is intended to advance an agenda not compatible by and large with American interests.[13]

In fact, the legal revisionists overstate the degree to which the intrusion of international customary law into the US legal system is actually taking place. As John Gerard Ruggie noted, the *Restatement of the Foreign Relations Law of the United States* attacked by legal revisionists represents an 'overreaching' by liberal internationalists of the time that exaggerated the extent to which US courts recognise the principle that international law is part of federal law.[14] Revisionists take the Alien Tort Claims Act (ATCA) as their main example and point of departure. But the ACTA is more of an anomaly than anything else.[15] The set of human rights treaties signed by the US at the end of the 1980s (the Genocide Convention, the International Covenant on Civil and Political Rights, the Torture Convention, and the International Convention on the Elimination of All Forms of Racial Discrimination) were all ratified by Congress with a series of reservations that effectively denied the self-executive character of those treaties in American courts.[16] The problem with revisionist arguments, critics point out, is not so much that they are flawed in legal terms but that they identify threats that in many respects remain hypothetical and fail to show what concrete public policy problems they would help solve.[17]

The intricacies of the debates over the legal substance, merits and flaws of revisionist proposals should not detain us. What is really important for the present discussion is not so much the legal and policy practicalities of revisionist proposals but rather the political significance of those nationalist contestations. For what is at stake here is not only the self-executive character of international customary law within the domestic courts of the United States or any other states. More fundamentally, it is the constitutionalisation of a system of international law that asserts the primacy of individual rights over those of the nation-state, and thereby subjects the latter to the authority of judicial bodies operating independently of the UN Security Council.[18] Opposition to these developments puts American legal revisionism firmly at odds with the legal climate of Europe, where those notions have already been institutionalised and welcomed as positive political developments.[19]

It is this political dimension of the debate that has been tapped into by neoconservatives over the last decade or so in their attack on global governance. Neoconservatives argue that the internalisation of international customary law is unconstitutional, and that it undermines the political matrix through which America has understood itself over the last three centuries. According to neoconservatives, globalisation and the spatio-temporal advance of liberal modernity have given rise to a 'globalist' cosmopolitan culture and ideology in Europe and within American academic circles that are increasingly hostile to American values and to the democratic constitutionalism of the United States. This post-national intelligentsia is belittling the principle of popular sovereignty and restricting America's domestic and international policy flexibility. Globalists, neoconservatives complain, wish to anchor international cooperation into a global constitutional order and subject the democratic will of the American people in all substantive fields—human rights, labour laws, the environment, health and political-military affairs—to the authority of a world state in the making.[20] 'This authority is exercised by new definitions ("evolving norms") of international law (really transnational law); transnational courts such as the International Criminal Court; myriad UN conventions that establish new global norms, particularly in the area of human rights; supranational institutions like the European Union; and non-government organisations (NGOs) that act as "global civil society"'.[21]

When sifting through neoconservative polemics, we find that the social base of this politico-cultural offensive is composed of leading American and European international lawyers and academics (e.g. Anne-Marie Slaughter, Harold Hongju Koh, Robert Falk, Jürgen Habermas, John Gerard Ruggie and Strobe Talbott); UN and EU officials and bureaucrats; international judges; NGOs; wealthy American foundations like Rockefeller, Ford, Mott and MacArthur; corporate executives who have a vested interest in eroding the sovereignty and territorial borders of the nation-state; and, more generally, practising Centre-Left politicians in America and Europe who have 'internalised' this emerging cosmopolitan culture.[22]

In fact, however, the characterisation of this intra-civilisational struggle for cultural hegemony as a clash between globalists and anti-globalists is misleading. Far from being out of step with globalisation, the 'Americanist' camp is strongly committed to free trade and free market economics. As Fonte emphasises in his own research on this ongoing debate, the 'critical argument' is over 'whether the form of Western global engagement in the coming decades will be transnationalist or internationalist'. It is whether global engagement will take a post-national character (what he calls transnational progressivism) or if it will remain bounded by statist categories like sovereignty, patriotism, nationalism, citizenship and the assimilation of minorities.[23]

Democratic Legitimacy and the Limits of Rationalism

As the above comments indicate, what neoconservatives present as a culture clash between globalists and Americanists over the continued relevance of the sovereign nation-state as the dominant form of political organisation expresses a broader ideological conflict over competing understandings of the relationship between democracy, law and individual rights. For neoconservatives, the idea that international legitimacy can be derived from the will of an international community transcending any individual nation-state is a dangerous leap of faith. Because the international community is not concretely anchored in a global democratic constitutional order, it cannot confer legitimacy upon international and state institutions from above. Whatever legitimacy international institutions may have, it is argued, this legitimacy is handed up to them by duly constituted democratic majorities at the level of the nation-state and can be withdrawn at any time by the latter.[24] As Francis Fukuyama put it, the chance that a democratic world government will ever come into being 'is as close to zero as you ever get in political life. What will be practically possible to construct in terms of international institutions will not be legitimate or democratic, and what will be legitimate and democratic will not be possible to construct'.[25]

Although certainly no great supporters of participatory democracy at home, neoconservatives criticise institutions of global governance on the grounds that (1) they reduce the possibility of individual and national parliamentary participation in the political process, and (2) they redistribute power and decision-making authority from elected governments to a conglomerate of international bureaucrats and technocrats. For them, the problem is not only that this supranational technocracy suffers from a serious democratic deficit. It is also the fact that global governance opens the formal political process to NGO participation 'from below' and thereby renders the constitutional order vulnerable to capture by a multitude of interest groups, all operating outside the bounds of democratic accountability.[26]

The EU is a primary target here and the source of much anxiety. According to Jeremy Rabkin, for example, the European model of shared sovereignty poses a threat to the popular sovereignty of non-member states because it transfers a great deal of state power to supranational institutions in the public sector and to NGOs in the private sector that are all bent on regulating environmental, human rights and social issues. Rabkin argues that because this 'Euro-tizing' process could incite other states to adapt their own regulations to the standards set by another group of states, the EU is an offence to the popular sovereignty of non-member states.[27]

At the more philosophical level, neoconservatives oppose the interpretation of democratic legitimacy defended by advocates of global liberal governance because of its rationalist, 'noumenal' character. International law and the institutions of global governance, they argue, sever the moral basis of international legitimacy from the political principle of democratic consent. Rather than reflecting the contractual will of the peoples concerned, they are the expression of a set of universalistic rules of morality that are deemed to be binding—even if actually rejected by the majority—because no free and rational human being would reject them.[28] The cosmopolitan scholar Jürgen Habermas, for example, formulates the rationalist position targeted by neoconservative polemics in the following terms: '[at the global level] the democratic procedure no longer draws its legitimising force only, indeed not even predominantly, from political participation and the expression of political will, but rather from the general accessibility of deliberative processes whose structure grounds an expectation of rationally accepted results'.[29]

Now as many critics have pointed out, the problem with this rationalist position is that what counts as a 'rationally acceptable result' is always contestable and must therefore remain a political decision. Neoconservatives accordingly reject this rationalist 'doctrine of derived consent' as a folly of the French Enlightenment, a totalitarian idiosyncrasy akin to Rousseau's 'doctrine of the general will of forcing the individual to be free'.[30] They insist that it is precisely because war is often a derivative of the egoistic disposition cultivated by liberalism that we ought to impose democratic safeguards on universal reason. As Peter Berkowitz argues, 'What if the universal rational norms are invoked not on principled grounds but on grounds of self-interest? What if the self-interest is not enlightened but cynical? And what if the cynical appeal to self-interest does not reflect the sort of human lapse concerning which we must always be on guard but is rather a by-product of the spirit that liberalism fosters?'[31]

Neo-Kantian advocates of global governance want to bring about a cosmopolitan order of right guided by rational universal norms. From an imaginary 'original position' (Rawls) or an 'ideal speech situation' (Habermas), they derive ethical principles that will guide political and socio-economic reforms. But these abstract theoretical constructs, neo-conservatives retort, are precisely just that: abstractions that take no heed of the natural constraints that human nature imposes on rational education.[32] Neoconservatives see the progressive displacement of Hobbes's 'state of nature' by rationalist conceits like the 'ideal speech situation' or the 'veil of ignorance' as the basis of a liberal theory of justice and a dangerous intellectual slippage. For them, conflict is not social but existential. It does not stem strictly—or even primarily—from irrational institutional arrangements but from the natural instincts and aspirations of human beings. As Jeane Kirkpatrick argued in the early 1980s, neo-Kantian rationalism disregards Hobbes's most valuable insight: 'because men are as prone to quarrelling about power, status, and virtue as about the distribution of wealth, they will quarrel forever'.[33] Fukuyama also makes the point repeatedly in *The End of History and the Last Man*:

> Experience suggests that if men cannot struggle on behalf of a just cause because that just cause was victorious in an earlier generation then they will struggle *against* the just cause. They will struggle for the sake of struggle... And if the greater part of the world in which they live is characterised by peaceful and prosperous liberal democracy, then they will struggle *against* that peace and prosperity, and against democracy. [...] No regime—no 'socio-economic system'—is able to satisfy all men in all places. This includes liberal democracy. This is not a matter of the incompleteness of the democratic revolution, that is, because the blessings of liberty and equality have not been extended to all people. Rather, the dissatisfaction arises precisely where democracy has triumphed most completely: it is a dissatisfaction *with* liberty and equality. Thus those who remain dissatisfied will always have the potential to restart history.[34]

These anti-rationalist exhortations resonate strongly with the Schmittian-Straussian reading of Hobbes that we have seen in Chapter 2. In this neo-Hobbesian world, the nation-state (politics) and the state of nature (anthropology) are not extrinsic to one another. Unlike in a neo-Kantian interpretation of the civilising process, liberal governance does not constitute a progressive transcendence of the 'natural dangerousness' of human societies. Rather, the nation-state here harnesses this natural dangerousness for its own life-preserving end and invokes it to justify its domination of society. In other words, liberal governance hinges on the transformation of the anthropological violence of the state of nature into a 'pre-emptive counter violence' that is monopolised by the state and legitimated by its order-generating function (the social contract).[35] This irreducible violence at the heart of the modern liberal state is a remnant of the state of nature in which states interact with one another. It manifests itself periodically and at different intensities through labour militancy, urban riots, student activism, terrorism, anti-war protests, and other such clashes between domestic and transnational social forces over the legitimacy of the dominant order. This generates a close interdependence between the indivisible character of the sovereignty of states in the international arena and the need to minimise elements of heterogeneity within the domestic sphere (more on this in a moment).

The limits of rationalism from this perspective have to do with the fact that, although state violence is 'legitimated' by the life-preserving function of sovereign power, it can never be completely 'civilised'. A genuine emancipation from the state of nature would involve the sovereign power in submitting itself to a set of legal rules determined by its ultimate end: the security, right to life and well-being of citizens. Yet this Lockean notion is irreconcilable with the Hobbesian view that individuals found the state in the first place to negate their own 'natural dangerousness'. Were sovereign power to be subordinated to any formal legal obligations towards civil society, it would no longer be sovereign and become subject to the very same dangerous human nature that it was meant to keep in check in the first place. As Strauss and his students have repeatedly pointed out, this is why Locke and his followers have never succeeded (and will never succeed) in eliminating the arbitrary political violence that constitutes the liberal state. For all that the liberal insistence on the rule of law has achieved is to incorporate this violence into the broader constitutional framework under the deceptive name of 'emergency powers' or what Locke called 'special prerogatives' ('This Power to act according to discretion, for the publick good, without the prescription of the law, and sometimes even against it…').[36] But the constitutionalisation of 'special prerogatives', of course, does not resolve the problem. It only assumes that virtuous leaders will use these powers wisely in the name of a shared conception of the good life that will give meaning and purpose to the lives of individual citizens.[37]

The upshot of this neo-Hobbesian narrative is that the transcendence of the Westphalian order of the sovereign nation-state through international law can only be achieved through the creation of a global leviathan. This global leviathan would centralise the legitimate means of violence and entrust a global elite to pursue and enforce an overarching conception of the good life on all existing cultural communities. And this, neoconservatives believe, is an implausible recipe for global tyranny.[38] According to Irving Kristol, the statesman who seriously entertains hopes for such a peace is simply not fit for office:

> Men have always dreamed of perpetual peace, and presumably always will. This dream is a noble one, and a man must be deficient in humanity not to have felt its appeal. But let us remember: It is a dream, whereas we live out our lives in a real and material world that is governed, not by dreams, but by limited possibilities. In this real material world, conflict between men and war between nations appear to be permanent features of the human condition. It has always been so; we must, if we are to be responsible statesmen, assume that it always will be so.[39]

No Governance without Government

This critique of rationalism feeds into a decisionist legal-constitutional interpretation of the international normative order that has been the source of much tension between America and Europe since the end of the Cold War, especially since 9/11. As we have just seen, neoconservatives are deeply ambivalent about the transformative and self-generating power of reason and liberalism in political life. In their view, given the empirical implausibility and ethical undesirability of a global leviathan, what allows for the liberal character of the contemporary global order is not the false security of international treaties, the benevolent civility of NGO networks or the invisible hand of commerce, but 'fear of overwhelming U.S. power'.[40] More precisely, it is the existence of a hegemonic power that has the capacity to exclude itself unilaterally from the legal order so as to institute a new set of norms or protect existing norms when the latter are under threat or have become inadequate. In Robert Kagan's famous terminology, governance requires a Hobbesian power that 'mans the wall' of Kant's constitutional paradise but that 'cannot walk through the gates' by virtue of its systemic responsibilities—a 'unilateralist iron fist inside the multilateralist velvet glove'.[41]

It is, of course, to Carl Schmitt that we owe this decisionist interpretation of sovereignty. 'Sovereign', Schmitt famously argued, 'is he who decides on the exception'.[42] Here is not the place to elaborate extensively on Schmitt's fascinating theory of sovereignty. But a number of brief conceptual clarifications concerning the main characteristics of his decisionism are nevertheless necessary in order to appreciate the set of philosophical and conceptual assumptions that underpins this particular position towards international norms.

Schmitt's decisionism can be understood as a neo-Hobbesian response to Max Weber's neo-Nietzschean/neo-Kantian interpretation of the 'crisis of modernity'.[43] Weber saw the 'crisis of modernity' as a crisis of legitimation generated by the demise of religious worldviews and the inability of reason to justify and ground its own activity in reason. He showed how this crisis of legitimation extended to all fields of human endeavour and how this had necessarily led to the fragmentation of modern social life into a multitude of belief systems, all normatively independent from one another. The consequence of this differentiation of value spheres is what Weber described as a 'pluriverse' of 'warring gods' in which all gods can confer meaning to their respective value sphere but none of them can give meaning to the totality, i.e. to life as a whole. As he put it, 'as long as life is left to itself and is understood in its own terms, it knows only that the conflict between these Gods is never-ending. Or, in non-figurative language, life is about the incompatibility of ultimate possible attitudes and hence the inability ever to resolve the conflict between them. Hence the necessity of deciding between them'.[44]

In the legal sphere, this foundational crisis expresses itself in the fact that 'the axioms of natural law have lost all capacity to provide the fundamental basis of a legal system'.[45] No longer capable of deriving its validity from transcendent theological-cultural beliefs, modern law must take a positivist form and draw its validity from a logically abstract set of formal rules immanent to the legal sphere. In this positivist framework, all expressions of substantive values must be integrated into a formal process that requires the application of laws to go beyond the specific case and that institutes a mechanism of checks and balances to mediate between competing interests and values. Authority in this self-enclosed legal system is therefore both formalised and rationalised. All norms immanent to the legal sphere must derive their validity from a previous norm. This leads to an impossible attempt to ban all subjective moral or emotional judgements concerning the substance of the law and to organise the latter by rationally and legally defined procedures. As Weber argued, modern logical formalism necessarily de-personalises the legal system and subsumes all concrete facticity under abstract rules. It 'enables the legal system to operate like a technically rational machine' and confines the judge or decision-maker to the mechanical application of already-existing law.[46] Yet, as Weber knew all too well, this abstract formalism in reality is never really cleansed of subjective judgement. For, there is always a gap between concrete reality and abstract law (fact and norm) that must be mediated by the subjective interpretation of the individual decision-maker.[47]

Schmitt developed his decisionist jurisprudence at the juncture between factual power and legal form. For him, the modern legal positivist attempt at objectifying political authority and subjecting it to the formal and rational rule of law rested on an ill-fated logical impasse that could only be resolved through an existential—i.e. normatively ungrounded—political decision. If the highest underived power is the norm that establishes the rule of law, it must necessarily be subject to law itself, otherwise it simply exempts itself in the same manner as sovereignty operates. Yet if this highest underived power is enclosed within the predefined procedures of the legal system, it cannot be the highest underived power, since its actions must be declared legal or illegal by an authority that must necessarily be higher. To arrive at a point of origin, an underived norm that will determine the right procedures, there must be a political act of creation *ex nihilo*—i.e. a normatively ungrounded decision on the substance of the legal form. For Schmitt, and this is the core feature of decisionism as a constitutional-legal theory, the arbitrary exercise of power is a permanent and immanent condition of the normative order.[48] As he emphasised in his *Nomos of the Earth*, the structure of international law is, and has always been, underpinned by a concrete, spatially delimited hierarchy of powers that is invested with symbolic meanings—i.e. a *nomos*. When this hierarchy dissolves, either war ensues or a new ordering principle is enforced by the dominant powers to replace the older one. So that at the foundation of all states, of all empires and of all legal systems there is an original violence, not a founding norm.[49]

Had Schmitt lived for another decade, he would not have been surprised to see that the collapse of the Cold War frame of intelligibility has brought the 'problem of sovereignty' back to the top of the political agenda. Today, however, the 'problem of sovereignty' is rendered transnationally and against the backdrop of an emerging global public sphere. As Fukuyama put it, the one defining question in global politics for the twenty-first century will be:

who gets to decide on whose sovereignty to violate, and on what grounds. To what extent does it remain the prerogative of sovereign nation-states, and to what degree must such decisions be constrained by international laws or norms? These questions take us into the domain of a different set of democratic legitimacy issues, this time focused not so much on individual states but on the international system. This debate has exposed an enormous gulf between the United States and its European allies, which is likely to be a neuralgic source of friction for some time to come.[50]

For neoconservatives the answers to these questions are straightforward. America is the only power that has the global reach and competence to police the international order and bridge the gap between fact and norm when the latter cannot be closed through normal procedures. As we have seen in the last chapter, neoconservatives maintain that the end of the Cold War, globalisation and recent technological developments have produced a security environment which is at odd with both the Westphalian *modus operandi* of contemporary international society and the woolly and encumbering multilateralism of global liberal governance favoured by Europeans. Terrorism, state-failure and the proliferation of weapons of mass destruction pose a series of 'exceptional' existential threats not only to America but to the modern international order as a whole that cannot be addressed within the limits of existing normative and legal frameworks. While the more cerebral among them recognise that hegemonic power needs a significant degree of legitimacy, they nevertheless insist that hegemonic legitimacy cannot presuppose multilateralism and law abidingness.[51] As Kagan argues in his latest book, if left unattended, the relative decline of American power over the last five years or so could spell the end not only of the American century but of the global liberal order as a whole:

> People who believe greater equality among nations would be preferable to the present American predominance often succumb to a basic logical fallacy. They believe the order the world enjoys today exists independently of American power… But that's not the way it works. International order does not rest on ideas and institutions. It is shaped by configurations of power. The international order we know today reflects the distribution of power since World War II, and especially since the end of the Cold War. A different configuration of power, a multipolar world in which the poles were Russia, China, the United States, India and Europe, would produce its own kind of order, with different rules and norms reflecting the interests of the powerful states that would have a hand in shaping it.[52]

As in Schmitt, the aim of these arguments is not to discard the relevance of norms in conditions of anarchy (as in a neorealist reading of the international system, for example). Rather, it is to re-assert the continued indispensability of American sovereignty even as America's closest allies are moving away from the power politics of sovereignty towards the 'brave new judicial world' anticipated by advocates of global governance.[53] Indeed, as James Ceaser explains, for neoconservatives the necessity of rallying the nation behind the case for American sovereignty follows precisely from the waning of the metaphysics of sovereignty in Europe:

> What has changed is not the importance of the nation for *us*, but its importance for others. Other nations do not bear the primary responsibility for maintaining a world order; when they engage in action under our umbrella they are less likely to use a national rhetoric and more apt to speak in terms of enforcing an international norm. At the same time, therefore, that we must think more nationally than before, we must accept that others will be thinking more internationally. Our understanding of the nation must be different from others' because our power and responsibilities are different. We must be prepared to make appropriate demands and claim appropriate prerogatives for the nation—this nation, at any rate—even when others oppose or condemn this.[54]

Beyond Autonomy and Policy Flexibility

What should we make of these sovereigntist arguments? As various critics have argued, given the highly interdependent environment in which we live today, the suggestion that sovereign, unilateral policies are optimal for the US makes little sense from a pragmatic point of view. Ruggie, for instance, argues that sovereigntists unwisely privilege 'doctrine over practical considerations' in making their case and along the way completely misconstrue the nature of international authority. Their attack on global governance, he argues, 'externalises and objectifies the very concept [of international authority], as though this authority were embodied in some*one* or some*thing* other than states'. 'With rare exception', he emphasises, 'authority in global governance involves no formal relations of super-and-subordination, but remains largely horizontal in character'.[55] Along similar lines, Andrew Moravcsik argues that the picture of the EU as a nascent, socialist super-state whose governing elites are not accountable to anyone is obviously a gross mischaracterisation of the democratic deficit and the residual commitments to social democracy in Europe. In his view, American sovereigntists are deluded '"conservative idealists" for whom "autonomy" and "sovereignty" is an end in itself, regardless of the concrete consequences'.[56] Invoking the work of Robert Keohane and Stephen Krasner on international regimes, he emphasises that welfare-maximisation in a globalised capitalist economy requires policy coordination and stresses that the collective action problems of international cooperation can only be resolved efficiently with a high degree of institutionalisation.[57]

These are legitimate criticisms, but they are somewhat missing the point. First, the American Right is by no means opposed to forms of policy coordination that bind others through liberal institutionalisation—as long as America is granted 'special prerogatives and exemptions' from this process wherever it sees fit.[58] Secondly, and more importantly, what is really at stake for neoconservatives in those debates is not only the policy autonomy and flexibility of the United States. It is also the symbolic and cultural resources attached to the communitarian interpretation of democracy that they have nurtured in support of their domestic political and economic agenda since the 1960s. My main contention here is that it is not really the link between the normative order and democracy as an emancipatory value in itself that is being defended by neoconservatives in those debates. Rather, it is the tie between the normative order and democracy as an ideal that is constitutive of a particular way of life and sustains a particular pattern of hegemonic relations between domestic social forces.

As we have seen, the challenge of global governance for neoconservatives has to do with the transformation of international law from a mechanism regulating interstate relations to a regime of individual rights which demands that we think of individual identity and rights as being prior to political association. In this setting, the state remains an important institution but it ceases to be an end in itself. It exists strictly to provide the environment in which individuals can pursue their interests at will. It is one of many intermediate associations competing with ethnic groups, religious groups, professional guilds, corporations and other such identity-conferring social formations for the loyalty of its members. As the constitutional scholar Paul W. Kahn points out, this whole process institutes a whole new, 'postmodern' understanding of the relationship between law and rights whereby law ceases to 'function as an expression of popular sovereignty that chooses to invest itself in particular rights ... and gains its legitimacy from the defence of rights'.[59]

Unsurprisingly, neoconservatives argue that this 'postmodern' interpretation of the relationship between law and rights is fundamentally at odds with America's republican constitutional tradition. They insist that the legitimacy of positive law is derived first and foremost from the fact that it expresses the will of an historical community. From this republican perspective, the exceptional character of America's political experience stems not so much from the fact that the American constitution expresses a set of universal values, but from the fact that Americans have agreed to govern themselves according to universal principles of natural right.[60] As in the ideal-typical model of liberal government, democratic politics here is about the representation of private social interests through the administrative framework of state institutions. But it is also conceived as a 'reflexive form of substantial ethical life' that expresses the self-understanding and the perspectival conceptions of the good life of particular groups.[61] Accordingly, the law in this context ties citizenship not only to a set of rights but also to a common obligation to maintain and carry the project of popular sovereignty into the future. As in all liberal interpretations, the law is seen as a critical means to prevent abuse of power and impose constraints on government. But it does so in the name of an historical community and its system of values rather than individual rights per se.[62] Bolton makes this point starkly with regard to the death penalty in his tirades against human rights regimes: 'Americans in the last several decades have soberly examined the death penalty, and by and large reaffirmed it in a textbook demonstration of popular sovereignty at work'.[63]

Neoconservatives nevertheless insist that, despite some relatively minor disagreements, Americans understand their political experience to be fully compatible with the moral substance of international law and human rights regime. But they stress that such a common moral ground cannot be the basis for a common political identity. Moral values can only become constitutive of a collective political identity when they express the will of the democratic majority. And this, they argue, necessarily entails the drawing of boundaries to determine who is a member of the political community and who is not. As Rabkin argues:

> To feel obligated by the decision of the requisite majority in the framing of a constitution, one must already accept the necessity or appropriateness of living under the same system with those others who make the majority. When we speak of America as a democracy, we imply that government is accountable to the majority of our own people. For there to be a democracy, there must first be a demos—a distinct people.[64]

Now, from a normative perspective, the problem with this substantive understanding of democracy is that it ultimately rests upon a normative a priori which ultimately is just as 'pre-political' as the cosmopolitan interpretation of human rights regimes. Whereas the latter confer rights on individuals prior to political association, neoconservatives define legal status in terms of civil rights that are made contingent upon membership in a democratic community whose boundaries are prior to and beyond normative justification. They are prior to and beyond normative justification simply because democracies cannot democratically determine their own membership.[65] This democratic paradox is what Habermas calls the normative 'conceptual gap in the legal construction of the constitutional state'. On the one hand, democratic constitutionalism as a joint practice necessarily requires some form of commonality. On the other hand, the social boundaries of any constitutional association are purely arbitrary since, beyond the fiction of the social contract, it is the reality of war, civil war and imperialism that has historically settled the civic and social boundaries of the different political communities.[66] During the past centuries, nationalism has 'concealed' the arbitrariness of the nation's boundaries. It has done so by appealing to the notion of an organic national consciousness crystallised around the idea of a common history, ancestry and language and together worked to naturalise the boundaries of the different political communities. This ethno-nationalist interpretation of citizenship has contributed immensely to providing the cultural impetus necessary for the consolidation of the modern constitutional state as we know it today.[67]

The United States is generally seen as an exception in this respect, since the social compact in America took hold in a multiethnic setting. American nationalism, neoconservatives like to remind us, is nothing like European nationalism. It is not based on blood and soil but on a civic religion sustained by 'deep truths' and a 'set of universal principles derived from natural rights as enunciated in the Declaration of Independence'.[68] Such claims, however, should be treated with caution. The 200-year-old constitutional history of the American republic is indeed remarkable proof that the nation-state can take a republican form even in the absence of a culturally homogenous population. But this should not obscure the fact that the civic religion from which American nationalism draws its exceptional character is itself rooted in the majority culture of the White, Protestant Anglo-Saxon population. Historically, this hegemonic culture has performed a very similar function to that of ethnic nationalism in Europe: it has provided the 'pre-political' basis of a cultural substrate for a legally defined republican citizenship status and set the terms for the assimilation of minorities into the shared political culture. This cultural substrate is 'pre-political' in the sense that normatively and empirically it skews the ethical embedding of the law in a manner that is strictly contingent on the social make-up of the population, which itself is extrinsic to the bundle of rights and legal principles of the constitutional state. As Habermas explains:

> Legal orders as wholes are also 'ethically imbued' in that they interpret the universalistic content of the same constitutional principles in different ways, namely, against the background of the experiences that make up a national history and in light of a historically prevailing tradition, culture, and form of life. Often the regulation of culturally sensitive matters, such as the official language, the public school curriculum, the status of churches and religious communities and the norms of criminal law (e.g., those regulating abortion), but also of less obvious matters such as the status of the family and marriage-like partnerships, the acceptance of security standards, or the demarcation of the private from the public realm, is merely a reflection of the ethical-political self-understanding of a majority culture that has achieved dominance for contingent, historical reasons.[69]

It is the 'pre-constitutional' hegemonic position of the majority culture in this liberal democratic framework that is at stake for neoconservatives in contemporary debates over the constitutionalisation of the global liberal order. Global liberal governance threatens to sever the tie between deliberative politics and the national consciousness of a macro-subject rooted in the ethical self-understanding of the majority culture. Instead, its leading advocates expect the success of democratic politics to follow from a higher and more abstract level of inter-subjectivity derived strictly from the institutionalisation of free and equal deliberative procedures ultimately grounded in a global constitutional order of rights—including cultural rights.[70]

This is an all-out negation of the neoconservative vision of America, along with the whole structure of cultural and socio-economic interests associated with it. As we have seen in previous chapters, neoconservatism emerged during the past four decades or so as a reaction and response to the perceived disintegration of the majority culture in the face of cultural diversification and popular demands for the extension of democratic citizenship to include not only liberal individual rights and rights of political participation but also social and cultural rights. According to neoconservatives, the cultural revolutions of the 1960s and the ensuing 'tragedy of multiculturalism' have undermined the universalist liberalism that inspired the American Revolution. It has introduced in its place a relativist liberalism that celebrates cultural individuality and no longer asserts the rights of man but of man as a Black, a Jew, a Muslim, a worker, a woman, a homosexual etc.[71] As Allan Bloom put it in *The Closing of the American Mind* (1987):

> That dominant majority gave the country a dominant culture with its traditions, its literature, its tastes, its special claim to know and supervise the language, and its Protestant religions. Much of the intellectual machinery of twentieth-century American political thought and social science was constructed for the purposes of making an assault on that majority. It treated the founding principles as impediments and tried to overcome the other strand of our political heritage, majoritarianism, in favor of a nation of minorities and groups each following its own beliefs and inclinations. In particular, the intellectual minority expected to enhance its status, presenting itself as the defender and spokesman of all the others.[72]

It is in this context that neoconservative resistance to global governance and the constitutionalisation of the international order must be understood. Global governance and a human rights regime are premised on a liberal interpretation of democracy in which the ethical self-understanding of the majority culture no longer mediates between the rule of law, popular sovereignty and democratic legitimation. To the particularism of a democratic community united by its historical commitment to a set of values held to be universal by its members, global liberal governance opposes a vision of democracy in which free individuals are united in the universalism of a multicultural and egalitarian legal community. The integrative force of this cosmopolitan framework is thought to be derived not from its substantive cultural content, but from its universal ethical value as a mechanism for mediating between different conceptions of the good and sources of political identity. As Fonte explains, 'Democratic national sovereigntists more or less support a form of patriotic assimilation that was successful in twentieth-century America...' By contrast, for the global progressives, '"integration" means the incorporation of a specific immigrant community as a specific community that retains loyalties to authorities outside the host democratic nation-state'.[73]

Against global progressives, neoconservatives maintain that the liberal constitutional state cannot sustain itself in the absence of a vibrant national consciousness which provides the ethical underpinnings for a legal system of liberal rights. They argue that downplaying national identity in favour of an open and tolerant post-national society can only lead to the disintegration of the political order into a multiplicity of conflicting ethical-cultural communities, each integrated around its own conception of the common good.[74] The 'counterproductive multiculturalist policies that sheltered radicalism' in Europe ever since the end of the Cold War, or so we are told, should serve as a warning of what such a post-national order has in store for 'the West' if those policies are not reversed at once: 'Remember Theo Van Gogh and Shudder for the Future' (Fukuyama).[75] For neoconservatives, global governance and the 'new' international law is not only a challenge to US sovereignty but also to the very existence of the American regime and its transmission to future generations. As Fonte argues:

> If our system is based not on individual rights, but on group consciousness; not on equality of citizenship, but on group preferences for non-citizens (including illegal immigrants) and for certain categories of citizens; not on majority rule within constitutional limits, but on power-sharing by different ethnic, racial, gender and linguistic groups; not on constitutional law but on transnational law; not on immigrants becoming Americans, but on migrants linked between transnational communities; then the regime will cease to be 'constitutional', 'liberal', 'democratic', and 'American', in the understood sense of those terms, but will become in reality a new hybrid system that is '"post-constitutional", "post-liberal", "post-democratic", and "post-American"'.[76]

For Fonte and his colleagues, the idea of subordinating American universals to some form of pluralistic, global constitutional order is simply the latest expression of a modernist relativism against which the American Right has sought to guard the republic since the 1960s. As Fukuyama explains, because the notion of democratic legitimacy from which international institutions draw their authority accommodates various types of moral and political cultures, it necessarily involves the abandonment of a standard of right and wrong independent of positive right. By associating and entrusting their commitment to a liberal moral order with global institutions, he argues, European and American advocates of global liberal governance adopt a procedural understanding of democratic legitimacy that in fact contradicts their belief in a hierarchy of moral values. For neoconservatives, the legitimacy of a constitutional order must necessarily come from the 'prior rights and norms that come from a moral realm higher than that of the legal order'.[77] Here 'there can be no clear dividing line between the domestic and the foreign'.[78] Abandoning sovereignty and American foreign policy to this emerging legal culture would empty the ideal democracy of its moral and cultural substance and deprive the Right of a key site for political mobilisation in its effort to roll back multiculturalism, re-moralise the social contract and contain the debilitating effects of cultural modernity. As Kagan and Kristol put it in their neo-Reaganite manifesto: 'The remoralisation of America at home ultimately requires the remoralisation of American foreign policy. For both follow from American's belief that the principles of the declaration of Independence are not merely the choices of a particular culture but are universal, enduring, "self-evident" truth. That has been, after all, the main point of the conservatives' war against a relativistic multiculturalism'.[79]

'Culturalising' Sovereignty, 'Americanising' Norms

Linking national autonomy with a culturally charged interpretation of democracy in this manner necessarily has implications for the ways in which sovereignty is being practised in the international arena. This is best illustrated by contrasting the neoconservative position with a cosmopolitan rendering of the relationship between state sovereignty and the contemporary normative order. As Habermas argues, in the latter, sovereignty is tied to the private and public autonomy enjoyed by all who participate as free and equal subjects in the democratic process. External sovereignty in this case has to do primarily with the quest for state power and securing the existence of the political community. The deliberative model of democracy associated with this reading of sovereignty sets up strict criteria concerning how domestic political rule is legitimated and what a legitimate international order would ideally look like. But those criteria do not necessarily affect the way external sovereignty is exercised.[80] By contrast, the substantive notion of democracy defended by neoconservatives assumes an essential link between the freedom and liberties of the people and the external independence of that people, since in this account the nation—a macro subject rooted in the ethical self-understanding of the majority culture—mediates between the rule of law and democracy. External sovereignty in this setting is therefore not only about preserving state power and the existence of the political community but also about securing its particular cultural character over and against other nations. 'The meaning of democratic self-determination based on the majority culture is not the political autonomy of individual citizens but rather national independence—the self-assertion, self-affirmation, and self-realisation of a nation in its specificity'.[81]

There is, of course, nothing exceptional about the fact that American nationalists consider the American experience to be exceptional and want to assert that myth through a politics of sovereignty. Many political communities have their own myth of exceptionalism and have appealed to it to justify various policies and claim various prerogatives in the past. But the crucial difference here is that American exceptionalism also claims to be universal in its particularity and must insist on the desirability and necessity of being emulated to validate and perpetuate itself. 'Americans', we are told, 'believe their nation has meaning ... only as it realises natural right and reason throughout the universe'.[82] It is this existential projection of American universals that differentiates the conservative internationalism of neoconservatives from the isolationist *paleoconservatism* of the likes of Pat Buchanan, Paul Craig Roberts and Paul Gottfried. As James Ceaser explains:

> Conservative internationalists see no difficulty in squaring the assertion of universal principles with a belief in the nation and national purpose. What is more an expression of the particular mission of *this* nation than to give voice to the universal principles on which it was founded? To renounce this element of the American founding in the name of avoiding internationalism would mean, ironically, to reject the foundation of our own nationalism. It would be to relinquish our specificity.[83]

American exceptionalism in this interpretation therefore sees itself as the expression of the historical unfolding of a universal morality that is fundamentally at odds with the procedural character of modern international law. As Kagan argues, 'By nature, tradition, and ideology the United States has generally favored the promotion of liberal principles over the niceties of Westphalian diplomacy. Despite its role in helping to create the UN and draft the UN Charter, the United States has never fully accepted the organisation's legitimacy or the charter's doctrine of sovereign equality'.[84] Neoconservatives nevertheless insist that the US is unreservedly committed to the establishment and preservation of a liberal order. But it is a liberal order 'with American power at the centre and with America as the indispensable nation'.[85]

These nationalist ruminations highlight the close conceptual link between the communitarian interpretation of democracy exposed above and the decisionist reading of the normative order discussed earlier. For neoconservatives, American popular sovereignty draws its meaning from the instantiation of the nation's historical role as the 'indispensable' decider and enforcer of natural rights over the relativistic normative structure of international society. Thus what renders the practice of sovereignty particularly volatile in this setting is not only that it links external autonomy with the self-realisation of an historical community. It is the fact that it does so by asserting the unmediated ethical identity of a particular way of life with a universal system of moral values from which political principles of international legitimacy ought to be derived. In other words, neoconservative discourses collapse the limits between fact and norms that are normally mediated by objective procedures and endow the law with general universal validity. International law here remains an indispensable means to restrain others, and therefore a valuable source of international stability. But it is envisaged as the institutionalisation of unmediated universals rather than as a set of procedural mechanisms for the management of political and cultural antagonisms.[86]

And this is where the neoconservative case for sovereignty against global liberal governance loses all plausibility. Its conceptual, political and normative failure stems from the fact that it rests upon two conflicting notions of politics: one particularistic and one universalistic. In the first, politics is defined by antagonism and the constant possibility of war. In this realist universe, conflicts can be resolved but human nature and the irremediable differentiation of modern society into incommensurable value spheres set limits on the possibility of a universally accepted notion of the common good. This both guarantees the autonomy of the political from other spheres of human activity and ensures that arbitrary violence will always remain an endemic feature of liberal civilisation. Politics in this setting is therefore not a contest over the actualisation of a universal good, but a mechanism that negotiates and limits conflicts stemming from the impossibility of such a universal rational agreement. The other notion of politics underpinning the discourses surveyed above is one that sees politics as the historical unfolding of a 'worldwide liberal revolution' characterised by the pacific expansion of a universal morality led by the US.[87] Here, politics is driven by a belief in the *possibility* of an eventual universal agreement on what constitutes a good society.

The nature and implications of this conceptual tension will be explored in more detail in the next chapter. For the moment, let us simply note that this identity-conferring moralisation of the political differentiates neoconservative decisionism from Schmitt's decisionism in a very important manner. As we will recall, Schmitt defended state sovereignty and the state's right to wage war as a correlate of his interpretation of the antagonistic nature and autonomy of the political. In his view, the need for a sovereign who stands both inside and outside the law and has the factual capacity to decide on the exception necessarily followed from the inevitable grouping of humanity into friends and enemies. But he insisted that the friend-enemy distinction should always be drawn on a strictly political manner, not on an ethical basis. Schmitt's defence of the sovereign state as a culturally homogenous unit against the pluralist and differentiated civil society of liberalism was at the service of a pluralist international order of formally equal sovereign states. For him, preserving the autonomy of the political was a means to allow for the possibility of legitimate dissent and the management of estranged relations between states.

Neoconservatives also presuppose the inevitable grouping of humanity into friends and enemies, and they build their defence of American sovereignty against global liberal governance and multiculturalism on its behalf. Yet, not unlike in Strauss's moralisation of Schmitt's concept of the political, they ultimately end up collapsing this fundamental political distinction into a universal ethics that purports to establish the moral authority of US sovereignty over the procedural universalisms of international law and institutions. This move generates a particularly aggressive and totalising form of conservative internationalism which is radically anti-pluralist both *inside* and *outside* the state and leaves no possibility for dissent to find any legitimate form of expression. As we have seen during the Bush presidency, it is a crusading conservatism that paradoxically thrives on the cultivation of otherness while at the same time seeking to overcome all estrangement from the 'other' by putting enemies beyond the realm of humanity and cultivating contempt for dissenting friends and allies who challenge unmediated expressions of American values.

The absence of a legitimate 'other' in the neoconservative construction of US sovereignty discredits whatever legitimate grievances neoconservatives may have against the contemporary project of global governance. Sovereigntists have good reason to question the viability and desirability of the constitutionalised global order wished for by the high priests of global governance. The constitutionalisation of the global order amounts to no less than a complete reversal of the ordering principle of the international system. International law in this setting would no longer exist to guarantee the formal equality of states but to ensure the compliance of the latter to a set of ideals whose political impartiality and ethical universalism remain highly contentious. To reduce politics to the application and policing of an abstract rational consensus is to deny the plurality of interests and values that characterise politics as a human activity. Kant himself warned against attempts at establishing constitutions that are geared towards ethical rather than political ends. For him, a normative order could only be established upon a set of tensions that leaves room for the indeterminacy and contingency of political action.[88]

Beyond these ethical considerations, the practical problem of enforcement raised by sovereigntist critics of global governance should also be taken seriously. As one commentator pointed out, the main problem here is that advocates of global governance must presuppose that coercive power as an attribute of states can be severed from its source in social relations and be 'borrowed' by international institutions '"from domestic government officials to implement supranational rules and decisions"'.[89] Such an asocial and functional view of power rests upon a silence about the real possibility of disagreement and dissent that mirrors the ideological zeal and asocial understanding of power of the most ardent American hegemonists. Those who call for a new set of norms involving a radical re-interpretation of the notion and function of international law tend to forget that this 'brave new judicial world' can itself only be imposed through conflict and political struggle. This much we have learned from the process of decolonisation.

Yet, and this is where both Schmittians and neoconservatives go wrong, politics needs law to legitimise its objectives. Law does this by 'universalising those objectives and inscribing in formal procedures the guarantees and sanctions tied to the pursuit of democratic objectives in a world of inequality and violence'.[90] As Jean Cohen argues, 'The concept of sovereignty is a reminder not only of the political context of law but also of the ultimate dependence of political power and political regimes on a valid, public, normative legal order for their authority'.[91] True, in times of uncertainty it is power that puts an end to endless deliberations and resolves differences of opinion. However, although it may indeed be born of legal nothingness, the sovereign decision on the exception is not a self-justificatory act. There is a gap between act and justification and between rule and legitimacy that is independent from neither politics nor law but that cannot be reduced to any one of them. In the international arena, this gap between pure power politics and positive law is where international institutions operate and can, however imperfectly, mediate between competing universalisms and conflicting conceptions of the good life.[92]

The American Right, and the United States more generally, paid a high price for not taking international institutions seriously during the Bush presidency. Yet, in spite of its humbling defeat in the November 2008 elections, it is very unlikely that the Right will ever become more accommodating in this respect. For, as our analysis suggests, its opposition to global liberal governance goes beyond the usual realist concerns over the inexpediency of multilateral diplomacy and the lack of viable enforcement mechanisms in the absence of a global leviathan. The Right has a vested interest in opposing American participation in legal frameworks of global governance simply because the procedural ethics that underpin the latter reduce the scope for a moralisation of politics outside of positive law. Global liberal governance deprives the American Right of its favourite political terrain. It mines the cultural categories and domestic patterns of hegemonic relations that the conservative movement wants to preserve and that ultimately constitute its very *raison d'être*.

6

A LIBERALISM BETRAYED?

'Granting the Bush critics part of their point, it can be admitted that pursuing democracy became too inflexible a doctrine. Foreign policy is a practical realm in which the primary aim is to promote the nation's security and interest. There is no room for an ethics of intention, only for an ethics of results or responsibility. No nation should follow a formula for its own sake. But this obvious counsel of prudence leaves open the question of what it is that promotes our security and interests... Does anyone believe that democrats in Tehran, Havana, or Caracas are celebrating today the triumph of the cool realists in Washington? It is a dictum of our new foreign policy that "moral hubris" is out and "humility" is in. This is fine so long as humility does not turn into its own form of hubris, giving the green light everywhere to the forces of oppression. Democrats now run the risk of turning their vaunted new doctrine of realism into a rigid ideology. It would be much better to follow the sober advice of that unerring scholar of international relations, Polonius: Neither an idealist nor a realist be'.

James Ceaser[1]

By way of a conclusion, this last chapter offers a conceptual reconstruction and critique of the idiosyncratic mixture of realism and idealism that characterises the neoconservative mode of political engagement with the world. As we have seen during the course of this study, this synthesis is constituted by two conflicting conceptions of politics: one communitarian and 'naturalistic', the other universal and utopian. In what follows, I argue that this is not an ideological inconsistency but the manifestation of a nihilistic and deeply atavistic form of *Realpolitik*. This *Realpolitik* is 'essential' to the nature of neoconservatism as an ideology. It accounts for much of the incoherent fit between the emancipatory rhetoric of neoconservative discourse and the oppressive neo-Hobbesian character of neoconservative politics.

That neoconservatism is nihilistic and has anything to do with an onerous, authoritarian tradition of European diplomacy its protagonists will deny vehemently. According to neoconservatives, their aversion for multilateralism and international institutions is the expression of a distinctively American and more assertive liberalism. This, neoconservatives tell us, is a progressive liberalism of substance rather than a timid liberalism of procedures; a liberalism that does not let its belief in human rights and universal values be naively constrained by a relativistic regime of international law which grants equal status to all states irrespective of regime types. As Robert Kagan explains:

> The problem is that the modern liberal vision of progress in international affairs has always been bifocal. On the one hand, liberalism has entertained since the Enlightenment a vision of world peace based on an ever-strengthening international legal system. The success of such a system rests on the recognition that all nations, big or small, democratic or tyrannical, humane or barbarous, are equal sovereign entities. On the other hand, modern liberalism cherishes the rights and liberties of the individual and defines progress as the greater protection of these rights and liberties across the globe. In the absence of a sudden global democratic and liberal transformation, that goal can be achieved only by compelling tyrannical or barbarous regimes to behave more humanely, sometimes through force. Given the tension between these two aspirations, what constitutes international legitimacy will inevitably be a matter of dispute within the liberal world. This is a problem for all liberals.[2]

Yet one does not have to look very far to find evidence of the false universalist pretence of neoconservative internationalism. Consider Kagan's own bestseller, *Of Paradise and Power* (2003), for example. After having reprimanded Europeans for not being true to their commitment to the universal ethics of liberalism when invoking international law to constrain America's *mission civilisatrice*, Kagan explains that:

> [a]ny 'rules-based' international order must apply the same sets of rules to different situations. Otherwise we return to a world where nations individually or in groups decide for themselves when a war is and is not justified, guided by their own morality and sense of justice and order. In fact that is the world we live in, and the only world we have ever lived in. It is a world where those with

power, believing they have right on their side, impose their sense of justice on others.[3]

According to Kagan, appeals to law and morality in global politics are the *natural* manifestation of a will to power that lacks other means to play the geopolitical game: 'Those who favor security through international law and institutions will constantly downplay the world's irrationality and brutality'.[4] Drawing on Thucydides and a Nietzschean psychology of power (or a Nietzschean reading of Thucydides? More on this in a moment), Kagan argues that a nation's strategic culture is shaped by its geopolitical condition. Thus, whereas a militarily powerful nation like the US will not hesitate to use force to pursue its national interest, military weak states will pursue their national interests by invoking the sanctity of international law and multilateral diplomacy: 'Their tactics, like their goal, are the tactics of the weak. They hope to constrain American power without wielding power themselves. In what may be the ultimate feat of subtlety and indirection, they want to control the behemoth by appealing to its conscience'. Europe's Kantian position thus distorts *reality* to justify a foreign policy dictated not by progressive ethical concerns but by its weakness relative to the United States. According to Kagan, these are the 'natural consequences of the transatlantic power gap':

> When the United States was weak, it practiced the strategies of indirection, the strategies of weakness; now that the United States is powerful, it behaves as powerful nations do. When the European great powers were strong, they believed in strength and martial glory. Now, they see the world through the eyes of weaker powers. These very different points of view, weak versus strong, have naturally produced differing strategic judgments, differing assessments of threats and of the proper means of addressing threats, and even differing calculations of interest.[5]

Peter Berkowitz sees this same natural will to power at work in Europe's insistence on the norm of sovereign equality underwriting the international legal order:

> The experience of equality fosters resentment of those who are stronger and more prosperous. This, as Nietzsche argued in his career-long polemic against equality, is where things get ugly... When resentment takes hold, the appeal to individual rights can serve as a vehicle for the unconscious as well as the calculated and cynical bid to power. Many of the wayward passions stirred up by equality are at work in Europe's ambition to portray international law and international institutions as the comprehensive means for securing global order.[6]

Needless to say, the Nietzschean doctrine of the will to power has little to do with the liberal tradition that neoconservatives claim for themselves in foreign affairs. In order to appreciate fully what is really at stake in these Nietzschean tropes, it is important to remind ourselves briefly of the basic premises of this realist appropriation of Nietzsche.

Will to Power

Nietzsche's controversial doctrine of the will to power found its way into the jargon of twentieth-century realism in various forms through the writings of prominent German theorists associated with the realist school such as Max Weber, Carl Schmitt, Reinhold Niebuhr (his parents were German immigrants), Hans Morgenthau and Leo Strauss.[7] The conservative and 'realist' dimension of Nietzsche's otherwise complex and multifaceted doctrine has to do with the claim that '"Exploitation" does not pertain to a corrupt or imperfect or primitive society: it pertains to the essence of the living thing as a fundamental organic function, it is a consequence of the intrinsic will to power which is precisely the will of life'.[8] Or as Morgenthau put it, the lust for power (*Lustprinzip*) is 'inseparable from social life itself'. It is a 'constitutive element of all human associations, from the family through fraternal and professional associations and local political organisations to the state'.[9] Crucially, the organic drive that grounds the will to power is by no means limited to, or determined by, a mere desire for self-preservation. As Nietzsche argued, 'Physiologists should think again before postulating the drive for self-preservation as the cardinal drive in an organic being. A living thing desires above to vent its strength—life as such is will to power—self-preservation is only one of the indirect and most frequent consequences of it'.[10]

This is consistent with the vitalist reading of Hobbes that we have encountered in this study. In this reading, we will remember, power is sought not only in utilitarian terms as a means for self-preservation but also, and more fundamentally, as a means for self-creation, self-overcoming, and self-assertion over others. Will to power is a doctrine of inevitable conflict that presupposes the ineluctable presence of counterforces, obstacles, undesirable others and 'monsters to destroy': 'will to power can manifest itself only against resistances; therefore it seeks that which resists it'.[11]

The will to power is a thoroughly tragic doctrine. It reminds us with unsettling lucidity that human existence is constituted by merciless forces and negative constraints—suffering, pain, death, loss, struggle—that impose limits on our highest moral aspirations and that can only be endured if one accepts the determinant impact of those forces on the human condition. As Morgenthau explains in the opening pages of *Politics Among Nations*, 'The world, imperfect as it is from the rational point of view, is the result of forces inherent in human nature. To improve the world one must work with those forces, not against them. This being inherently a world of opposing interests and of conflict among them, moral principles can never be fully realised…'[12] The will to power is therefore a negation of the Kantian notion of the 'free will' underpinning enlightenment narratives of progress. As Nietzsche argued, the notion of a will that is free in the sense that it is not caused by something prior to itself is an intellectual error that was engineered by the monotheistic religions to render man accountable to a transcendent god. Like everything in this modern godless world, the human will is caught in a chain of causality; if the will appears to be free and events often appear to be random, it is only because we cannot grasp the causal chain of events behind them. The will to power is a will that is not free but that is driven by unconscious psychological impulses.[13] It rests on a set of productive tensions between nature, culture and meaning that drives the historical process in perpetual cycles of energetic growth and decay rather than in a teleological manner. As Lawrence Hatab explains:

> Nature by itself is raw will to power, the ongoing struggle between opposing life forces in the unending cycle of victory and defeat, life and death. By itself, nature has no 'meaning', no purpose or value in its blind instinctive energies. Yet out of nature there emerges the human ability to form meaning and value in its cultural capacity to exceed the sheer immediacy of instinct, which by way of language is able to develop a reflective sense of time and thus create values that inform the present with past inheritances and future goals.[14]

The will to power thus sees culture and civilisation as being born out of, and transformative of, natural forces. Although culture—i.e. norms, traditions, law, institutions—can redirect the struggle for power into socially acceptable channels and contain its violent and destructive potential, nature and the 'evils of power' remain determinant of the fate of even the most 'civilised' societies. For the will to power is itself the main drive behind the civilising process. From this perspective, the modern nation-state, which has historically been shaped and constituted not only by the recurrence of war but also by the constant preparation of modern societies for the act of war, is not an emancipation from the state of nature but a collectivisation and external projection of the private lust for power onto the international arena. As Ned Lebow explains in his study of Morgenthau, 'The power of the state feeds on itself through a process of psychological transference. Impulses constrained by ethics and law are mobilised by the state for its own ends. By transferring their egotism to the nation, people gain vicarious release for their otherwise repressed impulses. What was formerly egotism, and ignoble and immoral, now became patriotism, and noble and altruistic'.[15] Thus just as state power grows when external counter-forces intensify, civil society decays and relapses towards the war of all against all when those counter-forces recede. Or as Strauss puts it in his critique of the liberal state: 'Liberalism, sheltered by and engrossed in a world of culture, forgets the foundations of culture, the state of nature, that is, human nature in its dangerousness and endangeredness'.[16]

This is where will to power and the realist doctrine of reason of state meet. As Reinhart Koselleck explains in *Critique and Crisis*, the rational need to found a state to render the will to power tolerable for individuals by projecting it onto the international arena removes all difference there exists between morality and politics. It transforms 'the moral alternative of good and evil into the political alternative of peace and war'.[17] In this Hobbesian universe, reason 'creates a neutral zone of State "technology" in which there is no law but the prince's will. In such a State only the formal legality of the laws is rational, not their content; therefore the political commandment of political morality to obey the laws regardless of their content is reasonable'.[18]

Now, from a neoconservative perspective, the problem with this subordination of moral reason to political reason is that it is unsustainable in a modern liberal polity whose national identity and historical experience have been so significantly shaped by the progressive discourse of the Enlightenment. As Kristol grudgingly reminds us, it was precisely against the immorality of a world governed by political reason that the Enlightenment defined itself and that its agents, under the spell of modern rationalism, reversed the Platonic subordination of utopia to reality.[19] From this perspective, the will to power is a negation of the American experience that can only lead down the same nihilistic path as the progressive illusions against which realism has constructed its own narrative. For, nihilism is the incapacity to accept conflict, suffering and the tragic conclusion that life has no final purpose or moral goal. It is the incapacity to find value and meaning in the immanence of life. Historically, the experience of nihilism stems from the fact that Western civilisation has always judged conditions of becoming in the world to be deficient, fallen, alien or base and thus has sought to address these shortcomings in favour of redemptive spiritual, rational or moralistic value traditions that locate the meaning of human existence either in the after-life, science or the rationality of the historical process. Today, the devaluation of Christianity and scientific rationalism is experienced as nihilistic because these traditions are still assumed to be our only measures of meaning, truth and valuation.[20] As Martin Heidegger put it in his study of Nietzsche:

> Nihilism moves history in the way of a scarcely recognised fundamental process in the destiny of the Western people. Hence nihilism is not just one historical phenomenon among others, not just one spiritual-intellectual current that occurs within Western history after others have occurred, after Christianity, after humanism, and after the Enlightenment. Nihilism, thought in its essence, is on the contrary the fundamental movement of the history of the West.[21]

The doctrine of will to power offers no way out of this impasse.[22] It offers us a choice between a self-deluding nihilism that refuses to work with the merciless forces of nature on the one hand, and its own naturalistic and equally nihilistic interpretation of the world as a universal and purposeless struggle for power on the other. As James Porter noted, the will to power, 'with its delusions of uninhibited power and agency untrammelled by the constraints and illusions of subjectivity', is both a critique and a symptom of this tragic reading of the history of Western metaphysics. It is a 'genealogy of the modern subject and its fascination with the one trait it absolutely lacks: power'.[23]

Neoconservative thought is caught in this nihilistic double bind. It lives by an executive-driven conservative political philosophy of sovereignty and reason of state that has been deprived of normative justification by Enlightenment criticism; but it talks the language of freedom, self-determination and human rights to mobilise an anomic and hedonistic civil society for the cause of empire. As Krauthammer explains:

> Realism is a valuable antidote to the woolly internationalism of the 1990s. But realism can only take you so far. Its basic problem lies in its definition of national interest as classically offered by its great theorist, Hans Morgenthau: interest defined as power. Morgenthau postulated that what drives nations, what motivates their foreign policy, is the will to power—to keep it and expand it. For most Americans, will to power might be a correct description

> of the world—of what motivates other countries—but it cannot be a prescription for America. It cannot be our purpose... Democratic globalism sees as the engine of history not the will to power but the will to freedom... Beyond interest defined as power ... expansive and utopian ... [yet sharing] realism's insights about the centrality of power ... [and] having appropriate contempt for the fictional legalism of liberal internationalism... The rationality of the enemy is something beyond our control. But the use of our power is within our control. And if that power is used wisely, constrained not by illusions and fictions but only by the limits of our mission—which is to bring a modicum of freedom as an antidote to nihilism—we can prevail.[24]

Yet as Krauthammer and his colleagues know all too well, the 'will to freedom', like the 'balance of power that favors freedom' promised by NSS 2002, does not mean anything. The will to power is a will that is not free. Whereas freedom as such cannot be balanced, power balancing is the natural and inevitable destiny of the international system of states.[25]

Further insights into this nihilistic *Realpolitik* can be drawn from an important article that Irving Kristol wrote for the *Weekly Standard* in the aftermath of the Iraq War in August 2003. There, Kristol describes what he considers to be the four main tenets of neoconservative foreign policy thinking:

1) 'Statesmen should, above all, have the ability to distinguish friends from enemies'.
2) 'Patriotism is a natural and healthy sentiment and should be encouraged by both private and public institutions'.
3) 'World government is a terrible idea since it can lead to world tyranny. International institutions that point to an ultimate world government should be regarded with the deepest suspicion'.
4) 'For a great power, the "national interest" is not a geographical term, except for fairly prosaic matters like trade and environmental regulation. A smaller nation might appropriately feel that its national interest begins and ends at its borders, so that its foreign policy is almost always in a defensive mode. A larger nation has more extensive interests. And large nations, whose identity is ideological, like the Soviet Union of yesteryear and the United States of today, inevitably have ideological interests in addition to more material concerns'.

Typically, Kristol does not give details nor justify the thinking that lies behind those basic principles. Yet he gives away an important clue as he informs his readers that 'the favorite neoconservative text on foreign affairs, thanks to professors Leo Strauss of Chicago and Donald Kagan of Yale, is Thucydides on the Peloponnesian War'.[26] Again here, Kristol does not explain what it is that attracts neoconservatives to this particular reading of Thucydides. But as we follow his lead into the Straussian literature on Thucydides, what we find is a fascinating neo-Nietzschean reading of the Peloponnesian War that differs a great deal from the interpretation of Thucydides that predominates in the mainstream IR literature.[27]

Sure enough, Strauss's Thucydides sees through Sparta's idealistic claim that it is fighting for justice and the liberation of Greece rather than its own self-interest. He also derides Spartan beliefs that gods and divine justice have anything to do with the outcome of battles and the meaning of human history. For, as the 'realist' Athenians put it to their 'idealist' Spartan enemies, it would be unreasonable and unjust for the gods either to reward or punish human beings for giving in to their immutable nature and pursuing what they hold to be in their self-interest. Thucydides the Athenian is therefore serenely resigned to the irredeemably dominating character of human nature and the weakness of justice among nations. But he is also aware of the unbearable psychological costs that such unpleasant truths impose on the polity. He therefore dissents from the Athenian thesis that morality has no place in international politics altogether.[28] For, a nation that lives by the wisdom of Athens cannot blame and resent its enemies for unjustly pursuing what they hold to be their self-interest any more than it can blame itself for pursuing ignoble imperialist policies. The political world of the Athenians is one in which the will to power of nations clash with one another in a godless moral vacuum. This means that the nation living by the realism of Athens must abandon all its claims to nobility, moral exceptionalism and manifest destiny. This is a requirement that no political community—especially not America—can embrace without seriously undermining its foundations. As Robert Kagan puts it, there is 'something about realism that runs directly counter to the fundamental principles of American society ... if the United States is founded upon universal principles, how can Americans practice amoral indifference when those principles are under siege around the world? And if they do profess indifference, how can they manage to avoid the implication that their principles are not, in fact, universal?'[29]

The Straussian reading of the Peloponnesian Wars teaches us that the imperialist Athenians could not live according to their own 'unrealistic realism', as they ultimately failed to free themselves completely of moral shame and religious anxiety. After the mysterious and profane mutilation of the statues of Hermes throughout the city on the eve of departure for the Sicilian expedition, the Athenians began to fear that the gods disapproved of their savage slaughter of the Melians. They interpreted the religious crime as a sign sent by the gods in disapproval of their ruthless imperialist policies. This then led to a zealous and politically dividing attempt to arrest and execute not only those suspected of having committed the religious crimes but also anyone suspected of impiety, in the hope of appeasing the gods and winning back their support for future expeditions. It also led to the arrest of the impious but militarily accomplished General Alcibiades who was meant to lead the Sicilian expedition. The expedition was subsequently entrusted to the pious but less capable General Nicias. Nicias's incompetence and his fear of the gods ultimately cost Athens both the conquest of Sicily and the war against Sparta.

The main lesson of this narrative is that moral and religious passions may be unreasonable, but as they are irreducible features of human existence, they have an important impact on the conduct of international politics. No statesman can do away with the constraints that *perceptions* of justice and injustice impose on the pursuit of the national interest. Thus against realists, the Straussian Thucydides holds that state power cannot be measured in narrow materialist terms since the capacity of a state to achieve its objective is contingent on the moral authority that it is able to exercise. However, and this is crucial, this moral authority is purely self-referential and self-interested: 'such authority is important for the state above all as a way of buttressing its *own* hopes for cosmic and divine support rather than as a way of gaining the consent of its allies or subjects'.[30]

In this interpretation, the need of the political community to transcend its own material self-interest is the one universal rational truth transcending the clash between irreconcilable conceptions of justice in international relations. It is this 'natural' truth which links the universal with the particular and drives the historical process forward. For Strauss's Thucydides, the fact that men always seek to transcend their self-interests through competing religious and moral discourses points towards the existence of a universal good higher than the Nietzschean will to power and domination. This higher good is the pursuit of trans-historical knowledge about the nature of political and human life. In other words, the universally good life is the trans-political and trans-civic life of the philosopher who understands and accepts with serenity that life has no intrinsic meaning beyond the earthly demands of citizenship and politics.[31]

The full implications of this peculiar neo-Nietzschean realism are best appreciated when contrasted with the modern, 'liberal' realism that predominates in the IR literature. Modern realism, in both its classical and neo-realist variants, holds that, even though all states are convinced that their national interest reflects the moral principles institutionalised in their political regime, their 'real' and ultimate objective is the pursuit of power understood in predominantly materialist terms. In contrast with the realism of Strauss and his followers, modern realism is based on a strict positivist rejection of the perspective of the engaged actor and hermeneutic conceptions of justice. Modern realism, in other words, hinges on a professed 'value-neutral' and morally relativistic approach to the study of politics. According to Morgenthau, for instance, because no human being can affirm the rational truth of any universal moral principle, notions of justice among states inevitably acquire a contestable character: 'To know that nations are subject to the moral law is one thing, while to pretend to know with certainty what is good and evil in the relations among nations is quite another'. For Morgenthau, talk of justice in international relations often simply means the imposition of the strongest nation's conception of good over that of weaker nations. Thus by defining interest in terms of material power, Morgenthau hopes to create a 'science of international politics' that analytically sees through the moral claims of states and prescriptively 'saves us from the moral excesses and political follies' of ideologically driven diplomacy.[32]

As Michael Williams argues, Morgenthau's 'science of politics' was an intellectual strategy of limits that sought to provide a more reliable—more realistic—basis for the maintenance of the post-war liberal order.[33] His positivism, of course, is hardly 'value-neutral'. It rests upon strong normative commitments to the preservation of human life and the nation as a political and cultural entity. It is also based on a set of rationally undemonstrable anthropological and metaphysical assumptions about the selfish, self-preserving and dominating character of human nature. Morgenthau's classical realism is liberal in the sense that it follows Hobbes in his intent to institute a procedural and 'value-neutral' peace that will render the struggle for power tolerable and allow for the preservation of individual human life.[34] From the relativity of justice in world politics, and from the 'natural' primacy of power and self-interest in relations among human beings and nations, Morgenthau infers a rational natural law commanding that state power be deployed in pursuit of peace, security and 'the moral principle of national survival'.[35] Morgenthau believed that human nature cannot be changed and that power politics will always be a permanent feature of the human condition. However, he believed that the most destructive effects of power politics could be eliminated by deploying a positivist theory of IR that proposes power, fear of death and the elimination of ideology and vainglory from diplomatic discourse as the best means to preserve human life and civilisation. Unsurprisingly, this typically Hobbesian strategy eventually led him to make the case for the abandonment of nationalist principles in favour of the establishment of a global leviathan that would hold humanity in check with its monopoly on weapons of mass destruction. For him this was the only viable means to avoid the destruction of human societies through nuclear war:

> The experience of two world wars within a quarter of a century and the prospects of a third one to be fought with nuclear weapons have imparted to the idea of a world state an unprecedented urgency. What is needed ... is not limitation of the exercise of national sovereignty through international obligations and institutions, but the transference of the sovereignties of individual nations to a world authority, which would be as sovereign over the individual nations as the individual nations are sovereign within their respective territories.[36]

From a Straussian-neoconservative perspective, the scenario envisaged by Morgenthau is conceptually inconsistent. Morgenthau's realism is an 'unrealistic' theoretical construct designed to recast the 'natural'—and therefore 'realistic'—struggle for justice and vain glory that he himself diagnoses (and in which actors *actually* perceive themselves to be engaged) into an abstract struggle for survival, power and peace free of identity-conferring ideology, moralism and utopia. This positivist conceptual move then leads him to assume—not unlike advocates of global liberal governance today (see Chapter 5)—that nations will want to preserve their *physical* existence even at the cost of their autonomy and *cultural* existence.[37] It presupposes that human beings will sacrifice the ideals, beliefs and values that constitute their identity and humanise their lives for the sake of 'perpetual peace' irrespective of the intellectual, spiritual and ethical substance of that peace. Yet, if one accepts Morgenthau's own interpretation of human nature and the will to power, it is more likely that his world state would be a tyranny permanently at war with those dissatisfied with its normative content.[38] Thus, while accepting the basic anthropological premises of Morgenthau's realism, neoconservatives reject its ethical prescriptions. For neoconservatives, a life worth living—a life free from political tyranny—is unthinkable without the permanent possibility of a nuclear conflict. As Pangle and Ahrensdorf argue, 'Civilisation can survive only if there are human beings who are willing to risk death, and even nuclear death, in order to defend that ideal against tyranny'.[39]

Neoconservatism's Political 'Way of Life'

According to neoconservatives, it is this unconditional commitment to the notion of the common good that humanises and gives meaning to the life of the individual citizen. Without this commitment, life is mere animal existence, without context or history. And it is the absence of this existential commitment that renders liberal societies so vulnerable to their enemies today. As Kristol argues, the liberal state 'defines the common good as consisting mainly of personal security under the law, personal liberty under the law, and a steadily increasing material prosperity for those who apply themselves to that end. It is, by the standards of previous civilisations, a "vulgar" conception of the common good: There is no high nobility of purpose, no selfless devotion to transcendental ends, no awe-inspiring heroism'.[40] This is what he called the 'The Lost Soul of the Welfare State': 'Readiness to die for one's country is regarded as a form of psychological "extremism", and it is to discourage such mental unbalance that the modern welfare state has practically abolished military parades'.[41]

According to neoconservatives, this neo-Schmittian political existentialism is not a celebration of war as such but an abandonment of the status quo that allows atomised citizens to transcend their individuality. War, as Pangle explains, is 'a source of renewal of high purpose, of exemplary civic spirit and thoughtful reflection, of citizen engagement and even participation. All this implies that even foreign and defense policy needs to be viewed in terms not only of defense, and of benefits to others, but also—if only secondarily—in terms of the moral effects on domestic political life'.[42] Fukuyama concurs: 'A liberal democracy that could fight a short and decisive war every generation or so to defend its own liberty and independence would be far healthier and more satisfied than one that experienced nothing but continuous peace'.[43]

As we have seen throughout this study, the upshot of this atavistic conception of ethical freedom is that it requires an enemy foil to bring itself into relief. This constitutes a radical negation of Enlightenment philosophy. For it relieves people from the burden of independent critical reflection by establishing the identity between individual freedom and obligation to the state.[44] In this framework, it is the executive decision on the existential distinction between friend and enemy that gives normative substance to the 'political way of life' that is thought to 'humanise' the life of the atomised individual. And this decision, of course, is simply beyond the realm of normative justification. As Schmitt himself insisted in *The Concept of the Political*, from the point of view of the state the justification for demanding that people sacrifice their own lives to defend the political community in times of national emergency is outside the bounds of discursive rationalisation: 'There is no rational end, no norm however correct, no program however exemplary, no social ideal however beautiful, and no legitimacy or legality that could justify men's killing one another'.[45] The only justification is the mere fact of an extreme existential situation. And since the existential realm is normatively self-referential, there is absolutely no rational standpoint from which to determine what counts as an existential condition and from which to question the ethicality of political authority. Hence, in reality, far from humanising and historicising the life of individuals, the intense moments of collective subjectivity cultivated by this existentialist ethics in fact only sublimate the political and socio-economic contradictions that define the true historicity of socially formed selves, while putting the foundation of political authority beyond all social and historical facticity.[46]

Neoconservatism is an idealist attack on the weak and naive idealist alienated from the world. Instead, it proposes a heroic idealism of struggle and sacrifice based on an anti-hedonistic ontological separation between the realm of the senses and the realm of ideas—between being and becoming. As George Friedman explains in his critique of the Frankfurt School's political philosophy:

> The human being is the being who gains sufficiency from a sense of insufficiency. True, it is fully human to struggle against one's suffering and alienation. The issue is, however, whether it is human to abolish suffering and live in gratification. Aristotle and Nietzsche would agree that it is not. It might be divine or superhuman or it might be bestial or it might possess elements of both, but in the end it is not simply nor truly human.[47]

In this stern ethical universe, relief from deprivation and alienation is relegated to individual imagination and deferred to a religious afterlife. Political stability and harmony are therefore not to be brought about through rational collective action to address injustices, but by cultivating those virtues of the soul that will conciliate individuals with the social contradictions of the existing order. As James Ceaser explains, for neoconservatives 'statecraft is soulcraft'.[48] Or as Kristol puts it:

> Just as it is ideas that alienate us from the world, so it is ideas which can make us at home in the world—which can permit us to envision the world as a 'homely place', where the practice of ordinary virtues in the course of our ordinary lives can indeed fulfil our potential as human beings. In such a world, dreams complement reality instead of being at war with it. The construction of such a world is the intellectual enterprise that most needs encouragement and support today... Only such a reformation can bring us back to that condition of sanity, to that confident acceptance of reality.[49]

According to Kristol, by freeing reason from the shackles of religion and tradition, the rationalist spirit of the intellectual class has cut ideas loose from actual social practice and experience. Kristol invokes Burke's 'composed' and 'organic' rationalism to argue that 'institutions which have existed over a long period of time have a reason and a purpose inherent in them, a collective wisdom incarnate them, and the fact that we don't perfectly understand or cannot perfectly explain why they "work" is no defect in them but merely a limitation in us'. This, we are told, is something that 'all reasonable common men know instinctively'. But as these same 'ordinary people' lack the intellectual skills to fend off the 'articulated and aggressive rationalism' of the liberal elite, they are 'likely to take refuge in some form of irrationalism'. According to Kristol, 'The 20th-century phenomenon of fascism is an expression of exactly such an exasperated and irrational rebelliousness against the tyranny—actual or prospective—of a radical-utopian rationalism'.[50]

Now, to say that social engineering often has unintended consequences, or that a social order cannot be based on reason alone, is one thing. But to say that traditions and existing institutions 'have a reason and a purpose inherent in them' is quite another. The obvious problem with this 'organic rationalism' is that it does not subject social practice to reason but assumes a priori the rationality of the social order. Despite what neoconservatives are telling us, enlightenment rationalism is not a rejection of tradition as such. It is a defence of the right of the individual to exercise his or her judgement as to what traditions and belief systems should be kept and which discarded.[51] The political community envisaged by neoconservatives presents itself as a community of historical destiny that carries its own legitimation in and of itself. Yet, the historical here is in fact de-historicised through the mythical elevation of the natural and organic character of the community over the reality of the racial and socio-economic relations that have concretely and historically shaped the American experience.

In sum, neoconservatism presents itself as a prudent conservatism that seeks to tame the utopian excesses of modern liberalism in order to protect bourgeois society from itself. Yet, in reality, its aim is not so much to 'conserve' this bourgeois society as to transform it into a post-welfare community of values *within* the existing class structure by transforming the relationship between the individual and the community without prying on the profit motive of capitalism. The aim is to keep state and society as differentiated as possible so as to prevent issues of socio-economic exclusion and pluralism of interests to enter the realm of democratic politics and weaken the state. This amounts to a politically motivated de-politicisation of social relations that ultimately separates liberalism from democracy. It does so by devaluating deliberative politics and interest groups' representations on the one hand, and by establishing unity between 'the people' and the political leadership on the other through various technologies of government based on the cultivation of intense existential moments of collective subjectivity.[52] As Jef Huysmans argues, in effect, this type of Right-wing populism transforms 'the societal' as a realm of socio-economic interests and identity mobilisation into a mere object of government. The political elite absorbs the democratic agency of the multitude in its attempt at nurturing this substantive consensus from above through the authoritarian allocation of 'authentic' cultural values independent from their objective socio-economic setting.[53] Apart from the justification of existing inequalities and injustices, what is at stake here is 'whether the *Volkstaat*, a state in which the "people" disregard their private interests and essentially want what their cultural "destiny" requires of them, should take precedence over the pursuit of particular interests under the liberal rule of law embodied in the *Rechstaat*'.[54]

The belligerent character of the neoconservative project must be understood in this light. Neoconservatism can only sustain itself by cultivating a level of limited but endemic conflict in the international system and nurturing its support base in the name of an expansive foreign policy. This is what the French political scientist Emmanuel Todd calls 'theatrical micromilitarism'.[55] Theatrical micromilitarism in Central America during the late 1970s and 1980s provided neoconservatives with long-lasting opportunities to tighten the boundaries of American identity and re-assert the power of the executive branch following the demise of the Nixon presidency, the humiliation of Vietnam and the Iran hostage crisis. This includes 'the manipulation of intelligence and the media, the building of an interagency war party that operated autonomously from Washington's foreign policy establishment, the illegal wiretaps, and the surveillance of antiwar activists'.[56] It did not matter that the democratic revolutions which America sought to roll back through proxies in that region at the time had more to do with US needs than with the real threat posed by an ailing Soviet Union. As David Ryan argues, 'Militarisation had deep roots in a US culture which wanted the respect without paying the price; it wanted the glory of Kennedy's inauguration without Vietnam. Reagan satisfied the contradictory demands of a low-cost foreign policy (in terms of US lives) and the "illusion of greatness" (in terms of arms procurement)'. The disquieting implication of this is that 'the militarisation and the narcissistic self-reflection that accompanied it would not end with the disappearance of the Soviet Union or the Cold War' because it was a process never determined primarily by the threat posed by the Soviet enemy, whether real or imagined.[57]

George Bush's 'neoconservative presidency' took theatrical micromilitarism to a new level. The Bush Doctrine abrogated a limitless personal authority for the American president to call a military action against any state that, in the subjective judgement of the president alone, constituted either an immediate or even distant threat to the nation. In terms of civil liberties and the contraction of American identity, the 'theatrical micromilitarist' management of the 'non-integrating periphery' in the war on terror has served as a vehicle for the introduction of arbitrary forms of authority, executive prerogatives and legal instruments that hark back to the age of absolutism. These include the destruction of attorney-client confidentiality, secret detentions and, not least, the claim that the government has a right to detain indefinitely US citizens whom it unilaterally identifies as potential terrorists. In the immediate aftermath of 9/11, the Bush administration arrested over 1,000 resident aliens from countries that the administration suspected of terrorist activity. Many of them remained in prison for months without ever being formally charged. Indeed, since the Bush administration signed the so-called 'Patriot Act' into law in October 2001, the myth of the foreign enemy has deprived over 9 million resident aliens of basic legal protection against potentially arbitrary decisions by federal security agencies.[58] Then there is the refusal to apply the Geneva Conventions to prisoners of war; the use of torture and the disregarding of basic human rights standards in the treatment of terrorist suspects; and the establishment of illegal prisoner camps and military tribunals in Guantanamo Bay in which the military act as interrogators, prosecutors, defence counsel, judges and, when death sentences are proclaimed, as executioners. As William Scheuerman noted at the time, 'That precisely such activities encouraged our Enlightenment predecessors to discard monarchy in the first place seems to have been lost on Republican partisans normally hostile to "big government," the [Bush] administration's cheerleaders at Fox News, and millions of ordinary Americans understandably angered by the 9/11 attacks'.[59]

The preservation of this neo-absolutist legal legacy has been a key component of the neoconservative agenda since Obama came into office in January 2009.[60] Whether we interpret it as 'an exceptional suspension of liberal democratic norms (revealing the constitutional limits of bourgeois political society whose hegemony is predicated on the universalising power of the legal-rational state)', or as 'a departure from the existing constitutional framework of liberalism (revealing the historical limits of the liberal state as a system of government)'[61], what is defining here is the paucity of neoconservative commitment to liberal rights. The same can be said of neoconservative strategies of societal management. For, in the end, the notion that the social disruption and disenchantment generated by the forces of liberal modernisation can be addressed by a Platonic return to discredited metaphysics and the constant replaying of the friend-enemy dialectic rests on a reductive political psychology that simply mirrors the obscurantism of the fundamentalists with which America has been at war for the past decade. However successful these political strategies can be in times of crisis and uncertainty, they rest on a vulgar misunderstanding of what the human search for transcendence is all about. Our quest for the meaning of struggle and human existence is driven as much by a desire for self-realisation, autonomy and difference as by a yearning for order and stability.

Arguably, the Straussian-Schmittian tactics with which neoconservatives have sought to foster national cohesion over the years have contributed to cultural fragmentation in an even more destructive manner than the multicultural and postmodernist intellectual movements that they blame for the decay of the American public sphere.[62] As Paul Gottfried noted, neoconservatives are 'for "values" and against "relativism" while keeping their options open as to which values need defending'.[63] This mendacious anti-foundationalism has encouraged a slanderous style of partisan politics that substitutes engagement in civilised public debate for loud-mouthed ranting à la Ann Coulter and Rush Lindbaugh in order to defend pre-formed opinions and prejudices against 'relativists' who do not share their values.[64]

It is important that we recognise American neoconservatism for what it is. In his otherwise excellent history of the movement, Justin Vaïsse, director of research in the Brookings Center on the United States and Europe, concludes that neoconservatism is a uniquely and thoroughly American ideology. Neoconservatism is conservative in domestic politics but liberal in foreign affairs: 'their Wilsonianism, their moralism, their tendency to disturb the status quo and, out of foreign policy necessity, their defence of a strong state possessing a powerful military apparatus—all of this puts them closer to liberals than conservatives'.[65] As I hope this study has demonstrated, this is a naïve conclusion that does not capture the dynamics between the domestic and foreign politics of neoconservatism, and that one can only arrive at by completely ignoring the intellectual underpinnings of neoconservative politics. Moralising supporters of a strong and expansionist militaristic state neoconservatives certainly are. But the worldview, values and objectives that sustain this transformative project have little to do with liberalism. Liberalism is about self-determination, collective security, institutions, international law and the transformation of the international state of anarchy into a global constitutional order of human rights. Neoconservatism is inimical to all this. To situate neoconservatism within the broad church of liberalism is to ignore everything that is specific to neoconservatism as an ideology.

NOTES

INTRODUCTION

1. Irving Kristol, *Reflections of a Neoconservative: Looking Back, Looking Ahead* (New York: Basic Books Inc., 1983), p. 253.
2. See, for instance, Peter Steinfels, *The Neoconservatives: The Men Who Are Changing America's Politics* (New York: Simon & Schuster, 1979); Paul Edward Gottfried, *Conservatism in America: Making Sense of the American Right* (New York: Palgrave Macmillan, 2007); Sara Diamond, *Roads to Dominion: Right-Wing Movements and Political Power in the United States* (New York: Guilford Press, 1995).
3. Jürgen Habermas, 'Neoconservative Cultural Criticism in the United States and West Germany', in *The New Conservatism* (Cambridge: Polity Press, 1985), p. 22.
4. Gottfried, *Conservatism in America*, p. 45.
5. Foreign Policy Initiative, 'Mission Statement', March 2009, http://www.foreignpolicyi.org/about.html [7 April 2009].
6. Michael C. Williams, 'What is the National Interest? The Neoconservative Challenge in IR Theory', *European Journal of International Relations*, vol. 11, no. 3, 2005, pp. 308–9. Williams is one of the very few IR scholars who engaged with neoconservatism at the theoretical level. See his *The Realist Tradition and the Limits of International Relations* (Cambridge: Cambridge University Press, 2005), pp. 197–204; *Culture and Security: Symbolic Power and the Politics of International Security* (London: Palgrave, 2007), pp. 92–119; 'Morgenthau Now: neoconservatism, national greatness, and realism', in M. C. Williams (ed.), *Realism Reconsidered: The Legacy of Hans Morgenthau* (Oxford: Oxford University Press, 2008), pp. 216–39; M. C. Williams, 'What is the National Interest?'; Brian C. Schmidt and Michael C. Williams, 'The Bush Doctrine and the Iraq War: Neoconservatives Versus Realists', *Security Studies*, vol. 17, no. 2, 2008, pp. 191–220. Another important contribution is Patricia Owens's 'Beyond Strauss, Lies, and the War in Iraq: Hannah Arendt's Critique of Neoconservatism', *Review of International Studies*, vol. 33, Special Issue, 2007,

pp. 265–83. Other valuable contributions include Peter Steinfels, *The Neoconservatives*; Stefan Halper and Jonathan Clarke, *America Alone: The Neo-Conservatives and the Global Order* (Cambridge: Cambridge University Press, 2004); Jim George, 'Leo Strauss, Neoconservatism and US Foreign Policy: Esoteric Nihilism and the Bush Doctrine', *International Politics*, vol. 42, no. 2, 2005, pp. 174–202; John Guelke, 'The Political Morality of Neo-Conservatives: An Analysis', *International Politics*, vol. 42, no. 1, 2005, pp. 97–115. A good number of intellectual histories of the movement have also appeared over the past two decades or so. See Gary Dorrien, *The Neoconservative Mind: Politics, Culture, and the War of Ideology* (Philadelphia: Temple University Press, 1993); *Imperial Designs* (London: Routledge, 2004); John Ehrman, *The Rise of Neoconservatism: Intellectuals and Foreign Affairs 1945–1994* (New Haven: Yale University Press, 1995); Mark Gerson, *The Neoconservative Vision: From Cold War to Culture Wars* (Lanham, MD: Madison Books, 1997); James Mann, *Rise of the Vulcans: The History of Bush's War Cabinet* (London: Penguin Books, 2004); Murray Friedman, *The Neoconservative Revolution: Jewish Intellectuals and the Shaping of Public Policy* (Cambridge: Cambridge University Press, 2005); Jacob Heilbrunn, *They Knew They Were Right: The Rise of the Neocons* (New York: Doubleday, 2008); Justin Vaïsse, *Neoconservatism* (Cambridge, MA: Harvard University Press, 2010).

7. Harvey C. Mansfield, 'The Legacy of the Late Sixties', in Stephen Macedo (ed.), *Reassessing the Sixties* (New York: W. W. Norton, 1997), p. 24.
8. Jeane Kirkpatrick, 'Neoconservatism as a Response to the Counter-Culture', in Irwin Stelzer (ed.), *Neoconservatism* (London: Atlantic Books, 2004), p. 235.
9. Joshua Muravchik, 'Operation Comeback', *Foreign Policy*, vol. 12, November 2006, http://www.foreignpolicy.com/users/login.php?story_id=3602&URL=http://www.foreignpolicy.com/story/cms.php?story_id=3602 [2 December 2007].
10. James W. Ceaser, 'The Great Divide: American Interventionism and its Opponents', in William Kristol and Robert Kagan (eds.), *Present Dangers: Crisis and Opportunity in American Foreign and Defense Policy* (New York: Encounter Books, 2000), p. 25.
11. Cited in William Kristol, 'Will Obama Save Liberalism?', *New York Times*, 26 January 2009, p. A6.
12. Dinesh D'Souza, *Letters to a Young Conservative* (New York: Basic Books, 2002), pp. 4–5.
13. Hilton Kramer and Roger Kimball (ed.), *The Betrayal of Liberalism: How the Disciples of Freedom and Equality Helped Foster the Illiberal Politics of Coercion and Control* (New York: Ivan R. Dee, 1985).
14. Tod Lindberg, 'Neoconservatism's Liberal Legacy', *Policy Review*, no. 27, 2004, p. 4. See also Peter Berger, *Facing Up to Modernity: Excursions in Society, Politics and Religion* (New York: Basic Books, 1977).
15. Kristol, *Reflections of a Neoconservative*, p. 75.

16. Ibid., p. xii.
17. Irving Kristol, 'The Neoconservative Persuasion: What It Was and What It Is', *The Weekly Standard*, 25 August 2003, pp. 2–3.
18. Kristol, *Reflections*, pp. 33–4.
19. Michael Freeden, *Ideologies and Political Theory: A Conceptual Approach* (Oxford: Oxford University Press, 1996); William B. Gallie, 'Essentially Contestable Concepts', *Proceedings of the Aristotelian Society*, vol. 56, 1955–6, pp. 167–98; William Connolly, *The Terms of Political Discourse* (Oxford: Blackwell, 1993).
20. Gerald F. Gaus, *Political Concepts and Political Theories* (Boulder, CO: Westview Press, 2000), p. 43.
21. Peter Kuryla, 'Three Variations on American Liberalism', in M. Halliwell and C. Morley, *American Thought and Culture in the 21st Century* (Edinburgh: Edinburgh University Press, 2008), p. 66. See also James P. Young, *American Liberalism: The Troubled Odyssey of the Liberal Idea* (Boulder, CO: Westview Press, 1996); Anthony Arblaster, *The Rise and Decline of Western Liberalism* (Oxford: Basil Blackwell, 1984), pp. 10–4; Gary Gerstle, 'The Protean Character of American Liberalism', *American Historical Review*, vol. 99, no. 4, 1994, pp. 1043–73.
22. John Gray, *Liberalism* (Buckingham: Open University Press, 1995), p. 10.
23. Pierre Hassner, 'The United States: The Empire of Force or the Force of Empire', EU-ISS Chaillot Papers, no. 54, September 2002.
24. Max Boot, 'What the Heck is a "Neocon"?', *Wall Street Journal*, 30 December 2002, p. A3; David M. Kenney, 'What "W" Owes to "WW"', *Atlantic Monthly*, March 2005, pp. 6–9.
25. Lawrence Kaplan, 'Regime Change: Bush, Closet Liberal', *New Republic*, 3 March 2003, p. 7.
26. Francis Fukuyama, *After the Neocons: America at the Crossroads* (London: Profile Books, 2006), pp. 139–40.
27. Anatol Lieven, *America Right or Wrong: An Anatomy of American Nationalism* (London: Harper Perennial, 2005), p. 9.
28. Robert Singh, 'Neo-Conservatism: Theory and Practice', in Linda B. Miller and Mark Ledwidge (eds.), *New Directions in US Foreign Policy* (London: Routledge, 2008), p. 34.
29. Anatol Lieven, for example, reads neoconservatism broadly along those lines in his *America Right or Wrong*, chapter one.
30. I am grateful to one of the anonymous reviewers for insisting on this potential objection.
31. Stephen Eric Bronner, *Reclaiming the Enlightenment: Toward a Politics of Radical Engagement* (New York: Columbia University Press, 2004), p. 49.
32. On liberal internationalism and the Iraq War, see Tony Smith, *A Pact with the Devil: Washington's Bid for World Supremacy and the Betrayal of the American Promise* (London: Routledge, 2006); Inderjeet Parmar, 'Foreign

Policy fusion: Liberal Interventionists, conservative nationalists and neo-conservatives—the new alliance dominating the US foreign policy establishment', *International Politics*, 46, no. 2/3, 2009, pp. 177–209; John Ikenberry et al., *The Crisis of American Foreign Policy: Wilsonianism in the Twenty-First Century* (Princeton: Princeton University Press 2009).

33. Robert Latham, *The Liberal Moment: Modernity, Security, and the Making of Postwar International Order* (New York: Columbia University Press, 1997). As Latham argues, liberal modernity is only one of many possible variations within the much larger macro-historical space of modernity as such: 'Indeed, besides its value in making clear that liberalism is not just a body of doctrine or a set of principles but a way of being modern, the term liberal modernity makes it possible to place liberalism and other organisational social forms within the same macro-historical fabric. Capitalist modernity, explored so thoroughly by Marx, is the broad body of social relations, such as those between workers and capitalists, structured by forms of political and economic organisation such as the state. Liberal, as distinct from capitalist, modernity represents the particular shaping of the political and social entities or spaces in which one lives through practices, principles, and institutions associated with liberal governance, rights, markets, and self-determination. These two forms of modernity, despite their close historical proximity, have different ontologies. Whereas capitalist modernity refers to material and organisational forces such as those associated with the circulation of commodities and its manifestation the social and political life of towns and cities (e.g., in the political domination of certain classes over others), liberal modernity refers to the patterning of that social and political life through a broad body of doctrines and practices' (pp. 14–6).
34. This definition is inspired by Francis Mulhern's *Culture/Metaculture* (London: Routledge, 2000), Introduction.
35. Daniel Bell, *The Cultural Contradictions of Capitalism*, 20th Anniversary Edition (New York: Basic Books, 1996 [1978]), p. 14.
36. Allan Bloom, *The Closing of the American Mind* (New York: Simon & Schuster, 1987), p. 33.
37. William Kristol, 'The Eighteenth Brumaire of Barack Obama', *Weekly Standard*, vol. 15, no. 27, 2010, http://www.weeklystandard.com/articles/eighteenth-brumaire-barack-obama [20 March 2010].
38. For an interesting study of the totalising tendencies of cultural politics in America which has influenced my own interpretation, see Sheldon Wolin, *Democracy Incorporated: Managed Democracy and the Specter of Inverted Totalitarianism* (Princeton: Princeton University Press, 2008).
39. On conservatism as a limited style of politics, see Noel O'Sullivan, *Conservatism* (London: Everyman, 1976).
40. See Jerry Z. Muller, *Conservatism: An Anthology of Social and Political Thought From Hume to the Present* (Princeton: Princeton University Press, 1997), pp. 32–69.

41. See, for instance, Earl Shorris, 'Ignoble Liars: Leo Strauss, George Bush and the philosophy of Mass Deception', *Harper's Magazine*, June 2004; Jeffrey Steinberg, 'Leo Strauss, Fascist and Godfather of Neo-Cons', *Executive Intelligence Review*, 21 March 2003; Will Hutton, 'Time to Stop Being America's Lap Dog', *The Observer*, 17 February 2002, p. 6.
42. Anne Norton, *Leo Strauss and the Politics of American Empire* (New Haven: Yale University Press, 2005), pp. 186, 179.
43. Shadia Drury, 'Noble lies and perpetual war: Leo Strauss, the neo-cons, and Iraq', www.informationclearinghouse.info/article5010.htm, 18 November 2003. Drury published a series of, in my view, overly polemical but very influential interpretation of Strauss's work and its impact on American conservatism. See her *The Political Ideas of Leo Strauss* (London: Macmillan, 1988); *Leo Strauss and the American Right* (London: Macmillan, 1997). Her work has influenced a large number of commentaries on Strauss and the neoconservatives during the Bush presidency.
44. For more convincing interpretations of the link between Strauss and neoconservative discourses, see Robert Devigne, *Recasting Conservatism: Oakeshott, Strauss, and the Response to Postmodernism* (New Haven and London: Yale University Press, 1994); Nicholas Xenos, *Cloaked in Virtue: Unveiling the Rhetoric of American Foreign Policy* (London: Routledge, 2008). Xenos offers a critical and, in my view, compelling reading of Strauss. However, the theoretical link with neoconservatism and US foreign policy offered in the last chapter of the book is under-theorised and rather thin in textual evidence.
45. See Owens, 'Beyond Strauss'.
46. See, for instance, Irving Kristol, 'Confessions of a True, Self-Confessed Neoconservative', in his *Reflections of a Neoconservative*, p. 76; Dinesh D' Souza, 'The Legacy of Leo Strauss: Is America the Good Society that the Ancient Philosophers Sought?', *Policy Review*, vol. 40, Spring 1987, pp. 36–43; Kenneth L. Deutsch and John A. Murley (eds.), *Leo Strauss, the Straussians, and the American Regime* (Lanham, MD: Rowman & Littlefield, 1999); Steven Lenzner and William Kristol, 'What Was Leo Strauss Up To?', *The Public Interest*, no. 153, Fall 2003, pp. 19–39; Fukuyama, *After the Neocons*, chapter 2; Thomas Pangle, 'Leo Strauss's Perspective on Modern Politics', American Enterprise Institute Conference, Washington, 1 December 2003, podcast available online at http://www.aei.org/event/478#doc [7 January 2008].
47. Raimondo Cudebbu cited in Alain Frachon and Daniel Vernet, *L'Amérique Messianique: Les guerres des neo-conservateurs* (Paris: Seuil, 2004), p. 64. My translation.
48. See Seymour Martin Lipset, 'Neoconservatism: Myth and Reality', *Society*, July/August, 1988, pp. 32–9.
49. Michael Harrington, 'The Welfare State and Its Neoconservative Critics', *Dissent*, Fall 1973, pp. 435–54.
50. Irving Kristol, 'Confessions of a True, Self-Confessed—Perhaps the Only—"Neoconservative"', *Public Opinion*, October/November, 1979, p. 50.

51. Norman Podhoretz, 'Following Irving', in DeMuth and Kristol, *The Neoconservative Imagination*.
52. Nathan Glazer, 'Neoconservatism: Pro and Con', *Partisan Review*, vol. 47, no. 4, 1980, p. 498.
53. Irwin Stelzer, 'Neoconservatives and Their Critics: An Introduction', in his *Neoconservatism*, p. 4.
54. Adam Wolfson, 'Conservatives and Neoconservatives', in Stelzer, *Neoconservatism*, p. 226.
55. Ibid.
56. Joshua Muravchik, 'The Neoconservative Cabal', in Stelzer, *Neoconservatism*, p. 254.
57. Kristol, 'The Neoconservative Persuasion', pp. 33–6.
58. Edward Hallet Carr, *The New Society* (London: Macmillan, 1951), p. 16.
59. Steinfels, *The Neoconservatives*, p. 42.
60. Stelzer, 'Neoconservatives', pp. 4–5.
61. In *After the Neocons*, Fukuyama argues that neoconservatism has developed into something that he can no longer support. According to him, his former colleagues inside and outside the Bush administration have misinterpreted neoconservatism's basic philosophical premises in order to justify the Iraq War. This is a contentious and rather disingenuous argument. Fukuyama was an active supporter of the Iraq War and was one of the co-signatories of the Project for a New American Century's statement of principles and campaign to transform the Middle East. He nevertheless argues that neoconservatism has been discredited by his former friends and that the label ought therefore to be abandoned in favour of a new foreign policy approach he calls 'realistic Wilsonianism'. As the label indicates, there is in fact very little that is new in Fukuyama's 'realistic Wilsonianism'. Fukuyama may no longer travel with some of his former friends, but at the ideological level he very much remains a neoconservative.
62. Ibid., pp. 13–4.
63. My approach here is inspired by David E. Cooper's exposition of the existentialist tradition in his *Existentialism* (Oxford: Blackwell, 1990), pp. 6–11.

1. A NEW CONSERVATISM

1. Irving Kristol, *Reflections of a Neoconservative: Looking Back, Looking Ahead* (New York: Basic Books Inc., 1983), pp. x-xi.
2. Alexander Bloom, *Prodigal Sons: The New York Intellectuals and Their World* (New York: Oxford University Press, 1986); Alan M. Wald, *The New York Intellectuals: The Rise and Decline of the Anti-Stalinist Left from the 1930s to the 1980s* (Chapel Hill: University of North Carolina Press, 1987); Neil Jumonville (ed.), *The New York Intellectuals Reader* (New York and London: Routledge, 2007).

3. Irving Kristol, 'Memoirs of a Trotskyist', in his *Neoconservatism: Selected Essays 1951–1995* (New York: Free Press, 1995); Daniel Bell, 'First Love and Early Sorrow', *Times Higher Education Supplement*, 16 January 1981, available online at http://www.pbs.org/arguing/nyintellectuals_bell_2.html [7 January 2008]; Seymour Martin Lipset, 'Out of the Alcoves', *The Wilson Quarterly*, vol. 23, no. 1, 1999, pp. 37–48.
4. Daniel Bell, 'Afterword, 1988: The End of Ideology Revisited', in his *The End of Ideology: On the Exhaustion of Political Ideas in the Fifties* (Cambridge, MA: Harvard University Press, 1988 [1960]), p. 415.
5. For a more detailed account of these disputes see John Ehrman, *The Rise of Neoconservatism: Intellectuals and Foreign Affairs 1945–1994* (New Haven: Yale University Press, 1994), pp. 1–32. On the decline of the American left at the hands of liberals during that period, see John Diggins, *The Rise and Fall of the American Left* (New York: W. W. Norton, 1992), chapter 5; Harvey Klehr and John Early Haynes, *The American Communist Movement* (New York: Twayne Publishers, 1992), pp. 96–147.
6. Arthur M. Schlesinger Jr., *The Vital Center: The Politics of Freedom* (Boston: Houghton Mifflin, 1949), p. 244.
7. Allen J. Matusow, *The Unravelling of America: A History of Liberalism in the 1960s* (New York: Harper & Row, 1984), p. 16.
8. Robert Latham, *The Liberal Moment: Modernity, Security, and the Making of Postwar International Order* (New York: Columbia University Press, 1997), p. 5.
9. Bruce Cummings, 'The Wicked Witch of the West is Dead. Long Live the Wicked Witch of the East', in Michael J. Hogan (ed.), *The End of the Cold War* (Cambridge: Cambridge University Press, 1992), pp. 87–101.
10. For a good overview see Arturo Escobar, *Encountering Development: The Making and Unmaking of the Third World* (Princeton: Princeton University Press, 1995).
11. National Security Council, 'A Report to the National Security Council—NSC 68', Washington, 12 April 1950, President's Secretary File, Truman Paper, p. 34, http://www.trumanlibrary.org/whistlestop/study_collections/coldwar/documents/pdf/10–1.pdf [2 October 2007].
12. Thomas J. McCormick, *America's Half-Century: United States Foreign Policy in the Cold War and After*, 2nd edn, (Baltimore: Johns Hopkins University Press, 1995), p. 136.
13. Steve Fraser and Gary Gerstle, *The Rise and Fall of the New Deal Order, 1930–1980* (Princeton: Princeton University Press, 1990).
14. This would become an especially important theme among liberal intellectuals during the 1950s. See, for instance, William H. Whyte, Jr., *The Organization Man* (New York: Simon & Schuster, 1956); John Kenneth Galbraith, *The Affluent Society* (Boston: Houghton Mifflin, 1958).
15. The Congress for Cultural Freedom had offices in Britain, France, India, Italy, Japan, Norway, the United States and West Germany. See Christopher Lasch, *The Agony of the American Left* (New York: Alfred A. Knopf,

1969), pp. 63–114; Peter Coleman, *The Liberal Conspiracy: The Congress for Cultural Freedom and the Struggle for the Mind of Postwar Europe* (New York: Free Press, 1989).

16. Irving Kristol, '"Civil Liberties", 1952—A Study in Confusion', *Commentary*, March 1952, p. 229.
17. Irving Kristol, 'On Negative Liberalism', *Encounter*, January 1954, p. 3.
18. Nathan Glazer, 'The Method of Senator McCarthy', *Commentary*, March 1953, p. 256. See also Alan F. Westin, 'Our Freedom—and the Rights of Communists', *Commentary*, July 1952, pp 134–43; Eliot Cohen, 'The Free American Citizen, 1952', *Commentary*, September 1952, pp. 212–24; Daniel Bell, '"Hard" and "Soft" Anti-Communist', *The New Leader*, 17 May 1954, pp. 22–36; Norman Podhoretz, 'Making the World Safe for Communism', *Commentary*, April 1976, pp. 31–42.
19. Cited in Anthony Arblaster, *The Rise and Decline of Western Liberalism* (Oxford: Basil Blackwell, 1984), p. 313.
20. Norman Podhoretz, *Making It* (New York: Random House, 1967), pp. 289–90.
21. George Nash, *The Conservative Intellectual Movement in America Since 1945* (New York: Harper, 1976), p. xvii. See also Clinton Rossiter, *Conservatism in America* (London: William Heinemann, 1955); Louis Hartz, *The Liberal Tradition in America* (New York: Harcourt Bruce Jovanovich, 1955).
22. See, for instance, Selig Adler, *The Isolationist Impulse: Its Twentieth Century Reaction* (New York: Abelard-Schuman, 1957); Michael W. Miles, *The Odyssey of the American Right* (New York: Oxford University Press, 1980).
23. Lionel Trilling, *The Liberal Imagination* (New York: Anchor Books, 1950), p. 6.
24. See Daniel Bell (ed.), *The Radical Right* (New York: Anchor Books, 1964); Seymour Martin Lipset and Earl Raab, *The Politics of Unreason: Right Wing Extremism in America 1790–1970* (New York: Harper & Row, 1970).
25. Kenneth Prewitt, 'Political Ideas and a Political Science for Policy', *The Annals of the American Academy of Political and Social Science*, vol. 600, no. 1, 2005, p. 26.
26. For good surveys of those debates see Chaim I. Waxman (ed.), *The End of Ideology Debate* (New York: Funk and Wagnalls, 1968); Mostafa Rejai (ed.), *Decline of Ideology?* (Chicago: Lieber-Atherton, 1971); Job L. Dittberber, *The End of Ideology and American Social Thought: 1930–1960* (UMI Research Press, 1977).
27. Edward Shils, 'The End of Ideology', *Encounter*, no. 5, November 1955, pp. 52–8; Stuart Hughes, 'The End of Political Ideology', *Measure*, Spring 1951; Raymond Aron, *L'opium des intellectuels* (Paris: Calman-Levy, 1955); Seymour Martin Lipset, *Political Man* (Baltimore: Johns Hopkins University Press, 1981 [1960]), chapters 13 and 15. Albert Camus also

pronounced on the end of ideology in 1946. His version of the thesis, however, did not predict the coming of a middle ground consensus as such. See Albert Camus, 'Ni victimes, ni bourreaux', in *Actuelles: Chroniques 1944–1948* (Paris: Gallimard, 1950).

28. Bell, *The End of Ideology*.
29. Ibid., pp. 405, 402.
30. Ibid., p. 440.
31. Ibid., p. 14.
32. Maurice Isserman and Michael Kazin, *America Divided: The Civil War of the 1960, 2nd edn* (New York and Oxford: Oxford University Press, 2004), p. 4.
33. Sara Diamond, *Roads to Dominion: Right-Wing Movements and Political Power in the United States* (New York: Guilford Press, 1995), p. 29.
34. W. A. Rusher, *The Rise of the Right*, 2nd edn (New York: Anchor Books, 1992); Mary C. Brennan, *Turning Right in the Sixties: The Conservative Capture of the GOP* (Chapel Hill: University of North Carolina Press, 1995).
35. Richard M. Abrams, *America Transformed: Sixty Years of Revolutionary Change, 1941–2001* (Cambridge: Cambridge University Press, 2006), p. 227.
36. Kevin Phillips, *The Emerging Republican Majority*, 2nd edn (New York: Anchor Books, 1970), p. 37.
37. Lee Edwards, *The Conservative Revolution* (New York: Free Press, 1999); Jonathan M Schoenwald, *A Time For Choosing: The Rise of Modern American Conservatism* (Oxford: Oxford University Press, 2001), chapter 1.
38. William O'Neill, *The New Left: A History* (Wheeling, Ill.: Harlan Davidson, 2001); Van Gosse, *Rethinking the New Left: An Interpretative History* (London: Palgrave Macmillan, 2006).
39. Students for a Democratic Society, *Port Huron Statement*, Port Huron, Michigan, 15 June 1962, http://www2.iath.virginia.edu/sixties/HTML_docs/Resources/Primary/Manifestos/SDS_Port_Huron.html [12 June 2008].
40. Jeffrey O. G. Ogbar, *Black Power: Radical Politics and African American Identity* (Baltimore: Johns Hopkins University Press, 2005); Gosse, *Rethinking the New Left*, chapters 4, 9.
41. Abrams, *America Transformed*, pp. 228–9.
42. Christopher Lasch, *The Agony of the American Left* (New York: Alfred A. Knopf, 1969); O'Neill, *Coming Apart*, pp. 293–8.
43. Ibid., p. 298.
44. Cited in Gerson, *The Neoconservatives*, p. 144.
45. Jeane Kirkpatrick, 'Neoconservatism as a Response to the Counter-Culture', in I. Stelzer (ed.), *Neoconservatism* (London: Atlantic Books, 2004), p. 235.
46. Daniel Bell and Irving Kristol, 'What is the Public Interest?', *The Public Interest*, vol. 1, Fall 1965, p. 3.

47. Irving Kristol, *On the Democratic Idea in America* (New York: Harper & Row, 1972), p. xix.
48. Irving Kristol, 'Skepticism, Meliorism and The Public Interest', *The Public Interest*, Fall 1985, p. 32. See also Seymour Martin Lipset, 'The Wavering Polls', *The Public Interest*, vol. 43, 1976, pp. 70–90; Daniel Patrick Moynihan, *Maximum Feasible Misunderstanding* (New York: Free Press, 1970); Moynihan, *The Politics of Guaranteed Income* (New York: Vintage, 1973).
49. Nathan Glazer and Daniel Patrick Moynihan, *Beyond the Melting Pot: The Negroes, Puerto Ricans, Jews, and Irish of New York* (Cambridge: MIT Press, 1963), p. 66. See also Norman Podhoretz, 'My Negro Problem—And Ours', *Commentary*, February 1963, p. 93–102.
50. Daniel Patrick Moynihan, *The Negro Family: The Case for National Action* (Washington: Office of Policy Planning and Research, United States Department of Labor, 1965).
51. See Lee Rainwater and William L. Yancey, *The Moynihan Report and the Politics of Controversy* (Cambridge: MIT Press, 1967).
52. James Q. Wilson, 'Liberalism versus Liberal Education', *Commentary*, June 1972, pp. 50–1.
53. Irving Kristol, 'Teaching in, Speaking Out: The Controversy Over Vietnam', *Encounter*, August 1965; Daniel Patrick Moynihan, 'The Politics of Stability', *The New Leader*, 9 October 1967; Daniel Bell and Irving Kristol (eds.), *Confrontation: The Student Rebellion and the Universities* (New York: Basic Books, 1968); Norman Podhoretz, 'The New Inquisitors', *Commentary*, April 1973, pp. 7–9.
54. Irving Kristol, *Two Cheers for Capitalism* (New York: Basic Books, 1978), p. 171. See also Nathan Glazer, 'The Limits of Social Policy', *Commentary*, September 1971, p. 53.
55. Norman Podhoretz, 'New Vistas for Neoconservatives', *Conservative Digest*, vol. 15, 1989, pp. 56–7.
56. Gerson, *The Neoconservative Vision*, pp. 112–16; Irving Kristol, 'Facing the Facts in Vietnam', *The New Leader*, 30 September 1963; 'We Can't Resign As Policeman of the World', *New York Times Magazine*, 12 May 1968; Nathan Glazer, 'The New Left and its Limits', *Commentary*, July 1968, pp. 31–40.
57. Norman Podhoretz, *My Love Affair With America: The Cautionary Tale of a Cheerful Conservative* (New York: Free Press, 2000), p. 172.
58. Jeane Kirkpatrick, 'The Revolt of the Masses', *Commentary*, February 1973, p. 60. See also Nathan Glazer, *Remembering the Answers: Essays on the American Student Revolt* (New York: Basic Books, 1970).
59. Theodore Draper, 'The Specter of Weimar', *Commentary*, December 1971, p. 43.
60. Cited in Gerson, *The Neoconservative Vision*, p. 131.
61. Irving Kristol, 'My Cold War', in his *Neoconservatism: Selected Essays 1951–1995* (New York: Free Press, 1995), p. 486. See also Nathan Glazer,

'On Being Deradicalized', in Jumonville, *The New York Intellectuals Reader*.

62. Lipset, *American Exceptionalism*, p. 198.
63. Coalition for a Democratic Majority, 'Come Home Democrats', *New York Times*, 7 December 1972, p. 14.
64. Norman Podhoretz, 'Between Nixon and the New Politics', *Commentary*, September 1972, pp. 4–7; Penn Kemble and Joshua Muravchik, 'The New Politics and the Democrats', *Commentary*, December 1972, pp. 78–85; Diamond, *Roads to Dominion*, pp. 191–4.
65. Jumonville, *The New York Intellectuals Reader*, p. 406.
66. Irving Kristol, 'American Conservatism 1945–1995', *The Public Interest*, September 1995, p. 1.
67. Irving Kristol, 'Introduction' to his *Reflections*, pp. xiii-xiv.
68. See James A. Smith, *The Idea Brokers: Think Tanks and the Rise of the New Policy Elite* (New York: Free Press, 1991).
69. Kristol, 'On Corporate Philanthropy', in his *Reflections*, pp. 144–5.
70. Friedman, *The Neoconservative Revolution*, p. 133.
71. Diamond, *Roads to Dominion*, pp. 199–200.
72. National Association of Scholars, www.nas.org/who.cfm [20 July 2008].
73. Paul Gottfried, *Conservatism in America: Making Sense of the American Right* (New York: Palgrave Macmillan, 2007), p. 60; *The Conservative Movement* (New York: Macmillan, 1993), pp. 118–41.
74. Cited in Gottfried, *Conservatism in America*, p. 59.
75. Diamond, *The Road to Dominion*, p. 200.
76. Norman Podhoretz, 'The Culture of Appeasement', *Harper's*, October 1977, http://www.harpers.org/archive/1977/10/0022763 [7 March 2009].
77. Gerson, *The Neoconservative Vision*, pp. 167–8.
78. P.T. Bauer, 'Western Guilt and Third World Poverty', *Commentary*, January 1976, pp. 31–9; Gerson, *The Neoconservative Vision*, p. 168.
79. Cited in Daniel Patrick Moynihan, *A Dangerous Place* (New York: Little, Brown, 1976), p. 158.
80. Daniel Patrick Moynihan, 'The United States in Opposition', *Commentary*, March 1975, p. 35.
81. Jeane Kirkpatrick, *The Reagan Phenomenon—and Other Speeches on Foreign Policy* (Washington, DC: AEI Press, 1982), pp. 111–12.
82. For the classic text, see Robert Keohane and Joseph Nye, *Power and Interdependence: World Politics in Transition* (Boston: Little, Brown, 1977).
83. Commentary Symposium, 'America Now: A Failure of Nerve?', *Commentary*, July 1975, pp. 16–98; Norman Podhoretz, 'Making the World Safe for Communism', *Commentary*, April 1976, pp. 31–42; Dana H. Allin, *Cold War Illusions: America, Europe, and Soviet Power, 1969–1989* (New York: St. Martin's Press, 1995), pp. 54–65; Tom Donnelly and Vance Serchuk, 'Unrealistic Realism', AEI Online, 9 July 2004, www.aei.org/publications/pubID.20875/pub_detail.asp [6 October 2005].

84. Norman Podhoretz, 'The Future Danger', *Commentary*, April 1981, p. 39.
85. Norman Podhoretz, 'Kissenger Reconsidered', *Commentary*, June 1982, p. 24. See also Kristol, 'My Cold War' in his *Neoconservatism*.
86. McCormick, *America's Half-Century*, pp. 179–80.
87. Walter Laqueur, 'Kissinger and the Politics of Détente', *Commentary*, December 1973, p. 46.
88. Henry Kissinger, 'Between the Old Left and the New Right', *Foreign Affairs*, vol. 78, no. 3, 1999, pp. 110–11.
89. Jeremy Suri, *Power and Protest: Global Revolution and the Rise of Détente* (Cambridge, MA: Harvard University Press, 2003).
90. See, for instance, Carl Everett Ladd, Jr., *Where Have All the Voters Gone? The Fracturing of America's Party System* (New York: W. W. Norton, 1978); Morris Fiorina, 'The Decline of Collective Responsibility in American Politics', *Daedalus*, vol. 10, Summer 1980, pp. 25–45; Martin Wattenberg, *The Decline of American Political Parties 1952–1994* (Cambridge, MA: Harvard University Press, 1996).
91. Christopher Coker, 'The United States and the ethics of post-modern war', in Karen E. Smith and Margo Light (eds.), *Ethics and Foreign Policy* (Cambridge: Cambridge University Press, 2001), pp. 154, 157.
92. Bell, *The Cultural Contradictions of Capitalism*, p. 281.
93. Cited in Ehrman, *The Rise of Neoconservatism*, p. 57.
94. See Commentary Symposium, 'America Now'; Peter Berger, 'The Greening of U.S. Foreign Policy', *Commentary*, March 1976, pp. 23–8; Podhoretz, 'The Culture of Appeasement'; *The Present Danger: Do We Have the Will to Reverse the Decline of American Power?* (New York: Simon & Schuster, 1980); *Why We Were in Vietnam* (New York: Simon & Schuster, 1982).
95. Peter Steinfels, *The Neoconservatives: The Men Who Are Changing America's Politics* (New York: Simon & Schuster, 1979), p. 69.
96. The original CPD was set up in the early 1950s and helped the Truman and Eisenhower administrations develop and implement the containment doctrine outlined in National Security Memorandum No. 8 (NSC-68). As the historian of the second CPD Jerry Sanders notes, the CPD was a real who's who of neoconservative intellectuals, anti-communist labour leaders and hard-nosed national security cold warriors. Sanders describes it as a 'Reagan shadow cabinet'. Among the most well known neoconservatives who served on the CDP were Norman Podhoretz, Midge Decter, Nathan Glazer, Jeane Kirkpatrick, Seymour Martin Lipset, Paul Seabury, Richard Schifter, Richard Pipes, Elliot Abrams, Richard Perle, Paul Wolfowitz, Paul Nitze, Eugene Rostow and Max Kampelman. Leading members of the new CDM–CPD militarist merger were also chosen by the then CIA Director, George Bush, in 1976 to form the so-called Team B, tasked to produce an 'outside of government' alternative assessment of Soviet military capabilities. Team B's assessment, it is well known, estimated the Soviet threat to be far more important than official CIA assessments. Jerry Sanders, *Ped-*

dlers of Crisis: The Committee on the Present Danger and the Politics of Containment (Boston: South End Press, 1983), pp. 7–9, 197–204.

97. Seymour Martin Lipset, *American Exceptionalism: A Double-Edged Sword* (New York: W. W. Norton, 1996), p. 194.
98. Diamond, *Roads to Dominion*, pp. 197–200.
99. McCormick, *America's Half-Century*, pp. 191–215.
100. Norman Podhoretz, 'The Neo-Conservative Anguish Over Reagan's Foreign Policy', *New York Times Magazine*, 2 May 1982, pp. 30–1.
101. On the 'second Cold War' see Fred Halliday, *The Making of the Second Cold War* (London: Verso, 1986).
102. Reagan famously used anti-communist rhetoric to fire nearly 13,000 striking air traffic controllers and jail their leaders in 1981.
103. Norman Podhoretz, 'The New American Majority', *Commentary*, January 1981, p. 27.
104. Sanders, *Peddlers*, p. 9.
105. See, for instance, Podhoretz, 'The Neo-Conservative Anguish'; Robert Tucker, 'The Middle East: Carterism Without Carter', *Commentary*, September 1981; Irving Kristol, 'The Foreign Policy Muddle', *Wall Street Journal*, 29 April 1984; Halper and Clarke, *American Alone*, pp. 157–81.

2. LEO STRAUSS, LIBERALISM AND THE 'CRISIS OF OUR TIMES'

1. Leo Strauss, 'What is Political Philosophy?', in his *An Introduction to Political Philosophy: Ten Essays by Leo Strauss*, edited and introduced by Hilail Gildin (Detroit: Wayne State University Press, 1989), p. 4.
2. Indeed, according to the historian of Jewish America Murray Friedman, Strauss is the political philosopher who had the greatest influence on the development of Jewish conservatism and the broader conservative movement in the United States since the end of the Second World War. *The Neoconservative Revolution: Jewish Intellectuals and the Shaping of Public Policy* (Cambridge: Cambridge University Press, 2005), p. 40.
3. See Kenneth L. Deutsch and John A. Murley (eds.), *Leo Strauss, the Straussians, and the American Regime* (Lanham, MD: Rowman & Littlefield, 1999); Kenneth L. Deutsch and Walter Soffer (eds.), *The Crisis of Liberal Democracy: A Straussian Perspective* (Albany, NY: State University of New York Press, 1987); Robert Devigne, *Recasting Conservatism: Oakeshott, Strauss, and the Response to Postmodernism* (New Haven and London: Yale University Press, 1994; Shadia Drury, *Leo Strauss and the American Right*, London:Macmillan, 1997). In *Leo Strauss and his Legacy: A Bibliography* (Lexington: Lexington Books, 2005), John A. Murley documents over 10,000 works by hundreds of Strauss's students, and their students' students.
4. Irving Kristol, 'America's Exceptional Conservatism', in his *Neoconservatism: Selected Essays 1949–1995* (New York: Free Press, 1995), pp. 379–80.

5. Irving Kristol, 'An Autobiographical Memoir', in ibid., p. 9. See also Peter Minowitz, *Defending Leo Strauss and Straussians Against Leo Strauss and Other Accusers* (Lexington: Lexington Books, 2010); Peter Berkowitz, 'The Shadow of Fascist Philosophy on Today's Conservative Politics', *Chronicle of Higher Education*, 14 May 2004, http://chronicle.com/weekly/v50/136/36b00401.htm[4 December 2006]; Catherine Zuckert and Michael Zuckert, *The Truth About Leo Strauss: Political Philosophy and American Democracy* (Chicago: Chicago University Press, 2006), pp. 184–94.
6. See Alan Gilbert, 'Leo Strauss and the Principle of the Right: An Introduction to Strauss's Letter', *Constellations*, vol. 16, no. 1, 2009, p. 79.
7. Leo Strauss, 'Letters to Karl Löwith', *Constellations*, vol. 16, no. 1, 2009, p. 84.
8. Scott Horton, 'The Letter', 16 July 2006, http://balkin.blogspot.com/2006/07/letter_16.html [5 August 2008]. The letter also appears in Eugene R. Shepperd, *Leo Strauss and the Politics of Exile: The Making of a Political Philosopher* (Waltham, MA: Brandeis University Press, 2007), in Nicholas Xenos, *Cloaked in Virtue: Unveiling the Rhetoric of American Foreign Policy* (London: Routledge, 2008), and in the journal *Constellations*, vol. 16, no. 1, 2009.
9. Harvey C. Mansfield, 'Timeless Mind', *Claremont Review of Book*, Winter 2007, http://www.claremont.org/publications/crb/id.1505/article_detail.asp [June 2008]. See also Minowitz, *Defending Leo Strauss*, pp. 141–78.
10. Scott Horton, 'Will the Real Leo Strauss Please Stand Up?', *Harper's Magazine*, 21 January 2008, http://www.harpers.org/archive/2008/01/hbc-90002212 [3 March 2009].
11. Leo Strauss, *The Rebirth of Classical Political Philosophy*, ed. Thomas Pangle (Chicago: Chicago University Press, 1989), p. 28.
12. See Peter Graf Kielmansegg, Horst Mewes and Elisabeth Glaser-Schmidt (eds.), *Hannah Arendt and Leo Strauss: German Émigrés and American Political Thought after World War II* (Cambridge: Cambridge University Press, 1995). See also Shepperd, *Leo Strauss and the Politics of Exile.*
13. Leo Strauss, *Spinoza's Critique of Religion* (New York: Schocken Books, 1965 [1930]), p. 2.
14. Ibid., p. 1.
15. Ibid., pp. 2–3. See also John Gunnell, 'Strauss before Straussianism: Reason, Revelation and Nature', *The Review of Politics*, vol. 53, no. 1, 1991, pp. 53–74.
16. See, especially, Leo Strauss, 'Reason and Revelation', reprinted in Heinrich Meier, *Leo Strauss and the Theologico–Political Problem* (Chicago: Chicago University Press, 2006).
17. Leo Strauss, *Liberalism Ancient and Modern* (New York: Basic Books, 1968) pp. 254–5. See also Leo Strauss, 'German Nihilism', *Interpretation*, vol. 26, no. 3, 1999, pp. 353–78; 'The Living Issues of German Postwar Phiosophy', in Meier, *Leo Strauss*; Gunnell, 'Strauss before Straussianism'.

For good recent (Straussian) studies of Strauss's treatment of the theological-political problem see Daniel Tanguay, *Leo Strauss, Une biographie intellectuelle* (Paris: Grasset et Fasquelle, 2003); Heinrich Meier, *Leo Strauss and the Theological–Political Problem* (Chicago: Chicago University Press, 2006); Steven B. Smith, *Reading Leo Strauss: Politics, Philosophy, Judaism* (Chicago: University of Chicago Press, 2006).

18. Strauss, *Spinoza's Critique of Religion*, p. 31.
19. Ibid.
20. John McCormick, 'Fear, Technology, and the State: Carl Schmitt, Leo Strauss, and the Revival of Hobbes in Weimar and National Socialist Germany', *Political Theory*, vol. 22, no. 4, 1994, pp. 619–52; Gary Ulmen, 'Between the Weimar Republic and the Third Reich: Continuity in Carl Schmitt's Thought', *Telos*, Spring 2001, pp. 18–31; David Dyzenhaus, 'Leviathan in the 1930s: The Reception of Hobbes in the Third Reich', in John P. McCormick (ed.), *Confronting Mass Democracy and Industrial Technology: Political and Social Theory From Nietzsche to Habermas* (Durham and London: Duke University Press, 2002), pp. 163–91; Heinrich Meir, *Carl Schmitt and Leo Strauss: The Hidden Dialogue* (Chicago and London: University of Chicago Press, 1995); Miguel Vatter, 'Strauss and Schmitt as Readers of Hobbes and Spinoza: On the Relation Between Political Theology and Liberalism', *The New Centennial Review*, vol. 4, no. 3, 2004, pp. 161–214.
21. Dyzenhaus, 'Leviathan', p. 166.
22. Ibid., pp. 162–3.
23. Carl Schmitt, *The Concept of the Political*, trans. George Schwab (Chicago: University of Chicago Press, 1996 [1932]). Schmitt's treatise was first published as an article in 1927 and then as a book in 1932.
24. Ibid., p. 27.
25. Ibid., p. 45.
26. Ibid., pp. 28–30.
27. See, especially, Carl Schmitt, *Political Theology: Four Chapters on the Concept of Sovereignty*, trans. George Schwab (Chicago: Chicago University Press, 2005 [1922]).
28. I am grateful to one of the anonymous referees for insisting on this point.
29. On this particular point, see Carl Schmitt, 'The Age of Neutralizations and Depoliticizations', *Telos*, no. 96, 1993, pp. 130–42.
30. Joseph Cropsey, 'Preface', in Meier, *Carl Schmitt and Leo Strauss*, pp. ix-x.
31. Schmitt, *The Concept of the Political*, p. 27.
32. Leo Strauss, 'Notes on Carl Schmitt's Concept of the Political', in Schmitt, *The Concept*, pp. 102–3. Italics original.
33. Ibid., p. 99.
34. Strauss, 'Spinoza's Critique of Religion', p. 350.
35. Ibid., p. 100.

36. Ibid., p. 124.
37. Cropsey, 'Preface', pp. x-xi.
38. Schmitt, *The Concept of the Political*, p. 52.
39. Strauss, 'Notes on Carl Schmitt's Concept of the Political', pp. 86–9.
40. Ibid., p. 84.
41. Ibid., p. 89.
42. Ibid., p. 92. See also McCormick, 'Fear, Technology, and the State', p. 628.
43. Ibid., p. 99.
44. Ibid., p. 91.
45. Ibid., pp. 100–1.
46. Leo Strauss, *The Political Philosophy of Hobbes: Its Basis and Its Genesis* (Chicago: University of Chicago Press, 1966 [1938]), p. 9.
47. Ibid., p. 11.
48. Ibid., p. 9.
49. Ibid., p. 11.
50. Ibid., pp. 20–1.
51. Ibid., p. 122.
52. McCormick, 'Fear, Technology, and the State', p. 630.
53. Strauss cited in ibid.
54. Carl Schmitt, *The Leviathan in the State Theory of Thomas Hobbes: Meaning and Failure of a Political Symbol*, trans. George Schwab and Erna Hilfstein (Westport: Greenwood, 1996 [1938]). John McCormick, 'Political Theory and Political Theology: The Second Wave of Carl Schmitt in English', *Political Theory*, vol. 26, no. 6, 1998, pp. 830–54.
55. Ibid., pp. 41–2.
56. See Renato Cristi, *Carl Schmitt and Authoritarian Liberalism* (Cardiff: University of Wales, 1998), pp. 25–52; Balakrishnan, *The Enemy*, pp. 176–89.
57. Schmitt, 'Strong State, Free Economy', in Cristi, *Carl Schmitt*, p. 218. Italics original.
58. Schmitt, *The Leviathan*, p. 71.
59. Ibid., pp. 31, 33.
60. Ibid., pp. 48–9.
61. Ibid., pp. 47–8.
62. Ibid., p. 48. See also Carl Schmitt, *The Nomos of the Earth: In the International Law of the Jus Publicum Europaeum* (New York: Telos Press, 2006 [1950].
63. Ibid., pp. 33–4.
64. This Schmittian-Straussian reading of Hobbes has also been developed further by one of Schmitt's most talented students, Reinhart Koselleck, in his doctoral dissertation *Critique and Crisis: Enlightenment and the Pathogenesis of Modern Society* (Cambridge, MA: MIT Press, 1988 [1959]). The critical theorist Jürgen Habermas, who is heavily antipathetical towards Schmitt, in fact borrows extensively from Koselleck's Schmit-

tian analysis in his first major work, *The Structural Transformation of the Public Sphere: Inquiry Into a Category of Bourgeois Society* (Cambridge: Polity Press, 1992 [1962]).

65. Ibid., pp. 73–4.
66. Dyzenhaus, 'Leviathan', pp. 187–8.
67. John P. McCormick, *Carl Schmitt's Critique of Liberalism: Against Politics as Technology* (Cambridge: Cambridge University Press, 1997, p. 279.
68. Leo Strauss, *What is Political Philosophy?* (Chicago: Chicago University Press, 1959), p. 172. Schmitt responded to Strauss's veiled commentary on his *Leviathan* indirectly in the 'Indications' added to the 1963 edition of *The Concept of the Political* and in the afterword to the 1965 German edition of his *Leviathan*. See Carl Schmitt, 'Die vollendete Reformation: Zu neuen Leviathan-Interpretationen', in *Der Leviathan in der Staatslehre des Thomas Hobbes* (Stuttgart: Klett-Cotta, 1965).
69. Strauss, *Spinoza's Critique of Religion*, p. 30.
70. Leo Strauss, *Natural Right and History* (Chicago: Chicago University Press, 1971 [1953]), p. 274.
71. Leo Strauss, 'The Three Waves of Modernity', in his *Introduction to Political Philosophy: Six Essays by Leo Strauss*, ed. Hilail Gildin (New York: Bobbs-Merrill, 1975); Strauss, 'What is Political Philosophy?'
72. Leo Strauss, *The City and Man* (Chicago: University of Chicago Press, 1964), Introduction.
73. Strauss, 'What is Political Philosophy?', p. 38.
74. Leo Strauss, *Liberalism Ancient and Modern* (Chicago: University of Chicago Press, 1995 [1968]) p. 4.
75. Ibid., p. 24.
76. Ibid., p. 5.
77. Strauss, *Natural Right*, pp. 31–2.
78. Leo Strauss, cited in Stanley Rosen, 'Leo Strauss and the Quarrel Between the Ancients and the Moderns', in Alan Udoff (ed.), *Leo Strauss's Thought: Toward a Critical Engagement* (Boulder, CO: Lynne Rienner Publishers, 1991), p. 160.
79. Strauss, *Natural Right*, p. 6.
80. Ibid., pp. 2–3.
81. Ibid., p. 79. On this particular dimension of Strauss's work see Laurence Berns, 'The Prescientific World and Historicism: Some Reflections on Strauss, Heidegger, and Husserl', in Alan Udoff (ed.), *Leo Strauss's Thought: Toward a Critical Engagement* (Boulder, CO: Lynne Rienner Publishers, 1991), p. 175; Robert Pippin, 'The Unavailability of the Ordinary: Strauss on the Philosophical Faith of Modernity', *Political Theory*, vol. 31, no. 3, 2003, pp. 335–58.
82. Ibid., pp. 6–8.
83. Strauss, *What is Political Philosophy?*, p. 11.
84. Strauss, *Natural Right and History*, p. 124.
85. Ibid., p. 100.

86. Strauss, *What is Political Philosophy?*, p. 10.
87. Gunnell, 'Strauss Before Straussianism', p. 70.
88. Strauss, *The City and Man*, p. 191.
89. Cited in Gunnell, 'Strauss Before Straussianism', p. 70.
90. Strauss, *Natural Right and History*, p. 160.
91. See, for instance, Berkowitz, 'The Shadow of Fascist Philosophy'; Zuckert and Zuckert, *The Truth About Leo Strauss*, pp. 184–94.
92. Berns, 'The Prescientific World and Historicism', p. 175.
93. Strauss, *The Rebirth*, p. 270.
94. Leo Strauss, *On Tyranny. Including the Strauss–Kojève Correspondence*, edited by Victor Gourevitch and Michael S. Roth (Chicago: Chicago University Press, 2000), p. 196.
95. Strauss, *Natural Right*, p. 6.
96. Stanley Rosen, 'Leo Strauss and the Quarrel Between the Ancients and the Moderns' in Udoff, *Leo Strauss's Thought*, pp. 162–3. See also Pippin, 'The Unavailability of the Ordinary'.
97. Strauss, *The City and Man*, pp. 20–9.
98. Strauss, *On Tyranny*, p. 212.
99. Ibid., p. 182.
100. Ibid., p. 200.
101. Strauss, *Natural Right*, p. 323.
102. Strauss, *The City and Man*, p. 49.
103. Strauss, *Natural Right*, pp. 145–6.
104. Strauss, *The City and Man*, p. 32.
105. Ibid., pp. 32–4.
106. Strauss, *Natural Right*, pp. 197–8.
107. As he put it in his debate with Kojève, 'The state through which man is said to become reasonably satisfied is, then, the state in which man loses his humanity'. *On Tyranny*, p. 208.
108. Strauss, *Natural Right*, pp. 145–6.
109. Ibid., p. 130.
110. Strauss, *The City*, p. 102.
111. Ibid., pp. 49, 31–4; *Natural Right*, pp. 163–4. See also Tanguay, *Leo Strauss*, pp. 183–262.
112. Strauss, *The City*, p. 20.
113. Pippin, 'The Unavailability of the Ordinary', p. 127.
114. *Strauss*, 'The Three Waves'.
115. See for instance Shadia Drury, *The Political Ideas of Leo Strauss* (London: Palgrave Macmillan, 1988); *Leo Strauss and the American Right* (London: Macmillan, 1997).
116. Leo Lampert, *Leo Strauss and Nietzsche* (Chicago: Chicago University Press, 1998), pp. 169–70.
117. Pippin, 'The Modern World of Leo Strauss', p. 467, note 6.
118. Strauss, 'What is Political Philosophy?', p. 28.
119. For an incisive discussion of the complex link between Strauss's Platonic practices and the Iraq War, see Patricia Owens, 'Beyond Strauss, Lies, and

the War in Iraq: Hannah Arendt's Critique of Neoconservatism', *Review of International Studies*, vol. 33, Special Issue, 2007, pp. 265–83.
120. See Mark Lilla, 'The Closing of the Straussian Mind', *New York Review of Books*, vol. 51, no. 17, 4 November 2004, pp. 55–9.
121. John Gray, *Black Mass: Apocalyptic Religion and the Death of Utopia* (London: Penguin Allen Lane, 2007), p. 131.
122. On Strauss and the founding of a Straussian philosophical school, see Meier, *Leo Strauss*, pp. xvii-xxi. On Straussianism see Michael Zuckert, 'Straussians', in Steven B. Smith (ed.), *The Cambridge Companion to Leo Strauss* (Cambridge: Cambridge University Press, 2009); Robert Devigne, 'Strauss and Straussianism: From the Ancients to the Moderns?', *Political Studies*, vol. 57, no. 3, 2009, pp. 592–616.
123. Lilla, 'The Closing of the Straussian Mind'.
124. Cited in Ronald Bailey, 'The Voice of Neoconservatism', *Reason Online*, 17 October 2001, http://www.reason.com/news/show/34900.html [3 October 2007].
125. Robert Devigne, *Recasting Conservatism: Oakeshott, Strauss, and the Response to Postmodernism* (New Haven and London: Yale University Press, 1994), pp. 64–5.

3. CAPITALISM, CULTURE WARS AND THE NEOCONSERVATIVE STATE

1. Irving Kristol, 'Utopianism Ancient and Modern', in his *Neoconservatism: Selected Essays 1951–1995* (New York: Free Press, 1995), p. 191.
2. Francis Fukuyama, *The End of History and the Last Man*, 2nd edn, (Free Press: New York and London, 2006 [1992]), pp. 157, 214–15.
2. Irving Kristol, *Reflections of a Neoconservative: Looking Back, Looking Ahead* (Basic Books: New York, 1983), p. xii; Adam Wolfson, 'Conservatives and Neo-conservatives', in I. Stelzer (ed.), *Neo-conservatism* (London: Atlantic Books, 2004), p. 216.
3. The term 'embedded liberalism' was coined by John Gerard Ruggie who drew upon Karl Polanyi's *The Great Transformation: The Political and Economic Origins of Our Times* (Boston: Beacon Press, 1957 [1944]). See Ruggie, 'International Regimes, Transactions and Change: Embedded Liberalism in the Postwar Economic Order', *International Organization*, vol. 36, no. 2, 1982, pp. 379–415.
5. Robert O. Keohane, 'The World Political Economy and the Crisis of Embedded Liberalism', in J. H. Goldthorpe (ed.), *Order and Conflict in Contemporary Capitalism* (Oxford: Clarendon Press, 1984); Mark Blyth, *Great Transformations: Economic Ideas and Institutional Changes in the Twentieth Century* (Cambridge: Cambridge University Press, 2002).
6. David Harvey, *A Brief History of Neoliberalism* (Oxford: Oxford University Press, 2005).

7. See Carl Friedrich, 'The Political Thought of Neo-Liberalism', *American Political Science Review*, vol. 49, no. 2, 1955, pp. 509–25; Michel Foucault, *La Naissance de la biopolitique: cours au collège de France, 1978–1979* (Paris: Seuil, 2004).
8. See Edward N. Megay, 'Anti-Pluralist Liberalism: The German Neoliberals', *Political Science Quarterly*, vol. 85, no. 3, 1970, p. 422; Rainer Hank, 'Neoliberalism or Ordoliberalism or: From Freiburg to Cologne and to Berlin', Working Paper, Centre for German and European Studies, University of California, Berkeley, 1991. The close proximity between the authoritarian economic liberalism of Carl Schmitt and that of the ordoliberals has been noted by Renato Cristi in his *Carl Schmitt and Authoritarian Liberalism: Strong State, Free Economy* (Cardiff: University of Wales Press, 1998), p. 194.
9. On Schmitt's influence on Hayek's work see William Scheuerman, 'The Unholly Alliance of Carl Schmitt and Friedrich A. Hayek', in his *Carl Schmitt: The End of Law* (Lanham, MD: Rowman & Littlefield, 1999), pp. 209–24.
10. Paul Treanor, cited in Harvey, *A Brief History of Neoliberalism*, p. 2.
11. Gerard Dumenil and Dominique Levy, *Capital Resurgent: Roots of the Neo-liberal Revolution* (Cambridge, MA: Harvard University Press, 2004); Susan George, 'A Short History of Neoliberalism: Twenty Years of Elite Economics and Emerging Opportunities for Structural Change', in W. Bello, N. Bullard and K. Malhotra (eds.), *Global Finance: New Thinking on Regulating Capital Markets* (London: Zed Books, 2000), pp. 27–35.
12. Harvey, *A Brief History of Neoliberalism*, p. 19.
13. Susan George, 'Winning the War of Ideas', *Dissent*, Summer 1997, http://www.tni.org/archives/george/dissent.htm, [4 October 2006].
14. Irving Kristol, 'The Neoconservative Persuasion', *Weekly Standard*, vol. 8, no. 47, August 2003, http://www.weeklystandard.com/Content/Public/Articles/000/000/003/000tzmlw.asp [3 June 2008].
15. Irving Kristol, 'Ideology and Supply-Side Economics', *Commentary*, April 1981, pp. 48–56; Murray Friedman, *The Neoconservative Revolution: Jewish Intellectuals and the Shaping of Public Policy* (Cambridge: Cambridge University Press, 2005, pp. 181–4; Mark Gerson, *The Neoconservative Vision: From the Cold War to the Culture War* (Lanham, MD: Madison Books, 1997), pp. 204–6.
16. Gerson, *The Neoconservative Vision*, pp. 205–6. For a sample of neoconservative writings on market capitalism see Daniel Bell and Irving Kristol (eds.), *Capitalism Today* (New York: Basic Books, 1972); Commentary Symposium, 'Capitalism, Socialism and Nihilism', *Commentary*, April 1978, pp. 29–72; June Wanniski, *The Way the World Works* (New York: Gateway Books, 1978); George Gilder, *Wealth and Poverty* (New York: Basic Books, 1981); Peter Berger, *The Capitalist Revolution: Fifty Propositions about Prosperity, Equality, and Liberty* (New York: Basic Books, 1986); Michael Novak, *The Spirit of Democratic Capitalism* (Lanham, MD: Madison Books, 1991); Fukuyama, *The End of History*.

17. See, for instance, Eric Fromm, *Escape from Freedom* (New York: Holt and Company, 1969 [1941]); Max Horkeimer and Theodor Adorno, 'The Culture Industry', in their *Dialectics of Enlightenment*, (London: Verso, 1997 [1947]); Theodor Adorno, *The Culture Industry* (London: Routledge, 2001); Herbert Marcuse, *One-Dimensional Man: Studies in the Ideology of Advanced Industrial Society* (London: Routledge, 2002 [1964]).
18. Daniel Bell, *The Cultural Contradictions of Capitalism* (New York: Basic Books, 1978), p. 35.
19. Ibid., p. 28.
20. Irving Kristol, '"When Virtue Loses All Her Loveliness"—Some Reflections on Capitalism and the "Free Society"', in his *On the Democratic Idea in America* (New York: Harper & Row, 1972).
21. Ibid., pp. 90–4.
22. Kristol's interpretation of Hayek can be contested on various grounds. For an alternative reading see John Gray, *Hayek on Liberty* (London: Routledge, 1998).
23. Ibid., pp. 94–8.
24. Ibid., pp. 97–8.
25. Irving Kristol, 'The Coming Conservative Century', *Wall Street Journal*, 1 February 1993, p. A10.
26. On this particular aspect of neoliberalism, see Foucault, *Naissance de la biopolitique*, chapters 5–12.
27. Kristol, 'When Virtue', p. 102. See also his 'Rationalism in Economics', in his *Reflections*, pp. 177–93.
28. Irving Kristol, 'Capitalism, Socialism, and Nihilism', in his *Neoconservatism*, p. 103.
29. Irving Kristol, 'Socialism: An Obituary for an Idea', in his *Reflections*, p. 117.
30. Irving Kristol, *Two Cheers for Capitalism* (New York: Basic Books, 1978), pp. 138–9.
31. Ibid., p. 85.
32. Irving Kristol, 'Adam Smith and the Spirit of Capitalism', in his *Reflections*, p. 169.
33. Bell, *The Cultural Contradictions*, pp. 28–9.
34. William Bennett, 'America's Cultural Decline Must Be Reversed', *Human Events*, vol. 50, 1994, pp. 12–3. See also, his 'Revolt Against God. America's Spiritual Despair', *Policy Review*, no. 67, 1994, pp. 19–24.
35. Kristol, 'The Coming Conservative Century'.
36. Irving Kristol cited in Ronald Bailey, 'The Voice of Neoconservatism', *Reason Online*, 17 October 2001, http://www.reason.com/news/show/34900.html [3 October 2007].
37. Bell, *The Cultural Contradictions*, p. 50. See also Kristol, 'Adam Smith', pp. 153, 161, 171; Jeane Kirkpatrick, 'The Sources of Stability in the American Tradition', in J. Kirkpatrick, *Dictatorships and Double Stand-*

ards: Rationalism and Reason in Politics (Washington: Simon & Schuster and AEI Press, 1982), pp. 224–5; Allan Bloom, *The Closing of the American Mind* (New York: Simon & Schuster, 1987), pp. 28, 110–1, 165, 286; Fukuyama, *The End of History*, pp. 145–50, 153–62, 185–9, 200.

38. Kristol, 'The Coming Conservative Century'.
39. Irving Kristol, 'Utopianism Ancient and Modern', pp. 195–6. Italics original. See also Irving Kristol, 'The American Revolution as a Successful Revolution', in ibid.; Nathan Glazer and Irving Kristol (eds.), *The American Commonwealth* (New York: Basic Books, 1976); Kirkpatrick, 'The Sources of Stability'.
40. Kristol, 'When Virtue', pp. 99–101.
41. Ibid, pp. 102–3.
42. Fukuyama, *The End of History*, p. 188.
43. Ibid., p. 189.
44. Bloom, *The Closing of the American Mind*, pp. 112. See also p. 28.
45. See Gary Dorrien, *The Neoconservative Mind: Politics, Culture and the War of Ideology* (Philadelphia: Temple University Press, 1993), pp. 30–44.
46. See William Scheuerman, 'Carl Schmitt and the Origins of Joseph Schumpeter's Theory of Elitism', in his *Carl Schmitt*, pp. 194–5; Richard Bellamy, 'Schumpeter and the Transformation of Capitalism, Liberalism and Democracy', in his *Rethinking Liberalism* (London and New York: Pinter, 2000), p. 93.
47. Scheuerman, 'Carl Schmitt'.
48. Joseph Schumpeter, *Capitalism, Socialism and Democracy* (London: Allen & Unwin, 1950 [1942]), p. 134.
49. Ibid., p. 151
50. Ibid., pp. 145–6.
51. Friedrich von Hayek, 'The Intellectuals and Socialism', in George B. de Huszar (ed.), *The Intellectuals* (Glencoe, Ill.: The Free Press, 1960 [1949]), pp. 371–3.
52. Lionel Trilling, *Beyond Culture* (New York: Viking, 1965).
53. Ibid., pp. xii-xvi.
54. B. Bruce-Briggs (ed.), *The New Class?* (New Brunswick, NJ.: Transaction Books, 1978); Alvin W. Gouldner, *The Future of Intellectuals and the Rise of the New Class* (London: Macmillan Press, 1979); Kristol, *Two Cheers*, p. 28; Jeane Kirkpatrick, 'Politics and the New Class', in her *Dictatorships*, pp. 186–203.
55. Seymour Martin Lipset and R. B. Dobson, 'The Intellectual as Critic and Rebel', *Daedalus*, vol. 101, no. 3, 1972; Seymour Martin Lipset, 'The New Class and the Professiorate', in Bruce-Briggs, *The New Class?*; E. C. Ladd Jr. and Seymour Martin Lipset, *The Divided Academy* (New York: McGraw-Hill, 1975); Norman Cantor, 'The Real Crisis in the Humanities Today', *New Criterion*, vol. 3, no. 10, 1985, p. 30. See also Robert Boyers, 'The Neoconservatives and Culture', *Salmagundi*, vol. 66, 1985, pp. 192–204.

56. Samuel Huntington, 'The Politics of Disharmony', *Comparative Politics*, vol. 6, January 1974, p. 184.
57. Cited in Gerson, *The Neoconservatives*, p. 236.
58. Kirkpatrick, 'Politics', p. 187.
59. Jeane Kirkpatrick, 'Introduction', in her *Dictatorships*, p. 11.
60. Aaron Wildavsky, *The Rise of Radical Egalitarianism* (New York: National Book Network, 1991), pp. 6–7. See also Richard J. Ellis, *The Dark Side of the Left: Illiberal Egalitarianism in America* (Lawrence, KS: University Press of Kansas, 2000); Irving Kristol, 'About Equality', in his *Neoconservatism*; Kirkpatrick, 'The Sources'.
61. Kristol, *Two Cheers*, pp. 235–6.
62. Kristol, 'About Equality', p. 167.
63. Kristol, 'Utopianism', p. 186; 'The American Revolution', p. 246.
64. See, for instance, Gertrude Himmelfarb, *The Roads to Modernity: The British, French and American Enlightenment* (London: Penguin, 2004); Kirkpatrick, 'Sources of Stability', pp. 215–36; Allan Bloom, *Confronting the Constitution: The Challenge to Locke, Montesquieu, Jefferson, and the Federalists from Utilitarianism, Historicism, Marxism, Freudianism, Pragmatism, Existentialism* (Washington, DC: AEI Press, 1990); *The Closing of the American Mind*; pp. 157–72.
65. Jeane Kirkpatrick, 'The Revolt of the Masses', *Commentary*, February 1973, p. 63.
66. Kirkpatrick, 'Politics'. See also Jeane Kirkpatrick, *Dismantling the Parties: Reflections on Party Reform and Party Decomposition* (Washington, DC: AEI Press, 1978); Samuel Huntington, 'The Democratic Distemper', in Kristol and Glazer, *The American Commonwealth*; Seymour Martin Lipset, 'Party Reform Since 1968: A Case Study in Intellectual Failure', in P. Bonomi, J. MacGregor Burns and Austin Ranney (eds.), *The American Constitutional System Under Strong and Weak Parties* (New York: Praeger, 1981); Nelson W. Polsky and Aaron Wildavsky, *Presidential Elections: Strategies of American Electoral Politics*, 5th edn (New York: Scribner, 1980).
67. Kirkpatrick, 'Politics', pp. 194–5.
68. Irving Kristol, 'On Corporate Capitalism', in Kristol and Glazer, *The American Commonwealth*, p. 126.
69. Kristol, 'Utopianism', pp. 196–7.
70. Jürgen Habermas, 'Neo-conservative Cultural Criticism in the United States and West Germany', and 'The New Obscurity', in his *The New Conservatism* (Cambridge: Polity, 1985).
71. Richard Wolin, 'The Cultural Politics of Neoconservatism', in his *Labyrinths: Explorations in the Critical History of Ideas* (Amherst: University of Massachusetts Press, 1995), p. 38.
72. Herbert Marcuse, 'The Affirmative Character of Culture', in his *Negations* (Harmondsworth: Penguin, 1968[1937]), pp. 94–5. See also Walter Benjamin, 'Edmund Fuchs: Collector and Historian', in A. Arato and E. Ger-

bhardt (eds.), *The Essential Frankfurt School Reader*, (New York: Urizen, 1978).

73. David Frisby, *The Alienated Mind: The Sociology of Knowledge in Germany 1918–1933* (London: Routledge, 1992), p. 15.
74. America's White working class displays a relatively low level of political consciousness, and it has experienced a frustrating decline in economic and social status since the 1960s. This has rendered this large segment of American society particularly receptive to mobilisations of conservative values. See Judith Stein, *Running Steel, Running America: Race, Economic Policy and the Decline of Liberalism* (Chapel Hill: University of North Carolina Press, 1998); Ruy A. Teixeira and Joel Rogers, *America's Forgotten Majority: Why the White Working Class Still Matters* (New York: Basic Books, 2000).
75. Kristol, *Two Cheers*, p. 235.
76. Gertrude Himmelfarb, *The De-Moralization of Society: From Victorian Virtues to Modern Values* (New York: Vintage, 1996), p. 236.
77. Harvey C. Mansfield, 'The Legacy of the Late Sixties', in Stephen Macedo (ed.), *Reassessing the Sixties* (New York: W. W. Norton, 1997), p. 32. See also Dinesh D'Souza, *The End of Racism: Principles for a Multiracial Society* (New York: Simon & Schuster, 1996).
78. Barbara Cruikshank, 'Cultural Politics: Political Theory and the Foundations of Democratic Order', in Jodi Dean (ed.), *Cultural Studies and Political Theory* (Ithaca, NY: Cornell University Press, 2000), p. 70. See also Nikolas Rose, *Powers of Freedom: Reframing Political Thought* (Cambridge: Cambridge University Press, 1999), pp. 182–4.
79. Kristol, 'The Coming Conservative Century'. See also Matthew Continetti, 'Misreading History: The Lesson of the Last Eight Years is Not that Americans Want a Smaller Government', *Weekly Standard*, vol. 14, no. 18, 2009, http://www.weeklystandard.com/Content/Public/Articles/000/000/016/015paamb.asp [17 January,2009].
80. Irving Kristol, 'A Conservative Welfare State', in Stelzer, *Neo-conservatism*, pp. 143–8. See also Bell, *The Cultural Contradictions of Capitalism*, pp. 220–82; Michael Novak, *The American Vision* (Washington, DC: AEI Press, 1978), p. 13; Seymour Martin Lipset, 'Neoconservatism: Myth and Reality', *Society*, vol. 25, 1988, pp. 29–37.
81. Irving Kristol, 'The Neoconservative Persuasion', *Weekly Standard*, vol. 8, no. 47, August 2003, http://www.weeklystandard.com/Content/Public/Articles/000/000/003/000tzmlw.asp [3 June 2008].
82. See, for instance, James Q. Wilson and Richard J. Herrnstein, *Crime and Human Nature: The Definitive Study of the Causes of Crime* (New York: Simon & Schuster, 1985); James Q. Wilson and George Kelling, 'Broken Windows: The Police and Neighbourhood Safety', in Stelzer, *Neo-Conservatism*; William J Bennett, *The Devaluing of America: The Fight for Our Culture and Our Children* (New York: Simon & Schuster, 1995); Mansfield, 'The Legacy of the Sixties', p. 39.

83. Daniel Patrick Moynihan, 'Defining Deviancy Down', *The American Scholar*, Winter 1993, http://www2.sunysuffolk.edu/formans/DefiningDeviancy.htm [12 December 2006].
84. Charles Krauthammer, 'Defining Deviancy Up: The New Assault on Bourgeois Life', *The New Republic*, 22 November 1993, p. 20.
85. Thomas McCarthy, *Race, Empire and the Idea of Human Development* (Cambridge: Cambridge University Press, 2009), p. 12. See also Richard H. King, *Race, Culture and the Intellectuals, 1940–1970* (Baltimore: Johns Hopkins University Press, 2004); Robert Gooding-Williams, *Look, A Negro!* (New York: Routledge, 2006).
86. See, for instance, Herbert J. Gans, *The War Against the Poor: The Underclass and Antipoverty Policy* (New York: Basic Books, 1995); Frances Piven and Richard Cloward, *Regulating the Poor: The Functions of Public Welfare* (New York: Vintage Books, 1993); Michael B. Katz, *The Undeserving Poor: From the War on Poverty to the War on Welfare* (New York: Pantheon Books, 1989). For a comparative study which highlights the distinctively punitive character of American welfare policies, see Alberto Alesina and Edward Glaeser, *Fighting Poverty in the US and Europe: A World of Difference* (Oxford: Oxford University Press, 2006).
87. Martin Gilens, *Why Americans Hate Welfare: Race, Media, and the Politics of Antipoverty* (Chicago: University of Chicago Press, 1999). See also Christopher Jencks, *Rethinking Social Policy: Race, Poverty and the Underclass* (Harvard, MA: Harvard University Press, 1992); Michael B. Katz, *The Price of Citizenship: Redefining the American Welfare State* (New York: Henry Holt, 1998); Michael K. Brown, Martin Carnoy, Elliot Currie et al., *Whitewashing Race: The Myth of a Color-Blind Society* (Berkeley: University of California Press, 2003).
88. See, for instance, M. Tonry, *Malign Neglect: Race, Crime, and Punishment in America* (New York: Oxford University Press, 1995); J. Yates, 'Racial Incarceration Disparity among States', *Social Science Quarterly*, vol. 78, 1997, pp. 1001–10; G. S. Bridges, R. Crutchfield and E. E. Simpson, 'Crime, Social Structure and Criminal Punishment: White and Nonwhite Rates of Imprisonment, *Social Problems*, vol. 34, 1987, pp. 345–61; P. I. Jackson and L. Carroll, 'Race and the War on Crime: The Sociopolitical Determinants of Municipal Police Expenditures', *American Sociological Review*, vol. 46, 1981, pp. 290–305.
89. Bruce Western, 'Politics and Social Structure in the Culture of Control', *Critical Review of International Social and Political Philosophy*, vol. 7, no. 2, 2004, p. 36.
90. David Garland, *The Culture of Control: Crime and Social Order in Contemporary Society* (Chicago: University of Chicago Press, 2001), pp. 100–01.
91. Fred Halliday, *The Making of the Second Cold War* (London: Verso, 1986), pp. 110–12; Thomas Ferguson and Joel Rogers (eds.), *The Hidden Election* (New York: Pantheon Books, 1981). See Frances Fox Piven and

Richard Cloward, *The New Class War: Reagan's Attack on the Welfare State and its Consequences* (New York: Pantheon Books, 1982).

92. Garland, *The Culture of Control*, p. 101.
93. Ibid., p. 98.
94. Cited in Corey Robin, 'The Ex-Cons: Right-Wing Thinkers Go Left', *Lingua Franca*, February 2001, p. 32.
95. See Émile Durkheim, *The Division of Labor in Society*, trans. G. Simpson (New York: Free Press, 1933); Michel Foucault, *Discipline and Punish* (London: Penguin, 1991).
96. William Connolly, 'The Will, Capital Punishment, and Culture War', in Dean, *Cultural Studies*, p. 36.
97. On this particular issue see Michael C. Williams, *The Realist Tradition and the Limits of International Relations* (Cambridge: Cambridge University Press, 2005), chapter 1; Corey Robin, *Fear: The History of a Political Idea* (Oxford: Oxford University Press, 2004), chapter 1.
98. Cited in Robin, *Fear*, p. 28.
99. Carl Schmitt, *The Leviathan in the State Theory of Thomas Hobbes: Meaning and Failure of a Political Symbol*, translation by George Schwab and Erna Hilfstein (Westport: Greenwood, 1996 [1938]), pp. 55–63, 85–6.
100. Richard Wolin, 'Carl Schmitt: The Conservative Revolution and the Aesthetics of Horror', in his *Labyrinths* (Amherst: University of Massachusetts Press, 1995); Jef Huysmans, *The Politics of Insecurity: Fear, Migration and Asylum in the EU* (London: Routledge, 1995), chapter 4; John P. McCormick, *Carl Schmitt's Critique of Liberalism: Against Politics as Technology* (Cambridge: Cambridge University Press, 1997), chapter 3.
101. Göran Dahl, *Radical Conservatism and the Future of Politics* (London: Sage, 1999), p. 57.
102. Peter Steinfels, *The Neoconservatives: The Men Who Are Changing America's Politics* (New York: Simon & Schuster, 1979), pp. 68–9.
103. Robert Kagan and William Kristol, 'Toward a Neo-Reaganite Foreign Policy', *Foreign Affairs*, no. 75, July/August 1996, http://www.foreignaffairs.org/19960701faessay4210/william-kristol-robert-kagan/toward-a-neo-reaganite-foreign-policy.html [3 April 2002], no page numbers.
104. On the radicalisation of 'the political' in our de-politicised age of neoliberal cosmopolitanism, see Chantal Mouffe, *The Return of the Political* (London: Verso, 2000); *On the Political* (London: Routledge, 2005).
105. Sheldon Wolin, *Politics and Vision*, expanded edition (Princeton: Princeton University Press, 2004 [1960]), pp. 472–3.
106. Hannah Arendt, *The Origins of Totalitarianism* (San Diego, New York and London: Harcourt Inc., 1966, [1950]), pp. 140–3.
107. Ibid.

4. THE DEMOCRATIC MIRAGE OF NEOCONSERVATIVE INTERNATIONALISM

1. Irving Kristol, 'A Post-Wilsonian Foreign Policy', *Wall Street Journal*, 2 August 1996, accessible online via http://www.aei.org/issue/17311 [3 December 2009].
2. Daniel Levy, Max Pensky and John Torpey (eds.), *Old Europe, New Europe, Core Europe: Transatlantic Relations After the Iraq War* (London: Verso, 2005); David M. Andrews (ed.), *The Atlantic Alliance Under Stress: US-European Relations After Iraq* (Cambridge: Cambridge University Press, 2005); Geir Lundestad (ed.), *Just Another Major Crisis? The United States and Europe Since 2000* (Oxford: Oxford University Press, 2008).
3. See Inderjeet Parmar, 'Foreign Policy fusion: Liberal Interventionists, conservative nationalists and neoconservatives—the new alliance dominating the US foreign policy establishment', *International Politics*, 46, no. 2/3, pp. 177–209; Tony Smith, *A Pact with the Devil: Washington's Bid for World Supremacy and the Betrayal of the American Promise* (London: Routledge, 2006); Timothy J. Lynch and Robert Singh, *After Bush: The Case for Continuity* (Cambridge: Cambridge University Press, 2008).
4. As Charles Krauthammer explained in July 2005, 'What neoconservatives have long been advocating is now being articulated and practiced at the highest levels of government by a war cabinet composed of individuals who, coming from a very different place, have joined and reshaped the neoconservative camp and are carrying the neoconservative idea throughout the world... This is the maturation of a governing ideology whose time has come'. 'The Neoconservative Convergence', *Wall Street Journal*, 21 July 2005, http://www.opinionjournal.com/extra/?id=110006921 [28 June 2006]. William Kristol also claimed credit for the neoconservatives: 'We at the *Weekly Standard* and the Project for the New American Century—and many other people, Wolfowitz way back in 1992—had articulated chunks and parts of what later became the Bush Doctrine... Certainly there was a lot out there that could be stitched together into the Bush Doctrine. But certainly, even people like me were kind of amazed by the speed and decisiveness with which the Bush administration, post-9/11, moved to pull these different arguments together'. Cited in Gary Dorrien, 'Benevolent Hegemony: William Kristol and the Politics of American Empire', *Logos*, vol. 3, no. 2, 2004, http://www.logosjournal.com/issue_3.2/dorrien.htm [28 October 2006]. See also Norman Podhoretz, 'In Praise of the Bush Doctrine', *Commentary*, September 2002, pp. 2–6; Max Boot, 'Think Again: Neocons', *Foreign Policy*, no. 140, January/February 2004, p. 21; Francis Fukuyama, *After the Neocons: America at the Crossroads* (London: Profile Books, 2006); Joshua Muravchik, 'Neoconservatism's Future: Still the Only Game in Town', *Wall Street Journal*, 3 October 2007, p. A6; Sidney Blumenthal, 'Preface to the 2008 Edition. The Hidden History of Neoconservatism: From Cheney to Cheney', in his *The Rise of the Counter-Establishment:*

The Conservative Ascent to Political Power (New York: Union Square Press, 2008 [1986]). For neoconservative assessments of the continuity between Bush and Obama see William Kristol, 'Plus ça change', *Washington Post*, 10 December 2009; Abe Greenwald, 'Going Neocon: Is Obama getting mugged by reality?', *National Review*, 10 December 2009.

5. Charles Krauthammer, *Democratic Realism: An American Foreign Policy for a Unipolar World*, American Enterprise Institute's Irving Kristol Lecture, Washington, DC, 12 February 2004, http://www.aei.org/publications/pubID.19912,filter.all/pub_detail.asp [8 February 2006].
6. Fukuyama, *After the Neocons*, pp. 139–40.
7. See, for instance, Joshua Muravchik, 'The Abandonment of Democracy', *Commentary*, July/August 2009; Robert Kagan, 'Obama, Siding with the Regime', *Washington Post*, 17 June 2009; James Ceaser, 'Giving Realism a Bad Name: The Demise of Idealism in Obama's Washington', *Weekly Standard*, vol. 39, no. 39, 2009, http://www.weeklystandard.com/Content/Public/Articles/000/000/016/650rpvzs.asp?pg=2 [25 June 2009].
8. Robert Kagan, 'Obama's Year One—Contra', *World Affairs Journal*, 6 January 2010, available online via http://www.foreignpolicyi.org/node/14966 [3 February 2010].
9. For classic statements, see Robert Cox, 'State, Social Forces and World Orders: Beyond International Relations Theory', *Millennium: Journal of International Studies*, vol. 10, no. 2, 1981, pp. 126–55; Richard K. Ashley, 'Untying the Sovereign State: A Double Reading of the Anarchy Problematique', *Millennium: Journal of International Studies*, vol., 17, no. 2, 1988, pp. 227–62; Alexander Wendt, 'Anarchy is What States Make of It: The Social Construction of Power Politics', *International Organization*, vol. 46, no. 2, Spring 1992, pp. 391–425.
10. See, for instance, Irving Kristol, *Reflections of a Neoconservative: Looking Back, Looking Ahead* (New York: Basic Books, 1983), p. xiv; Commentary Symposium, 'American Power—For What?', *Commentary*, January 2000, pp 21–48; Paul Wolfowitz, 'Think Again—Realism', *Foreign Policy*, September 2009, http://www.foreignpolicy.com/articles/2009/08/17/think_again_realism [6 October 2009]; Krauthammer, *Democratic Realism*. Michael C. Williams provided an incisive analysis of this dimension of neoconservative thought in his 'What is the National Interest? The Neoconservative Challenge in IR Theory', *European Journal of International Relations*, vol. 11, no. 3, 2005, pp. 307–35, and 'Morgenthau Now: neoconservatism, national greatness, and realism', in M. Williams (ed.), *Realism Reconsidered: The Legacy of Hans Morgenthau* (Oxford: Oxford University Press, 2008), pp. 216–39.
11. Robert Kagan and William Kristol, 'Toward a Neo-Reaganite Foreign Policy', *Foreign Affairs*, no. 75, July/August 1996, pp. 26–7.
12. Williams, 'What is the National Interest?'
13. Krauthammer, *Democratic Realism.*
14. Kristol, *Reflections of a Neoconservative*, p. xiv.

15. Ibid., p. xiii.
16. Francis Fukuyama, *The End of History and the Last Man* (London: Hamish Hamilton, 1992), pp. 245–65; Kristol, 'A Post-Wilsonian Foreign Policy'; Gary J. Schmitt and Abram N. Shulsky, 'Leo Strauss and the World of Intelligence (By Which We Do Not Mean Nous)', in K. L. Deutsch and J. A. Murray (eds.), *Leo Strauss, the Straussians and the American Regime* (Lanham, MD: Rowman & Littlefield, 1999); Thomas Pangle and Peter Ahrensdorf, *Justice Among Nations: On the Moral Basis of Power and Peace* (Lawrence, KS: University Press of Kansas, 1999), chapter 8.
17. Fukuyama, *The End of History*, pp. 255–6, 257, 258–9.
18. Kenneth R. Weinstein, 'Philosophic Roots, the Role of Leo Strauss, and the War in Iraq', in Irwin Stelzer (ed.) *Neoconservatism* (London: Atlantic Books, 2004); Fukuyama, *After the Neocons*, pp. 25–9); William Kristol and Robert Kagan, 'National Interest and Global Responsibilities', in W. Kristol and R. Kagan (eds.), *Present Dangers: Crisis and Opportunities in American Foreign and Defense Policy* (New York: Encounter Books, 2000); Charles Krauthammer, 'In Defense of Democratic Realism', in Gary Rosen (ed.), *The Right War? The Conservative Debate on Iraq* (New York: Cambridge University Press, 2005).
19. Thomas Pangle, *Leo Strauss: An Introduction to His Thought and Intellectual Legacy* (Baltimore: Johns Hopkins University Press, 2006), p. 95.
20. Steven Lenzner and William Kristol, 'What was Leo Strauss up to?', *The Public Interest*, Fall 2003, p. 38.
21. Kagan and Kristol, 'National Interests', p. 13.
22. Wolfowitz, 'Think Again: Realism', p. 2. See also Ben Wattenberg, 'Richard Perle: The Making of a Neoconservative', Think Tank with Ben Wattenberg, 14 November 2002, http://www.pbs.org/thinktank/show_1017.html [7 January 2008].
23. See Michael E. Latham, *Modernization as Ideology: American Social Science and Nation-Building in the Kennedy Era* (Chapel Hill, NC: University of North Carolina Press, 2000); Nils Gilman, *Mandarins of the Future: Modernization Theory in Cold War America* (Baltimore: Johns Hopkins University Press, 2003).
24. The key text here is Walt Whitman Rostow, *The Stages of Economic Growth: A Non-Communist Manifesto* (Cambridge: Cambridge University Press, 1960).
25. For good overviews see Odd Arne Westad, *The Global Cold War: Third World Interventions and the Making of Our Times* (Cambridge: Cambridge University Press, 2006); Gabriel Kolko, *Confronting the Third World: United States Foreign Policy 1945–1980* (New York: Pantheon, 1988); Fred Halliday, *The Making of the Second Cold War*, 2nd edn (London: Verso, 1986), pp. 81–97.
26. See Ronald L. Scheman, *The Alliance for Progress: A Retrospective* (New York: Praeger, 1988); Tony Smith, 'The Alliance for Progress: The 1960s', in Abraham F. Lowenthal, *Exporting Democracy: The United States and*

Latin America (Baltimore: Johns Hopkins University Press, 1991). See also David Williams, *International Development and International Order: History, Theory and Practice* (London, Routledge, 2011).

27. Max F. Millikan and Walt Whitman Rostow, *A Proposal: Key to An Effective Foreign Policy* (New York: Harper and Bros., 1957), p. 2.
28. A. Hoogvelt, *Globalization and the Postcolonial World: The New Political Economy of Development* (London: Palgrave, 2001), p. 177.
29. Gilman, *Mandarins of the Future*, p. 12.
30. See, for instance, Andre Gunder Frank, *Capitalism and Underdevelopment in Latin America* (New York: Monthly Review Press, 1967); Samir Amin, *Le développement inégal. Essai sur les formations sociales du capitalisme périphérique* (Paris: Editions de Minuit, 1973); Immanuel Wallerstein, *The Modern World System I: Capitalist Agriculture and the European World Economy in the Sixteenth Century* (New York: Academic Press, 1974).
31. Westad, *The Global Cold War*, p. 36.
32. Gilman, *Mandarins of the Future*, pp. 251–2.
33. Simon Bromley, *American Power and the Prospects for International Order* (Cambridge: Polity Press, 2008), p. 45.
34. Irving Kristol, 'Facing the Facts in Vietnam', *The New Leader*, 30 September 1963, p. 13. Cited in Mark Gerson, *The Neoconservative Vision: From Cold War to Culture Wars* (Lanham, MD: Madison Books, 1997), p. 113.
35. Samuel Huntington, *Political Orders in Changing Societies* (New Haven: Yale University Press, 2006 [1968].
36. See, for instance, Nathan Glazer, 'The New Left and Its Limits', *Commentary*, July 1968, p. 39; 'American Values and American Foreign Policy', *Commentary*, July 1976, pp. 32–8; Daniel Patrick Moynihan, 'Was Woodrow Wilson Right?', *Commentary*, May 1974, pp. 25–32; Norman Podhoretz, 'Making the World Safe for Communism', *Commentary*, April 1976, pp. 31–42. See also Justin Vaïsse, *Histoire du néoconservatisme aux États-Unis* (Paris: Odile Jacob, 2008), pp. 149–55.
37. Norman Podhoretz, *The Present Danger: Do We Have the Will to Reverse the Decline of American Power* (New York: Simon & Schuster, 1980), p. 100.
38. Jeane J. Kirkpatrick, 'Dictatorships and Double Standards', in her *Dictatorships and Double Standards: Rationalism and Reason in Politics* (Washington, DC: AEI Press, 1982), p. 26. The article was originally published in *Commentary*, November 1979.
39. Ibid., pp. 32, 49.
40. Ibid., p. 45.
41. Ibid., pp. 35–6.
42. Jeane J. Kirkpatrick, 'The Hobbes Problem', in *American Enterprise Institute's Public Policy Papers* (Washington, DC: AEI Press, 1981). Also reprinted in Robert S. Leiken and Barry Rubin (eds.), *The Central American Crisis Reader* (New York: Summit Books, 1987).

43. Kirkpatrick, 'Dictatorships', p. 52.
44. See also *Commentary* Symposium, 'Human Rights and American Foreign Policy', *Commentary*, November 1981, pp. 25–64; Jeane J. Kirkpatrick, 'U.S. Security in Latin America', *Commentary*, January 1981, pp. 29–41; Irving Kristol, 'The Timmerman Affair', *Wall Street Journal*, 29 May 1981, pp. 24–5; Robert Kagan, *A Twilight Struggle: American Power and Nicaragua 1977–1990* (New York: Free Press, 1996).
45. Cited in James Mann, *The Rise of the Vulcans* (London: Penguin Books, 2004), p. 130.
46. William I. Robinson, *Promoting Polyarchy: Globalization, US Intervention, and Hegemony* (Cambridge and New York: Cambridge University Press, 1996); 'Globalization, The World System, and "Democracy Promotion in U.S. Foreign Policy', *Theory and Society*, vol. 25, 1996, pp. 615–65; Barry Gills and Joel Rocamora, 'Low Intensity Democracy', *Third World Quarterly*, vol. 13, no. 3, 1992, pp. 501–23; Christopher I. Clement, 'Organic Intellectuals and the Discourse on Democracy: Academia, Foreign Policy Makers, and Third World Intervention', *New Political Science*, vol. 25, no. 3, 2003, pp. 351–64; Council on Hemispheric Affairs *National Endowment for Democracy (NED): A Foreign Policy Branch Gone Awry* (Washington, DC: Albuquerque and Inter-Hemispheric Education Resource Center, 1990); Thomas Carothers, 'The NED at 10', *Foreign Policy*, vol. 73, 1994, pp. 109–20.
47. William Douglas, *Developing Democracy* (Washington, DC: Heldref, 1972); Robinson, 'Globalization', pp. 641–2; Clement, 'Organic Intellectuals', pp. 358–9.
48. Michel Crozier, Samuel P. Huntington, Joji Watanuki, *The Crisis of Democracy: Report on the Governability of Democracies to the Trilateral Commission* (New York: New York University Press, 1975),
49. Ibid., pp. 53, 55. See also Richard N. Cooper, Karl Kaiser, Matasaka Kosaka, *Towards a Renovated International System*, Triangle Papers 14 (New York: Trilateral Commission, 1977). The literature sponsored by the Trilateral Commission during this period is discussed extensively in Robert W. Cox, 'Ideologies and the New International Economic Order: Reflections on Some Recent Literature', *International Organization*, vol. 33, no. 2, 1979; Stephen Gill, *American Hegemony and the Trilateral Commission* (New York: Cambridge University Press, 1991).
50. Alain Frachon and Daniel Vernet, *L'Amérique Messianique* (Paris: Seuil, 2004), p. 124.
51. Tom Farer, *Confronting Global Terrorism and American Neo-Conservatism* (Oxford: Oxford University Press, 2007), p. 31. See also Aryeh Neier, 'Human Rights in the Reagan Era: Acceptance in Principles', *Annals of the American Academy of Political and Social Science*, vol. 506, November 1989, pp. 31–40; James M. Scott, *Deciding to Intervene: The Reagan Doctrine and American Foreign Policy* (Durham, NC: Duke University Press, 1996).

52. Seymour Martin Lipset, *The First New Nation: The United States in Historical and Comparative Perspective* (Garden City, NY: Doubleday, 1963), p. 238.
53. Fukuyama, *The End of History*, p. 43.
54. Seymour Martin Lipset and Martin Lakin, *The Democratic Century* (Oklahoma City: University of Oklahoma Press, 2006), pp. 19–20.
55. Joseph Schumpeter, *Capitalism, Socialism and Democracy* (London: Routledge, 1994 [1952]), pp. 250–72.
56. Cited in William E. Scheuerman, 'Carl Schmitt and the Origins of Joseph Schumpeter's Theory of Democratic Elitism', in his *Carl Schmitt: The End of Law* (Lanham, MD: Rowman & Littlefield, 1999), p. 201.
57. Ibid.
58. See, for instance, Bernard Berelson, Paul Lazarfeld and William McPhee, *Voting* (Chicago: Chicago University Press, 1954); Robert Dahl, *A Preface to Democratic Theory* (Chicago: Chicago University Press, 1956); Gabriel Almond and Sidney Verba, *The Civic Culture: Political Attitudes and Democracy in Five Nations* (Princeton: Princeton University Press, 1963).
59. Robert Dahl, *Polyarchy: Participation and Opposition* (New Haven: Yale University Press, 1971), p. 2.
60. The classic text remains Larry Diamond, Juan Linz and Seymour Martin Lipset (eds.), *Democracy in Developing Countries* (Boulder, CO: Lynne Rienner and National Endowment for Democracy, 1988).
61. Richard Bellamy, *Rethinking Liberalism* (Pinter: London and New York, 2000), p. 97.
62. Robinson, 'Globalization', p. 626.
63. Robinson, *Promoting Polyarchy*, p. 105.
64. Lipset and Lakin, *The Democratic Century*, pp. 23–4.
65. Diamond et al., *Democracy*, p. xvi.
66. Larry Diamond, *Developing Democracy: Toward Consolidation* (Baltimore: Johns Hopkins University Press, 1997), p. 8.
67. Robert Dahl, *A Preface to Economic Democracy* (Cambridge: Polity Press, 1985), p. 55. See also Philippe Schmitter, 'Democracy's Future: More Liberal, Preliberal or Postliberal?, *Journal of Democracy*, vol. 6, no. 1, 1995, p. 75.
68. Robinson, *Promoting Polyarchy*, p. 6.
69. David Ryan, *US Foreign Policy in World History* (London: Routledge, 2000), p. 167.
70. Irving Kristol, 'Foreign Policy in an Age of Ideology', *National Interest*, no. 1, Fall 1985, pp. 14–5. See also Michael Leeden, 'How to Support the Democratic Revolution', *Commentary*, March 1985, pp. 43–51.
71. Philip Armstrong, Andrew Glyn and John Harrison, *Capitalism Since 1945* (Cambridge, MA: Blackwell, 1991), p. 293.
72. Ian Clark, *Globalization and Fragmentation* (Oxford: Oxford University Press, 1997), p. 167

73. Joshua Muravchik, *Exporting Democracy: Fulfilling America's Destiny* (Washington, DC: AEI Press, 1991), p. 1.
74. Francis Fukuyama, 'The End of History?' *The National Interest*, no. 16, Summer 1989, pp. 3–18; *The End of History*.
75. Fukuyama, *The End of History*, p. 17.
76. Allan Bloom, 'Response to Fukuyama', *National Interest*, vol. 16, Summer 1989.
77. Kristol, 'A Post-Wilsonian Foreign Policy'.
78. Samuel Huntington, 'The Erosion of the American National Interest', *Foreign Affairs*, vol. 76, no. 5, 1997, p. 30.
79. Jeane Kirkpatrick, 'A Normal Country in a Normal Time', *National Interest*, vol. 21, Fall 1990; Irving Kristol, 'Defining Our National Interest', *National Interest*, vol. 21, Fall 1990; Nathan Glazer, 'A Time for Modesty', in Owen Harries (ed.), *America's Purpose: New Visions of US Foreign Policy* (San Francisco: Institute of Contemporary Studies, 1991); Robert Tucker and David C. Hendrickson, *The Imperial Temptation: The New World Order and America's Purpose* (Council on Foreign Relations, 1992).
80. Irving Kristol, 'In Search of Our National Interest', *Wall Street Journal*, 7 June 1990, p. 9.
81. Gregory Fossedal, *The Democratic Imperative: Exporting the American Revolution* (New York: Basic Books, 1989); Joshua Muravchik, 'At Last Pax Americana', *New York Times*, 24 January 1991; Michael Novak, 'Pax Americana', *Forbes*, vol. 147, 29 April 1991, p. 121; Charles Krauthammer, 'The Unipolar Moment', *Foreign Affairs*, no. 70, 1991; Ben J. Wattenberg, 'Neo-Manifest Destinarianism', *National Interest*, vol. 21, Fall 1990, pp. 51–2; Carl Gershman, 'Freedom Remains the Touchstone', in Harries, *America's Purpose*; Paul Wolfowitz, 'After Communism, Global Turmoil', *Wall Street Journa*l, 21 April 1993.
82. Stefan Halper and Jonathan Clarke, *America Alone: The Neo-Conservatives and the Global Order* (Cambridge: Cambridge University Press, 2004), pp. 86–98; Ivo Daalder, 'Fear and Loathing in the Former Yugoslavia', in Michael Brown (ed.), *The International Dimensions of Internal Conflict* (Cambridge, MA: MIT Press, 1996), pp. 243–9; Brendan Simms, *Unfinest Hours: Britain and the Destruction of Bosnia* (London: Penguin, 2002).
83. Ivo Daalder and Michael E. O'Hanlon, 'Unlearning the Lesson of Kosovo', *Foreign Policy*, vol. 99, no. 116, 1999, pp. 128–40.
84. Robert Kagan, *Paradise and Power: America and Europe in the New World Order* (London: Atlantic Books, 2003), pp. 51–2.
85. Fred Ilke and Albert Wohlstetter, *Discriminate Deterrence: Report of the Commission on Integrated Long-Term Strategy* (Washington, DC: Government Printing Office, 1988), p. 50. See also Samuel Huntington, 'U.S. Defense Strategy: The Strategic Innovation of the Reagan Years', in Joseph Kruzel (ed.), *American Defense Annual: 1987–1988* (Lexington, MA:

Lexington Books, 1988); Gary Dorrien, *Imperial Designs* (London: Routledge, 2004), pp. 43–50; Halper and Clarke, *America Alone*, pp. 62–4.

86. See Paul Wolfowitz, 'Interview', *Vanity Fair*, 15 May 2003; Neil Swidey, 'The Analyst', *Globe Magazine*, 18 May 2003; Halper and Clarke, *America Alone*, pp. 91–2.
87. Robert Devigne, *Recasting Conservatism: Oakeshott, Strauss, and the Response to Postmodernism* (New Haven and London: Yale University Press, 1994), p. 185.
88. Jeane Kirkpatrick, 'Where Is Our Foreign Policy?', *Washington Post*, 30 July 1993; Donald Kagan and Frederic Kagan, *While America Sleeps: Self-Delusion, Military Weakness, and the Threat to Peace Today* (New York: St. Martin's Press, 2000), pp. 293–5; James W. Ceaser, 'The Great Divide: American Interventionism and its Opponents', in William Kristol and Robert Kagan (eds.), *Present Dangers: Crisis and Opportunity in American Foreign and Defense Policy* (New York: Encounter Books, 2000); David Wurmser, *Tyranny's Ally: America's Failure to Defeat Saddam Hussein* (Washington, DC: AEI Press, 1999); Paul Wolfowitz, 'Remembering the Future', *National Interest*, vol. 59, Summer 2000, pp. 67–73.
89. Robert Kaplan, 'The Coming Anarchy', *Atlantic Monthly*, vol. 273, no. 2, 1994, pp. 44–76.
90. Kristol and Kagan., 'Towards a Neo-Reaganite Foreign Policy', pp. 20–3.
91. Project for the New American Century, 'Statement of Principles' (June 1997), http://www.newamericancentury.org [2 February 2004]. The original signatories of its Statement of Principles were Elliott Abrams, Jeane Kirkpatrick, Gary Bauer, William J. Bennett, Jeb Bush, Dick Cheney, Eliot A. Cohen, Midge Decter, Paula Dobriansky, Steve Forbes, Aaron Friedberg, Francis Fukuyama, Frank Gaffney, Fred C. Ikle, Donald Kagan, Zalmay Khalilzad, I. Lewis Libby, Norman Podhoretz, Dan Quayle, Peter W. Rodman, Stephen P. Rosen, Henry S. Rowen, Donald Rumsfeld, Vin Weber, George Weigel and Paul Wolfowitz.
92. Ibid.
93. 'Excerpts from Pentagon's Plan: "Prevent the Re-emergence of a New Rival"', *New York Times*, 8 March 1992. Not surprisingly, the PNAC's statement of purpose also has striking substantive and stylistic affinities with the 1984 Policy Statement of the Committee on the Present Danger. See 'Common Sense and the Common Danger', in Committee on the Present Danger, *Alerting America: The Papers of the Committee on the Present Dangers* (Washington, DC: Pergamon Brasseys, 1984).
94. Paul Wolfowitz, 'Statesmanship in the New Century', in Kagan and Kristol, *Present Dangers*, p. 311.
95. David Brooks, 'The Age of Conflict', *Weekly Standard*, 5 November 2001, p. 6.

96. Norman Podhoretz, 'Syria Yes, Israel No?', *Weekly Standard*, 12 November 2001, http://www.weeklystandard.com/Content/Public/Articles/000/000/000/457edhtn.asp [3 September 2005].
97. Robert Kagan, 'Fightin' Democrats', *Washington Post*, 10 March 2002, p. A2.
98. Krauthammer, *Democratic Realism*, pp. 6–7. See also Norman Podhoretz, *World War IV: The Long Struggle Against Islamofascism* (New York: Vintage, 2008).
99. Charles Krauthammer, 'Three Cheers for the Bush Doctrine', *New York Times*, 7 March 2005, http://www.time.com/time/printout/0,8816,1035052,00.html [8 December 2006].
100. Jeane Kirkpatrick, 'The Modernizing Imperative: Tradition and Change', *Foreign Affairs*, September-October 1993, http://www.foreignaffairs.org/19930901faresponse5204/jeane-j-kirkpatrick/the-modernizing-imperative-tradition-and-change.html [26 January 2009]. See also Michael Novak, *The Universal Hunger for Liberty: Why the Clash of Civilization is Not Inevitable* (New York: Basic Books, 2004); Max Boot, 'Neocons May Get the Last Laugh', *Los Angeles Times*, 3 March 2005, http://articles.latimes.com/2005/mar/03/opinion/oe-boot3 [7 December 2006]; Joshua Muravchik, 'Can the Neocons Get their Groove Back?', *Washington Post*, 19 November 2006, p. B3; Timothy J. Lynch, 'Kristol Balls: Neoconservative Vision of Islam and the Middle East', *International Politics*, vol. 45, no. 2, 2008, pp. 182–211.
101. Charles Krauthammer, 'Violence and Islam', *Jewish World Review*, 6 December 2002, http://www.jewishworldreview.com/cols/krauthammer120602.asp [5 January 2008].
102. Francis Fukuyama, *State-Building: Governance and World Order in the Twenty-First Century* (London: Profile Books, 2004), p. 3.
103. Fukuyama, *The End of History*, p. 348.
104. Robert D. Kaplan, *Balkan Ghosts: A Journey Through History* (New York: St. Martin's Press, 1993); *The Ends of the Earth: A Journey at the Dawn of the Twenty-First Century* (New York: Random House, 1996); *The Coming Anarchy: Shattering the Dreams of the Post Cold War* (New York: Random House, 2000).
105. Kaplan, *The Coming Anarchy*, p. 24. See also Robert D. Kaplan, *Warrior Politics: Why Leadership Demands a Pagan Ethos* (New York: Random House, 2002); 'Supremacy by Stealth', *Atlantic Monthly*, vol. 292, July-August 2003, p. 83; Fukuyama, *State-Building*; George P. Shultz, 'Terror and the State', *Washington Post*, 26 January 2002, p. 16.
106. International Commission on Intervention and State Sovereignty, *The Responsibility to Protect* (Ottawa: International Development Research Centre, 2001), www.idrc.ca [2 May 2003].
107. Robert Kagan, 'The Sovereignty Dodge: What Pakistan Won't Do, the World Should', *Washington Post*, 2 December 2008, p. A21. See also American Enterprise Institute, Transcripts From the Conference on War,

International Law, and Sovereignty: Reevaluating the Rules of the Game in a New Century, 24 June 2004, http://www.aei.org [12 October 2007].

108. Barnett served as a Pentagon aide with Frank Gaffney to Secretary of Defense Donald Rumsfeld between 2000 and 2003. After 9/11, he joined one of the teams commissioned by Rumsfeld to develop an interpretative and operational framework for the so-called 'new American way of war'. See http://www.thomaspmbarnett.com/projects/newrulesset/nrs_index.html [on 28 September 2006]; Thomas Barnett and H. H. Gaffney Jr., *The Top 100 Rules of the New American Way of War, Transformation Trends*, 3 February 2003, http://www.cdi.org/mrp/transformation-trends.cfm [2 October 2006].
109. Thomas Barnett, 'The Pentagon's New Map', *Esquire*, March 2003, http://www.thomaspmbarnett.com/published/pentagonsnewmap.htm [7 December 2008]; *The Pentagon's New Map: War and Peace in the Twenty First Century* (London: Putnam Adult, 2004); *A Blueprint for Action* (Washington: Putnam Publishing Group, 2005); 'Obama's New Map of the World', *Esquire*, March 2009, http://www.esquire.com/features/obama-foreign-policy-0309 [7 April 2009].
110. Barnett, 'The Pentagon's New Map', p. 1.
111. Ibid., pp. 2–4.
112. Thomas Barnett, 'Where—not when—preemption makes sense', *Transformation Trends*, 18 November 2002, http:www.nwc.navy.mil/newrulesets/PreemptionMakesSense.pdf [2 October 2006].
113. Thomas Barnett, cited in Richard Salit, 'Finally His Vision Finds an Audience', *Providence Journal*, 2 March 2003, available on Barnett's website at http://www.thomaspmbarnett.com/projects/newrulesset/Providence%20Journal%20profile%20of%20Thomas%20Barnett.htm [2 January 2005].
114. See, for instance, David Rose, 'Neo Culpa', *Vanity Fair*, 3 November 2006, http://www.vanityfair.com/politics/features/2006/12/neocons2006 12 [6 November 2006]; Joshua Muravchik, 'Operation Comeback', *Foreign Policy*, vol. 12, November 2006, http://www.foreignpolicy.com/users/login.php?story_id=3602&URL=http://www.foreignpolicy.com/story/cms.php?story_id=3602 [2 December 2007]; Lynch and Singh, *After Bush*.
115. Robert R. Reilly, 'Ideas Matter: Restoring the Content of Public Diplomacy', Heritage Special Report, The Heritage Foundation, SR-64, 27 July 2009, pp. 9–10. Available online at http://www.heritage.org/research/publicdiplomacy/sr0064.cfm [26 September 2009].
116. Robert Kagan, 'The Case for a League of Democracies', *Financial Times*, 13 May 2008, http://us.ft.com/ftgateway/superpage.ft?news_id=fto051320081421543873 [13 May 2008]; Robert Singh, 'In Defence of a Concert of Liberal Democracies', *Whitehead Journal of Diplomacy and International Relations*, vol. 10, no. 1, 2009, pp. 19–29.

117. The Foreign Policy Initiative, 'Mission Statement', March 2009, http://www.foreignpolicyi.org/about.html [7 April 2009].
118. Mark T. Berger, 'From Nation-Building to State-Building: The Geopolitics of Development, The Nation-State System and the Changing Global Order', *Third World Quarterly*, vol. 27, no. 1, p. 13; Karen Ballentine and Jake Sherman, 'Introduction', in Ballentine and Sherman (eds.), *The Political Economy of Armed Conflict: Beyond Greed and Grievance* (Boulder, CO: Lynne Rienner, 2003); Rama Mani, 'The Root Causes of Terrorism and Conflict Prevention', in Jane Boulden and Thomas G. Weiss (eds.), *Terrorism and the UN: Before and After September 11* (Bloomington and Indianapolis: Indiana University Press, 2004), pp. 225–31; Andrew Johnston, 'Disparities of Wealth Are Seen as Fuel for Terrorism', *International Herald Tribune*, 20 December 2001; Jane Eisner, 'Terrorism's Tenuous Link to Poverty', *Philadelphia Inquirer*, 7 July 2002.
119. Berger, 'From Nation-Building to State-Building', p. 14. See also Geoffrey Hawthorne, 'Running the World Through Windows', *New Left Review*, vol. 5, Sept.-Oct. 2000; Beverly Crawford and Ronnie Lipschultz, *The Myth of "Ethnic Conflict": Politics, Economics, and Cultural Violence* (Berkeley, CA: International and Area Studies, University of California, Berkeley, 1998), http://repositories.cdlib.org/uciaspubs/research/98/ [accessed 18 April 2007]; Jean-François Bayart, *L'Etat en Afrique* (Paris: Fayard, 1989); Christopher Clapham, *Africa and the International System: The Politics of State Survival* (Cambridge: Cambridge University Press, 1996).
120. See, for instance, Kolko, *Confronting the Third World*; Westad, *The Global Cold War*; Ryan, *US Foreign Policy*; Thomas J. McCormick, *America's Half-Century: United States Foreign Policy in the Cold War and After*, 2nd edn (Baltimore and London: Johns Hopkins University Press, 1995).
121. On the complex and mutually constitutive relationship between 'zones of war' and liberal 'zones of peace' see Tarak Barkawi and Mark Laffey, 'The Imperial Peace: Democracy, Force and Globalization', *European Journal of International Relations*, vol. 5, no. 4, 1999, pp. 403–34. On the Cold War origins of the global war on terror, see Chalmers Johnson, *Blowback* (New York: Time Warner, 2002); Westad, *The Global Cold War*.
122. Simon Dalby, 'Geopolitics, Grand Strategy and the Bush Doctrine', in Charles Philippe David and David Grondin (eds.), *Hegemony or Empire? The Redefinition of US Power Under George W. Bush* (Farnham: Ashgate, 2006), p. 41.
123. See Toby Dodge, 'Coming Face to Face with Bloody Reality: Liberal Common Sense and the Ideological Failure of the Bush Doctrine in Iraq', *International Politics*, vol. 46, no. 2–3, 2009, pp. 253–75.
124. Olivier Roy, *Le Croissant et le Chaos* (Paris: Hachette, 2006), pp. 52–3. My translation.

125. Samuel Huntington, *The Clash of Civilizations and the Remaking of World Order* (New York: Simon & Schuster, 1998).
126. For an excellent discussion of the politicisation of culture in global politics in the broader context of the global war on terror, which has influenced my own thinking on the issues discussed here, see Vivienne Jabri, *War and the Transformation of Global Politics* (London: Palgrave, 2007), pp. 136–62.
127. William Kristol and Robert Kagan, 'National Interest and Global Responsibility', in Kagan and Kristol, *Present Dangers*, p. 18.
128. Gerry Simpson, *Great Powers and Outlaw States: Unequal Sovereigns in the International Legal Order* (Cambridge: Cambridge University Press, 2004); Nico Krisch, 'More Equal Than the Rest? Hierarchy, Equality and US Predominance in International Law', in Michael Byers and Georg Nolte (eds.), *United States Hegemony and the Foundations of International Law* (Cambridge: Cambridge University Press, 2004).
129. Barnett, *The Pentagon's New Map*, pp. 369–70.
130. Gareth Stedman Jones, 'The History of US Imperialism', in R. Blackburn (ed.), *Ideology in Social Science: Readings in Critical Social Theory* (London: Fontana, 1972).
131. Robert Cox, 'Multilateralism and World Order', in his *Approaches to World Order* (Cambridge: Cambridge University Press, 1996), pp. 494–7.
132. Ian Clark, 'Another Double Movement: The Great Transformation After the Cold War?', *Review of International Studies*, vol. 27, 2001, p. 238.
133. Martti Koskenniemi, '"The Lady Doth Protest Too Much" Kosovo, and the Turn to Ethics in International Law', *Modern Law Review*, vol. 65, no. 2, 2002, p. 174. See also Jürgen Habermas, 'Does the Constitutionalisation of International Law Have a Chance?', in his *The Divided West* (Cambridge: Polity Press, 2006).
134. John Ikenberry, *Liberal Order and Imperial Ambition* (Cambridge: Polity, 2006), pp. 15–6.
135. John Ikenberry is co-director with Anne-Marie Slaughter of the liberal internationalist Princeton Project for on National Security. See http://www.princeton.edu/~ppns/mission.html.
136. Richard Perle, 'We Won Years Ago', *The American Interest*, vol. 3, no. 4, 2008. See also Deputy Secretary Paul Wolfowitz interview with Sam Tannenhaus, *Vanity Fair*, 9 May 2003, http://www.defenselink.mil/transcripts/transcript.aspx?transcriptid=25 [7 January 2009].
137. Wolfowitz, 'Realism: Think Again', p. 1.
138. Charles Krauthammer, cited in Michael Cox, 'American Power Before and After 9/11: Dizzy With Success?', *International Affairs*, vol. 18, no. 2, 2002, p. 275, note 48.
139. On this particular point see Emmanuel Todd, *Àprès l'empire: Essai sur la décomposition du système Américain* (Paris: Gallimard Folio, 2002), pp. 12–40; Immanuel Wallerstein, 'The Eagle Has Crash Landed', *Foreign Policy*, July/August 2002, pp. 60–8.

140. Kristol, 'The Imminent War'; Michael A. Ledeen, *The War Against the Terror Masters: Why It Happened, Where We Are Now, How We'll Win* (New York: St. Martin's Press, 2002), p. 221; Max Boot, 'For Better and Worse', *Newsweek International*, 11 April 2006.
141. Niccolò Machiavelli, *The Prince* (London: Penguin Books, 2004 [1531–2]), p. 71.

5. THE NEOCONSERVATIVE CRITIQUE OF GLOBAL LIBERAL GOVERNANCE

1. Harvey Mansfield, 'What Obama Isn't Saying', *Weekly Standard*, vol. 15, no. 2, 2010, 0http://www.weeklystandard.com/articles/what-obama-isnt-saying?page=3 [20 February, 2010].
2. Global Governance Watch, http://www.globalgovernancewatch.org/about/ [20 November 2008].
3. American Enterprise Institute, 'Keeping an Eye on National Sovereignty', *AEI Newsletter*, 1 June 2008, http://www.aei.org/publications/filter.all,pubID.28080/pub_detail.asp [3 June 2008].
4. John Fonte, 'Global Governance vs the Liberal Democratic Nation-State: What is the Best Regime?', in *Encounter at 10: The Bradley Symposium*, Hudson Institute, 4 June 2008, pp. 17–8, accessible via http://www.globalgovernancewatch.org/resources/global-governance-vs-the-liberal-democratic nationstate-what-is-the-best-regime-2 [3 November 2008], p. 1. See also the Federalist Society for Law and Public Policy, 'Dictating Norms: 'Who Decides What's Right for the World: The Inauguration of Global Governance Watch', 14 April 2008, audio and video recordings, http://www.fed-soc.org/publications/pubid.1002/pub_detail.asp [3 November 2008].
5. See, for instance, Dick Cheney, 'Keeping America Safe', Address at the American Enterprise Institute, Washington, 21 May 2009, podcast available online at http://www.aei.org/video/101099 [7 July 2009]; John Bolton, 'The Coming War on Sovereignty', *Commentary*, March 2009, http://www.commentarymagazine.com/viewarticle.cfm/the-coming-war-on-sovereignty-15080 [4 June 2009]; Robert Kagan, 'Woodrow Wilson's Heir', *Washington Post*, 7 June 2009, http://www.washingtonpost.com/wp-dyn/content/article/2009/06/05/AR2009060502615.html [7 June 2009]; Eliot A. Cohen, 'What's Different About Obama's Foreign Policy?' *Wall Street Journal*, 2 August 2009, http://online.wsj.com/article/SB100014240529702039469045743004026084755582.html,[7 August, 2009]; Eric Posner, 'Obama and international law', *Volokh*, 5 December 2008, http://volokh.com/posts/1228509500.shtml [8 December 2008]; Andrew C. McCarthy, 'Obama and Gitmo', *National Review Online*, 13 November 2008, http://article.nationalreview.com/print/?q=NTMxNWYzY2MxMGVkZmVkNTFkYTg0MzliMWRmNTU1M2I= [3 December 2008]; John Fonte, 'The World is My Constituency', *National Review*, 2 November 2008, accessible via http://www.

hudson.org/index.cfm?fuseaction=publication_details&id=5852 [6 November 2008].

6. Fonte, 'Global Governance', pp. 17–8.
7. For an overview, see American Enterprise Institute Conference, 'Trends in Global Governance: Do They Threaten American Sovereignty?', *Chicago Journal of International Law*, Fall 2000; Transcript of American Enterprise Institute Conference, 'Outsourcing of American Law', AEI, Washington 21 February 2006, http://www.aei.org/events/eventID.1256,filter.all/event_detail.asp [November 2007]; James P. Kelly, 'The Matrix of Human Rights Governance Networks', *Engage*, vol. 9, no. 1, 2008, http://www.fed-soc.org/publications/pubID.691/pub_detail.asp [2 November 2008]; Steven Groves, 'The U.S. Should Reject the U.N. "Responsibility to Protect" Doctrine', *Heritage Foundation Backgrounder*, no. 2130, 2008, http://www.heritage.org/research/InternationalOrganizations/bg2130.cfm [3 December 2008].
8. See, for instance, Curtis Bradley and Jack Goldsmith, 'Customary International Law as Federal Common Law: A Critique of the Modern Position', *Harvard Law Review*, vol. 110, no. 4, 1997, pp. 815–76; 'U.N. Human Rights Standards and the U.S. Law: The Current Illegitimacy of International Human Rights Litigations', *Fordham Law Review*, vol. 66, November 1997, pp. 319–59; 'International Delegations, the Structural Constitutions and Non-Self Executions', *Stanford Law Review*, vol. 55, May 2003, pp. 1557–96; Lee A. Casey and David B. Rivkin, 'The Rocky Shoals of International Law', *The National Interest*, no. 62, Winter 2000, pp. 35–45; Eric Posner, 'Do States Have a Moral Obligation to Obey International Law?', *Stanford Law Review*, vol. 55, 2003, pp. 1901–19; John Yoo, *The Powers of War and Peace: The Constitution and Foreign Affairs After 9/11* (Chicago: University of Chicago Press, 2006).
9. Robert Delanty and John Yoo, 'Against Foreign Law', AEI Working Paper no. 158, 2009, http://www.aei.org/docLib/20090820-Chapter8.pdf [12 October 2009]; Justice Antonin Scalia, 'Foreign Law in Constitutional Interpretation', AEI Working Paper no. 159, 2009, http://www.aei.org/docLib/20090820-Chapter2.pdf [12 October 2009]; William S. Dodge, 'After Sosa: The Future of Customary International Law in the United States', AEI Working Paper no. 153, 2009, http://www.aei.org/docLib/20090820-Chapter3.pdf [12 October 2009]; Thomas C. Goldstein and Cody S. Harris, 'Foreign Law and Constitutional Interpretation: The Debate Behind the Diatribes', AEI Working Paper no. 157, 2009, http://www.aei.org/docLib/20090820-Chapter7.pdf [14 October 2009]; Julian G. Ku, 'The President's Unexamined Power to Interpret Customary International Law', AEI Working Paper no. 155, 2009, http://www.aei.org/docLib/20090820-Chapter5.pdf [14 October 2009].
10. John Yoo, 'Outsourcing American Law: Conclusion', AEI Working Paper no. 159, 2009, p. 1, http://www.aei.org/docLib/20090820-Chapter9.pdf [12 October 2009].

11. John Gerard Ruggie, 'American Exceptionalism, Exemptionalism, and Global Governance', in Michael Ignatieff (ed.), *American Exceptionalism and Human Rights* (Princeton and Oxford: Princeton University Press, 2005), p. 326.
12. See, in particular, Bradley and Goldsmith, 'International Delegations'.
13. John Bolton, 'Global Governance and Shared Sovereignty', *On the Issues*, AEI, 28 April 2008, http://www.aei.org/publications/pubID.27885/pub_detail.asp [2 September 2008].
14. Ruggie, 'American Exceptionalism', p. 326.
15. Andrea Bianchi, 'International Law and US Courts: The Myth of Lohengrin Revisited', *European Journal of International Law*, vol. 15, no. 4, 2004, p. 777.
16. Christian G. Vergonis, 'The Federalism Implications of International Human Rights Law', *The Federalist Society for Law and Public Policy Studies*, 2002, p. 9. Online at http://www.fed-soc.org/publications/PubID.72/pub_detail.asp.
17. Ruggie, 'American Exceptionalism', pp. 327–8; Peter J. Spiro, 'The New Sovereigntists: American Exceptionalism and Its False Prophets', *Foreign Affairs*, vol. 79, no. 6, November/December 2000, pp. 9–15. See also Anne-Marie Slaughter, 'Building Global Democracy', *Chicago Journal of International Law*, vol. 1, no. 2, 2000, pp. 249–76; Andrew Moravcsik, 'Conservative Idealism and International Institutions', *Chicago Journal of International Law*, vol. 1, no. 2, 2000, pp. 291–314; Harold Hongju Koh, 'On American Exceptionalism', *Stanford Law Review*, vol. 55, no. 5, 2003, pp. 1483–94.
18. John R. Bolton, 'Courting Danger: What's Wrong With the International Criminal Court', *The National Interest*, Winter 1998/1999, vol. 54, p. 60; Robert Kagan, 'Europeans Courting International Disaster', *Washington Post*, 8 June 2003, p. B07; Jack Goldsmith, 'The Self-Defeating International Criminal Court', *University of Chicago Law Review*, vol. 70, no. 1, 2003, pp. 89–104; Tod Lindberg, 'A Way Forward with the International Criminal Court: Cooperation', *Policy Review*, no. 159, 2010, http://www.hoover.org/publications/policyreview/83084577.html# [6 February 2010]. See also Jason Ralph, 'International Society, the International Criminal Court and American Foreign Policy', *Review of International Studies*, vol. 31, no. 1, 2005, pp. 27–44; 'Between Cosmopolitan and American Democracy: Understanding US Opposition to the International Criminal Court', *International Relations*, vol. 17, no. 2, 2003, pp. 195–211.
19. See Peter Spiro, 'Treaties, International Law and Constitutional Rights', *Stanford Law Review*, vol. 55, 2003, pp. 1618–49.
20. Bolton, 'The Coming War on Sovereignty'; 'Should We Take Global Governance Seriously?', *Chicago Journal of International Law*, vol. 1, no. 2, 2000, pp. 205–6; *Surrender is Not an Option: Defending America at the United Nations and Abroad* (New York: Simon & Schuster, 2008); 'Symposium: American Power—for what?', *Commentary*, January 2000;

American Institute Conference, 'American Sovereignty: Issues for the New Administration and the New Decade', *Chicago Journal of International Law*, vol. 2, no. 2, 2001; Jeremy Rabkin, *The Case for Sovereignty: Why the World Should Welcome American Independence* (Washington, DC: AEI Press, 2004); *Law Without Nations: Why Constitutional Government Requires Sovereign States* (Princeton: Princeton University Press, 2007); John Fonte, 'Liberal Democracy vs. Transnational Progressivism: The Ideological War Within the West', *Orbis*, Summer 2002, pp. 449–64; *Sovereignty or Submission: Will Americans Rule Themselves or Be Ruled By Others?* (New York: Encounter Books, 2009); Andrew M. MacCarthy, 'International Law vs. the United States', *Commentary*, February 2006, http://www.commentarymagazine.com/viewarticle.cfm/international-law-v—united-states-10026?search=1 [6 November 2008].

21. Fonte, 'Global Governance', p. 3.
22. Fonte's work is particularly instructive in this respect. See his 'The Enablers of Transnational Progressivism: Is the Nation-State Threatened?', Hudson Institute, 4 October 2006, http://www.hudson.org/index.cfm?fuseaction=publication_details&id=4232 [3 December 2008].
23. Fonte, 'Global Governance', p. 457.
24. John Bolton, '"Legitimacy" in International Affairs: The American Perspective. Theory and Operation', remarks to the Federalist Society, Washington, DC, 13 November 2003, www.state.gov [accessed 6 May 2004]; Marc F. Plattner, *Democracy Without Borders? Global Challenges to Liberal Democracy*, (Lanham, MD: Rowman & Littlefield, 2008).
25. Francis Fukuyama, 'Does the West Still Exist?' in Tod Lindberg (ed.), *Beyond Paradise and Power: Europe, America and the Future of a Troubled Partnership* (New York and London: Routledge, 2005), pp. 146–7.
26. Bolton, 'Should We Take Global Governance Seriously?', p. 215; Jeane Kirkpatrick, in 'American Power—for what? A Symposium', *Commentary*, January 2000; Lee A. Casey and David B. Rivkin, Jr., 'Europe in the Balance: The Alarmingly Undemocratic Drift of the European Union', *Policy Review*, June/July 2001, pp. 41–53; Fonte, 'Global Governance', p. 6.
27. Jeremy Rabkin, 'Is EU Policy Eroding the Sovereignty of Non-Members States?', *Chicago Journal of International Law*, vol. 1, no. 2, 2000, pp. 273–90.
28. Peter Berkowitz, 'Liberalism and Power', in Lindberg, *Beyond Paradise and Power*, pp. 203–8; Fukuyama, 'Does the West Still Exist?', p. 145.
29. Jürgen Habermas, *The Postnational Constellation* (Cambridge: Polity Press, 2000), p. 110.
30. Berkowitz, 'Liberalism and Power', pp. 205–6. See also Irving Kristol, 'The American Revolution as a Successful Revolution', in his *NeoConservatism: Selected Essays 1951–1995* (New York: Basic Books, 1995); Gertrude Himmelfarb, *The Roads to Modernity: The British, French and American Enlightenment* (London: Penguin, 2004).

31. Berkowitz, 'Liberalism and Power', p. 207.
32. Allan Bloom, 'Justice: John Rawls versus the Tradition of Political Philosophy', in his *Giants and Dwarfs: Essays 1960–1990* (New York: Simon & Schuster, 1990), pp. 296–315; Berkowitz, 'Liberalism in Power', pp. 205–7; 'Leviathan Then and Now', *Policy Review*, vol. 151, 2008, http://www.hoover.org/publications/policyreview/30118304.html [4 November 2009]; Fukuyama, 'Does the West Still Exist?', pp. 145–6; Irving Kristol, 'Diplomacy vs. Foreign Policy in the United States', in his *Reflections of a Neoconservative: Looking Back, Looking Ahead* (New York: Basic Books, 1983).
33. Jeane Kirkpatrick, 'Sources of Stability in the American Tradition', in her *Dictatorships and Double Standards: Rationalism and Reason in Politics* (Washington, DC: Simon & Schuster and AEI, 1982), pp. 224–5.
34. Francis Fukuyama, *The End of History and the Last Man* (London: Hamish Hamilton, 1992), pp. 330, 334.
35. Étienne Balibar, 'Le Hobbes de Schmitt et le Schmitt de Hobbes', in Carl Schmitt, *Le Léviathan Dans La Doctrine De L' État de Thomas Hobbes* (Paris: Seuil, 2002), pp. 30–1.
36. John Locke, *Two Treatises on Government*, ed. Peter Laslett (Cambridge: Cambridge University Press, 1988 [1690]), Section 160, p. 393.
37. This is why Strauss maintains that 'Locke is closer to Machiavelli than he is generally said or thought to be'. Leo Strauss, 'John Locke's Doctrine of Natural Law', in Strauss, *What is Political Philosophy?* (Chicago: Chicago University Press, 1959), p. 218. See also *Natural Right and History* (Chicago: University of Chicago Press, 1965 [1953]), pp. 227–33; Harvey C. Mansfield, *Taming the Prince: The Ambivalence of Modern Executive Power* (Baltimore: Johns Hopkins University Press, 1989); Carnes Lord, *The Modern Prince: What Leaders Need to Know Now* (New Haven: Yale University Press, 2004).
38. Fukuyama, *The End of History*, pp. 287–340; Kristol, 'Diplomacy vs. Foreign Policy'; 'The Neoconservative Persuasion', *Weekly Standard*, vol. 8, no. 47, August 2003, http://www.weeklystandard.com/Content/Public/Articles/000/000/003/000tzmlw.asp [3 June 2008].
39. Irving Kristol, 'Utopianism and American Politics', in his *On the Democratic Idea in America* (New York: Harper & Row, 1972), p. 128.
40. Charles Krauthammer, 'When Unilateralism is Right and Just', in E. J. Dionne, Jr., J. B. Elshtain and K. Droggosz (eds.), *Liberty and Power: A Dialogue on U.S. Foreign Policy in an Unjust World* (Washington, DC: Brooking Institution Press, 2004), p. 97. See also Jeane Kirkpatrick, *Right versus Might: International Law and the Use of Force* (Washington: Council on Foreign Relations, 1994); Peter Brookes, 'Why the World Still Needs America's Military Might', Heritage Lecture no. 1102, Heritage Foundation, 24 November 2008, http://www.heritage.org/research/features/nationalsecurity/ [3 December 2008]; Robert Kagan, 'The September 12 Paradigm: America, the World, and George W. Bush', *Foreign Affairs*,

September/October 2008, http://www.foreignaffairs.org/20080901faessay87502/robert-kagan/the-september-12-paradigm.html?mode=pr [4 November 2008].

41. Inter alia, Kagan, *Of Paradise and Power*, p. 76; 'Multilateralism, American Style', *Washington Post*, 14 September 2002.
42. Carl Schmitt, *Political Theology: Four Chapters on the Concept of Sovereignty*, trans. George Schwab (Chicago: University of Chicago Press, 2006 [1922]), p. 3. Analysts of all political and theoretical persuasions have noted the similarity between Schmitt's theory of sovereignty and neoconservative discourses on American unilateralism during the Bush presidency. See, for instance, Couze Venn, 'World Dis/Order: On Some Fundamental Questions', *Theory, Culture and Society*, vol. 19, no. 4, 2002, pp. 121–36; Nehal Bhuta, 'A Global State of Exception? The United States and Global Order', *Constellations*, vol. 10, no. 3, 2003, pp. 371–91; Jef Huysmans, 'International Politics of Exception: Competing Visions of International Political Order Between Law and Politics', *Alternatives*, vol. 31, no. 2, 2006, pp. 135–65; Stanley Hoffman, 'American Exceptionalism: The New Version', in Ignatieff, *American Exceptionalism*, pp. 225–40.
43. The Weberian roots of Schmitt's decisionsim are discussed in Gary L. Ulmen, 'The Sociology of the State: Carl Schmitt and Max Weber', *State, Culture and Society*, vol. 1, 1985, pp. 3–57; John McCormick, 'Transcending Weber's Categories of Modernity? The Early Lukács and Schmitt on the Rationalization Thesis', *The New German Critique*, vol. 75, 1988, pp. 133–77.
44. Max Weber, 'Science as a Vocation', in his *The Vocations Lectures*, edited and introduced by David Owen and Tracy Strong (Indianapolis and Cambridge: Hackett, 2004), p. 27.
45. Max Weber, *Economy and Society: An Outline of Interpretive Sociology*, (eds.) R. Roth and C. Wittich (Berkeley: California University Press, 1978), pp. 874–5.
46. Ibid., p. 811.
47. Ibid., p. 758.
48. Schmitt, *Political Theology*. For a useful discussion of Schmitt's theory of sovereignty that has influenced my own interpretation, see William Rasch, *Sovereignty and Its Discontent: On the Primacy of Conflict and the Structure of the Political* (London: Birkbeck Law Press, 2004), pp. 91–2; Hidemi Suganami, 'Understanding Sovereignty Through Kelsen/Schmitt', *Review of International Studies*, vol. 33, 2007, pp. 511–30.
49. Carl Schmitt, *The Nomos of the Earth in the International Law of the Jus Publicum Europaeum* (New York: Telos Press, 2006 [1950]).
50. Francis Fukuyama, *State-Building: Governance and World Order in the Twenty-First Century* (London: Profile Books, 2004), p. 142.
51. Robert Kagan, 'A Tougher War for the US is One of Legitimacy', *New York Times*, 24 January 2004, http://query.nytimes.com/gst/fullpage.html?res=9F00E2DA1E39F937A15752C0A9629C8B63 [26 January 2008];

Fukuyama, 'Does the West Still Exist?'; American Enterprise Institute, Transcripts From the Conference on War, International Law, and Sovereignty: Reevaluating the Rules of the Game in a New Century, Washington, 24 June 2004, http://www.aei.org [12 October 2007]; Robert D. Kaplan, 'Supremacy by Stealth', *Atlantic Monthly*, vol. 292, July-Aug. 2003, pp. 66–83; Gordon C. Chang, 'The End of Multilateralism' *Weekly Standard*, vol. 15, no. 17, 2010.

52. Robert Kagan, *End of Dreams, Return of History* (London: Atlantic Books, 2008), p. 96.
53. Anne-Marie Slaughter, 'A Brave New Judicial World', in Ignatieff, *American Exceptionalism and Human Rights*, pp. 177–203.
54. James W. Ceaser, 'The Great Divide: American Interventionism and its Opponents', in William Kristol and Robert Kagan (eds.), *Present Dangers: Crisis and Opportunity in American Foreign and Defense Policy* (New York: Encounter Books, 2000), pp. 41–2.
55. Ruggie, 'American Exceptionalism', p. 330. Italics original.
56. Moravcsik, 'Conservative Idealism', p. 298.
57. Ibid., p. 296.
58. See, Kagan, 'Europeans Courting Disaster'; Nico Krisch, 'Weak as Constraint, Strong as a Tool: The Place of International Law in U.S. Foreign Policy', in David Malone and Yuen Foong Khong (eds.), *Unilateralism and U.S. Foreign Policy: International Perspectives* (Boulder, CO.: Lynne Rienner Publishers, 2003).
59. Paul W. Kahn, 'American Hegemony and International Law. Speaking Law to Power: Popular Sovereignty, Human Rights, and the New International Order', *Chicago Journal of International Law*, vol. 1, no. 2, 2000, p. 6.
60. See, for instance, Bolton, '"Legitimacy" in International Affairs'; Rabkin, *The Case for Sovereignty*, chapter 2; Anthony A. Peacock, *Deconstructing the Republic: Voting Rights, the Supreme Court and the Founders' Republicanism Reconsidered* (Washington, DC: AEI Press, 2008).
61. Jürgen Habermas, *The Inclusion of the Other: Studies in Political Theory* (Cambridge: Polity Press, 1999), p. 240.
62. See Kahn, 'American Hegemony', pp. 2–6.
63. Bolton, 'Should We Take Global Governance Seriously?', pp. 213–4.
64. Rabkin, cited in Moravcsik, 'Conservative Idealism', p. 304. See also Fonte, 'Global Governance', p. 3; Sharansky and Wolosky, *Defending Identity*.
65. Robert Dahl, *Democracy and its Critics* (New Haven: Yale University Press, 1991), p. 204.
66. Habermas, *The Inclusion of the* Other, pp. 115–6.
67. Ibid., p. 113.
68. William Bennett, 'Morality, Character and American Foreign Policy', in Robert Kagan and William Kristol (eds.), *Present Dangers* (New York: Encounter Books, 2000), p. 290.

69. Habermas, *The Inclusion of the Other*, p. 227.
70. For classic cosmopolitan formulations of these issues, see Jürgen Habermas, 'Multiculturalism and the Liberal State', *Stanford Law Review*, vol. 47, no. 5, 1995, pp. 849–53; Daniel Archibugi and David Held (eds.), *Cosmopolitan Democracy: an Agenda for a New World Order* (Cambridge: Polity, 1995); Robert Falk, *Law in an Emerging Global Village: A Post-Westphalian Perspective* (Ardsley, NY: Transnational Publishers, 1998); Seyla Benhabib, *Another Cosmopolitanism* (Oxford: Oxford University Press, 2008). Two documents often targeted by neoconservative polemics in this context are Ford Foundation, *Close to Home: Case Studies of Human Rights Work in the United States* (New York: Ford Foundation, 2004) and United Nations Convention for the Elimination of Racial Discrimination, 'Structural Racism in the United States. A Report to the UN Committee for the Elimination of Racial Discrimination on the occasion of its review of the Periodic Report of the United States of America', organised by the Kirwan Institute and 250 NGOs, February 2008, http://www2.ohchr.org/english/bodies/cerd/docs/ngos/usa/USHRN2.doc [November 2008]. See Steven Groves, 'Furthering the UN's Leftist Agenda: The UN CERD Committee Report', Webmemo no. 1899, Heritage Foundation, 22 April 2008, *http://www.heritage.org/Research/InternationalOrganizations/wm1899.cfm* [3 December 2008]; Fonte, 'Global Governance'.
71. Irving Kristol, 'The Tragedy of Multiculturalism', in his *Neo-Conservatism*; John Fonte, 'Why There is a Culture War: Gramsci and Tocqueville in America', *Policy Review*, no. 104, 2000, http://www.hoover.org/publications/policyreview/3484376.html [6 October 2007].
72. Allan Bloom, *The Closing of the American Mind* (New York: Simon & Schuster, 1987), p. 31.
73. Fonte, 'Global Governance', p. 5. In *Who Are We? The Challenge to American National Identity* (New York: Simon & Schuster, 2004), Samuel Huntington warns that American liberalism has fallen under the spell of 'de-nationalized elites' who are out to dismantle the American creed through anti-assimilation, multilingual and multicultural policies and legislations.
74. James Ceaser, 'Multiculturalism and American Democracy', and Marc Plattner, 'Liberalism, Universalism, and Multiculturalism', in A. M. Melzer, J. Weinberger and R. Zinman (eds.), *Multiculturalism and American Democracy* (Lawrence, KS: University of Kansas Press, 1998); Ben Wattenberg, 'Melt, Melting, Melted', *Washington Post*, 15 March 2001, accessible via http://www.aei.org/publications/filter.all,pubID.12609/pub_detail.asp [3 December 2007]; John Fonte, 'Dual Allegiance: A Challenge to Immigration Reform and Patriotic Assimilation', Centre for Immigration Studies, Washington, 2005, http://www.cis.org/articles/2005/back1205.html [3 May 2007]; Heather MacDonald, Victor Davis Hanson and Steven Malanga, *The Immigration Solution: A Better Plan Than Today's*, with introduction by Myron Magnet (Chicago: Ivan R. Dee, 2007).

75. Francis Fukuyama, 'A Year of Living Dangerously: Remember Theo Van Gogh and Shudder for the Future', *Washington Post*, 2 November 2005, http://www.opinionjournal.com/editorial/feature.html?id=110007491 [3 November 2005]. See also Daniel Pipes, 'Britain's Encounter with Islamic Law', *Jerusalem Post*, 13 February 2008, and 'Will Europe Resist Islamization', *Jerusalem Post*, 3 April 2008, both accessible via http://www.danielpipes.org/article/5462 [October 2008]; Robert Kagan, 'Europe slides into irrelevance', *Washington Post*, 15 June 2008, p. B07.
76. Fonte, 'Liberal Democracy', p. 465.
77. Fukuyama, 'Does the West Still Exist?', pp. 145–6.
78. Kagan, 'A Tougher War for the US is One of Legitimacy'.
79. Robert Kagan and William Kristol, 'Toward a Neo-Reaganite Foreign Policy', *Foreign Affairs*, no. 75, July/Aug. 1996, p. 31.
80. Habermas, *The Inclusion of the Other*, p. 136.
81. Ibid.
82. Robert Kagan, 'America Supports Democracy, How Novel', *Financial Times*, 6 December 2006, p. 19.
83. Ceaser, 'The Great Divide', pp. 38–9. Italics original.
84. Robert Kagan, 'America's Crisis of Legitimacy', *Foreign Affairs*, March/April, 2004, p. 19.
85. Robert Kagan, 'One Year After: A Grand Strategy for the West?', *Survival*, vol. 44, no. 4, 2002–3, pp. 138–9.
86. For different treatments of this point in the more specific context of the Iraq War, see Jacques Rancière, 'Prisoners of the Infinite', *Counterpunch*, 30 April 2002, http://www.counterpunch.org/ranciere0430.html [12 October 2002]; Étienne Balibar, *L'Europe. L'Amérique, la guerre* (Paris: La Découverte, 2003), pp. 114–24; Pål Wrange, 'Of Power and Justice', *German Law Journal*, vol. 4, no. 9, 2003, pp. 936–62; Jef Huysmans, 'International Politics of Insecurity: Normativity, Inwardness, and the Exception', *Security Dialogue*, vol. 37, 2006, pp. 11–29.
87. Kagan, 'A Tougher War for the US is One of Legitimacy'.
88. Immanuel Kant, 'Perpetual Peace: A Philosophical Sketch', in I. Kant, *Political Writings*, ed. H. S. Reiss (Cambridge: Cambridge University Press, 1991), pp. 93–125.
89. Michael Savage, 'Legalizing Politics and Politicising Law', in C. Bickerton, P. Cunliffe and A. Gourevitch (eds.), *Politics Without Sovereignty* (London: UCL Press, 2007), p. 174.
90. Balibar, *L'Europe, L'Amérique*, p. 118. My translation.
91. Jean L. Cohen, 'Whose Sovereignty? Empire Versus International Law', *Ethics and International Affairs*, vol. 18, no. 3, 2004, p. 14.
92. Balibar, *L'Europe, L'Amérique*, p. 118.

6. A LIBERALISM BETRAYED?

1. James Ceaser, 'Giving Realism a Bad Name: The Demise of Idealism in Obama's Washington', *Weekly Standard*, vol. 39, no. 39, 2009, http://www.

weeklystandard.com/Content/Public/Articles/000/000/016/650rpvzs.asp?pg=2 [25 June,2009].

2. Robert Kagan, 'America's Crisis of Legitimacy', *Foreign Affairs*, March/April 2004, http://www.foreignaffairs.com/articles/59710/robert-kagan/americas-crisis-of-legitimacy [8 March 2006], no page numbers.
3. Robert Kagan, *Of Paradise and Power: America and Europe in the New World Order* (London: Atlantic Books, 2004), pp. 130–31.
4. Robert Kagan, 'Power and Weakness', *Policy Review*, June-July 2002, http://www.hoover.org/publications/policyreview/3460246.html [6 October 2008], no page numbers.
5. Ibid.
6. Peter Berkowitz, 'Liberalism and Power', in T. Lindberg (ed.), *Beyond Paradise and Power: Europe, America and the Future of a Troubled partnership* (London: Routledge, 2005), p. 210. For Berkowitz's interpretation of Nietzsche, see his *Nietzsche: The Ethics of an Immoralist* (Cambridge, MA: Harvard University Press, 1996).
7. See, for instance, Karl Löwith, *Max Weber and Karl Marx* (London: Routledge, 1993); Michael J. Smith, *Realist Thought From Weber to Kissinger* (Baton Rouge: Louisiana State University, 1986), chapter 2; Robert Eden, *Political Leadership and Nihilism: A Study of Weber and Nietzsche* (Gainsville: University Press of Florida, 1983); Tracy B. Strong, 'Love, Passion, and Maturity: Nietzsche and Weber on Politics and Morality', in John McCormick (ed.), *Democracy and Technology* (Durham, NC: Duke University Press, 2002); Mark F. W. Lovatt, *Confronting the Will-to-Power: A Reconsideration of the Theology of Reinhold Niebuhr* (New York: Wipf and Stock Publisher, 2001); John P. McCormick, *Carl Schmitt's Critique of Liberalism: Against Politics as Technology* (Cambridge: Cambridge University Press, 1997), pp. 96–116; Christopher Frei, *Hans Morgenthau: An Intellectual Biography* (Baton Rouge: Louisiana State University Press, 2001); Mark Lampert, *Leo Strauss and Nietzsche* (Chicago: University of Chicago Press, 1998).
8. Friedrich Nietzsche, *Beyond Good and Evil*, trans. Walter Kaufmann (New York: Random House, 1966), p. 259.
9. Cited in Richard Ned Lebow, *The Tragic Vision of Politics: Ethics, Interests and Orders* (Cambridge: Cambridge University Press, 2003), p. 224. The extent to which Nietzsche influenced Morgenthau's work is a source of contention in the IR literature. For a good engagement with this debate which downplays (too much in my view) Morgenthau's intellectual debt to Nietzsche, see Stephen Turner and George Mazur, 'Morgenthau as a Weberian Methodologist', *European Journal of International Relations*, 15/3 (2009), pp. 477–504.
10. Nietzsche, *Beyond Good and Evil*, p. 163.
11. Friedrich Nietzsche, *The Will to Power*, trans. Walter Kaufmann and R. J. Hollingdale (New York: Vintage, 1967), p. 656.
12. Hans J. Morgenthau, *Politics Among Nations*, 5th edn, ed. Kenneth Thompson (New York: Alfred A. Knopf, 1978 [1948]), p. 3.

13. Nietzsche, *The Will to Power*, pp. 401–2. Nietzsche here was drawing on Spinoza, who had already set the basis of this argument in a non-secular language some two hundred years earlier in his *Ethics*, edited and translated by G. H. R. Parkinson (Oxford: Oxford University Press, 2000 [1677]).
14. Lawrence J. Hatab, *Nietzsche's On the Genealogy of Morality* (Cambridge: Cambridge University Press, 2008), p. 174.
15. Lebow, *The Tragic Vision*, p. 222.
16. Leo Strauss, 'Notes on Carl Schmitt, The Concept of the Political', in Carl Schmitt, *The Concept of the Political* (Chicago: University of Chicago Press, 1996), p. 92.
17. Reinhardt Koselleck, *Critique and Crisis: Enlightenment and the Pathogenesis of Modern Society* (Cambridge, MA: MIT Press, 1987), p. 25.
18. Ibid., p. 33.
19. Irving Kristol, 'Utopianism, Ancient and Modern', in his *Neoconservatism: Selected Essays 1949–1995* (New York: Free Press, 1995), pp. 184–99. See also Kirkpatrick, *Dictatorships*, pp. 11–2.
20. Nietzsche, *The Will to Power*, p. 12; Hatab, *Nietzsche's On the Genealogy*, pp. 11–2; Bülent Diken, *Nihilism* (London: Routledge, 2009), pp. 1–16.
21. Martin Heidegger, 'Nietzsche's Word: "God is Dead"', in his *Off the Beaten Tracks*, edited and translated by Julian Young and Kenneth Hayes (Cambridge: Cambridge University Press, 2002), p. 163.
22. Martin Heidegger famously read Nietzsche's doctrine of the 'eternal return of the same' as Nietzsche's attempt to transcend the nihilistic dilemma of his own doctrine of the will to power. See Martin Heidegger, *Nietzsche*, 2 volumes, ed. David Farrell Krell (New York: HarperCollins, 1991). See also Gianni Vattimo, 'Nihilism and the Problem of Temporality', in his *Dialogue with Nietzsche* (New York: Columbia University Press, 2006).
23. James I. Porter, 'Nietzsche's Theory of the Will to Power', in Keith Ansell Pearson (ed.), *A Companion to Nietzsche* (Oxford: Wiley-Blackwell, 2009), pp. 555–6.
24. Krauthammer, *Democratic Realism*, no page numbers.
25. The US diplomatic historian Melvin Leffler described the 'balance of power that favors freedom' of the NSS 2002 as a 'confused' and 'meaningless' concept. See his '9/11 and the Past and Future of American Foreign Policy', *International Affairs*, vol. 79, 2003, p. 10.
26. Irving Kristol, 'The Neoconservative Persuasion', *Weekly Standard*, vol. 8, no. 47, August 2003, http://www.weeklystandard.com/Content/Public/Articles/000/000/003/000tzmlw.asp [3 June 2008].
27. See, for instance, Morgenthau, *Politics*, pp. 8–9, 38–9; Kenneth Waltz, *Man, The State and War* (New York: Columbia University Press, 1959), pp. 159–60, 210–12; Michael Walzer, *Just and Unjust Wars: A Moral Argument with Historical Illustrations* (New York: Basic Books, 1977), chapter 1; Robert Gilpin, 'The Richness of the Tradition of Political Realism', *International Organization*, vol. 38, no. 2, 1984, pp. 287–304.

28. Strauss's main study of Thucydides is in his *The City and Man* (Chicago: University of Chicago Press, 1964), chapter 3. For a sample of some of the most influential Straussian interpretations of Thucydides, see Donald Kagan, *The Outbreak of the Peloponnesian War* (Ithaca: Cornell University Press, 1969); *The Archidamian War* (Ithaca: Cornell University Press, 1974); *The Peace of Nicias and the Sicilian Expedition* (Ithaca: Cornell University Press, 1981); *The Fall of the Athenian Empire* (Ithaca: Cornell University Press, 1987); David Bolotin, 'Thucydides', in Leo Strauss and Joseph Cropsey (eds.), *History of Political Philosophy*, 3rd edn (Chicago: Chicago University Press, 1987); Pangle and Ahrensdorf, *Justice Among Nations*, chapter 1; Christopher Bruell, 'Thucydides' View of Athenian Imperialism', *American Political Science Review*, vol. 68, no. 1, 1974, pp. 11–7; Steven Forde, *The Ambition to Rule: Alcibiades and the Politics of Imperialism in Thucydides* (Ithaca: Cornell University Press, 1989); Peter Ahrensdorf, 'Thucydides' Realistic Critique of Realism', *Polity*, vol. 30, 1997, pp. 231–65; Steven Forde, 'International Realism: Thucydides, Machiavelli, and Neorealism', *International Studies Quarterly*, vol. 39, no. 2, 1995, pp. 141–60.
29. Robert Kagan, 'Inside the Limo', *The New Republic*, 10 April 2000, p. 36.
30. Pangle and Ahrensdorf, *Justice Among Nations*, p. 270, n. 39, italics original; Daniel Garst, 'Thucydides and Neorealism', *International Studies Quarterly*, 33/1 (1989), p. 22.
31. Pangle and Ahrensdorf, *Justice Among Nations*, pp. 13–32.
32. Morgenthau, *Politics Among Nations*, p. 13.
33. Michael C. Williams, *The Realist Tradition and the Limits of International Relations* (Cambridge: Cambridge University Press, 2005), chapter 1.
34. Morgenthau, *Politics Among Nations*, pp. 231–2, 491, 498.
35. Ibid., p. 12.
36. Ibid., p. 333.
37. Pangle and Ahrensdorf, *Justice Among Nations*, p. 235.
38. Fukuyama, *The End of History*, pp. 287–328; Pangle and Ahrensdorf, *Justice Among Nations*, chapters 7–8. In fact Morgenthau himself admitted so much: 'a world state created by conquest' and ruling over 'an unwilling humanity' would be a 'totalitarian monster resting on feet of clay'. *Politics Among Nations*, p. 344.
39. Pangle and Ahrensdorf, *Justice Among Nations*, p. 237.
40. Irving Kristol, 'About Equality', in his *Neoconservatism*, p. 171.
41. Irving Kristol, 'The Soul of the Welfare State', *On the Issues*, 3 February 1997, http://www.aei.org/issue/7392 [6 January 2008].
42. Thomas Pangle, *Leo Strauss: An Introduction to his Thought and Intellectual Legacy* (Baltimore: Johns Hopkins University Press, 2006), p. 87.
43. Fukuyama, *The End of History*, p. 329. See also Robert Kaplan, *Warrior Politics* (New York: Vintage, 2003) and Max Boot, *The Savage Wars of Peace: Small Wars and the Rise of American Power* (New York: Basic Books, 2002).

44. Cassirer, *The Myth of the State*, pp. 287–8.
45. Cited in Herbert Marcuse, 'The Struggle Against Liberalism in the Totalitarian View of the State', in his *Negations* (London: Penguin, 1968 [1934]), p. 30.
46. Marcuse, 'The Struggle', pp. 32–5. This was also the basis of Theodor Adorno's critique of German existentialism in *The Jargon of Authenticity*, translated by Knut Tarnowski and Frederic Will (London and New York: Routledge, 2003 [1964]).
47. George Friedman, *The Political Philosophy of the Frankfurt School* (Ithaca and London: Cornell University Press, 1981), p. 294.
48. James Ceaser, *Reconstructing America* (New Haven and London: Yale University Press, 1997), p. 231.
49. Kristol, 'Utopianism', pp. 198–9.
50. Ibid., p. 191. See also Jeane Kirkpatrick, 'Introduction', in her *Dictatorship and Double Standards: Rationalism and Reason in Politics* (Washington, DC: AEI and Simon & Schuster, 1982).
51. Stephen Eric Bronner, *Reclaiming the Enlightenment: Towards a Politics of Radical Engagement* (New York: Columbia University Press, 2004), p. 142.
52. This was also the aim and strategy of Carl Schmitt's critique of the liberal democratic state. See his *The Crisis of Parliamentary Democracy* (Cambridge, MA: MIT Press, 1985 [1923]). See also Chantal Mouffe, *The Democratic Paradox* (London: Verso, 2000).
53. Jef Huysmans, 'The jargon of exception—on Schmitt, Agamben and the absence of political society', *International Political Sociology*, vol. 2, no. 2, 2008, pp. 165–78.
54. Bronner, *Reclaiming the Enlightenment*, p. 118. The notion of *Gemeinschaft* (community) was developed by the German sociologist Ferdinand Tönnis (1855–1936) who, perhaps not so coincidentally, is responsible for putting Hobbes back on the agenda in Germany at the end of the nineteenth century. A *Gemeinschaft* refers to a form of association regulated by a shared culture, common mores and beliefs about responsibility in which selfless individuals prioritise the public interest over their own. *Gemeinschaft* contrasts with the 'artificial' *Gesellschaft* (society or civil society), which denotes a purposive association whose cohesion derives not from a shared belief system but from a complex division of labour, materialism and the pursuit of individual interests. Ferdinand Tönnis, *Community and Civil Society* (Cambridge: Cambridge University Press, 2001 [1887]), p. 22.
55. Emmanuel Todd, *Après l'empire: Essai sur la décomposition du système Américain* (Paris: Gallimard 2002), pp. 41–70.
56. Greg Grandin, 'The Imperial Presidency: The Legacy of Reagan's Central America Policy', in Michael J. Thompson (ed.), *Confronting the New Conservatism: The Rise of the Right in America* (New York: NYU Press, 2007), p. 200.

57. David Ryan, *US Foreign Policy in World History* (London: Routledge, 2000), p. 170.
58. See Ronald Dworkin, 'The Threat to Patriotism', *New York Review of Books*, vol. 49, no. 3, 2002, pp. 44–9; 'A Necessary Evil?', *The Economist*, 12 July 2003, p. 26; P. Knox, 'Rights Trampled in the U.S., Report Says', *Globe and Mail*, 15 August 2002, p. 2; K. Q. Seelye, 'Pentagon Raises Idea of Indefinite Detention', *International Herald Tribune*, 22 March 2002, p. 3. Two of the main legal masterminds behind the Bush administration's approach to the war on terror are neoconservative ideological travellers and AEI fellows John Yoo and Jack Goldsmith. See John Yoo, *The Powers of War and Peace: The Constitution and Foreign Affairs* (Chicago: University of Chicago Press, 2006); *War by Other Means: An Insider's Account of the War on Terror* (Washington: Atlantic Monthly Press, 2006); Jack Goldsmith, *The Terror Presidency: Law and Judgement Inside the Bush Administration* (New York: W. W. Norton, 2007); Jeffrey Rosen, 'Conscience of a Conservative', *New York Times*, 9 September 2007, http://www.nytimes.com/2007/09/09/magazine/09rosen.html?_r=1&ei=5087%0A&em=&en=f195c56e871af91e&ex=118913760&oref=slogin [9 September 2008].
59. See William Scheuerman, 'Rethinking Crisis Government', in D. J. Sherman and T. Nardin (eds.), *Terror, Culture, Politics: Rethinking 9/11* (Bloomington and Indianapolis: Indiana University Press, 2006), p. 214.
60. See, for instance, for Dick Cheney, 'Keeping America Safe', Address at the American Entreprise Institute, Washington, 21 May 2009, podcast available online at http://www.aei.org/video/101099 [7 July 2009]; Charles Krauthammer, 'Torture? No. Except…', *Washington Post*, 1 May 2009, http://www.washingtonpost.com/wp-dyn/content/article/2009/04/30/AR2009043003108.html [3 May 2009]; John Yoo and Robert J. Delahunty (eds.), 'Outsourcing American Law: Against Foreign Law', AEI Working Paper no. 158, 20 August 2009, http://www.aei.org/papers?page=1&rid=48 [6 October 2009]; Thomas Joscelyn, 'Clear and Present Dangers', *Weekly Standard*, vol. 14, no. 11, 2008, http://www.weeklystandard.com/Content/Public/Articles/000/000/015/845xcgce.asp [3 January 2010].
61. Daniel Woodley, *Fascism and Political Theory: Critical Perspectives on Fascist Ideology* (London: Routledge, 2010), p. 77.
62. Kevin Mattson, 'The Rise of Postmodern Conservatism', in Martin Halliwell and Catherine Morley (eds.), *American Thought and Culture in the 21st Century* (Edinburgh: Edinburgh University Press, 2008), pp. 81–96.
63. Paul Gottfried, *Conservatism in America* (New York: Palgrave Macmillan, 2007), p. 53.
64. Coulter's advice to her hundreds of thousands of readers, for example, is that 'You must outrage the enemy. If the liberal you're arguing with doesn't become speechless with sputtering, impotent rage, you're not doing it right'. According to Coulter, if Americans actually knew the truth

about what 'slandering liberals' really believe, 'the public would boil them in oil'. Cited in Mattson, 'The Rise of Postmodern Conservatism', pp. 84–5.

65. Justin Vaisse, *Histoire du néoconservatisme aux Etats-Unis: Le triomphe de l'idéologie* (Paris: Odile Jacob, 2008), p. 287.

BIBLIOGRAPHY

Abrams, R. M., *America Transformed: Sixty Years of Revolutionary Change 1941–2001*, Cambridge University Press, Cambridge, 2006.

Adler, S., *The Isolationist Impulse: Its Twentieth Century Reaction*, Abelard-Schuman, New York, 1957.

Adorno, T., *The Culture Industry*, Routledge, London, 1991.

Adorno, T., *The Jargon of Authenticity*, translated by K. Tarnowski and F. Will, Routledge, London and New York, 2003 [1964].

Ahrensdorf, P., 'Thucydides' Realistic Critique of Realism', *Polity*, vol. 30, 1997, pp. 231–65.

Alesina, A. and E. Glaeser, *Fighting Poverty in the US and Europe: A World of Difference*, Oxford University Press, Oxford, 2006.

Allin, D. H., *Cold War Illusions: America, Europe, and Soviet Power, 1969–1989*, St. Martin's Press, New York, 1995.

Ambrose, S. E., and D. G. Brinkley, *Rise to Globalism: American Foreign Policy Since 1938*, 8th edn, Penguin Books, London and New York, 1997.

American Enterprise Institute, Transcripts From the Conference on War, International Law, and Sovereignty: Reevaluating the Rules of the Game in a New Century, Washington, 24 June 2004, http://www.aei.org [12 October 2007].

Andrews, D. M., ed., *The Atlantic Alliance Under Stress: US–European Relations After Iraq*, Cambridge University Press, Cambridge, 2005.

Arblaster, A., *The Rise and Decline of Western Liberalism*, Basil Blackwell, Oxford, 1984.

Archibugi, D., and Held, D., eds., *Cosmopolitan Democracy: An Agenda for a New World Order*, Polity Press, Cambridge, 1995.

Arendt, H., *The Origins of Totalitarianism*, Harcourt Inc., San Diego, New York and London, 1966, 1950.

Armstrong, P., A. Glyn and J. Harrison, *Capitalism Since 1945*, Blackwell, Cambridge, MA, 1991.

Aron, R., *L'opium des intellectuels*, Calman-Levy, Paris, 1955.

Bailey, Ronald, 'The Voice of Neoconservatism', *Reason Online*, 17 October 2001, http://www.reason.com/news/show/34900.html [3 October 2007].

Balakrishnan, G., *The Enemy: An Intellectual Portrait of Carl Schmitt*, Verso, London, 2000.

Balibar, E., 'Le Hobbes de Schmitt et le Schmitt de Hobbes', in C. Schmitt, *Le Léviathan Dans La Doctrine De L'État de Thomas Hobbes*, Seuil, Paris, 2002.

———, *L'Europe, l'Amérique, la guerre*, La Découverte, Paris, 2003.

Ballentine, K. and J. Sherman, eds., *The Political Economy of Armed Conflict: Beyond Greed and Grievance*, Lynne Rienner Publishers, Boulder, CO, 2003.

Barkawi, T. and M. Laffey, 'The Imperial Peace: Democracy, Force and Globalization', *European Journal of International Relations*, vol. 5, no. 4, 1999, pp. 403–34.

Barnett, T., 'Where—not when—preemption makes sense', *Transformation Trends*, 18 November 2002, http:www.nwc.navy.mil/newrulesets/PreemptionMakesSense.pdf [2 October 2006].

———, 'The Pentagon's New Map', *Esquire*, 1 March 2003, http://www.thomaspmbarnett.com/published/pentagonsnewmap.htm [7 December 2008].

———, *The Pentagon's New Map: War and Peace in the Twenty First Century*, Putnam Adult, London, 2004.

———, *A Blueprint for Action*, Putnam Publishing Group, Washington, 2005.

———, 'Obama's New Map of the World', *Esquire*, March 2009, http://www.esquire.com/features/obama-foreign-policy-0309 [7 April 2009].

Bauer, P. T., 'Western Guilt and Third World Poverty', *Commentary*, January 1976, pp. 31–9.

Bell, D., '"Hard" and "Soft" Anti-Communist', *The New Leader*, 17 May 1954, pp. 7–11.

———, 'Ethnicity and Social Change', in N. Glazer and D. P. Moynihan, eds., *Ethnicity: Theory and Experience*, Harvard University Press, Cambridge, MA, 1975.

———, *The Winding Passage*, Harper & Row, New York, 1979.

———, 'First Love and Early Sorrow', *Times Higher Education Supplement*, 16 January 1981, available online at http://www.pbs.org/arguing/nyintellectuals_bell_2.html [7 January 2008].

———, *The Cultural Contradictions of Capitalism*, 20th Anniversary Edition, Basic Books, New York 1996 [1978].

———, *The End of Ideology: On the Exhaustion of Political Ideas in the Fifties*, Harvard University Press, Boston, 2000 [1960].

———, ed., *The Radical Right*, Anchor Books, New York, 1964.

Bell, D. and I. Kristol, 'What is the Public Interest?', *The Public Interest*, vol. 1, Fall 1965, pp. 3–6.

———, eds., *Confrontation: The Student Rebellion and the Universities*, Basic Books, New York, 1968.

———, eds., *Capitalism Today*, Basic Books, New York, 1972.

Bellamy, R., 'Schumpeter and the Transformation of Capitalism, Liberalism and Democracy', in Bellamy, *Rethinking Liberalism*, Pinter, London and New York, 2000.

———, *Rethinking Liberalism*, Pinter, London and New York, 2000.

Benhabib, S., *Another Cosmopolitanism*, Oxford University Press, Oxford, 2008.

Benjamin, W., 'Edmund Fuchs: Collector and Historian', in A. Arato and E. Gerbhardt, eds., *The Essential Frankfurt School Reader*, Urizen, New York, 1978.

———, 'Theories of German Fascism', in A. Kaes, M. Jay and E. Dimenberg, eds., *The Weimar Republic Sourcebook*, University of California Press, Berkeley, 1994.

Bennett, W., 'America's Cultural Decline Must Be Reversed', *Human Events*, vol. 50, 1994, pp. 12–13.

———, 'Revolt Against God. America's Spiritual Despair', *Policy Review*, no. 67, 1994, pp. 19–24.

———, *The Devaluing of America: The Fight for Our Culture and Our Children*, Simon & Schuster, New York, 1995.

———, 'Morality, Character and American Foreign Policy', in R. Kagan and W. Kristol, eds., *Present Dangers*, Encounter Books, New York, 2000.

———, 'From Nation-Building to State-Building: The Geopolitics of Development, The Nation-State System and the Changing Global Order', *Third World Quarterly*, vol. 27, no. 1, pp. 5–25.

Berger, P., 'The Greening of U.S. Foreign Policy', *Commentary*, March 1976, pp. 23–8.

———, *Facing Up to Modernity: Excursions in Society, Politics and Religion*, Basic Books, New York, 1977.

———, *The Capitalist Revolution: Fifty Propositions about Prosperity, Equality, and Liberty*, Basic Books, New York, 1986.

Berkowitz, P., *Nietzsche: The Ethics of an Immoralist*, Harvard University Press, Cambridge, MA, 1996.

———, 'The Shadow of Fascist Philosophy on Today's Conservative Politics', *Chronicle of Higher Education*, 14 May 2004, http://chronicle.com/weekly/v50/i36/36b00401.htm [7 September 2005].

———, 'Liberalism and Power', in T. Lindberg, ed., *Beyond Paradise and Power: Europe, America and the Future of a Troubled Partnership*, Routledge, New York and London, 2005.

———, 'Leviathan Then and Now', *Policy Review*, vol. 151, 2008, http://www.hoover.org/publications/policyreview/30118304.html [4 November 2009].

Berman, R.A., *Modern Culture and Critical Theory: Art, Politics and the Legacy of the Frankfurt School*, University of Wisconsin Press, Madison, 1989.

Berns, L., 'The Prescientific World and Historicism: Some Reflections on Strauss, Heidegger, and Husserl', in A. Udoff, ed., *Leo Strauss's Thought:*

Toward a Critical Engagement, Lynne Rienner Publishers, Boulder, CO, 1991.

Bhuta, N., 'A Global State of Exception? The United States and Global Order', *Constellations*, vol. 10, no. 3, 2003, pp. 371–91.

Bianchi, A., 'International Law and US Courts: The Myth of Lohengrin Revisited', *European Journal of International Law*, vol. 15, no. 4, 2004, pp. 751–81.

Bloom, A., *Prodigal Sons: The New York Intellectuals and Their World*, Oxford University Press, New York, 1986.

———, *The Closing of the American Mind*, Simon & Schuster, New York, 1987.

———, *Giants and Dwarfs: Essays 1960–1990*, Simon & Schuster, New York, 1990.

———, *Confronting the Constitution: The Challenge to Locke, Montesquieu, Jefferson, Federalism from Utilitarianism, Historicism, Marxism, Freudianism, Pragmatism, Existentialism*, AEI Press, Washington, 1990.

Blumenthal, S., *The Rise of the Counter-Establishment: From Conservative Ideology to Political Power*, Harper & Row, New York, 1988.

Blyth, M., *Great Transformations: Economic Ideas and Institutional Changes in the Twentieth Century*, Cambridge University Press, Cambridge, 2002.

Bolotin, D., 'Thucydides', in L. Strauss and J. Cropsey, eds., *History of Political Philosophy*, 3rd edn, Chicago University Press, Chicago, 1987.

Bolton, J., 'Courting Danger: What's Wrong With the International Criminal Court', *The National Interest*, Winter 1998/1999, vol. 54, pp. 60–71.

———, 'Should We Take Global Governance Seriously?', *Chicago Journal of International Law*, vol. 1, no. 2, 2000, pp. 205–21.

———, 'Is There Really "Law" in International Affairs?', *Transnational Law and Contemporary Problems*, vol. 10, no. 1, 2000, pp. 37–52.

———, '"Legitimacy" in International Affairs: The American Perspective. Theory and Operation', Federalist Society, Washington DC, 13 November 2003, www.state.gov [6 May 2004].

———, 'Global Governance and Shared Sovereignty', *On the Issues AEI*, 28 April 2008, http://www.aei.org/publications/pubID.27885/pub_detail.asp [2 September 2008].

———, *Surrender is Not an Option: Defending America at the United Nations and Abroad*, Simon & Schuster, New York, 2008.

———, 'The Coming War on Sovereignty', *Commentary*, March 2009, pp. 9–15.

Boot, M., *The Savage Wars of Peace: Small Wars and the Rise of American Power*, Basic Books, New York, 2002.

Boyers, R., 'The Neoconservatives and Culture', *Salmagundi*, vol. 66, 1985, pp. 192–204.

Bradley, C. and J. Goldsmith, 'Customary International Law as Federal Common Law: A Critique of the Modern Position', *Harvard Law Review*, vol. 110, no. 4, 1997, pp. 815–76.

———, 'U.N. Human Rights Standards and the U.S. Law: The Current Illegitimacy of International Human Rights Litigations', *Fordham Law Review*, vol. 66, November 1997, pp. 319–59.
———, 'International Delegations, the Structural Constitutions and Non-Self Executions', *Stanford Law Review*, vol. 55, May 2003, pp. 1557–96.
Brennan, M. C., *Turning Right in the Sixties: The Conservative Capture of the GOP*, University of North Carolina Press, Chapel Hill, 1995.
Bridges, G. S., R. Crutchfield and E. E. Simpson, 'Crime, Social Structure and Criminal Punishment: White and Nonwhite Rates of Imprisonment, *Social Problems*, vol. 34, 1987, pp. 345–61.
Bromley, S., *American Power and the Prospects for International Order*, Polity Press, Cambridge, 2008.
Bronner, S. E., *Reclaiming the Enlightenment: Towards a Politics of Radical Engagement*, Columbia University Press, New York, 2004.
Bruce-Briggs, B., ed., *The New Class?*, Transaction Books, New Brunswick, NJ, 1978.
Bruell, C., 'Thucydides' View of Athenian Imperialism', *American Political Science Review*, vol. 68, no. 1, 1974, pp. 11–7.
Busch, N., *No End in Sight: The Continuing Menace of Nuclear Proliferation*, University Press of Kentucky, Lexington, 2004.
Callinicos, A., *Against Postmodernism: A Marxist Critique*, Polity Press, Cambridge, 1989.
Cantor, N., 'The Real Crisis in the Humanities Today', *New Criterion*, vol. 3, no. 10, 1985, pp. 28–33.
Carothers, T., 'The NED at 10', *Foreign Policy*, vol. 73, 1994, pp. 109–20.
Carr, E. H., *The New Society*, Macmillan, London, 1951.
Casey, L. A. and D. B. Rivkin Jr., 'The Rocky Shoals of International Law', *The National Interest*, no. 62, Winter 2000, pp. 35–45.
———, 'Europe in the Balance: The Alarmingly Undemocratic Drift of the European Union', *Policy Review*, June/July 2001, pp. 41–53.
Cassirer, E., *The Myth of the State*, Yale University Press, New Haven and London, 1974 [1946].
Ceaser, James W., *Reconstructing America*, Yale University Press, New Haven and London, 1997.
———, 'Multiculturalism and American Democracy', in A. M. Melzer, J. Weinberger and R. Zinman, eds., *Multiculturalism and American Democracy*, University of Kansas Press, Lawrence, KS, 1998.
———, 'The Great Divide: American Interventionism and its Opponents', in R. Kagan and W. Kristol, eds., *Present Dangers: Crisis and Opportunity in American Foreign and Defense Policy*, Encounter Books, New York, 2000.
———, 'Giving Realism a Bad Name: The Demise of Idealism in Obama's Washington', *Weekly Standard*, vol. 39, no. 39, 2009, http://www.weeklystandard.com/Content/Public/Articles/000/000/016/650rpvzs.asp?pg=2 [25 June, 2009].

Ceaser, J., 'The Roots of Obama Worship', *Weekly Standard*, vol. 15, no. 18, 2010, http://www.weeklystandard.com/articles/roots-obama-worship [10 February 2010].

Cheney, D., 'Keeping America Safe', Address at the American Enterprise Institute, Washington, 21 May 2009, podcast available online at http://www.aei.org/video/101099 [7 July 2009].

Clapham, C., *Africa and the International System: The Politics of State Survival*, Cambridge University Press, Cambridge, 1996.

Clark, I., 'Another Double Movement: The Great Transformation After the Cold War?', *Review of International Studies*, vol. 27, 2001, pp. 237–55.

Clement, C.I., 'Organic Intellectuals and the Discourse on Democracy: Academia, Foreign Policy Makers, and Third World Intervention', *New Political Science*, vol. 25, no. 3, 2003, pp. 351–64.

Coalition for a Democratic Majority, 'Come Home Democrats', *New York Times*, 7 December 1972, p. 14.

Cohen, E., 'The Free American Citizen, 1952', *Commentary*, September 1952, pp. 212–24.

———, 'The Moral Realism of Irving Kristol', *National Affairs*, vol. 2, 2010, http://nationalaffairs.com/publications/detail/the-moral-realism-of-irving-kristol [4 February 2010].

Cohen, J. L., 'Whose Sovereignty? Empire Versus International Law', *Ethics and International Affairs*, vol. 18, no. 3, 2004, pp. 1–24.

Coker, C., 'The United States and the ethics of post-modern war', in K. E. Smith and M. Light, eds., *Ethics and Foreign Policy*, Cambridge University Press, Cambridge, 2001.

Colas, A. and R. S. Saull, eds., *The War on Terrorism and the American 'Empire' after the Cold War*, Routledge, London, 2006.

Coleman, P., *The Liberal Conspiracy: The Congress for Cultural Freedom and the Struggle for the Mind of Postwar Europe*, Free Press, New York, 1989.

Commentary, 'Symposium: Capitalism, Socialism and Nihilism', *Commentary*, April 1978, pp. 29–72.

———, 'Symposium: American Power—For What?', *Commentary*, January 2000, pp 21–48.

Committee on the Present Danger, *Alerting America: The Papers of the Committee on the Present Dangers*, Pergamon Brasseys, Washington, DC, 1984.

Connolly, W., *The Terms of Political Discourse*, Blackwell, Oxford, 1993.

———, 'The Will, Capital Punishment, and Culture War', in J. Dean, ed., *Cultural Studies and Political Theory*, Cornell University Press, Ithaca, NY, 2000.

Continetti, M., 'Misreading History: The Lesson of the Last Eight Years is Not that Americans Want a Smaller Government', *Weekly Standard*, vol. 14, no. 18, 2009, http://www.weeklystandard.com/Content/Public/Articles/000/000/016/015paamb.asp [17 January, 2009].

Cooper, D. E., 'Exposition in the existentialist tradition in philosophy', in David E. Cooper, *Existentialism*, Blackwell, Oxford, 1990.

Cooper, R. N., K. Kaiser and M. Kosaka, *Towards a Renovated International System*, Triangle Papers 14, The Trilateral Commission, New York, 1977.

Council on Hemispheric Affairs, *National Endowment for Democracy (NED): A Foreign Policy Branch Gone Awry*, Albuquerque and Inter-Hemispheric Education Resource Center, Washington, DC, 1990.

Cox, M., 'American Power Before and After 11 September: Dizzy with Success?', *International Affairs*, vol. 78, no. 2, 2002, pp. 237–55.

———, 'The Empire's Back In Town: Or America's Imperial Temptation—Again', *Millennium: Journal of International Studies*, vol. 32, no. 1, 2003, pp. 1–27.

———, 'Is the United States in Decline—Again? An Essay', *International Affairs*, vol. 83, no. 4, 2007, pp. 643–53.

———, 'State, Social Forces and World Orders: Beyond International Relations Theory', *Millennium: Journal of International Studies*, vol. 10, no. 2, 1981, pp. 126–55.

———, 'Multilateralism and World Order', in his *Approaches to World Order*, Cambridge University Press, Cambridge, 1996.

Crawford, B. and R. Lipschultz, *The Myth of 'Ethnic Conflict': Politics, Economics, and Cultural Violence*, International and Area Studies, University of California, Berkeley, 1998.

Cristi, R., *Carl Schmitt and Authoritarian Liberalism: Strong State, Free Economy*, University of Wales Press, Cardiff, 1998.

Crozier, M., S. Huntington and J. Watanuki, *The Crisis of Democracy: Report on the Governability of Democracies to the Trilateral Commission*, New York University Press, New York, 1975.

Cruikshank, B., 'Cultural Politics: Political Theory and the Foundations of Democratic Order', in J. Dean, ed., *Cultural Studies and Political Theory*, Cornell University Press, Ithaca, NY, 2000.

Cummings, B., 'The Wicked Witch of the West is Dead. Long Live the Wicked Witch of the East', in M. J. Hogan, ed., *The End of the Cold War*, Cambridge University Press, Cambridge, 1992.

Daalder, I. H. and James M. Lindsay, *America Unbound: The Bush Revolution in Foreign Policy*, Brookings Institution Press, Washington, 2003.

Daalder, I. and R. Kagan, 'The Next Intervention', *Washington Post*, 6 August 2007, p. A17.

Dahl, R., *Polyarchy: Participation and Opposition*, Yale University Press, New Haven, 1971.

———, *A Preface to Economic Democracy*, Polity Press, Cambridge, 1985.

———, *Democracy and its Critics*, Yale University Press, New Haven, 1991.

———, *Radical Conservatism and the Future of Politics*, Sage, London, 1999.

Dalby, S., 'Geopolitics, Grand Strategy and the Bush Doctrine', in C. P. David and D. Grondin, eds., *Hegemony or Empire? The Redefinition of US Power Under George W. Bush*, Ashgate, Farnham, 2006.

Delanty, R. and J. Yoo, 'Against Foreign Law', AEI Working Paper no. 158, 2009, http://www.aei.org/docLib/20090820-Chapter8.pdf [12 October 2009].

DeMuth, C. and W. Kristol, eds., *The Neoconservative Imagination: Essays in Honour of Irving Kristol*, Washington, DC: AEI Press, 1995.

Derrida, J., 'Force of Law: "The Mystical Foundations" of Authority', *Cardozo Law Review*, vol. 11, 1990, pp. 919–1046.

Deutsch, K. L. and J. A. Murley, eds., *Leo Strauss, the Straussians, and the American Regime*, Rowman & Littlefield, Lanham, MD, 1999.

Devetak, R., 'Incomplete States: Theories and Practices of Statecraft', in J. Macmillan and A. Linklater, eds., *Boundaries in Question: New Directions in International Relations*, Macmillan Press, London, 1995.

———, *Recasting Conservatism: Oakeshott, Strauss, and the Response to Postmodernism*, Yale University Press, New Haven and London, 1994.

———, J. Linz and S. M. Lipset, eds., *Democracy in Developing Countries*, Lynne Rienner and National Endowment for Democracy, Boulder, CO, 1988.

———, *Developing Democracy: Toward Consolidation*, Johns Hopkins University Press, Baltimore, 1997.

———, *Roads to Dominion: Right-Wing Movements and Political Power in the United States*, Guilford Press, New York, 1995.

———, *The Rise and Fall of the American Left*, W. W. Norton, New York. 1992.

Diken, B., *Nihilism*, Routledge, London, 2009.

Dittberber, J. L., *The End of Ideology and American Social Thought: 1930–1960*, UMI Research Press, Kansas City, 1977.

Dodge, T., 'Coming Face to Face with Bloody Reality: Liberal Common Sense and the Ideological Failure of the Bush Doctrine in Iraq', *International Politics*, vol. 46, no. 2–3, 2009, pp. 253–75.

Dodge, W. S., 'After Sosa: The Future of Customary International Law in the United States', AEI Working Paper no. 153, 2009, http://www.aei.org/docLib/20090820-Chapter3.pdf [12 October 2009].

Donnelly, T. and V. Serchuk, 'Unrealistic Realism', AEI Online, 9 July 2004, www.aei.org/publications/pubID.20875/pub_detail.asp [6 October 2005].

Dorrien, G., *The Neoconservative Mind: Politics, Culture, and the War of Ideology*, Philadelphia, Temple University Press, 1993.

———, *Imperial Designs*, Routledge, London, 2004.

———, 'Benevolent Hegemony: William Kristol and the Politics of American Empire', *Logos*, vol. 3, no. 2, 2004, http://www.logosjournal.com/issue_3.2/dorrien.htm [28 October 2006].

Douglas, W., *Developing Democracy*, Heldref, Washington, DC, 1972.

Douzinas, C., *Human Rights and Empire: The Political Philosophy of Cosmopolitanism*, Routledge-Cavendish, London, 2007.

Draper, T., 'The Specter of Weimar', *Commentary*, December 1971, pp. 43–50.

Drury, S., *The Political Ideas of Leo Strauss*, Macmillan, London, 1988.

———, *Leo Strauss and the American Right*, Macmillan, London, 1997.
D'Souza, D., 'The Legacy of Leo Strauss: Is America the Good Society that the Ancient Philosophers Sought?', *Policy Review*, vol. 40, Spring 1987, pp. 36–43.
———, *Letters to a Young Conservative*, Basic Books, New York, 2002.
Dumenil, G. and D. Levy, *Capital Resurgent: Roots of the Neo-liberal Revolution*, Harvard University Press, Cambridge, MA, 2004.
Durkheim, E., *The Division of Labor in Society*, trans. G. Simpson, Free Press, New York, 1933.
Dworkin, R., 'The Threat to Patriotism', *New York Review of Books*, vol. 49, no. 3, pp. 44–9.
Dyzenhaus, D., 'Leviathan in the 1930s: The Reception of Hobbes in the Third Reich', in J. McCormick, ed., *Confronting Mass Democracy and Industrial Technology: Political and Social Theory From Nietzsche to Habermas*, Duke University Press, Durham and London, 2002, pp. 163–91.
Economist, 'A Necessary Evil?', *The Economist*, 12 July 2003, p. 26.
Edwards, L., *The Conservative Revolution*, Free Press, New York, 1999.
Ehrman, J., *The Rise of Neoconservatism: Intellectuals and Foreign Affairs 1945–1994*, Yale University Press, New Haven, 1995.
Ellis, R. J., *The Dark Side of the Left: Illiberal Egalitarianism in America*, University Press of Kansas, Lawrence, KS, 2000.
Escobar, A., *Encountering Development: The Making and Unmaking of the Third World*, Princeton University Press, Princeton, 1995.
Falk, R., *Law in an Emerging Global Village: A Post-Westphalian Perspective*, Transnational Publishers, Ardsley, NY, 1998.
Farer, T., *Confronting Global Terrorism and American Neo-Conservatism*, Oxford University Press, Oxford, 2007.
Ferguson, T. and J. Rogers, eds., *The Hidden Election*, Pantheon Books, New York, 1981.
Fiorina, M., 'The Decline of Collective Responsibility in American Politics', *Daedalus*, vol. 10, Summer 1980, pp. 25–45.
Fonte, J., 'Liberal Democracy vs. Transnational Progressivism: The Ideological War Within the West', *Orbis*, Summer 2002, pp. 449–64.
———, 'Dual Allegiance: A Challenge to Immigration Reform and Patriotic Assimilation', Centre for Immigration Studies, Washington, 2005, http://www.cis.org/articles/2005/back1205.html [3 May 2007].
———, 'The Enablers of Transnational Progressivism: Is the Nation-State Threatened?', The Hudson Institute, 4 October 2006, http://www.hudson.org/index.cfm?fuseaction=publication_details&id=4232 [3 December 2008].
———, 'Global Governance vs the Liberal Democratic Nation-State: What is the Best Regime?', in *Encounter at 10: The Bradley Symposium*, Hudson Institute, 4 June 2008, http://www.globalgovernancewatch.org/resources/global-governance-vs-the-liberal-democratic nationstate-what-is-the-best-regime-2 [3 November 2008].

———, 'The World is My Constituency', *National Review*, 2 November 2008, http://www.hudson.org/index.cfm?fuseaction=publication_details&id=5852 [6 November 2008].

———, *Sovereignty or Submission: Will Americans Rule Themselves or Be Ruled By Others?* Encounter Books, New York, 2009.

Ford Foundation, *Close to Home: Case Studies of Human Rights Work in the United States*, Ford Foundation, New York, 2004.

Forde, S., *The Ambition to Rule: Alcibiades and the Politics of Imperialism in Thucydides*, Cornell University Press, Ithaca, 1989.

Forde, S., 'International Realism: Thucydides, Machiavelli, and Neorealism', *International Studies Quarterly*, vol. 39, no. 2, 1995, pp. 141–60.

Foreign Policy Initiative, 'Mission Statement', Washington, March 2009, http://www.foreignpolicyi.org/about.html [7 April 2009].

Fossedal, G., *The Democratic Imperative: Exporting the American Revolution*, Basic Books, New York, 1989.

Foucault, M., *Discipline and Punish*, Penguin, London, 1991.

———, *La Naissance de la biopolitique: Cours au collège de France, 1978–1979*, Seuil, Paris, 2004.

Frachon, A. and D. Vernet, *L'Amérique Messianique: Les guerres des neo-conservateurs*, Seuil, Paris, 2004.

Fraser, S. and G. Gerstle, *The Rise and Fall of the New Deal Order, 1930–1980*, Princeton University Press, Princeton, 1990.

Freeden, M., *Ideologies and Political Theory: A Conceptual Approach*, Oxford University Press, Oxford, 1996.

Frei, C., *Hans Morgenthau: An Intellectual Biography*, Louisiana State University Press, Baton Rouge, 2001.

Friedman, G., *The Political Philosophy of the Frankfurt School*, Cornell University Press, Ithaca and London, 1981.

Friedman, M., *The Neoconservative Revolution: Jewish Intellectuals and the Shaping of Public Policy*, Cambridge University Press, Cambridge, 2005.

Friedrich, C., 'The Political Thought of Neo-Liberalism', *American Political Science Review*, vol. 49, no. 2, 1955, pp. 509–25.

Fromm, E., *Escape from Freedom*, Holt and Company, New York, 1969 [1941].

Frum, D. and R. Perle, *An End to Evil: How to Win the War on Terror*, Random House, New York, 2003.

Fukuyama, F., 'The End of History?', *The National Interest*, no. 16, Summer 1989, pp. 3–18.

———, *The End of History and the Last Man*, Free Press, New York, 1992.

———, *State-Building: Governance and World Order in the Twenty-First Century*, Profile Books, London, 2004.

———, Does the West Still Exist?', in T. Lindberg, ed., *Beyond Paradise and Power: Europe, America and the Future of a Troubled Partnership*, Routledge, New York and London, 2005.

———, 'A Year of Living Dangerously: Remember Theo Van Gogh and Shudder for the Future', *Washington Post*, 2 November 2005, http://www.opinionjournal.com/editorial/feature.html?id=110007491 [3 November 2005].
———, *After the Neocons: America at the Crossroads*, London, Profile Books, 2006.
Galbraith, J. K., *The Affluent Society*, Houghton Mifflin, Boston, 1958.
Gallie, W. B., 'Essentially Contestable Concepts', *Proceedings of the Aristotelian Society*, vol. 56, 1955–6, pp. 167–98.
Gans, H. J., *The War Against the Poor: The Underclass and Antipoverty Policy*, Basic Books, New York, 1995.
Garland, D., *The Culture of Control: Crime and Social Order in Contemporary Society*, University of Chicago Press, Chicago, 2001.
Garst, 'Thucydides and Neorealism', *International Studies Quarterly*, vol. 33, no. 1, 1989, pp. 3–27.
Gaus, G. F., *Political Concepts and Political Theories*, Westview Press, Oxford, 2000.
George, J., 'Leo Strauss, Neoconservatism and US Foreign Policy: Esoteric Nihilism and the Bush Doctrine', *International Politics*, vol. 42, no. 2, 2005, pp. 174–202.
George, S., 'Winning the War of Ideas', *Dissent*, Summer 1997, http://www.tni.org/archives/george/dissent.htm [4 October 2006].
George, S., 'A Short History of Neoliberalism: Twenty Years of Elite Economics and Emerging Opportunities for Structural Change', in W. Bello, N. Bullard and K. Malhotra, eds., *Global Finance: New Thinking on Regulating Capital Markets*, Zed Books, London, 2000, pp. 27–35.
Gerson, M., *The Neoconservative Vision: From Cold War to Culture Wars*, Madison Books, Lanham, MD, 1997.
Gerstle, G., 'The Protean Character of American Liberalism', *The American Historical Review*, vol. 99, no. 4, 1994, pp. 1043–73.
Gilder, G., *Wealth and Poverty*, Basic Books, New York, 1981.
Gilens, M., *Why Americans Hate Welfare: Race, Media, and the Politics of Antipoverty*, University of Chicago Press, Chicago, 1999.
Gill, S., *American Hegemony and the Trilateral Commission*, Cambridge University Press, New York, 1991.
Gills, B. and J. Rocamora, 'Low Intensity Democracy', *Third World Quarterly*, vol. 13, no. 3, 1992, pp. 501–23.
Gilman, N., *Mandarins of the Future: Modernization Theory in Cold War America*, Johns Hopkins University Press, Baltimore, 2003.
Gilpin, R., 'The Richness of the Tradition of Political Realism', *International Organization*, vol. 38, no. 2, 1984, pp. 287–304.
Glazer, N., 'The Method of Senator McCarthy', *Commentary*, March 1953, pp. 244–56.
———, 'The New Left and its Limits', *Commentary*, July 1968, pp. 31–40.
———, *Remembering the Answers: Essays on the American Student Revolt*, Basic Books, New York, 1970.

———, 'The Limits of Social Policy', *Commentary*, September 1971, pp. 51–9.
———, 'American Values and American Foreign Policy', *Commentary*, July 1976, pp. 32–8.
———, 'Neoconservatism: Pro and Con', *Partisan Review*, vol. 47, no. 4, 1980, pp. 496–501.
———, 'Neoconservative From the Start', *The Public Interest*, vol. 159, Spring 2005, pp. 115–9.
Glazer, N. and I. Kristol, eds., *The American Commonwealth*, Basic Books, New York, 1976.
Glazer, N. and D. P. Moynihan, *Beyond the Melting Pot: The Negroes, Puerto Ricans, Jews, and Irish of New York*, MIT Press, Cambridge, MA, 1963.
Gleason, A., *Totalitarianism: The Inner History of the Cold War*, Oxford University Press, New York, 1995.
Glidden, J. A., 'Neo-conservatives and U.S. foreign policy: an intellectual history, 1930–95', unpublished D.Phil. manuscript, Department of International Relations, University of Oxford, Oxford, 1995.
Goldsmith, J., 'The Self-Defeating International Criminal Court', *University of Chicago Law Review*, vol. 70, no. 1, 2003, pp. 89–104.
———, *The Terror Presidency: Law and Judgement Inside the Bush Administration*, New York, W. W. Norton, 2007.
Goldstein, T. C. and C. S. Harris, 'Foreign Law and Constitutional Interpretation: The Debate Behind the Diatribes', AEI Working Paper no. 157, 2009, http://www.aei.org/docLib/20090820-Chapter7.pdf [14 October 2009].
Goldwin, R. A. and R. A. Licht, eds., *Foreign Policy and the Constitution*, AEI Press, Washington, DC, 1990.
Gosse, V., *Rethinking the New Left: An Interpretative History*, Palgrave Macmillan, London, 2006.
Gottfried, P., *The Conservative Movement*, Macmillan, New York, 1993.
Gottfried, P., *Conservatism in America: Making Sense of the American Right*, Palgrave Macmillan, New York, 2007.
Gouldner, A. W., *The Future of Intellectuals and the Rise of the New Class*, Macmillan Press, London, 1979.
Graf Kielmansegg, P., H. Mewes and E. Glaser-Schmidt, eds., *Hannah Arendt and Leo Strauss: German Émigrés and American Political Thought after World War II*, Cambridge University Press, Cambridge, 1995.
Grandin, G., 'The Imperial Presidency: The Legacy of Reagan's Central America Policy', in M. J. Thompson, ed., *Confronting the New Conservatism: The Rise of the Right in America*, New York, NYU Press, 2007.
Gray, J., *Liberalism*, Open University Press, Buckingham, 1995.
———, *Hayek on Liberty*, Routledge, New York, 1998.
———, *Black Mass: Apocalyptic Religion and the Death of Utopia*, Penguin Allen Lane, London, 2007.
Griffin, R., *The Nature of Fascism*, Routledge, London, 1991.
———, *Modernism and Fascism*, Palgrave, London, 2007.

Groves, S., 'Furthering the UN's Leftist Agenda: The UN CERD Committee Report', Webmemo no. 1899, Heritage Foundation, 22 April 2008, *http://www.heritage.org/Research/InternationalOrganizations/wm1899.cfm* [3 December 2008].

Gunnell, J., 'Strauss before Straussianism: Reason, Revelation and Nature', *The Review of Politics*, vol. 53, no. 1, 1991, pp. 53–74.

Habermas, J., *The New Conservatism*, Polity Press, Cambridge, 1985.

———, *The Philosophical Discourse of Modernity*, Polity Press, Cambridge, 1987.

———, 'Multiculturalism and the Liberal State', *Stanford Law Review*, vol. 47, no. 5, 1995, pp. 849–53.

———, *The Inclusion of the Other: Studies in Political Theory*, Polity Press, Cambridge, 1999.

———, *The Postnational Constellation*, Polity Press, Cambridge, 2000.

———, *The Divided West*, Polity Press, Cambridge, 2006.

Halliday, F., *The Making of the Second Cold War*, Verso, London, 1986.

Halper, S. and J. Clarke, *America Alone: The Neo-Conservatives and the Global Order*, Cambridge University Press, Cambridge, 2004.

Hardt, M. and A. Negri, *Empire*, Harvard University Press, Cambridge, MA, 2000.

Harries, O., ed., *America's Purpose: New Visions of US Foreign Policy*, Institute of Contemporary Studies, San Francisco, 1991.

Harrington, M., 'The Welfare State and Its Neoconservative Critics', *Dissent*, Fall 1973, pp. 435–54.

Hartz, L., *The Liberal Tradition in America*, Harcourt Bruce Jovanovich, New York, 1955.

Harvey, D., *A Brief History of Neoliberalism*, Oxford University Press, Oxford, 2005.

Hassner, P., 'The United States: The Empire of Force or the Force of Empire', EU-ISS Chaillot Papers, no. 54, September 2002.

Hatab, L.J., *Nietzsche's On the Genealogy of Morality*, Cambridge University Press, Cambridge, 2008.

Hayek, F. von 'The Intellectuals and Socialism', in G. B. de Huszar, ed., *The Intellectuals*, The Free Press, Glencoe, Ill., 1960 [1949].

Heidegger, M., *Off the Beaten Tracks*, edited and translated by Julian Young and Kenneth Hayes, Cambridge University Press, Cambridge, 2002.

———, *Nietzsche*, 2 volumes, edited by David Farrell Krell, Harper Collins, New York, 1991.

Heilbrunn, J., *They Knew They Were Right: The Rise of the Neocons*, Doubleday, New York, 2008.

Held, D., *Models of Democracy*, Polity Press, Cambridge, 2006.

Herf, J., *Reactionary Modernism: Technology, Culture and Politics in the Third Reich*, Cambridge University Press, Cambridge, 2008.

Himmelfarb, G., *The De-Moralization of Society: From Victorian Virtues to Modern Values*, Vintage, New York, 1996.

———, *The Roads to Modernity: The British, French and American Enlightenment*, Penguin, London, 2004.
Himmelstein, J. L., *To the Right: The Transformation of American Conservatism*, University of California Press, Berkeley, 1990.
Hoffman, S., 'American Exceptionalism: The New Version', in M. Ignatieff, *American Exceptionalism and Human Rights*, Princeton University Press, Princeton and Oxford, 2005.
Hogan, M. J., ed., *The Ambiguous Legacy: U.S. Foreign Relations in the 'American Century'*, Cambridge University Press, Cambridge, 1999.
Hoogvelt, A., *Globalization and the Postcolonial World: The New Political Economy of Development*, Palgrave, London, 2001.
Horkeimer, M., *Critical Theory: Selected Essays*, Continuum, London, 1997.
Horkeimer, M. and T. Adorno, *Dialectics of Enlightenment*, Verso, London, 1997 [1947].
Horton, S., 'The Letter', 16 July 2006, http://balkin.blogspot.com/2006/07/letter_16.html [5 August 2008].
Huntington, S., 'The Politics of Disharmony', *Comparative Politics*, vol. 6, no. 2, 1974, pp. 181–96.
———, 'The Democratic Distemper', in N. Glazer and I. Kristol, eds., *The American Commonwealth*, Basic Books, New York, 1976.
———, *The Clash of Civilizations and the Remaking of World Order*, Simon & Schuster, New York, 1998.
———, *Who Are We? The Challenge to American National Identity*, Simon & Schuster, New York, 2004.
———, *Political Orders in Changing Societies*, Yale University Press, New Haven, 2006 [1968].
Hurrell, A., 'Pax Americana or the Empire of Insecurity?', *International Relations of the Asia-Pacific*, vol. 5, 2005, pp. 153–76.
Huysmans, J., *The Politics of Insecurity: Fear, Migration and Asylum in the EU*, Routledge, London, 1995.
———, 'International Politics of Insecurity: Normativity, Inwardness, and the Exception', *Security Dialogue*, vol. 37, 2006, pp. 11–29.
———, 'International Politics of Exception: Competing Visions of International Political Order Between Law and Politics', *Alternatives*, vol. 31, no. 2, 2006, pp. 135–65.
———, 'The jargon of exception—on Schmitt, Agamben and the absence of political society', *International Political Sociology*, vol. 2, no. 2, 2008, pp. 165–78.
Ignatieff, M., ed., *American Exceptionalism and Human Rights*, Princeton University Press, Princeton and Oxford, 2005.
Ikenberry, J., 'The End of the Neo-Conservative Moment', *Survival*, vol. 46, no. 1, 2004, pp. 7–22.
———, *Liberal Order and Imperial Ambition*, Polity Press, Cambridge, 2006.

International Commission on Intervention and State Sovereignty, *The Responsibility to Protect*, International Development Research Centre, Ottawa, 2001, www.idrc.ca [2 May 2003].

Isserman, M. and M. Kazin, *America Divided: The Civil War of the 1960*, 2nd edn, Oxford University Press, New York and Oxford, 2004.

Jabri, V., *War and the Transformation of Global Politics*, Palgrave, London, 2007.

Jackson, P. I. and L. Carroll, 'Race and the War on Crime: The Sociopolitical Determinants of Municipal Police Expenditures', *American Sociological Review*, vol. 46, 1981, pp. 290–305.

Jay, M., 'The "Aesthetic Ideology" as Ideology: Or What Does it Mean to Aestheticize Politics', *Cultural Critique*, no. 21, 1992, pp. 41–61.

Jencks, C., *Rethinking Social Policy: Race, Poverty and the Underclass*, Harvard University Press, Cambridge, MA, 1992.

Jervis, R., 'Understanding the Bush Doctrine', *Political Science Quarterly*, vol. 118, no. 2, 2003, pp. 365–88.

Johnson, C., *Blowback*, Time Warner, New York, 2002.

Johnson, L. M., *Thucydides, Hobbes, and the Interpretation of Realism*, Northern Illinois University Press, DeKalb, Ill., 1993.

Joscelyn, T., 'Clear and Present Dangers', *Weekly Standard*, vol. 14, no. 11, 2008, http://www.weeklystandard.com/Content/Public/Articles/000/000/015/845xcgce.asp [3 January 2010].

Jumonville, N., ed., *The New York Intellectuals Reader*, Routledge, New York and London, 2007.

Kagan, D., *The Outbreak of the Peloponnesian War*, Cornell University Press, Ithaca, 1969.

———, *The Archidamian* War, Cornell University Press, Ithaca, 1974.

———, *The Peace of Nicias and the Sicilian Expedition*, Cornell University Press, Ithaca, 1981.

———, *The Fall of the Athenian Empire*, Cornell University Press, Ithaca, 1987.

Kagan, D. and F. Kagan, *While America Sleeps: Self-Delusion, Military Weakness, and the Threat to Peace Today*, St. Martin's Press, New York, 2000.

Kagan, F. W., 'The Fog: Translating Obama's vague foreign policy pronouncements', *The Weekly Standard*, vol. 14, no. 6, 20 October 2008, http://www.weeklystandard.com/Content/Public/Articles/000/000/015/691vjfsv.asp?pg=1 [8 January 2009].

Kagan, R., 'Inside the Limo', *The New Republic*, April 10, 2000, pp. 32–41.

———, 'Power and Weakness', *Policy Review*, June-July 2002, http://www.hoover.org/publications/policyreview/3460246.html [6 October 2008].

———, 'One Year After: A Grand Strategy for the West?', *Survival*, vol. 44, no. 4, 2002–3, pp. 138–9.

———, 'Europeans Courting International Disaster', *Washington Post*, 8 June 2003, p. B07.

———, *Of Paradise and Power: America and Europe in the New World Order*, Atlantic Books, London, 2004.

———, 'A Tougher War for the US is One of Legitimacy', *New York Times*, 24 January 2004, http://query.nytimes.com/gst/fullpage.html?res=9F00E2DA1E39F937A15752C0A9629C8B63 [26 January 2008].

———, 'America's Crisis of Legitimacy', *Foreign Affairs*, March/April 2004, http://www.foreignaffairs.com/articles/59710/robert-kagan/americas-crisis-of-legitimacy [8 December 2004].

———, 'America Supports Democracy, How Novel', *Financial Times*, 6 December 2006, p. 19.

———, *End of Dreams, Return of History*, Atlantic Books, London, 2008.

———, 'The Case for a League of Democracies', *Financial Times*, 13 May 2008, http://us.ft.com/ftgateway/superpage.ft?news_id=fto051320081421543873 [13 May 2008].

———, 'Europe slides into irrelevance', *Washington Post*, 15 June 2008, p. B07.

———, 'The September 12 Paradigm: America, the World, and George W. Bush', *Foreign Affairs*, September/October 2008, http://www.foreignaffairs.org/20080901faessay87502/robert-kagan/the-september-12-paradigm.html?mode=pr [4 November 2008].

———, 'The Sovereignty Dodge: What Pakistan Won't Do, the World Should', *Washington Post*, 2 December 2008, p. A21.

Kagan, R. and W. Kristol, 'Toward a Neo-Reaganite Foreign Policy', *Foreign Affairs*, no. 75, July/August, 1996, pp. 18–32.

———, eds., *Present Dangers: Crisis and Opportunities in American Foreign and Defense Policy*, Encounter Books, New York, 2000.

Kahn, P. W., 'American Hegemony and International Law. Speaking Law to Power: Popular Sovereignty, Human Rights, and the New International Order', *Chicago Journal of International Law*, vol. 1, no. 2, 2000, pp. 1–118.

Kant, I., *Political Writings*, ed. H.S. Reiss, Cambridge University Press, Cambridge, 1991.

Kaplan, L. and W. Kristol, *The War Over Iraq: Saddam's Tyranny and America's Mission*, Encounter Books, New York, 2003.

Kaplan, R. D., *Balkan Ghosts: A Journey Through History*, St. Martin's Press, New York, 1993.

———, *The Ends of the Earth: A Journey at the Dawn of the Twenty-First Century*, Random House, New York, 1996.

———, *The Coming Anarchy: Shattering the Dreams of the Post Cold War*, Random House, New York, 2000.

———, *Warrior Politics: Why Leadership Demands a Pagan Ethos*, Vintage, New York, 2003.

———, 'Supremacy by Stealth', *Atlantic Monthly*, vol. 292, July-August 2003, pp. 66–83.

Katz, M. B., *The Undeserving Poor: From the War on Poverty to the War on Welfare*, Pantheon Books, New York, 1989.

———, *The Price of Citizenship: Redefining the American Welfare State*, Henry Holt, New York, 1998.

Kelly, J. P., 'The Matrix of Human Rights Governance Networks', *Engage*, vol. 9, no. 1, 2008, http://www.fed-soc.org/publications/pubID.691/pub_detail.asp [2 November 2008].

Kemble P., and J. Muravchik, 'The New Politics and the Democrats', *Commentary*, December 1972, pp. 78–85.

Kenney, D. M., 'What "W" Owes to "WW"', *Atlantic Monthly*, March 2005, pp. 6–9.

Keohane, R. and J. Nye, *Power and Interdependence: World Politics in Transition*, Little, Brown, Boston, 1977.

Keohane, R. O., 'The World Political Economy and the Crisis of Embedded Liberalism', in J. H. Goldthorpe, ed., *Order and Conflict in Contemporary Capitalism*, Clarendon Press, Oxford, 1984.

Kershaw, I., *The Nazi Dictatorship*, Edward Arnold, London, 2000.

Kirkpatrick, J., 'The Revolt of the Masses', *Commentary*, February 1973, pp. 58–62.

———, *Dismantling the Parties: Reflections on Party Reform and Party Decomposition*, AEI Press, Washington, DC, 1978.

———, 'The Hobbes Problem', in *American Enterprise Institute's Public Policy Papers*, AEI Press, Washington, DC, 1981.

———, 'U.S. Security in Latin America', *Commentary*, January 1981, pp. 29–41.

———, *Dictatorships and Double Standards: Rationalism and Reason in Politics*, Simon & Schuster and AEI Press, Washington, DC, 1982.

———, *The Reagan Phenomenon—and Other Speeches on Foreign Policy*, AEI Press, Washington, DC, 1982.

———, 'The Modernizing Imperative: Tradition and Change', *Foreign Affairs*, September-October 1993, http://www.foreignaffairs.org/19930901faresponse5204/jeane-j-kirkpatrick/the-modernizing-imperative-tradition-and-change.html [26 January 2009].

———, *Right versus Might: International Law and the Use of Force*, Council on Foreign Relations, Washington, DC, 1994.

———, 'Neoconservatism as a Response to the Counter-Culture', in I. Stelzer, *Neoconservatism*, Atlantic Books, London, 2004.

Kissenger, H., 'Between the Old Left and the New Right', *Foreign Affairs*, vol. 78, no. 3, 1999, pp. 99–116.

Klehr, H. and J. E. Haynes, *The American Communist Movement*, Twayne Publishers, New York, 1992.

Koh, H. H., 'On American Exceptionalism', *Stanford Law Review*, vol. 55, no. 5, 2003, pp. 1483–94.

Kolko, G., *Confronting the Third World: United States Foreign Policy 1945–1980*, Pantheon, New York, 1988.

Koselleck, R., *Critique and Crisis: Enlightenment and the Pathogenesis of Modern Society*, MIT Press, Cambridge, MA, 1988 [1959].

Koskenniemi, M., *The Gentle Civilizer of Nations: The Rise and Fall of International Law, 1870–1960*, Cambridge University Press, Cambridge, 2001.

———, '"The Lady Doth Protest Too Much": Kosovo, and the Turn to Ethics in International Law', *The Modern Law Review*, vol. 65, no. 2, 2002, pp. 159–75.

Kramer, H. and Roger Kimball (eds.), *The Betrayal of Liberalism: How the Disciples of Freedom and Equality Helped Foster the Illiberal Politics of Coercion and Control*, Ivan R. Dee, New York, 1985.

Krauthammer, C., 'The Unipolar Moment', *Foreign Affairs*, no. 70, 1991, pp. 36–58.

———, 'Defining Deviancy Up: The New Assault on Bourgeois Life', *The New Republic*, 22 November 1993, pp. 3–9.

———, 'Violence and Islam', *Jewish World Review*, 6 December 2002, http://www.jewishworldreview.com/cols/krauthammer120602.asp [5 January 2008].

———, *Democratic Realism: An American Foreign Policy for a Unipolar World*, American Enterprise Institute's Irving Kristol Lecture, Washington, 12 February 2004, http://www.aei.org/publications/pubID.19912,filter.all/pub_detail.asp [8 February 2006].

———, 'When Unilateralism is Right and Just', in E. J. Dionne Jr, J. B. Elshtain and K. Droggosz, eds., *Liberty and Power: A Dialogue on U.S. Foreign Policy in an Unjust World*, Brooking Institution Press, Washington, DC, 2004.

———, 'In Defense of Democratic Realism', in G. Rosen, ed., *The Right War? The Conservative Debate on Iraq*, Cambridge University Press, New York, 2005.

———, 'Three Cheers for the Bush Doctrine', *New York Times*, 7 March 2005, http://www.time.com/time/printout/0,8816,1035052,00.html [8 December 2006].

———, 'The Neoconservative Convergence', *Wall Street Journal*, 21 July 2005, http://www.opinionjournal.com/extra/?id=110006921 [28 June 2006].

Krisch, N., 'Weak as Constraint, Strong as a Tool: The Place of International Law in U.S. Foreign Policy', in D. Malone and Y. F. Khong, eds., *Unilateralism and U.S. Foreign Policy: International Perspectives*, Lynne Rienner Publishers, Boulder, CO, 2003.

Kristol, I., '"Civil Liberties", 1952—A Study in Confusion', *Commentary*, March 1952, pp. 228–36.

———, 'On Negative Liberalism', *Encounter*, January 1954, pp. 3–4.

———, *On the Democratic Idea in America*, Harper & Row, New York, 1972.

———, *Two Cheers for Capitalism*, Basic Books, New York, 1978.

———, 'Ideology and Supply-Side Economics', *Commentary*, April 1981, pp. 48–56.
———, 'The Timmerman Affair', *Wall Street Journal*, 29 May 1981, pp. 24–5.
———, *Reflections of a Neoconservative: Looking Back, Looking Ahead*, Basic Books Inc., New York, 1983.
———, 'Skepticism, Meliorism and The Public Interest', *The Public Interest*, Fall 1985, pp. 31–42.
———, 'Foreign Policy in an Age of Ideology', *The National Interest*, no. 1, Fall 1985, pp. 14–5.
———, 'Defining Our National Interest', *The National Interest*, Fall 1990, pp. 16–25.
———, 'In Search of Our National Interest', *Wall Street Journal*, 7 June 1990, p. 9.
———, 'The Coming Conservative Century', *Wall Street Journal*, 1 February, 1993, p. A10.
———, 'American Conservatism 1945–1995', *The Public Interest*, 22 September 1995, p. 80–92.
———, *Neoconservatism: Selected Essays 1951–1995*, Free Press, New York, 1995.
———, 'A Post-Wilsonian Foreign Policy', *Wall Street Journal*, 2 August 1996.
———, 'The Neoconservative Persuasion', *Weekly Standard*, vol. 8, no. 47, August 2003, http://www.weeklystandard.com/Content/Public/Articles/000/000/003/000tzmlw.asp [3 June 2008].
———, 'A Conservative Welfare State', in I. Stelzer, ed., *Neo-Conservatism*, Atlantic Books, London, 2004.
Ku, J. G., 'The President's Unexamined Power to Interpret Customary International Law', AEI Working Paper no. 155, 2009, http://www.aei.org/docLib/20090820-Chapter5.pdf [14 October 2009].
Kuryla, P., 'Three Variations on American Liberalism', in M. Halliwell and C. Morley, eds., *American Thought and Culture in the 21st Century*, Edinburgh University Press, Edinburgh, 2008.
Laclau, E., *Emancipation(s)*, Verso, London, 1995.
Laclau, E. and Chantal Mouffe, *Hegemony and Socialist Strategy: Towards a Radical Democratic Politics*, Verso, London, 2001 [1986].
Ladd, C. E., Jr. and S. M. Lipset, *The Divided Academy*, McGraw-Hill, New York, 1975.
Ladd, C. E., Jr., *Where Have All the Voters Gone? The Fracturing of America's Party System*, W. W. Norton, New York, 1978.
Lampert, L., *Leo Strauss and Nietzsche*, Chicago University Press, Chicago, 1998.
Laqueur, W., 'Kissenger and the Politics of Détente', *Commentary*, December 1973, pp. 46–53.

Lasch, C., *The Agony of the American Left*, Alfred A. Knopf, New York, 1969.
Latham, M. E., *Modernization as Ideology: American Social Science and Nation-Building in the Kennedy Era*, University of North Carolina Press, Chapel Hill, 2000.
Latham, R., *The Liberal Moment: Modernity, Security, and the Making of Postwar International Order*, Columbia University Press, New York, 1997.
Lebow, R. N., *The Tragic Vision of Politics: Ethics, Interests and Orders*, Cambridge University Press, Cambridge, 2003.
Ledeen, M., 'How to Support the Democratic Revolution', *Commentary*, March 1985, pp. 43–51.
Ledeen, M., *The War Against the Terror Masters: Why It Happened, Where We Are Now, How We'll Win*, St. Martin's Press, New York, 2002.
Lenzner, S. and W. Kristol, 'What Was Leo Strauss Up To?', *The Public Interest*, no. 153, Fall 2003, pp. 19–39
Levy, D., M. Pensky and J. Torpey, eds., *Old Europe, New Europe, Core Europe: Transatlantic Relations After the Iraq War*, Verso, London, 2005.
Lieven, A., *America Right Or Wrong: An Anatomy of American Nationalism*, Harper Perennial, London, 2005.
Lilla, M., 'The Closing of the Straussian Mind', *New York Review of Books*, vol. 51, no. 17, 4 November 2004, pp. 55–9.
Lindberg, T., 'Neoconservatism's Liberal Legacy', *Policy Review*, no. 27, 2004, pp. 1–16.
———, ed., *Beyond Paradise and Power: Europe, America and the Future of a Troubled Partnership*, Routledge, New York and London, 2005.
———, 'Some Social Requisites of Democracy: economic development and political legitimacy', *American Political Science Review*, vol. 53, no. 1, 1959, pp. 69–105.
———, *The First New Nation: The United States in Historical and Comparative Perspective*, Doubleday, New York, 1963.
———, 'The Wavering Polls', *The Public Interest*, vol. 43, 1976, pp. 70–90.
———, *Political Man*, Johns Hopkins University Press, Baltimore, 1981 [1960].
———, 'Party Reform Since 1968: A Case Study in Intellectual Failure', in P. Bonomi, J. MacGregor Burns and Austin Ranney, eds., *The American Constitutional System Under Strong and Weak Parties*, Praeger, New York, 1981.
———, 'Neoconservatism: Myth and Reality', *Society*, July/August, 1988, pp. 32–9.
———, *American Exceptionalism: A Double-Edged Sword*, W. W. Norton, New York, 1996.
———, 'Out of the Alcoves', *The Wilson Quarterly*, vol. 23, no. 1, 1999, pp. 37–48. Lipset, S. M. and R. B. Dobson, 'The New Class and the Professiorate', in B. Bruce-Briggs, ed., *The New Class?*, Transaction Books, New Brunswick, NJ, 1978.

Lipset, S. M. and M. Lakin, *The Democratic Century*, University of Oklahoma Press, Oklahoma City, 2006.

Lipset, S. M., and E. Raab, *The Politics of Unreason: Right Wing Extremism in America 1790–1970*, Harper & Row, New York, 1970.

Locke, J., *Two Treatises on Government*, ed. Peter Laslett, Cambridge University Press, Cambridge, 1988 [1690].

Lord, C., *The Modern Prince: What Leaders Need to Know Now*, Yale University Press, New Haven, 2004.

Lovatt, M. F. W., *Confronting the Will-to-Power: A Reconsideration of the Theology of Reinhold Niebuhr*, Wipf and Stock Publisher, New York, 2001.

Lundestad, G., ed., *Just Another Major Crisis? The United States and Europe Since 2000*, Oxford University Press, Oxford, 2008.

Lynch, T. J., 'Kristol Balls: Neoconservative Vision of Islam and the Middle East', *International Politics*, vol. 45, no. 2, 2008, pp. 182–211.

Lynch, T. J. and R. Singh, *After Bush: The Case for Continuity*, Cambridge University Press, Cambridge, 2008.

MacDonald, H., V. D. Hanson and S. Malanga, *The Immigration Solution: A Better Plan Than Today's*, Ivan R. Dee, Chicago, 2007.

Machiavelli, N., *The Prince*, Penguin Books, London, 2004 [1531–32].

Mani, R., 'The Root Causes of Terrorism and Conflict Prevention', in J. Boulden and T. G. Weiss, eds., *Terrorism and the UN: Before and After September 11*, Indiana University Press, Bloomington and Indianapolis, 2004.

Mann, J., *Rise of the Vulcans: The History of Bush's War Cabinet*, Penguin Books, London, 2004.

Mansfield, H. C., *Taming the Prince: The Ambivalence of Modern Executive Power*, Johns Hopkins University Press, Baltimore, 1989.

———, 'The Legacy of the Late Sixties', in S. Macedo, ed., *Reassessing the Sixties*, W. W. Norton, New York, 1997.

———, 'Timeless Mind', *Claremont Review of Books*, Winter 2007, http://www.claremont.org/publications/crb/id.1505/article_detail.asp [June 2008].

———, 'What Obama Isn't Saying', *Weekly Standard*, vol. 15, no. 2, 2010, 0http://www.weeklystandard.com/articles/what-obama-isnt-saying?page=3 [20 February 2010].

Marcuse, H., *Negations*, Penguin, Harmondsworth, 1968 [1937].

———, *One-Dimensional Man: Studies in the Ideology of Advanced Industrial Society*, Routledge, London, 2002 [1964].

Matusow, A. J., *The Unravelling of America: A History of Liberalism in the 1960s*, Harper & Row, New York, 1984.

Mazarr, M. J., 'George W. Bush, Idealist', *International Affairs*, vol. 79, no. 3, 2003, pp. 503–22.

McCarthy, A., 'International Law vs. the United States', *Commentary*, February 2006, http://www.commentarymagazine.com/viewarticle.cfm/international-law-v—united-states-10026?search=1 [6 November 2008].

———, 'Obama and Gitmo', *National Review Online*, 13 November 2008, http://article.nationalreview.com/print/?q=NTMxNWYzY2MxMGVkZmVkNTFkYTg0MzliMWRmNTU1M2I [3 December 2008].

McCarthy, A. and A.Velshi, 'We Need a National Security Court', AEI Working Paper no. 156, 2009, http://www.aei.org/docLib/20090820-Chapter6.pdf [12 October 2009].

McCormick, J., 'Transcending Weber's Categories of Modernity? The Early Lukács and Schmitt on the Rationalization Thesis', *The New German Critique*, vol. 75, 1988, pp. 133–77.

———, 'Fear, Technology, and the State: Carl Schmitt, Leo Strauss, and the Revival of Hobbes in Weimar and National Socialist Germany', *Political Theory*, vol. 22, no. 4, 1994, pp. 619–52.

———, *Carl Schmitt's Critique of Liberalism: Against Politics as Technology*, Cambridge University Press, Cambridge, 1997.

———, 'Political Theory and Political Theology: The Second Wave of Carl Schmitt in English', *Political Theory*, vol. 26, no. 6, 1998, pp. 830–54.

McCormick, T. J., *America's Half-Century: United States Foreign Policy in the Cold War and After*, 2nd edn, Johns Hopkins University Press, Baltimore, 1995.

Megay, E. N., 'Anti-Pluralist Liberalism: The German Neoliberals', *Political Science Quarterly*, vol. 85, no. 3, 1970, p. 422–42.

Meir, H., *Carl Schmitt and Leo Strauss: The Hidden Dialogue*, University of Chicago Press, London and Chicago, 1995.

Micklethwait, J. and A. Wooldridge, *The Right Nation: Conservative Power in America*, Penguin, New York, 2005.

Miles, M. W., *The Odyssey of the American Right*, Oxford University Press, New York, 1980.

Millikan, M. F. and W. W. Rostow, *A Proposal: Key to An Effective Foreign Policy*, Harper and Bros., New York, 1957.

Minowitz, Peter, *Straussophobia: Defending Leo Strauss Against Shadia Drury and Other Accusers*, Lexington Books, Lanham, MD, 2009.

Monten, J., 'The Roots of the Bush Doctrine: Power, Nationalism and Democracy Promotion in U.S. Strategy', *International Security*, vol. 29, no. 4, 2005, pp. 112–56.

Moravcsik, A., 'Conservative Idealism and International Institutions', *Chicago Journal of International Law*, vol. 1, no. 2, 2000, pp. 291–314.

Morgenthau, H. J., *Politics Among Nations*, 5th edn, ed. Kenneth Thompson, Alfred A. Knopf, New York, 1978 [1948].

Mouffe, C., *The Return of the Political*, Verso, London, 2000.

———, *The Democratic Paradox*, Verso, London, 2000.

———, *On the Political*, Routledge, London, 2005.

Moynihan, D. P., *The Negro Family: The Case for National Action*, Office of Policy Planning and Research, United States Department of Labor, Washington, DC, 1965.

———, *Maximum Feasible Misunderstanding*, Free Press, New York, 1970.
———, *The Politics of Guaranteed Income*, New York, Vintage, 1973.
———, 'Was Woodrow Wilson Right?', *Commentary*, May 1974, pp. 25–32.
———, 'The United States in Opposition', *Commentary*, March 1975, pp. 31–45.
———, *A Dangerous Place*, Little, Brown, New York, 1976.
———, 'Defining Deviancy Down', *The American Scholar*, Winter 1993, http://www2.sunysuffolk.edu/formans/DefiningDeviancy.htm [12 December 2006].
Mulhern, F., *Culture/Metaculture*, London, Routledge, 2000.
Muller, J. Z., *Conservatism: An Anthology of Social and Political Thought From Hume to the Present*, Princeton University Press, Princeton, 1997.
Müller, J. W., *A Dangerous Mind: Carl Schmitt in Post-War European Thought*, Yale University Press, New Haven, 2003.
Muravchik, J., *Exporting Democracy: Fulfilling America's Destiny*, AEI Press, Washington, 1991.
———, 'The Neoconservative Cabal', in I. Stelzer, *Neoconservatism*, Atlantic Books, London, 2004.
———, 'Operation Comeback', *Foreign Policy*, vol. 12, November 2006, http://www.foreignpolicy.com/users/login.php?story_id=3602&URL=http://www.foreignpolicy.com/story/cms.php?story_id=3602 [2 December 2007].
———, 'Neoconservatism's Future: Still the Only Game in Town, *Wall Street Journal*, 3 October 2007, p. A6.
Murray, D., *Neoconservatism: Why We Need It*, The Social Affairs Unit, London, 2005.
Nash, G., *The Conservative Intellectual Movement in America Since 1945*, Harper, New York, 1976.
Neier, A., 'Human Rights in the Reagan Era: Acceptance in Principle', *Annals of the American Academy of Political and Social Science*, vol. 506, November 1989, pp. 31–40.
Nietzsche, F., *Beyond Good and Evil*, trans. Walter Kaufmann, Random House, New York, 1966.
———, *The Will to Power*, trans. Walter Kaufmann and R. J. Hollingdale, Vintage, New York, 1967.
Norton, A., *Leo Strauss and the Politics of American Empire*, Yale University Press, New Haven, 2005.
Novak, M., *The American Vision*, AEI Press, Washington, DC, 1978.
———, *The Spirit of Democratic Capitalism*, Madison Books, Lanham, MD, 1991.
———, 'Pax Americana', *Forbes*, vol. 147, 29 April 1991, p. 121.
———, *The Universal Hunger for Liberty: Why the Clash of Civilization is Not Inevitable*, Basic Books, New York, 2004.
Ogbar, J. O. G., *Black Power: Radical Politics and African American Identity*, Johns Hopkins University Press, Baltimore, 2005.

O'Neill, W., *The New Left: A History*, Harlan Davidson, Wheeling, Ill., 2001.

Orwin, C., *The Humanity of Thucydides*, Princeton University Press, Princeton, 1994.

O'Sullivan, N., *Conservatism*, Everyman, London, 1976.

Owens, P., 'Beyond Strauss, Lies, and the War in Iraq: Hannah Arendt's Critique of Neoconservatism', *Review of International Studies*, vol. 33, Special Issue, 2007, pp. 265–83.

Palmer, M., *Love of Glory and the Common Good: Aspects of the Political Thought of Thucydides*, Rowman & Littlefield, Lanham, MD, 1992.

Pangle, T., Leo Strauss's Perspective on Modern Politics, American Enterprise Institute Conference, Washington, 1 December 2003, podcast available online at http://www.aei.org/event/478#doc [7 January 2008].

———, *Leo Strauss: An Introduction to His Thought and Intellectual Legacy*, Johns Hopkins University Press, Baltimore, 2006.

Pangle, T. and P. Ahrensdorf, *Justice Among Nations: On the Moral Basis of Power and Peace*, University Press of Kansas, Lawrence, KS, 1999.

Parmar, I., 'Foreign Policy fusion: Liberal Interventionists, conservative nationalists and neoconservatives—the new alliance dominating the US foreign policy establishment', *International Politics*, vol. 46, no. 2/3, pp. 177–209.

Peacock, A. A., *Deconstructing the Republic: Voting Rights, the Supreme Court and the Founders' Republicanism Reconsidered*, AEI Press, Washington, DC, 2008.

Perle, R., 'We Won Years Ago', *The American Interest*, vol. 3, no. 4, 2008, pp. 20–1.

Phillips, K., *The Emerging Republican Majority*, 2nd edn, Anchor Books, New York, 1970.

Pippin, R., 'The Unavailability of the Ordinary: Strauss on the Philosophical Fate of Modernity', in Robert B. Pippin, *The Persistence of Subjectivity: On the Kantian Aftermath*, Cambridge University Press, Cambridge, 2006.

Piven, F. F. and R. Cloward, *The New Class War: Reagan's Attack on the Welfare State and its Consequences*, Pantheon Books, New York, 1982.

———, *Regulating the Poor: The Functions of Public Welfare*, Vintage Books, New York, 1993.

Plattner, M., 'Liberalism, Universalism, and Multiculturalism', in A. M. Melzer, J. Weinberger and R. Zinman, eds., *Multiculturalism and American Democracy*, University Press of Kansas, Lawrence, KS, 1998.

Plattner, M. F., *Democracy Without Borders? Global Challenges to Liberal Democracy*, Rowman & Littlefield, Lanham, MD, 2008.

Podhoretz, N., 'My Negro Problem—And Ours', *Commentary*, February 1963, pp. 93–102.

———, *Making It*, Random House, New York, 1967.

———, 'Between Nixon and the New Politics', *Commentary*, September 1972, pp. 4–7.

———, 'The New Inquisitors', *Commentary*, April 1973, pp. 7–9.

———, 'Making the World Safe for Communism', *Commentary*, April 1976, pp. 31–42.
———, 'The Culture of Appeasement', *Harper's*, October 1977, http://www.harpers.org/archive/1977/10/0022763 [7 March 2009].
———, *The Present Danger: Do We Have the Will to Reverse the Decline of American Power?*, Simon & Schuster, New York, 1980.
———, 'The New American Majority', *Commentary*, January 1981, pp. 19–29.
———, 'The Future Danger', *Commentary*, April 1981, pp. 29–48.
———, *Why We Were in Vietnam*, Simon & Schuster, New York, 1982.
———, 'The Neo-Conservative Anguish Over Reagan's Foreign Policy', *The New York Times Magazine*, 2 May 1982, pp. 30–1.
———, 'Kissenger Reconsidered', *Commentary*, June 1982, pp. 19–29.
———, 'New Vistas for Neoconservatives', *Conservative Digest*, vol. 15, 1989, pp. 56–7.
———, 'Following Irving', in C. DeMuth and W. Kristol, eds., *The Neoconservative Imagination: Essays in Honour of Irving Kristol*, AEI Press, Washington, DC, 1995.
———, *My Love Affair With America: The Cautionary Tale of a Cheerful Conservative*, Free Press, New York, 2000.
———, 'Syria Yes, Israel No?', *Weekly Standard*, 12 November 2001, http://www.weeklystandard.com/Content/Public/Articles/000/000/000/457edhtn.asp [3 September 2005].
———, 'In Praise of the Bush Doctrine', *Commentary*, September 2002, pp. 2–6.
Podhoretz, *World War IV: The Long Struggle Against Islamofascism*, Doubleday, New York, 2007.
Polanyi, K., *The Great Transformation: The Political and Economic Origins of Our Times*, Beacon Press, Boston, 1957 [1944].
Polsky, N. W. and A. Wildavsky, *Presidential Elections: Strategies of American Electoral Politics*, 5th edn, Scribner, New York, 1980.
Posner, E., 'Do States Have a Moral Obligation to Obey International Law?', *Stanford Law Review*, vol. 55, 2003, pp. 1901–19.
———, 'Obama and international law', *Volokh*, 5 December 2008, http://volokh.com/posts/1228509500.shtml [8 December 2008].
Project for the New American Century, 'Statement of Principles', Washington, DC, June 1997, http://www.newamericancentury.org [2 February 2004].
———, *Rebuilding America's Defenses: Strategy, Forces and Resources for a New Century*, Project for the New American Century, Washington, DC, 2000.
———, Letter to President George W. Bush on the War on Terrorism, Washington, DC, 20 September 2001, http://www.newamericancentury.org/Bushletter.htm [3 November 2003].
Rabkin, J., 'Is EU Policy Eroding the Sovereignty of Non-Member States?', *Chicago Journal of International Law*, vol. 1, no. 2, 2000, pp. 273–90.

———, *The Case for Sovereignty: Why the World Should Welcome American Independence*, AEI Press, Washington, DC, 2004.
———, *Law Without Nations: Why Constitutional Government Requires Sovereign States*, Princeton University Press, Princeton, 2007.
Rainer, H., 'Neoliberalism or Ordoliberalism or: From Freiburg to Cologne and to Berlin', Working Paper, Centre for German and European Studies, University of California, Berkeley, 1991.
Rainwater, L. and W. L. Yancey, *The Moynihan Report and the Politics of Controversy*, MIT Press, Cambridge, MA, 1967.
Ralph, J., 'Between Cosmopolitan and American Democracy: Understanding US Opposition to the International Criminal Court', *International Relations*, vol. 17, no. 2, 2003, pp. 195–211.
———, 'International Society, the International Criminal Court and American Foreign Policy', *Review of International Studies*, vol. 31, no. 1, 2005, pp. 27–44.
Rancière, J., 'Prisoners of the Infinite', *Counterpunch*, 30 April 2002, http://www.counterpunch.org/ranciere0430.html [12 October 2002].
Rasch, W., *Sovereignty and Its Discontent: On the Primacy of Conflict and the Structure of the Political*, Birkbeck Law Press, London, 2004.
Rejai, M., ed., *Decline of Ideology?*, Lieber-Atherton, Chicago, 1971.
Rengger, N., *International Relations, Political Theory and the Problem of Order*, Routledge, London, 2000.
Robin, C., 'The Ex-Cons: Right-Wing Thinkers Go Left', *Lingua Franca*, February 2001, pp. 30–32.
———, *Fear: The History of a Political Idea*, Oxford University Press, Oxford, 2004.
Robinson, N., 'State-Building and International Politics', in Aidan Hehir and Neil Robinson, eds., *State-Building: Theory and Practice*, Routledge, London, 2007.
Robinson, W. I., *A Faustian Bargain: U.S. Intervention in the Nicaraguan Elections and American Foreign Policy in the Post-Cold War Era*, Westview Press, Boulder, CO, 1992.
———, 'Globalization, the World System, and "Democracy Promotion" in U.S. Foreign Policy', *Theory and Society*, vol. 25, 1996, pp. 615–65.
———, *Promoting Polyarchy: Globalization, US Intervention, and Hegemony*, Cambridge University Press, Cambridge and New York, 1996.
Rose, D., 'Neo Culpa', *Vanity Fair*, 3 November 2006, http://www.vanityfair.com/politics/features/2006/12/neocons200612 [6 November 2006].
Rose, N., *Powers of Freedom: Reframing Political Thought*, Cambridge University Press, Cambridge, 1999.
Rosen, J., 'Conscience of a Conservative', *New York Times*, 9 September 2007, http://www.nytimes.com/2007/09/09/magazine/09rosen.html?_r=1&ei=5087%0A&em=&en=f195c56e871af91e&ex=118913760&oref=slogin [9 September 2008].

Rosen, S., 'Leo Strauss and the Quarrel Between the Ancients and the Moderns', in A. Udoff, ed., *Leo Strauss's Thought: Toward a Critical Engagement*, Lynne Rienner Publishers, Boulder, CO, 1991.

Rossiter, C., *Conservatism in America*, William Heinemann, London, 1955.

Rostow, W. W., *The Stages of Economic Growth: A Non-Communist Manifesto*, Cambridge University Press, Cambridge, 1960.

Roucaute, Y., *Le néoconservatisme est un humanisme*, Presses Universitaires de France, Paris, 2005.

Roy, O., *Le Croissant et le Chaos*, Hachette, Paris, 2006.

Ruggie, J. G., 'International Regimes, Transactions and Change: Embedded Liberalism in the Postwar Economic Order', *International Organization*, vol. 36, no. 2, 1982, pp. 379–415.

———, 'American Exceptionalism, Exemptionalism, and Global Governance', in M. Ignatieff, ed., *American Exceptionalism and Human Rights*, Princeton University Press, Princeton and Oxford, 2005.

Rusher, W. A., *The Rise of the Right*, 2nd edn, Anchor Books, New York, 1992.

Ryan, D., *US Foreign Policy in World History*, Routledge, London, 2000.

Sanders, J., *Peddlers of Crisis: The Committee on the Present Danger and the Politics of Containment*, South End Press, Boston, 1983, pp. 7–9, 197–204.

Savage, M., 'Legalizing Politics and Politicising Law', in C. Bickerton, P. Cunliffe and A. Gourevitch, eds., *Politics Without Sovereignty*, London, UCL Press, 2007.

Scalia, A., 'Foreign Law in Constitutional Interpretation', AEI Working Paper no. 159, 2009, http://www.aei.org/docLib/20090820-Chapter2.pdf [12 October 2009].

Schaller, M., *Right Turn: American Life in the Reagan–Bush Era 1980–1992*, Oxford University Press, New York, 2006.

Scheman, R. L., *The Alliance for Progress: A Retrospective*, Praeger, New York, 1988.

Scheuerman, W., *Carl Schmitt: The End of Law*, Rowman & Littlefield, Lanham, MD, 1999.

Schlesinger, A. M., Jr., *The Vital Center: The Politics of Freedom*, Houghton Mifflin, Boston, 1949.

Schmitt, C., *The Crisis of Parliamentary Democracy*, MIT Press, Cambridge, MA, 1985 [1923].

———, *The Concept of the Political*, trans. George Schwab, University of Chicago Press, Chicago, 1996 [1932].

———, *The Leviathan in the State Theory of Thomas Hobbes: Meaning and Failure of a Political Symbol*, trans. George Schwab and Erna Hilfstein, Greenwood, Westport, 1996 [1938].

———, 'Strong State, Free Economy', reprinted in R. Cristi, *Carl Schmitt and Authoritarian Liberalism: Strong State, Free Economy*, University of Wales Press, Cardiff, 1998 [1928].

———, *The Nomos of the Earth: In the International Law of the Jus Publicum Europaeum*, Telos Press, New York, 2006 [1950].

———, *Political Theology: Four Chapters on the Concept of Sovereignty*, trans. George Schwab, University of Chicago Press, Chicago, 2006 [1922].

Schmitt, G. J. and A. N. Shulsky, 'Leo Strauss and the World of Intelligence (By Which We Do Not Mean Nous)', in K. L. Deutsch and J. A. Murray, eds., *Leo Strauss, the Straussians and the American Regime*, Rowman & Littlefield, Lanham, MD, 1999.

Schmitter, P., 'Democracy's Future: More Liberal, Preliberal or Postliberal?, *Journal of Democracy*, vol. 6, no. 1, 1995, pp. 69–77.

Schoenwald, J. M., *A Time For Choosing: The Rise of Conservatism*, Oxford University Press, Oxford, 2001.

Schumpeter, J., *Capitalism, Socialism and Democracy*, Allen & Unwin, London, 1950 [1942].

Scott, J. M., *Deciding to Intervene: The Reagan Doctrine and American Foreign Policy*, Duke University Press, Durham, NC, 1996.

Selfa, L., *The Democrats: A Critical History*, Haymarket Books, London, 2008.

Shepperd, E., *Leo Strauss and the Politics of Exile: The Making of a Political Philosopher*, Brandeis University Press, Waltham, MA, 2007.

Shils, E., 'The End of Ideology', *Encounter*, no. 5, November 1955, pp. 52–8.

Shulsky, A., *Silent Warfare: Understanding the World of Intelligence*, Brassey's/Macmillan, Washington DC, 1991.

Shultz, G. P., 'Terror and the State', *Washington Post*, 26 January 2002, p. 16.

Simpson, G., *Great Powers and Outlaw States: Unequal Sovereigns in the International Legal Order*, Cambridge University Press, Cambridge, 2004.

Singh, R., 'Neo-Conservatism: Theory and Practice', in L. B. Miller and M. Ledwidge, eds., *New Directions in US Foreign Policy*, Routledge, London, 2008.

———, 'In Defence of a Concert of Liberal Democracies', *The Whitehead Journal of Diplomacy and International Relations*, vol. 10. no. 1, 2009, pp. 19–29.

Slaughter, A., 'Building Global Democracy', *Chicago Journal of International Law*, vol. 1, no. 2, 2000, pp. 249–76.

Smith, J. A., *The Idea Brokers: Think Tanks and the Rise of the New Policy Elite*, Free Press, New York, 1991.

Smith, M. J., *Realist Thought from Weber to Kissinger*, Louisiana State University, Baton Rouge, 1986.

Smith, S. B., *Reading Leo Strauss: Politics, Philosophy, Judaism*, Oxford University Press, Oxford, 2006.

Smith, T., 'The Alliance for Progress: The 1960s', in A. F. Lowenthal, *Exporting Democracy: The United States and Latin America*, Johns Hopkins University Press, Baltimore, 1991.

———, *A Pact with the Devil: Washington's Bid for World Supremacy and the Betrayal of the American Promise*, Routledge, London, 2006.

Spinoza, B., *Ethics*, edited and translated by G. H. R. Parkinson, Oxford University Press, Oxford, 2000 [1677].

Spiro, P. J., 'The New Sovereignists: American Exceptionalism and its False Prophets', *Foreign Affairs*, vol. 79, no. 6, November/December 2000, pp. 9–15.

———, 'Treaties, International Law and Constitutional Rights', *Stanford Law Review*, vol. 55, 2003, pp. 1618–49.

Stedman Jones, G., 'The History of US Imperialism', in R. Blackburn, ed., *Ideology in Social Science: Readings in Critical Social Theory*, Fontana, London, 1972.

Stein, J., *Running Steel, Running America: Race, Economic Policy and the Decline of Liberalism*, University of North Carolina Press, Chapel Hill, 1998.

Steinfels, P., *The Neoconservatives: The Men Who Are Changing America's Politics*, Simon & Schuster, New York, 1979.

Stelzer, I., *Neoconservatism*, Atlantic Books, London, 2004.

Sternhell, Z., *The Birth of the Fascist Ideology*, Princeton University Press, Princeton, 1994.

Strauss, L., *What is Political Philosophy?*, Chicago University Press, Chicago, 1959.

———, *Spinoza's Critique of Religion*, Schocken Books, New York, 1965 [1930].

———, *The Political Philosophy of Hobbes: Its Basis and Its Genesis*, University of Chicago Press, Chicago, 1966 [1938].

———, *Liberalism Ancient and Modern*, Basic Books, New York, 1968.

———, *Natural Right and History*, Chicago University Press, Chicago, 1971 [1953].

———, *The City and Man*, Chicago University Press, Chicago, 1978 [1964].

———, *An Introduction to Political Philosophy: Six Essays by Leo Strauss*, edited and introduced by H. Gildin, Wayne State University Press, Detroit, 1989.

———, *The Rebirth of Classical Political Philosophy*, ed. T. Pangle, Chicago University Press, Chicago, 1989.

———, 'Notes on Carl Schmitt's Concept of the Political', in C. Schmitt, *The Concept of the Political*, Chicago University Press, Chicago, 1996 [1932].

———, *On Tyranny. Including the Strauss–Kojève Correspondence*, edited by V. Gourevitch and M. S. Roth, Chicago University Press, Chicago, 2000.

———, 'Letters to Karl Löwith', *Constellations*, vol. 16, no. 1, 2009, pp. 84–6.

Students for a Democratic Society, *Port Huron Statement*, Port Huron, Michigan, 15 June 1962, http://www2.iath.virginia.edu/sixties/HTML_docs/Resources/Primary/Manifestos/SDS_Port_Huron.html [12 June 2008].

Suganami, H., 'Understanding Sovereignty Through Kelsen/Schmitt', *Review of International Studies*, vol. 33, 2007, pp. 511–30.

Suri, J., 'Explaining the End of the Cold War: A New Historical Consensus?', *Journal of Cold War Studies*, vol. 4, no. 4, 2002, pp. 56–81.

———, *Power and Protest: Global Revolution and the Rise of Détente*, Harvard University Press, Cambridge, MA, 2003.

Tanguay, D., *Leo Strauss, Une biographie intellectuelle*, Grasset et Fasquelle, Paris, 2003.

Teixeira, R. A. and J. Rogers, *America's Forgotten Majority: Why the White Working Class Still Matters*, Basic Books, New York, 2000.

Todd, E., *Après l'empire: Essai sur la décomposition du système Américain*, Gallimard Folio, Paris, 2002.

Tönnis, F., *Community and Civil Society*, Cambridge University Press, Cambridge, 2001 [1887].

Tonry, M., *Malign Neglect: Race, Crime, and Punishment in America*, Oxford University Press, New York, 1995.

Trilling, L., *The Liberal Imagination*, Anchor Books, New York, 1950.

———, *Beyond Culture*, Viking, New York, 1965.

Tucker, R., 'The Middle East: Carterism Without Carter', *Commentary*, September 1981.

Tucker, R. and D. C. Hendrickson, *The Imperial Temptation: The New World Order and America's Purpose*, Council on Foreign Relations, New York, 1992.

Ulmen, G. L., 'The Sociology of the State: Carl Schmitt and Max Weber', *State, Culture and Society*, vol. 1, 1985, pp. 3–57.

———, 'Between the Weimar Republic and the Third Reich: Continuity in Carl Schmitt's Thought', *Telos*, vol. 119, 2001, pp. 18–31.

United Nations Convention for the Elimination of Racial Discrimination, 'Structural Racism in the United States. A Report to the UN Committee for the Elimination of Racial Discrimination on the occasion of its review of the Periodic Report of the United States of America', Organised by the Kirwan Institute and 250 NGOs, February 2008, http://www2.ohchr.org/english/bodies/cerd/docs/ngos/usa/USHRN2.doc [November 2008].

Vaisse, J., *Histoire du néoconservatisme aux Etats-Unis: Le triomphe de l'idéologie*, Odile Jacob, Paris, 2008.

Vattimo, G., *Dialogue with Nietzsche*, Columbia University Press, New York, 2006.

Venn, C., 'World Dis/Order: On Some Fundamental Questions', *Theory, Culture and Society*, vol. 19, no. 4, 2002, pp. 121–36.

Wald, A. M., *The New York Intellectuals: The Rise and Decline of the Anti-Stalinist Left from the 1930s to the 1980s*, University of North Carolina Press, Chapel Hill, 1987.

Wallerstein, I. 'The Eagle Has Crash Landed', *Foreign Policy*, July/August 2002, pp. 60–8.

Waltz, K., *Man, The State and War*, Columbia University Press, New York, 1959.

Walzer, M., *Just and Unjust Wars: A Moral Argument with Historical Illustrations*, Basic Books, New York, 1977.
Wanniski, J., *The Way the World Works*, Gateway Books, New York, 1978.
Wattenberg, B., 'Melt, Melting, Melted', *Washington Post*, 15 March 2001, accessible via http://www.aei.org/publications/filter.all,pubID.12609/pub_detail.asp [3 December 2007].
———, 'Neo-Manifest Destinarianism', *National Interest*, vol. 21, Fall 1990, pp. 51–2.
Wattenberg, M., *The Decline of American Political Parties 1952–1994*, Harvard University Press, Cambridge, MA, 1996.
Waxman, C. I, ed., *The End of Ideology Debate*, Funk and Wagnalls, New York, 1968.
Weber, M., *Economy and Society: An Outline of Interpretive Sociology*, R. Roth and C. Wittich, eds., California University Press, Berkeley, 1978.
———, *The Vocations Lectures*, edited and introduced by David Owen and Tracy Strong, Hackett, Indianapolis and Cambridge, 2004.
Weinstein, K.R., 'Philosophic Roots, the Role of Leo Strauss, and the War in Iraq', in I. Stelzer, ed., *Neoconservatism*, Atlantic Books, London, 2004.
Wendt, A., 'Anarchy is What States Make of It: The Social Construction of Power Politics', *International Organization*, vol. 46, no. 2, Spring 1992, pp. 391–425.
Westad, O. A., *The Global Cold War: Third World Interventions and the Making of Our Times*, Cambridge University Press, Cambridge, 2006.
Western, B., 'Politics and Social Structure in the Culture of Control', *Critical Review of International Social and Political Philosophy*, vol. 7, no. 2, 2004, pp. 27–43.
White, H., *Tropics of Discourse: Essays in Cultural Criticism*, Johns Hopkins University Press, Baltimore, 1978.
Whyte, W.H., Jr., *The Organization Man*, Simon & Schuster, New York, 1956.
Wildavsky, A., *The Rise of Radical Egalitarianism*, National Book Network, New York, 1991.
Williams, D., *International Development and International Order: History, Theory and Pra*ctice, Routledge, London, 2011.
Williams, M. C., *The Realist Tradition and the Limits of International Relations*, Cambridge University Press, Cambridge, 2005.
———, 'What is the National Interest? The Neoconservative Challenge in IR Theory', *European Journal of International Relations*, vol. 11, no. 3, 2005, pp. 307–35.
———, *Culture and Security: Symbolic Power and the Politics of International Security*, Palgrave, London, 2007.
———, ed., *Realism Reconsidered: The Legacy of Hans Morgenthau*, Oxford University Press, Oxford, 2008.
Wilson, J. Q., 'Liberalism versus Liberal Education', *Commentary*, June 1972, pp. 50–55.

Wilson, J. Q. and R. J. Herrnstein, *Crime and Human Nature: The Definitive Study of the Causes of Crime*, Simon & Schuster, New York, 1985.

Wilson, J. Q. and G. Kelling, 'Broken Windows: The Police and Neighbourhood Safety', in I. Stelzer, ed., *Neo-Conservatism*, Atlantic Books, London, 2004.

Wolfowitz, P., 'After Communism, Global Turmoil', *Wall Street Journal*, 21 April 1993, p. 17.

———, 'Remembering the Future', *The National Interest*, vol. 59, Summer 2000, pp. 67–73.

Wolfson, A., 'Conservatives and Neoconservatives', in I. Stelzer, *Neoconservatism*, Atlantic Books, London, 2004.

Wolin, R., *Labyrinths: Explorations in the Critical History of Ideas*, University of Massachusetts Press, Amherst, 1995.

Wolin, S., *Politics and Vision*, expanded edition, Princeton University Press, Princeton and Oxford, 2004.

———, *Democracy Incorporated: Managed Democracy and the Specter of Inverted Totalitarianism*, Princeton University Press, Princeton, 2008.

Woodley, D., *Fascism and Political Theory: Critical Perspectives on Fascist Ideology*, Routledge, London, 2010.

Wrange, P., 'Of Power and Justice', *German Law Journal*, vol. 4, no. 9, 2003, pp. 936–62.

Wurmser, D., *Tyranny's Ally: America's Failure to Defeat Saddam Hussein*, AEI Press, Washington, DC, 1999.

Xenos, N., *Cloaked in Virtue: Unveiling the Rhetoric of American Foreign Policy*, Routledge, London. 2008.

Yates, J., 'Racial Incarceration Disparity among States', *Social Science Quarterly*, vol. 78, 1997, pp. 1001–10.

Yoo, J., *The Powers of War and Peace: The Constitution and Foreign Affairs After 9/11*, Chicago University Press, Chicago, 2006.

———, *War by Other Means: An Insider's Account of the War on Terror*, Atlantic Monthly Press, Washington, DC, 2006.

———, 'Outsourcing American Law: Conclusion', AEI Working Paper no. 159, 2009, p. 1, http://www.aei.org/docLib/20090820-Chapter9.pdf [12 October 2009].

Zuckert, C. and M. Zuckert, *The Truth About Leo Strauss: Political Philosophy and American Democracy*, Chicago University Press, Chicago, 2006, pp. 184–94.

INDEX